HARBOR OF REFUGE

HARBOR OF REFUGE

Being the Recreation of Four Seasons

on an Offshore Lighthouse from the

Authentic Journal of S. P. Jones, S.N.

STEPHEN JONES

Illustrations by RICHARD BROWN

For Bill Hossack, "The Penny Opera,"
whose performance in the script brief, I yet cherish — to say
nothing of his performance in my classes.
Best of luck
Stephen Jones
January 29, 1998

W·W·NORTON & COMPANY·NEW YORK·LONDON

Library of Congress Cataloging in Publication Data
Jones, Stephen, 1935–
  Harbor of Refuge, being the recreation of four
seasons on an offshore lighthouse from the authentic
journal of S. P. Jones, S.N.
   1. Harbor of Refuge Lighthouse, N.J.   2. Jones,
Stephen, 1935–   I. Title.
VK1025.H37J66 1981   387.1'55   80–26278
ISBN 0-393-01417-7

W. W. Norton & Company, Inc. 500 Fifth Avenue, New York, N.Y. 10110
W. W. Norton & Company Ltd. 25 New Street Square, London EC4A 3NT

1 2 3 4 5 6 7 8 9 0

DEDICATION

This book is dedicated to the crew of The Harbor Refuge Light. In order to capture the spirit of that crew, characters have been synthesized and action generalized. Through the four seasons I spent on the Harbor of Refuge there were nine different men serving aboard at various times. Various statements and actions by some of them appear here under different names. Others have passed through these pages without leaving a trace. The character referred to in the first person is based on someone I partially knew twenty years ago.

ACKNOWLEDGMENTS

I would like to thank Norma and Davis Bame, the Philadelphia Bay and River Pilots, Robert Rollinson, Robert Belcher, Peter Casino, Richard G. Sharp, Richard Goode, Harvey Loomis, Edward Jones, Jessica Jones, Preston Massey, Audrey Massey, Lois Jones, Archie T. Wahab, Engineman Holden.

Carol Hines helped with the art work as she did on the cover of *Backwaters*.

The United States Coast Guard provided structural drawings of the Harbor of Refuge Light.

Mrs. John Floherty provided interesting conversation about her late husband and with his publishers permitted us to use a section of his chapter on the Harbor of Refuge Light from *Sentries of the Sea* (J. B. Lippincott) is reprinted by permission of Mrs. Floherty and Harper & Row.

The lines "As much dim distance as a man perceives/ from a high lookout over winedark sea," quoted as the third epigraph for the book, are from Homer's *Iliad*, translated by Robert Fitzgerald, reprinted with permission of the Doubleday Anchor Press, 1974.

Susan Preston helped immeasurably in getting this long-dormant project together.

The lighthouse invites the storm.
—Old Saying often quoted
by Malcolm Lowry

And I was forced to think of household tasks.
—Sophocles, *Philoctetes*

As much dim distance as a man perceives
from a high lookout over winedark sea,
—Homer, *The Iliad*
(Robert Fitzgerald, trans.)

CONTENTS

PART FOUR *Spring*

HARBOR OF REFUGE

EXTRACTS

I saw that this was a place of wonders . . .

—Thoreau, "The Highland Light," *Cape Cod*

THESE EXTRACTS are dedicated to the Sub-Sub-Librarian who burrowed and grubbed for the shards of Melville's *cetus*. May this Pale Sherry prove not too rosy-strong. After-all, as Mr. Cyril Connolly points out, "A book collector is like a lighthouse keeper who offers sanctuary to buffeted and exhausted migrants as they home toward the friendly beam."

The Bartholdi Statue has written to a friend that the twin lights at Navesink are two fine bouncing youngsters, bright as buttons.

—Stephen Crane, *Notebooks*

As we were going to spend the night in a lighthouse, we wished to make the most of so novel experience . . .

—Thoreau, "The Highland Light," *Cape Cod*

For years I had wanted to spend the night on a lighthouse when the birds were flying.

—Roger Tory Peterson

No Other New Year's Like It . . .

Come early . . . Dine from 5, be out by 9 to get your gala evening off to a glamorous start here in this regal mansion by the sea. Regular prices, of course, until 9.

Come 9:15 or later . . . The party starts! Scintillating company in the Gold Room, John Paul Jones Room, Living Room and the Lounge. Festivities and favors, merriment until 3 A.M.

Dine in Splendor . . . Superb full-course dinners presented with a flair in the Lighthouse mode, served until midnight. The band plays on until 8 and it's the time of your life!

Celebrate in the Captain's Gallery . . . Lounge in the svelte environs of this enchanted enclave, listen to Tommy Hughes' piano magic, wander out to the dance floor as the spirit moves, pick your pleasure of hot and cold hors d'ouvres and enjoy, enjoy!

Dance . . . to the titillating rhythms of the deft Steve Boska Orchestra who've promised a delectable potpourri of melody all night long.

The LIGHTHOUSE INN

*Stay the night, perhaps! 52 flawless rooms, $11 to $15 double.

The practical duties of buildings are twofold. They have either (1) to hold and protect something; or (2) to place or carry something.

1. Architecture of Protection. This is architecture intended to protect men or their possessions from violence of any kind whether of men or of the elements. It will include all churches, houses, and treasuries; fortresses, fences, and ramparts; the architecture of the hut and sheepfold; of the palace and citadel; of the dyke, breakwater, and sea-wall. And the protection, when of living creatures, is to be understood as including commodiousness and comfort of habitation, wherever these are possible under the given circumstance.

2. Architecture of Position. This is architecture intended to carry men or things to some certain places, or to hold them there. This will include all bridges, aqueducts, and road architecture; lighthouses, which have to hold light in appointed places; chimneys, to carry smoke or direct currents of air; staircases; towers, which are to be watched from or cried from, as in mosque, or to hold bells, or to place men in positions of offence, as ancient movable towers . . .

—Ruskin, *The Stones of Venice*

LIGHTHOUSE, n. A tall building on the seashore in which the government maintains a lamp and the friend of a politician.

—Ambrose Bierce, *The Devil's Dictionary*

So to night—wandering sailors pale with fears
Wide o'er the watery waste a light appears,
Which on the far-seen mountain blazing high
Streams from lonely watch towers to the sky.

—Homer, *The Iliad*, XIX, 405–9, trans.
Pope. (the first reference to a lighthouse
according to Stevenson)

To judge from the Homeric legend of King Proteus, the earliest Pelasgian settlers in the Delta used Pharos, the lighthouse island off what later became Alexandria, as their sacred oracular island. Proteus, the oracular Old Man of the Sea, who was king of Pharos and lived in a cave—where Menelaus consulted him—had the power of changing his shape.

—Robert Graves, *The White Goddess*

The Ancient of the Ancients, the unknown of the unknown, was a lighthouse standing high above the world and man could know of its existence through the light that fell on him from above and shone before his eyes with so much brightness and abundance.

—"The Cabala"

Chuckling to himself, the Captain drew up the little boat and made her fast: then, taking sundry brown paper parcels from under the thwart, he turned and made his way up toward the lighthouse. A picturesque figure he was striding along among the heaped and tumbled rocks. His hair and beard, still thick and curly, were absolutely white, as white as the foam that broke over the rocks at the cliff's foot. His face was tanned and weather-beaten to the colour of mahogany, but the features were strong and sharply cut, while the piercing blue eyes which gleamed beneath his shaggy eyebrows showed all the fire of youth, and seemed to have no part in the seventy years which had bent the tall form, and rounded slightly the broad and massive shoulders. The Captain wore a rough pea-jacket and long boots, while his head

was adorned with a nondescript covering which might have begun life either as a hat
or a cap, but would now hardly be owned by either family.

—Laura E. Richards, *Captain January*

. . . the lighthouse keeper's red and tranquil face.

—Marcel Proust, *Jean Santeuil*

The keeper entertained us handsomely in his solitary little ocean house. He was a
man of singular patience and intelligence, who, when our queries struck him, rung
clear as a bell in response. The light-house lamps a few feet distance shone full into
my chamber, and made it bright as day, so I knew exactly how the Light bore all
that night, and I was in no danger of being wrecked . . . I thought, as I lay there,
half awake and half asleep, looking upward through the window at the lights above
my head, how many sleepless eyes from far out on the Ocean stream—mariners of
all nations spinning their yarns through the various watches of the night—were
directed toward my couch.

—Thoreau, "The Highland Light"

Visited a lighthouse. I climbed the spiral staircase and knocked on the door up
at the top. A man came to open who seemed the image of what a lighthouse-keeper
ought to be. He smoked a pipe and had a grayish-white beard. Like a seaman, he
wore a thick navy-blue jacket with gold buttons, trousers to match, and boots. Yet
he had also something of the land about him—a well-set look, a firmly planted look,
and his boots could have been a farmer's. Bathed by the ocean and buttressed by the
rock, the lighthouse and its keeper stood in between, upon the thin, long fringe of
land and sea—belonged to both and neither.
     "Come in, come in," he said, and immediately, with that strange power some
people have to put you at ease, he made me feel at home in the lighthouse. He
seemed to consider it most natural that a boy should come and visit his lighthouse.
Of course a boy my age would want to see it, his whole manner seemed to say—
there should be more people interested in it, and more visits. He practically made
me feel he was there to show the place to strangers, almost as if that lighthouse were
a museum or a tower of historical importance.

—Arturo Vivante, "The Lighthouse"

At night, when Tim was at home, before he got into bed, he would draw back
the curtains of his window.
     Then, once every minute, the great beam of light from the lighthouse would
shine into his room.
     It made him happy to see it because he knew that ships far out to sea could see
it too, and so steer clear of the dangerous rocks at its base.
     Often he would lie half asleep in his bed wishing and wishing he could be a
lighthouse keeper.

—Edward Ardizzone, *Tim to the Lighthouse*

The first light to go on was that of the lighthouse on the Ille Caillebotte; a little
boy stopped near me and murmured in ecstasy, "Oh, the lighthouse!"
     Then I felt my heart swell with a great feeling of adventure.

—J. P. Sartre, *Nausea*

The boy often brought fish to the lighthouse, feeling a debt of gratitude toward
the lighthouse keeper.

From another room the good-natured voice of the lighthouse keeper answered familiarly.

—Yukio Mishima

From *The Lantern Deck:* Tony Marvin, the keeper of Keyport Light, was in his little room next the fog-horn when Sanford and the skipper, wet and glistening as two seals, knocked at the outer door of his quarters.

'Well, I want to know!' broke out Tony in his bluff, hearty way . . . 'anybody drownded?'

—F. Hopkinson Smith,
Caleb West: Master Diver
(The building of Race Rock Light)

On watch in the light tower on Gay Head, Fred Poole saw the white light on Devil's Bridge around 5 o'clock in the morning. He noticed the light did not move, and so called his chief, Keeper Horatio N. Pease, a veteran of twenty years service at Gay Head. Keeper and assistant watched and talked about the light which was where no such light should be. They agreed it must be a vessel on the rocks. . . .

As dawn neared, Keeper Pease sent his helper to arouse the little Indian community. It was slow work going round the scattered homes, arousing occupants, and explaining the alarm. . . .

As the sun rose, Keeper Pease extinguished the light. From the tower balcony, he waved a blanket in futile hope it would be seen if there were people on the wreck. The signal was a violation of regulations. At the moment the veteran keeper did not care about regulations.

—George A. Hough, Jr., *Disaster on Devil's Bridge*

There is something inexpressibly lonely about a lighthouse as the light is turned on at dusk.

—John J. Floherty, *Sentries of the Sea*

It is an employment in some respects best suited to the habits of the gulls which coast up and down here and circle over the sea. . . .

—Thoreau, The Highland Light, *Cape Cod*

Today the lighthouse had as its guest
A savage poet, his wings loaded with lead;

—Tristan Corbière, "The Contumacious Poet"

He was very drunk, an' he went right out to the lighthouse, an' threw hisself off the steps. They never picked 'n up.

—Elizabeth Prettejohn

In the latest lighthouses there are no keepers; the electric lighting is automatically attended to—by a most ingenious arrangement of valves the lightswitches itself off at sunrise and switches itself on at dusk. And it can't go wrong. A reserve lamp lights up if the first fails.

—*Boy's Book of the Sea: The Latest Afloat and Beneath the Waters,*
Charles Boff, 1938

Lighthouse keeper that I am in a policeman's bed sitter record . . .

—William Burrough's, *St. Louis Journal*

Because of [the] requirement for a broader educational background and a subtle change in attitude toward the more rugged and isolated type of life required of lighthouse keepers, it became extremely difficult to recruit young men as assistant keepers.

—Capt. Walter Capan, *Watts Seapower Library*

It became hard to get young people to work on the lighthouses.

—Ruth Glunt, *Lighthouse of the Hudson River*

I am the dark man, the disconsolate widower,
The prince of Aquitanio whose tower has been torn down.

—de Nerval

In general, it [a lighthouse keeper's life] is the life of a monk, and indeed more than that—the life of a hermit . . .

—Henryk Sienkiewicz, "The Lighthouse Keeper of Aspinwall,"
From Jeremiah Curtain's translation of *Yanko the Musician*

Lighthouse Is Poor Port For Termites in Storm

Atlanta (AP)—Seagoing termites? And in a lighthouse? That problem faced the Orkin Exterminating Company and the United States Coast Guard.

Termites, normally landlubbers, got into the wooden structure of the third level of Smith Point Lighthouse, which is in the Chesapeake Bay, two and a half miles from land near Sunnyland, Va.

Entomologists could not explain how the pests managed to reach the lighthouse or how they survived since termites need fresh water to live.

At any rate the colony was quickly dispatched.

—*New London Day*

Now unless Aimwell has made good use of his time, all our fair machines goes souse into the sea like the Eddystone.

—Farquhar, *The Beaux Stratagem*

There is nothing that moves the imagination like a lighthouse.

—Samuel Adams Drake
(quoted by Edward Rowe Snow)

The darkness, equally dense on all sides, amid which the lighthouse appears to float like some great luminous body . . .

—H. Gatke

A green star appeared ahead of me, flashing like a lighthouse. Was it a lighthouse? or really a star? I took no pleasure from this supernatural gleam, this star the Magi might have seen, this dangerous decoy.

"A lighthouse!"

Both of us spied it at the same moment, that winking decoy! What madness! Where was that phantom light, that invention of the night?

—Antoine De Saint Exupery, *Wind, Sand and Stars*

There is a light though, a real and tangible light, ahead: the revolving lamp of the lighthouse beyond the channel. . . . In the misty blowy night the lighthouse lamp, but only intermittently, for the briefest second, stands out like torch suddenly brighter and larger than it should be, and then quickly vanishes as its beam sweeps the wide sealike lake before it turns inland, and then once again stares you in the face like a hurried, angry Cyclops who has no time for you, who is not really interested because he turns away so quickly, as you scuff on along the sand.

—Charles Jackson, *A Second-Hand Life*

You usually sail from Mallorca to Ibiza starting late at night because the late-night breeze is easterly, and about halfway through the voyage, as I recall, you pick up the light on Isla Tage Mago, a hunk of rock about a mile off the easternmost tip of Ibiza. Anyhow, that day we had sailed and swum and burned our brains in the sun and in the evening we messed around with friends in a little resort town, I forget its name, on the western horn of Palma Bay, and ate a huge late many-coursed supper with a lot of wine, so that when we embarked at midnight we were already tired out and sleepy. Then somewhere out there in the open Mediterranean the clear pleasant night went cloudy and the nice easterly breeze turned into a horrid shoving northeast bitch with heavy seas, and we started taking turns at the helm for twenty or thirty minutes at a time, which was about as long as we could manage it without going to sleep or into dreamy dangerous hallucinations, since there was nothing to be seen but the Tage Mago light, at least when you were on the crests, and occasionally some curling prosphorescence on top of a mast-high following wave behind the little boat, if you dared to look around.

—John Graves, unpublished correspondence

The ivory tower cannot be suffered unless it is transformed into a lighthouse or a broadcasting station.

—Vladimir Nabokov, *The Real Life of Sebastian Knight*

'O yes,' you will sigh, 'we have had what once we would have called success. I moved the vices out of the city into a chain of reconditioned lighthouses . . .'

—W. H. Auden, "Caliban to the Audience"

My father was the keeper of the Eddystone Light
And he slept with a mermaid one fine night
From this union there came three
A porpoise and a porgy and the other was me.

—Traditional

Jarl van Hoother had his burnt head high up in his lamphouse, laying cold hands on himself.

—James Joyce, *Finnegans Wake*

"This lighthouse nourishes itself upon the pure matter which is the substance of the isle . . ."

—Alfred Jarry, "Concerning The Squitty Sea The Olfactory Light house, and The Isle of Cack, Where We Drank Not"

. . . you must hold onto the lighthouse to prevent being blown into the Atlantic.

—Thoreau, "The Highland Light," *Cape Cod*

When from our better selves we have too long
Been parted by the hurrying world, and droop,

Sick of its business, of its pleasures tired,
How gracious, how benign, is Solitide;
How potent a mere image of her sway;
Most potent when impressed upon the mind
With an appropriate human centre—hermit,
Deep in the bosum of the wilderness;
Votary (in vast cathedral, where no foot
Is treading, where no other face is seen)
Kneeling at prayers; or watchman on the top
Of lighthouse, beaten by Atlantic waves . . .
                    —Wordsworth, *The Prelude*, Book IV

Smith closing arms around the lanky soul. Just in a string of pearls. Now you know. Your breasts shine. Twin beams from a lighthouse on a lonely coast.
                                                              —J. P. Donleavy

I lit the lamps in the light-house tower,
    For the sun dropped down and the day was dead;
They shone like a glorious cluster flower,
    Two golden and five red.
            —Celia Thaxter, (daughter of Thomas B. Laighton,
            Keeper of Isle of Shoals Light), "The Watch of Bos'n Island"

. . . But the city's chief glory radiated in quite a literal sense from a huge lamp, shining on the lighthouse outside the island of Pharos. The first concave mirror multiplied the light. Even today the name of Alexander's choice shines through the night to the navigators of distant lands, the symbol of rescue.
                                                    —Emil Ludwig, *The Nile*

. . . we were miraculously saved by civilization itself (of which a lighthouse is perhaps always the highest symbol) . . .
                —Malcolm Lowry, *Hear Us Lord from Heaven Thy Dwelling Place*

Now, all over the world, similar institutions carry on his [Pasteur's] work, lighthouses of safety for humanity.
                        —Donald Culross Peattie, *An Almanac for Moderns*

In a few minutes there were dozens of them, standing in a wide circle round the lighthouse, staring, laughing, clicking their cameras, throwing (as to an ape) peanuts . . . their numbers increased. As in a nightmare, the dozens became scores, the scores hundreds.

The Savage had retreated towards cover, and now, in the posture of an animal at bay, stood with his back to the wall of the lighthouse, staring from face to face in speechless horror . . .
                                        —Aldous Huxley, *Brave New World*

. . . in a war, when you feel behind you the vigilance, the judgement, the profound study of the Higher Command, you are as much moved by them as by the simple lamps of a lighthouse, which while only a material combustion, is nevertheless an emanation of the spirit, sweeping through space to warn ships of danger.
                                    —Marcel Proust, *The Guermantes Way*

Libre Belgique, a conservative newspaper in Belgium, lauded the Vatican ruling on birth control as "the lighthouse to which man can turn to find a doctrinal and moral basis."
                                                              —A.P. article

My guide, my pharos be, and save from wreck
My boat, which labors in so deep a sea.

—Ronsard (to Charles IX)

Silhouetted against a morning sky, New London Light on Pequot Avenue has
been a favorite subject of artists and photographers. It is a familiar beacon for vessels
heading for New London Harbor. For many people, the sturdy structure seems to
typify much of the enduring tradition of New England.

—caption in New London *Day*

I had a classmate who fitted for college by the lamps of a light-house, which was
more light, we think, than the University afforded . . .

—Thoreau, "The Highland Light"

Trumpeter Don Cherry hopes to record a composition written for him by Ornette
Coleman, entitled *The Lighthouse* . . .

–*Downbeat February 8, 1968*

"You would do much better, sir, to go to the lighthouse, for as you must very
well know you would return from it in a far happier mood, and would have at least
written something fine."

—Marcel Proust, *Jean Santeuil*

In times of old, when time was young,
And poets their own verses sung,
              * / * / *   ,
Each number had its diff'rent power;
Heroic strains could build a tower

—Jonathan Swift

Lighthouse Slated as Ash Repository

SEASIDE, Ore. (AP)—A group of investors that bought a 100-year-old, de-
funct lighthouse perched on a rock off the wave-lashed Oregon coast says the guano-
covered structure will become a repository for human ashes.

Mimi Morissette, one of the owners of the Tillamook Rock Lighthouse, said the
group originally considered selling it to some California investors who wanted to
ship it to Los Angeles in pieces to build a restaurant.

"That didn't appeal to us much, and we started looking for other uses," she
said.

She and others have formed Eternity Of The Sea Columbarium, which will
operate the offshore tomb. She says they will soon be asking for ashes.

"Using the lighthouse as a columbarium started out as a joke, but people
seemed to think it was a great idea," she said. "They told us they wanted two (reser-
vations) for their parents and another for their kids and it just started growing.

"I think it's crazy but it seems to be catching on," she said.

—*New London Day*

PART ONE

Summer

REVEILLE

A long straight arm of stone stretches out from the coast of Delaware as a sort of peacemaker between the turbulent Atlantic and Delaware Bay. Two miles in length, it is composed of loose boulders of great weight. Inside this barrier is safety for vessels during the gales that lash the coast. The protected zone is known as Harbor of Refuge from which the lighthouse on the end of the breakwater takes its name.

—John J. Floherty, *Sentries of the Sea*

IT WAS DOWN at the bottom of New Jersey in one of those temporary buildings left over from two earlier wars. Originally the base had been designed as a lighter-than-air station for the navy, but had been modified down through heavier occasions until it was the Coast Guard Receiving Center. The breeze was coming in from the sea, but it had picked up heat from the asphalt grinder where the shouts of men drilling still made me jump. The yeoman had just handed me more long-range orders. The typed sentence on the printed form said I was to report to the Harbor of Refuge Light Station, Third District. The yeoman had merely pointed to a wall chart and gone back to typing orders. On the chart there were no fewer than three light towers marked *aban*.

"*Aban*.?" I poked at the chart. It hung just above my head like a breaking sea.

Abandoned.

"Oh." I stood on tip-toe. The charts of my homewaters had been complex affairs in yellow, blue, and white, crowded with islands, inlets, bays, spits, reefs, even the most austere of which was yet invested with a name: Sixpenny, Sea Flower, Dumpling, Cerebrus, Shagwong, Vixen, Valiant, Little Gull, Intrepid, Plum. Here above my head was chiefly the blank white sea itself, sprinkled with soundings, spattered with *abans*. "Where in all this is the Harbor of Refuge?"

The yeoman waved his hand at the chart. There indeed was a hook of yellow land, just enough to indicate the bottom of the bay's gaping mouth. Off the land were three wrecks, an obstruction and two precautionary areas. In the midst of this melancholy zone reposed a thin line, apparently representing a breakwater. At neither end was it attached to anything. On the most exposed tip was a magenta circle. In the water next to the circle were some numbers that were apparently not soundings:

Fl 5sec 72 ft 14M Horn

"Is that it?" I said. "The Harbor of Refuge?"

The yeoman suggested I see the radio man. Perhaps he would permit me to talk to them.

"Good Lord, talk to who?"

"Talk to the lighthouse, of course. That is, if the radio man could *raise it*."

"Where do I go to raise the lighthouse?"

The radio shack, of course. It was only down the passageway. I must have expected a separate building set up out in heavy weather with balloons and aerials ascending in lark-like flights. I walked right past, thinking the half-door was an aperture out of which socks and underwear might be issued. There was, however, a sign warning of high voltage. Over the half door thrust a head capped in earphones.

Harbor of Refuge?

He had been trying for a half hour to raise it. In fact he'd been trying off and on for three whole days. He would, however, try again.

There were a number of dials, knobs, even extra microphones at his command. The instruments received his mutterings. His words vanished into the wiring. Some of the curses remained in the room. He glared at me as if I had done something with the lighthouse.

"I cannot," he said, "for Christ's fucking sake, raise Harbor Refuge Light."

When I had enlisted in New London, the recruiter took me aside back of the front door of the Custom House, a great portal made from pieces of the *Constitution*, and assured me that the Coast Guard was equal to any other outfit because you could, "get killed just as good as in the Navy or the Marines." In fact the percentages were even better. The trick, he said, was that whereas the Marines got picked off one by one, the Coast Guard had *whole units* that just went down, drowning every last man and that this was what "brought the numbers right back on up."

Some of the first books I'd ever read by myself were the accounts of maritime disasters, especially lighthouses, which for some reason seemed to bring out the purple in the pen. There was Edward Rowe Snow on such grisly events as the fall of Minot's Light, and John J. Floherty, whose prose was full of forlorn bells sounding from collapsing beacons. The final scene always seemed to be a tableau of widows on the beach the dawn after the storm. They would be shielding their eyes against the glare, but shield as they might, there was now nothing to protect them from the fact the darkness knew: the sea, where once had stood the proud tower, was absolutely flat.

Growing up on the shore, I had also seen less literary lighthouses, but always from a distance, for, as my father pointed out, a lighthouse was a place to stay away from—after all, was not that its message? Here was a creation whose sole purpose was to tell you to avoid it. And, indeed, the time we had come closest to a lighthouse was a foggy day in New London harbor when we did not see the tower at all. We must not have been a boat-length off Southwest Ledge when we were shaken by a noise so great we could not hear it. Though I had heard the horn many times before, its soothing, distant diaphon lulling me to sleep ten miles away, it now caused me to shriek in pain, and our whole crew seemed to echo volumes of noise upon one another. "Damn lighthouse," my father finally managed, spinning the wheel, and we were as shaken by the sound as if we had rammed the invisible tower itself.

From then on I watched for that lighthouse as we drove down to the shore each summer. Unless there was fog, you could see it from the top of the new highway bridge. There it was, far off, a couple of miles down river. It became for us the first sign of the sea and, more than that, the sign that summer was coming. Sometimes the lighthouse seemed close and so well-defined you could see the windows, and its squared-off three-storey construction made it like one of the city's apartments broken loose from the slums to cleanse itself in the harbor. On other days it appeared to have been wheeled off down the estuary into the misty Sound. Then it no longer even looked like a brown building, but a small green bell poised on the edge of invisibility. My father said the Coast Guard moved it up and down the harbor depending upon the weather.

There was another lighthouse we could usually see and hear from the cottage, a white building with a red mansard roof and the light up in the cupola. This station was perched upon a green drumlin set some three miles out from us called Dumpling Island. Surely this picturesque spot was made for visiting. My mother even set aside one of her stacks of *Saturday Evening Posts*. "Lighthouse keepers get lonely," she explained, "and like to read." It was the first I had ever thought of the people inside those forbidding buildings. Then I remembered Minot's keepers as they made "their plans for what proved to be their last night in this world." Among those plans, of course, the message to be launched in the bottle.

Weeks went by as my mother accumulated magazines. Should she throw in the *New Yorker?* The ads might make them dissatisfied with their life. But what was their life like, I wanted to know. If I were a lighthouse keeper I would not worry that I had no Rolls Royce or Arpège or brandy of the Napoleons.

My father, however, persisted in avoiding the actual trip. He discoursed at length on the strength of currents, the treachery of lee shores, the suddenness of weather shifts. Meanwhile my friends were zooming out daily in outboards and sailboats a fourth the size of his.

Ironically, it was one of these carefree excursions which, as John J. Floherty might say, sealed the doom forever upon my chances for youthful voyage to one of the sentries of the sea. Nor was it a case of faulty seamanship. One of the outboards had gone out with magazines and laughing youth and come back chagrined. It was never quite clear what had happened out on picturesque Dumpling, but it was quickly agreed among the mothers that there would be no more trips to the swelling green drumlin upon which sat the red-roofed house. The phrase "treacherous undertow," was used in polite conversation, but one night my mother said, "The magazines evidently had made the lighthouse men unsatisfied with their life."

In spite of my youthful curiosity I had not applied for lighthouse duty in the Coast Guard. My idea was to run flashing forty-footers through surf and storms to rescue sinking trawlers and lobstermen. At twilight I would lounge in my chambray shirt and dungarees along the wharves of remote watercourses. And now after much actual marching over dusty plains with M-1s, and twilight scrubbings of white hats, I was assigned from boot camp not to a roaring rescue craft, but to one of these strange towers, the existence of which I had almost forgotton.

"Are you sure," I said, "this Harbor Refuge unit is still really functioning?"

The Group yeoman was standing in front of the chart, his hands on his hips, lower lip drifting.

"I mean your man down the hall in the radio shack said he could not raise them. Not for three days."

"The proper phras'ology is passageway, not *hall*. Use proper phras'ology."

"Down the passageway, he could not raise the tower."

"Look, boy, just take this envelope and your nice new sea bag and get your ass over there."

"Fine," I said, "but this Harbor of Refuge place, according to your own chart, is out in the water."

"Swim," he said turning back to his desk. "Jump. Fly. Hey, I could give a shit. Just get there."

After an evening meal in the chow hall, I picked my way through the twilight, floating in my new freedom between the pale lighter-than-air barracks. The asphalt on the grinder still held the heat of the day, but the parade was empty and I could smell the sea that lay somewhere out beyond the line of saber grass. For the past six weeks I had not actually seen it,

though we had shot out toward it with M-1s on Thursdays, and sometimes at
night, on fire watch, I had seen from the second deck of a barracks what I
took to be the moving mast lights of fishing boats. Now the bugle playing
evening colors drifted over the deserted parade. Even at that distance I
could hear the scratches on the record.

When I had joined the service they had made me the bugler. The training officer had summoned me to his office. On his desk had been an open
trumpet case with the brass instrument inside. "Do you know what this is?"
he had said. I assumed he wanted some highly technical nuance and asked if
I might inspect it. The mouthpiece was missing; the valves stuck; the spring
on the water key yawned. I informed him of all these matters. He was
pleased. He hated recordings. His daughter played recordings all night at
home. Recordings were unmilitary. My recruitment application was before
him. My interests included the trumpet. Could a trumpet be employed to
bugle? It would mean no more watches for me and a military atmosphere for
the base at large.

With a new mouthpiece and oiled valves for the trumpet and my finger
over its water key, I had stood two dawns later in the Officer-of-the-Day
shack. The O.D. himself was at attention, encased within the webbing of his
Sam Browne belt, his arm band like a tourniquet. A microphone was stuck in
his fist. Above his head was a large clock across the face of which swept a thin
red hand. We were alone in the compartment. Only a small pass-through
window gave out onto the corridor. The barracks shifted uneasily within its
asbestos siding. I placed my lips on the mouthpiece. My mouth was morning
mushy. I had been able to practice less than an hour. The horn tasted sour.
The O.D. nodded to the clock and squeezed open the microphone.

It was as if he had cracked the valve that let out all the pressure in the
room. I was drained right out the end of the horn, out into the passageway,
out the barracks, up and out over row upon row of barracks, over the mess
hall, grinder, rifle range, buoy docks—I was suspended over the entire base.
Except there was no *I*. I was lost, dissipated in this cosmic suspiration:

O-o-o-o-o-o-o-o-o-o-o-o-o-o-o-o

The OD tipped the microphone. My mouth began nibbling. My lungs
pushed what air was miraculously left in the room. At once I realized I'd
started too high; the harmonics were all wrong. "Reveille," is at best a lip
tripper, a set of brass staircases cut into the sharp morning air. Made by a
mush mouth, it staggered off key, a grotesque twitch slamming and spilling
about the room like a dragon kite in a downdraft. I tried to kill it with speed.
If I could but get it all out of my sour horn as fast as possible it would die. As

long as there was still a note, a bit of the tail in my endlessly curling tubes, the dragon lived in the room with us. The worse it got, the faster I went and the worse it got.

I knew it was bad because the OD kept holding the microphone farther and farther away from himself while attempting to compensate for my slithering intervals by making his belts and bands even more rigid. About halfway through I began to be aware of the more remote effects. Feet were slapping onto the decks above and there were yelps and cries. The small pass-through window behind the OD was filling up with faces, the eyes and mouths distorted in the squeeze so that they looked oriental. The OD's face by now was a battlefield of twitches, grimaces, snorts, suppressed shrieks, and simperings. It was clear he felt himself responsible, for was not the magic valve in his hand? Had he not been the one to let this cat out of the bag? "It's a Chinese fire drill!" the window faces shouted. "A real Chinese fire drill!" Deck upon deck rattled with laughter and from the bell of my marvelous horn rose tonalities indeed not usually heard outside the valley of the Yangtze.

The training officer, if not the OD, had been forgiving. "At least it was a real mistake," he said, "not a *recorded* mistake." He even granted my request for additional practice time. During the grinder sessions I was allowed to go off to an abandoned parachute loft and blat my lungs out. A quarter hour before sunrise the fire watch woke me so that I might stalk out into the dew to wheeze into my mouthpiece among the ruins of a nearby barracks. Slowly I'd built up my embouchure to handle the rapid articulations of not only "Reveille," but "Mess Call" and "Assembly," and with those sessions came the sustaining power needed for the long holds in the evening calls, "Tatoo," and "Taps." I put my all into those two, coloring the earlier tune with a chromatic or two, but leaving the last call of the day in all its starkness. Coming to my bunk in the dark I heard voices hoarse with emotion in praise of "real music."

The power went to my head. There were certain mates who had been hard on me before. If, during "Assembly," I caught them stumbling from the barracks, I speeded up the call and they were marked late, often losing their already thin privileges. If, on the other hand, some friend of mine was slow out the door, I retarded the tune, thus saving him. If these actions were not bad enough, I began shamelessly embellishing, employing the valves that, of course, no proper bugle possessed. Finally I began putting so much effort into the music, that my navigation course suffered. Most damaged was my Combat Information Control. Aircraft and surface vessels swarmed through my plotter at will like a giant Bach fugue come unsprung. The trainer officer had no choice. "I'm sorry," he said, "but this is for your own sake." I placed the trumpet in his outstretched hands. Shortly after, the personnel officer, who must have considered himself lucky to have yet a few manned lighthouses where he might send malfunctioning buglers, cut my orders.

When the record finished "Evening Colors" the scratching continued or so it seemed until I realized it was the sound of the sea itself. The ocean was just beyond the roll of the dune.

I don't know how long I'd been standing there after the sun had gone into the sea when I was challenged by the guard, who, true to his eleven general orders, was walking his post in a military manner, keeping always on the alert, observing everything that took place within sight and hearing, being especially watchful at night. On his hip cackled a walkie-talkie. I thought of using my old excuse, that I was the base bugler out articulating his embouchure.

"I'm just looking to see where I'm going."

In the manner of a theater usher he offered a path with his flashlight.

"No," I said, "I'm looking for my lighthouse."

Now the flashlight was smack bright in my face.

General Order Number Nine seemed to cover this situation for him: *To call the corporal of the guard in any case not covered by instructions.*

As soon as the exchange on the radio was over, it was very very still. The sea might as well have been a lake for all it offered acoustically. I stood there pointing out toward the black water. After a while I dropped my arm. He did not lower the light.

Not that I could blame him. Once a week some recruit tried to get out of the service by slashing at his wrists or attempting to seduce the guy in the next bunk.

The corporal of the guard was an old boatswain. He added his light to the guard's.

"No," I said, "out there. The Harbor of Refuge Light." It occurred to me I had my orders in my other hand. The water knocked along the cobbles. The boatswain put his light back on my face, then shifted it out across the dark.

"Hell," he said, "that's fourteen miles out there. You'd better go around the bay to Greenmeal, Delaware. The lifeboat station will take you out. It's only a couple of miles off shore from there."

He turned out his light and we could just see, low in the wet black, a blink.

"Is that it?" I said.

"That could be it." He turned his light on the guard who was only a recruit. "You got a spot on your hat, boy. What do you mean going on guard duty with a spot on your hat!"

TO THE LIGHTHOUSE

Long considered one of the most exposed lighthouses on the Atlantic coast, Harbor of Refuge station has had a history in which death, destruction and conflict with the sea recur with startling frequency.

—John J. Floherty, *Sentries of the Sea*

T HE NEXT MORNING I found that everything I owned still fit in my old Ford station wagon. It even ran up through the soft underside of New Jersey's bay shore. It kept running through the sleeping sickness backwaters, sour inlets of marsh gas and mosquitoes, and unpainted stores at silent crossroads. I was glad the sun was out so the mosquitoes would be less apt to attack. I even welcomed the sudden noise of metallic light in outer Camden and it was in that din I found the sign for the great bridge. Crossing the Delaware, I was fighting too much late-hour traffic to look down, so I had to comfort myself with visions of Walt Whitman leisurely buffooning his way across on the ferry boat that must have run somewhere under where the bridge now shot its iron. Well, I would have time on the lighthouse to read. On the lighthouse there would be time beyond what I could imagine. I wondered how deep it was under the bridge.

The Delaware roads passed in a mist. I woke up at a sign that announced: Smyrna.

But there were gas stations and used-car lots instead of exotic Mid-Eastern quays. The auto blight at last thinned into chicken farms and the sunlight that had been strident among the chrome thinned with the landscape, finding only occasional cross-hatchings of coop wire over which to twitch. By the time I saw the sign for the Greenmeal turn-off even these farms had softened into dusk. The side road went left and I knew I was beginning the final run that would take me to the sea. Meager as the landscape had just been, I wanted to hold on to it, for I sensed it was going to be more than I'd have for weeks to come.

There was a stop light. I looked for the cross traffic on the dark road. It took me a moment to realize that the darkness was not a road but water—evidently, by its neat cut, a canal. From beyond it a beam of light came swinging in over a stretch of peeling sand. The light ripped the sand up into existence, reaching to my hood until the buildings all about me were whacked into shape. As quickly the beam moved off, leaving the town hunkered down in its night lights, and though it was only around ten o'clock the only sound was the click of the traffic light as it changed and the plop of something falling into the canal.

In the magnolia-haunted shadows of a canal bank bar I found a lean, weatherbeaten man. He blew booze and directions at me. Sure the lighthouse was working: look out—wasn't that its beam blasting past? But how did one get to it? He grinned. So I was the new man, eh? Did I think I was man enough to get old Chanty off? Old who? Old Chanty. Pete Chanty, BM2, "a crazy nigger holed up in the tower for eight years." Was he alone out there? Others came and went, but he stayed on. The Group Commander had been his buddy, but now he had retired, and the new C.O. had discovered Chanty asleep in his chair with no horn or light on in the fog. That had been a week ago. Chanty had refused to leave, though the other members of the rotating four-man crew were on duty out there. What, I asked, about the abandoned lights? I must have meant Cape Henlopen. A mile out to sea she was by now. Why was that? Why was what? Why was a lighthouse out to sea? It was *under* the sea—the sea covered it up completely. Yes, but what had actually happened? The sea had covered it up. And the other abandoned towers? A tanker had hit the Elbow-of-Cross-Ledge Light and knocked the tower off its base. The watch stander had been asleep. Was this, I asked, the same fellow who'd been asleep on the tower I was to board?

"There's always a fellow asleep in a tower," he said. "How else could you stand to be surrounded by so much damn water?"

Using this waterfront Elijah's directions, I found the lifeboat station that was to put me aboard the tower the next day. It was a big, white frame house with a red roof and outbuildings all nestled down back of high dunes over which swung the ocean beacon.

The big parking lot was empty except for a gray, Coast Guard pick-up, so I parked right alongside of it and advanced, orders in hand, upon the station's back door.

There was a noise from the roof. Up there was an oversized cupola and there seemed to be somebody moving around in it, a restless shadow, the idiot son maintained in the attic twisting his bright pieces of cloth. I continued my march toward the back door.

Peering out through the screen were two eyes. They were having trouble because the screen was covered with June bugs that looked like big, brown popped eyes themselves. The pale face was topped by a chief's hat and held up by a neck that emerged from loopy underwear. The ample belly, however, was covered by khaki. One hand held a straight razor and at first I thought this instrument was being used to remove the bugs. What made the face pale was the lather. Up close, he looked like Santa Claus.

In thirteen weeks of intensive training we'd received hours of instruction on just what to do when reporting into our first duty station. There was a sequence of officers to salute. Flags, quarterdecks and other objects also required us to raise our visor. There were methods of executing the pivots involved, techniques for enunciating the appropriate utterances. I stood paralysed before the Santa of the June bugs.

"You must be the new man," he said.

"Is the Harbor of Refuge Light still--?" I jabbed my orders toward the screen.

"I figured I'd better shave even though it was almost time to go to bed," said the chief. "Better late than never, don't you think, son?"

My well-drilled salute limped off into a slap at the June bugs on the screen.

"Don't pay them no mind, son. There's a certain amount going to be on this old door screen for the next two weeks. But what's two weeks? Nuthing we can't live with, eh, son?"

Inside the back passageway he took the manilla folder and fanned it in the bright overhead light. I marveled that I had gotten inside while the June bugs had not.

"Oh, boy," sighed the chief, "but you *are* the new man afterall, ain't you." He shook his head sadly, but the lather clung to his face.

He sat me down at a long green table that faced a half dozen windows down which had been dropped venetian blinds. There were no lights on in this room, just a pale wash from the galley behind me. As the chief hummed in the galley the smell of coffee came out to me with his voice. I sat with my hands folded on the table and watched the blinds swell with light from the outside, swell and ripple from right to left and then die back into dimness. It was like a night in the Keokuk Hotel. A crash from the galley.

A load of crockery, heavy institutional plates soused with military utensils.

I turned, expecting to see a cursing man up to his ankles in shards and silverware.

The chief, however, stood in the galley door, mild with the accomplishment of his two mugs of coffee. It was quite another voice pouring down in a cascade of static as through a hole in the roof.

"There you go," said the chief with his own mild voice. He tossed his head up. While in the galley, he must have removed the lather. His cheeks were pink enough. "There's your new home now." He put the coffee on the table. I peered into it, thinking he meant my new home was to be in a coffee cup, a figure of speech I thought his soft drawl easily capable of. Nor did it seem to me, in my present agitation, that a steaming coffee cup would be such a bad harbor in which to hole up for the remainder of my military obligation.

The other voice rolled down on us. Deep, resonant, it seemed nevertheless full of holes, like lava cooled too quickly.

"Chanty," explained the chief. "He's been extra anxious since he heard you were coming."

"He's up there? Up in the attic?"

"Sounds like it, don't it. I told the boy up there on watch to leave the hatch open so we could all hear the radio."

"Up in the cupola?"

"Up in the tower."

"On the roof, that big . . . cupola."

"That's where the radio is, son; Chanty, he's out on the lighthouse." The chief turned toward the venetian blinds. "That's her beacon splashing by out there. We keep these here blinds drawn at night so she don't give us a headache."

"Then it does work, the lighthouse. The Harbor of Refuge."

The chief just smiled and pointed a pink finger at the overhead. The strange voice reverberated from on high.

"That's the first we've heard from him di-rectly in a week," said the chief, "but we been hearing in-directly. That's how we knew he was anxious about you."

"But he doesn't even know me. No one knew who was going out there. They just cut my orders yesterday."

"I mean he wanted to know all about just who was going out there to try to get him to leave."

The coffee was ok. "If he didn't let you know *directly*, as you say, how did he let you know *in*-directly?"

"There's all kinds of funny ways the boys out there communicates."

"But he didn't actually want to leave?"

"Old Chant, he's a little different. He don't even always take his liberty."

"Two weeks on, one week off, right?" I said. "Just like your bugs out there on the door."

"It is, if you can make things work out for you when you come ashore. Some people can't seem to do that, you know, son. They prefers to remain out there on them towers stuck into the sea."

"And the towers stuck into the sea? Do they remain?"

"That was an Air Force tower you're thinking of off here. 'Old Shakey.' The Air Force don't know how to make no good sea towers."

"I was referring to a Crossed-Elbow thing and one called Hen some-thing. A sailor coming out of a bar down town by the canal, sharp-faced fellow—"

"Creel that was, no doubt. The best boat handler in the Group, maybe the District, a down-home boy from the Banks. We'll use him to get you out there tomorrow," he winked "Them lighthouses can be tricky places to land."

"I'm not sure he was actually drunk—"

"Now don't worry, son." The chief reached across the table but his belly prevented his arm from making it all the way to my hand. "He can handle a boat in nearly any condition."

"And the tower itself, is it in *ok* condition?"

"You got to stop worrying about the Elbow-of-Cross-Ledge Light, son. That was hit by a tanker on account of dozing at the switch. The Cape Henlopen Light, well, now that was long ago. Why, the British even burnt her before she got around to falling over from what you call your e-ros-yun."

"And if this Chanty fellow doesn't want to get off the——"

"Harbor of Refuge Light," said the chief. "That's your new home, son: The Harbor of Refuge Light. It ain't gonna be Chanty's home no more."

"And if he wants to stay?"

"Why, you're just going to have to tell him, son. You're just going to have to say, 'Chanty, old boy, this is *my* new home.' "

The next morning two chambray-shirted men met me in the galley. Neither was the sharp-faced Creel. I looked for the friendly chief. The coffee smelled as good, but neither his voice nor his face was there. The blind was still down; I pushed up a slat. At first I thought they were snow drifts. The light swung in, paler now in the first loosening of the night sky. In spite of the snow fence, I knew they were dunes. I could not see the ocean over them.

"And Creel?" I said. "Creel, the famous boathandler from the Outer Banks?"

"Ha!" said the shorter man. His stencil read: *Luntsky*.

"Come on," said the taller one, "you got to go to the grocery store first. Chanty called in the list last night." His stencil read: *Farilla*.

"Is that what that was?" I said, "I heard his voice, but couldn't under-stand a word he said."

"It's got all his favorite shit on it," said Luntsky. "You're going to have to throw him off, boy." He waved a paper. He was younger than I.

"And Creel, he's going to be there to—"

"Forget Creel."

"But what about the other guy? This Chanty—"

"He was a fighter in the navy, you know." Luntsky looked me up and down. "Chanty was a boxer, a *fleet* boxer."

"And an all-round mean nigger," said Farilla. "Chanty may not need anything on that list. He may just chew *you* up for breakfast." He motioned Luntsky to give me the list.

It seemed to have been written by a civilized hand, but then I realized it had not been penned by this Chanty, but merely copied down by last night's watch. Nevertheless, since it was my first chance to know the workings of the man into whose shoes I was going to step, I studied it as if it had been a message in a bottle:

> 1 gal low fat milk
> 1 box garlic
> 1 box garlic salt
> 1 box time (?)
> 1 bag onions
> 1 can onions (Bearmuda)
> 1 box salt (E-Z pour)

"This is for the whole week?" I said, "for two or three men?"

"Chanty was a cook before he went out there. No use arguing with him. What you call one of them goar-mayz."

"Well, who's in charge of the Light?" I asked. "I'm sure not being sent out there to take over."

The two men looked at each other. "That's for sure," said Farilla. "That's for fuckinsure."

"Guy named Blump. BM1. Used to be a cook, too."

"They send all the losers out there. What was your fuckup?"

"I was the camp bugler," I said. "They didn't care for the improvisation, or what they took to be jazz."

"Yeah, well you may get along with that nigger yet."

"But if you do, Blump will be pissed."

"He believes the nigger's laying the black pipe where it don't belong, if you know what I mean."

"You see, Blump's got a pretty wife ashore."

"Well, does Chanty have a wife?" I said.

"Chanty's wife is that thar light-*house*."

"He gets the crap kicked out of him by the pimps when he goes home. He's got one of them 'underpriviliged homes' at home, if you know what I mean. Harbor of Refuge, now that's a much better home for him."

I tried to see the tower through the slats in the blind, but the dunes were, of course, still heaped so that all we had was the cresting from the beacon as it hit the top of the sand. "How far out is that place anyway?"

"You won't swim it."

"About two and a half miles."

In the pickup they explained to me that Blump was supposed to be out there the same as everybody else, two out of the three weeks, but he took advantage of Chanty so that he could stay ashore with his own pretty wife.

"She wants to be a movie star."

"Don't worry, Blump will take a run out to check on you one of these days. You can bet he won't be spending the night, though."

"It's hard to imagine all this intrigue," I said. "I mean there's just a tower out there that from here doesn't even look like it holds anybody at all."

"One thing you got to learn about workin' on one of them offshore stations, son: You got to keep track of your head."

The store was a small, unpainted building behind a dune. Its wood took on color only when the beacon passed over it. There was a chewing tobacco ad on the screen door and a man with a hat on within. As he moved under the single naked bulb, his hat brim spread the dangling strips of fly paper and his hands reached out to fill the order in the dim air like an undersea creature. He handed me a bill that already looked old. "You boys pay up on time now and you can look forward to the Christmas free gift."

I nodded and was half-way out the door when he waved a sleeve full of magazines, "How about some *fresh reading material?*"

The beacon swept over the faces of various starlets and floozies, their smiles fading with the beam.

"I got books," I stammered and fled into the night.

"What?" said Luntsky, "no *fresh reading material?*"

We drove back of the dunes. Above us the beacon light was almost imperceptible in the pearl-colored sky. We turned left before a huge block silhouette, and the air was heavy.

"Fish factory," said Farilla.

We ran toward the water, and I could see the fishing boats at the pier with their deck lights still on. They were big boats, well over seventy feet with smokestacks and a wild shear. The crews were hollering under the bright deck lights.

"Don't get excited," said Farilla, "they's just niggers."

"And them boats ain't nothin either, just ol' coal heavers. They was sub chasers back to World War One. Men-*hay*-den boats. Boney fish. Strictly trash."

A mixture of low tide, coal, and fish oil, the air was strong enough to bring tears.

We drove straight into it, right down the pier, bouncing over the rough planks so I began to feel queasy. There was a light at the end of the pier, and it kept coming up out of the water to blind us so that Farilla had his sun flap down and his left arm up. "That's your goddamn Light killing us now," he said.

"I didn't realize that was it," I said. "It's much stronger."

"Before you was down behind the dunes. This here's an open shot."

For a moment I thought he was going to drive me right out to it, but we came to the end of the pier and he swung along the T-head. There were no Coast Guard craft down at the bottom of the ladder.

There were two iron boats with long foredecks and box cabins that looked like Band-Aid boxes. On the foredeck was an oversized bow rail. On the side of the white box cabin was tall red lettering:

PILOT

"We'll help you with your gear," said Farilla.

"Where's the boat we're going out on?" I said.

We had stopped above the pilot boat, and the Coast Guard crew was unloading the groceries and my embarrassingly new sea bag.

"These fellers'll take you out."

"We just cleaned up our boat and don't want to get her all fuctup just for no lighthouse run."

They were gone back up the pier in the truck before I could ask how I was to persuade the pilots to put me on that distant tower. In fact I could not even find any pilots. There was no one at all except the crews of the menhaden boats at the pier a hundred yards away, and as the sun started to come up it got so cold I began to shiver.

There was a limit to the effectiveness of my keep-warm dance and the cabin on the pilot boat below looked cozy, so I slithered down the piling onto the steel deck. It was littered with cigarette butts and soda caps. After months of boot camp you notice those kinds of things. I actually began picking them up. As I was bending over for my second handful of litter, a door opened behind me, and a sleepy young man dressed only in his underwear drifted out past me and proceeded to pee, employing his stream in the same task that had occupied me so that many of the cigarette butts were swept overboard in the effort, to say nothing of a few soda caps which tumbled after. I stood there with my collection in my hands. The young man looked at me.

"You must be the guy right out of boot camp who's going to try to throw Chanty off."

"The crew from the lifeboat station left me here," I said. "They said their boat was too clean to go to the lighthouse."

"Too lazy you mean." He shuffled back inside the cabin, his bare feet leaving prints on the dewy red steel. The door slid shut. I stood there with the trash still in my hand. The door slid open. "Put that shit down and come in out of the cold, you asshole."

"Thank you," I said.

He was asleep by the time I'd disposed of the litter overboard and gotten the door back open and shut again. On the other bench was another man, much older, so fat that his covers were oozing off the rise of his belly. All he had over him was a bed spread with elegant tassels that twittered with the quiver of his body as he snored. Faint music came from the radio, country and western long before the fad, and there were ads for Blue Seal feed and bibles in between the forlorn stories. There was even an ad for setting your poetry to music, followed by one for rupture trusses. I sat on the pilot's stool, eased my forehead onto the rubber radar hood and dozed.

An explosion from the overhead:

"*Steel Age* standing in, Johnny. Get yer butt out here."

The young man staggered to the microphone dangling above my head, muttered something, and with a curse snatched the tasseled spread from the fat man's frantic paws.

While I tried to keep out of the way, the two of them slammed their legs into dungarees, balled up their bedspreads and flung them through a hatch which, when opened, reeked of diesel. There was a neatly dressed man up on the pier with an attaché case. He was reading the newspaper and could have been waiting for the commuter train at Scarsdale. The young man took the attaché case and told me to get my gear aboard. The fat man helped me.

"You'd better know your knots when we come to swing this chow up onto the Harbor Refuge," he said. "If you lose the week's chow in the sea, it's gonna be your ass in a sling."

We headed out past the menhaden boats and around the inner breakwater. The Lighthouse was shining pink in the sunrise, and the sea spread clear to the flat horizon. There was a smudge on that horizon, and the boy was talking on the radio. It was hard to believe that these frail voices were bridging that long expanse of sea.

"That smoke is the *Steel Age* all right," said the fat man, "but what you're going to need your knots for is the lighthouse, or your ass will be in a sling."

I tried to engage the well-dressed man in a discussion of the history of the lighthouses in the area, which ones had actually fallen down, et cetera. He remained behind his paper, but did confirm the Henlopen erosion case and the Elbow-of-Cross-Ledge fiasco.

The young man was reading, too. Not the financial page, but a comic book. He had it up in front of him as he steered the boat and sucked on an orange soda. The fat man alone was free to interpret the scene for me, but I could see he was preparing another sling warning.

The tower, meanwhile, had risen considerably. In fact, it had come to dominate the view. It was stuck on the end of a long, free-standing breakwater that angled up the bay and ended in a skeletal beacon. Off the far end were five separate piles of rock that made the whole affair look like a dragon's tail. "What are those little islands beyond the breakwater?" I asked.

"Ice breakers," said the fat man. "Wait until winter, you'll know enough about 'em. In winter you can be stuck out here a month at a time and then you damn well better have your chow aboard because nobody's getting out here to you."

"There's mainly gourmet stuff in that box now," I said.

"That's because Chanty's crazy," said the fat man.

"True," said the well-dressed man and he lowered his newspaper for the first time, adjusted his horn rims. "Of all the crazy keepers on this Light I've seen through the years, he wins hands down."

"I don't know," said the young man turning a page in his comic book and adjusting the helm a few degrees to starboard. "I found this here guy out on the fantail this morning picking up cigarette butts."

CHEZ CHANTY

The first lighthouse built on the end of the breakwater was completed in 1901. From the beginning it seemed to be a special target for the violence of the sea, for scarcely had the light been lit, when a gale of hurricane force attacked it.
—John J. Floherty, *Sentries of the Sea*

T HE TOWER was over us now: a great flared brown base, the seat for three stories of white cylinder and an additional smaller cylinder upon which perched the glassed-in lantern capped by a round, black roof that came to a comic point. Three open galleries circled the tower, but I saw no one. Twin foghorns protruded on the seaward side. A pair of black stacks jutted up beyond the roof. A flagpole without a flag jabbed from the highest of three galleries. Though there was no wind, the open ocean heaved us toward the lee of the landing stage, which loomed high over our radio mast.

"You better have those knots ready," said the fat man. He had helped me carry the boxes around the cabin and up onto the foredeck, where we crouched by the oversized bow rail. The deck had not dried from the dew before taking on a bit of spray, and the bottoms of the cardboard boxes were already sucking up the dark stain, which would weaken them.

"I know. I know," I said. "The bloody sling."

As if magically summoned, down from the sky snaked a line. I didn't have time to see who, if anyone, had dropped it. There was a hook on the end, and as it swept past my ear, I caught it, pulled, and, receiving some slack, at once went into several of the cargo slings I'd been running over in my mind in between bouts of worrying about the lighthouses falling over. The problem was I combined several of the flashier moves from an assortment of standard cadenzas without achieving a single bend that could be trusted with a week of dinners.

"What the hellz that?" the fat man kept saying, "The *three-leaf dragonfly knot?* What the hellz that, the *two-leafed Chinese temple knot?*" From the pilot house came more abuse.

In all that harassment, however, there cooed a different voice. Were there pigeons up there, ancient cliff-dwelling wings come to live in the high crossbeams, all other escarpments being drowned? The voice dripped from

45

the same height whence had descended the marvelous rope. Once before I had heard it falling upon me, and then I remembered: the voice from the cupola the night before—Chanty, *"Now, now, take your time, son. It's better to be safe than sorry. Don't let those pilot boys upset you. What do they know about the long nights out here in the lonely sea? Waterbugs, that's all they are. Scurrying back and forth. Back and forth. It is up to us to remain imperturbable midst the sep-liquor of the sea. Better to be safe than sorry."*

"Here," said the fat man, aborting the celebrated Davenport Brothers trick knot that was aborning in my trembling hands. "There." He had performed an instant cargo sling. "Haul away, you nigger rigger."

And up it went. A week of dinners into the sky.

To be replaced up there by a dark face. "You see? *Safety Pays."* Covering the top half of the face was an inverted sailor's hat. Under it swung a long Chinese goatee. Black hands performed an act of legerdemain, and down again snaked the empty line. It was easy to make it fast to the handle on my sea bag. I had a small box of books which I took under my arm and, grabbing the iron ladder that ran up the face of the staging, I swung onto the highest rung I could grab.

Beneath me the pilot boat fell away on the swell. The fat man crinkled his hand in farewell and shook his head. The young man at the wheel leaned out the pilot house window and, screaming, flung an obscene gesture up at the top of the staging. From there the standard curse was returned. As the pilot boat rolled away I could see the well-dressed man was back to his paper. In fact it looked as if in all our circus of knots and slings he had maintained his preference for distant finances.

"Come on, son. Come on up the ladder now. You got to come up sometime."

"I'm coming," I said, and juggled the box of books so I could arrive at the top without attracting attention to them. My bright-khaki bag, however, spun slowly up past my face. There would be no hiding the fact that it had never been to sea before.

"You musn't pay any mind to those who in this world might cast their lot with the detractors of lighthouses."

He was behind me, toting my sea bag. I had the carton of groceries, and the small box of books was on top, held down only by my chin.

As he talked, I kept my eyes straight ahead. High above me, I knew, was the tower, its black comic cap tearing at the speeding clouds. Behind me was this half-naked man with the deep sing-song. I had caught a glimpse of him as I'd stepped from the top of the ladder. In fact, had there not been a handshake, one of those bonecrushers which catches you early and renders

your hand helpless? I had managed, however, to look him in the eye, no
mean task as his eyes were almost completely covered by the inverted sailor
cap, which hung like a yellowed bell over his already-drooping lids. Around
the brown irises was a yellow to match the stained cap. And the cap had stenciled on it:

BLUMP BM1

We were climbing the stairs to the first balcony. There was a shack
stuck on the back of the white, rounded tower, and beyond it a big fuel tank.
Behind me Chanty continued to philosophize upon the historical plight of
those attending the world's beacons. The first such people, he said, were
priests burning piles of faggots. I was to understand this was not so much in
reprisal for homosexuals infiltrating the ranks as in the spirit of international
navigation.

Unsure if this remark had been designed as a joke, I coughed.

It was also important that I understand that there were fifty people on a
Chinese lighthouse.

"Fifty people, eh?" I said. "That's a lot of people." It was also a lot of
steps.

"Not so many people when you considers they got this in-tensive drive
mechanism of complexities so they got to bicycle it around the basement to
keep it in the major oscillation operation."

The Chinese were not the only Orientals we had to deal with. The Japanese were even worse. They were "precise." This strange trait seemed to
manifest itself in their constantly calling us up on the radio demanding we
correct our beacon characteristic, which was only off by a tenth of a second,
and, in any case, locked into adjustment by the district engineers from Base
Gloucester. "Now the Limey ships, they come up here without no chart or
nothin and all covered in that soft Birmingham coal and are lucky they even
knows what lighthouse they has found out to be lookin at at all. Then these
Nips not only *knows*, they knows which lighthouse you is, but tells you in
what way *you* is not the *precise* that you ought to be."

"I thought this was going to be a lonely duty," I puffed, "but instead we
seem to be at an international crossroads."

"Well, now technically this is the National Harbor of Refuge—that is,
the harbor part out of which we is climbing. Other side is the bay meetin the
ocean, just like on the corner."

"I meant the ships were international."

International indeed! He himself had killed two dozen Italians in the
Anzio campaign in World War Two and had recently been the victim of a pistol whipping by the South Philadelphia police "following an encounter with a

nigger pimp," a conflict made more inevitable somehow by Chanty's long absence from "the field of egregious moments."

"Yes," I puffed, "I imagine that——"

"Don't waste no sympathy on me, boy. I got somethin on the side myself."

"Out here?"

"Oh, no, I don't receive no mail out here. Like I say, lighthouse keepers is not exactly the eye-leet of the Coast Guard. I put down we is really on a weather cutter, one of them what's called 'white elephants' count of bein' U.S. Navy discards from World War Two. I puts down: *U.S. Coast Guard Cutter Harbor of Refuge*. That way she thinks I'm roving the high voluminous upon de white elly-phant. That way she don't think I is just out here stuck on a pile a gull shit lookin out the window night after night."

"But the mail, does it get to you that way?"

"Hey, there's chances you got to take out here, boy. Chances in love and war."

"These sure are a long set of stairs," I said.

"Ain't nothin," he said. "Just look up."

Foolishly I did and, without a free hand, would have fallen back down the full length of the stairs had it not been for the strong garlic breath behind me.

"Upsa daisy," he said and restored my equilibrium. I recalled that below the yellowed cap and the yellow eyes, below the wispy goatee, he had broad, fighter's shoulders brown and bare. "Just keep calm now and step through that shelter door, son. Ain't no point in fallin overboard before you see your new bed."

Inside I was shocked by the persistence the building had in maintaining its roundness. A central cylinder ran up through the middle of the tower, just like, as Chanty explained, an angel-cake pan. Indeed, the stove and sink were around clockwise, and as we walked that way toward the open sea there were chrome and plastic chairs, a Formica table and two big leather chairs leading on around the curve of the tower. In the near chair lounged a young man in rumpled chambray and jeans. His face was white, especially pale for that time of year. He, like Chanty, sported a scraggle of goat hair.

"This is the very chair responsible for your new life," Chanty went on, tapping the leather back while ignoring the occupant. "The infamous or, if you prefer, famous, chair in which I fell asleep on watch."

"It does look comfortable," I said.

"Dis herez Toy," said Chanty in what I had already come to recognize as his imitation darky voice. "Toy, dis herez de newman what's gonna replace your ol Papa here on the Harbor Refuge."

Toy cast an eye up at me though his tangled hair. He might have been a corpse found floating in a stagnant pond choked with rotting lily pads and goitered frogs.

"How are you?" I said.

A smirk crept across Toy's thin lips.

"I doubt I'll be able to replace Chanty here," I said, "but this is where they sent me."

A few teeth deigned to slip up into Toy's smirk for a look around. Behind me, Chanty coughed.

"Well," I said, "I'd better put this chow somewhere."

"I can just imagine," said Toy, a croak as if he had not spoken in days.

"You can just imagine what?" I said.

"What's in that box," he said. " 'Chow.' " His nostrils flared.

"You had your opportunity for input," said Chanty. "The entire crew has its opportunity to effect an input into any meal conceived and directed here."

But Toy was looking back at the bulkhead, tongue-in-groove vertical sheathing painted light green. There was a bracket up there and some wires.

"Come on, Mr. Replacement," Chanty cooed. "He ain't gonna do no more for us today than just stare at that bracket where the TV used to be."

"Yeah, you bastard!" shouted Toy and he was standing up, pushing me aside, this rumpled ragamuffin in chambray, his eyes burning now through his forelock. "You nigger bastard, so dumb you dropped the fuckinTVoverboard and now we ain't got nothin to do, nothin to do all day and nothin fuckintodo all night and all fuckinday but listen to you, listen to you, listen to you and your crazyfuckin stories about Wopssneakinuponya an Chinamenpedaling-gears an burning-fuckin-faggots an pistol-whipping-pimps, ya fuckindumbnigger. You know what you done? Ha, ya know what you done? You dropped the TV overboard."

And as suddenly as he'd jumped up, he collapsed back into the vast leather chair, his eyes went back to the empty bracket, and his teeth sank back down through his thin lips and were covered by them.

"Come on," cooed Chanty, "I'll address you to your new quarters."

The central cylinder, which Chanty had likened to the middle of an angel-cake pan, actually contained an iron spiral staircase. Our steps echoed upwards into the light Chanty had produced by hitting a switch. At the conclusion of a full revolution of the spiral we arrived at a door which opened into a circular room flooded once again with daylight pouring in out of the sky and off the sea. There were bunks with pale-blue spreads against the far bulkhead, and their color matched that of the sea so perfectly that if it weren't for the Coast Guard emblem with its anchor in the center of each spread the bunks would have flown out the windows into the circumambient blue.

"A place of unmitigated repose," said Chanty in his strange mellow voice. Then clearing his throat he added, "Dis here to de right is de shitter."

The bathroom had a good view of the breakwater running off to the north and, if one peered down directly below, there was the landing stage, which, looked at from above, seemed like the dance floor of a summer pavilion. A pair of bright-yellow metal boxes completed the garden effect.

"Paint lockers," said Chanty. "You'll learn to know them all too well. They are situated out there owing to regulations arising from the Stannard Rock Lighthouse disaster on Lake Michigan. There, a tower in which paint was stored suffered a near-fatal conflagration during the depths of a winter blizzard. The men had to flee to a small pinnacle of ice-encrusted rock from which they were forced to observe the distruction of their home while warming their hands at the fire."

"And what about the disasters around here?" I said, and recounted the list I had been assembling.

"That, my friend," he said, "is something you iz jus gonna have to work out for ye-sef." And he turned on the shower and sink faucets and flushed the toilet to demonstrate just how such contrivances might work.

"But don't *you* go flushin an drainin without no personal needs. There may be water-water every where you peeks, but *it* don't do nuthin but *menace*. That's what good that water out there is. A mess o' menace. In here what we uses is from the cellar in de casks."

"Casks?" I said. "Sounds like a winery."

He laughed bitterly. "Nothin but bat-wing water down in dem casks, son. Brought here by *buoy snatcher*, by Mr. Milkins's buoy snatcher, not off de roof for our sisters no mo'."

"Sister?"

"Never minds the sister. I payed for that already. I got the courts-marshal offense for the sister. You, see, nobody told me nuthin when I come on here. No body." He put his arm on my shoulder, and his face was very close. "I'm be-friendin you with a tour of what you might say, is my sinful, ignorant past."

"I see," I said, "and these sisters? They were the ones you had on the side?"

"Sister! Sister!" He withdrew his arm. "Down in de basement is de sister what co-lects de water from de roof in old days gone by, *before* I put *de fuel oil* in by courts-marshallable error." He took a step back. "You got to stop thinkin about sex all the time when you're out here."

"You put the fuel oil in the water supply?"

"Don't laugh, my little replacement man. You ain't had none of what I had eight year of. You know what that eight year was of?" He put his face up close. "Huh? You know?"

"No, not exactly."

"*Opportunity.*"

The tour continued on the three remaining decks aloft. There was a storage room in which reposed the switches and valves that activated the foghorns. Above it was the old watchstander's room where the "Wickies," as Chanty called them, the old Lighthouse Service keepers, maintained their night-long vigils in the days before the automatic alarm system. There they had wound the chain-driven mechanism that propelled the light casing, or chariot, in its orderly circle. There they had stored the brass Aladdin's lamp with its whale oil, which they used if the generator failed to provide the electricity that lit the bulb. He opened a wooden cabinet and showed me the brightly polished Aladdin's lamp.

"That's a beautiful piece of work," I said. "Wouldn't that look good on the mantelpiece!"

"Mantelpiece? It goes inside the chariot when the bulbs all been burned out, only it don't fit the new system."

"And the small cask of whale oil?"

"Overboard."

"Overboard?"

"A fit of *personal nausea.*"

He put back the lamp and shut the locker doors. "You have no idea," he said, "of the depths to which even a small cask of whale oil can reach into you. I refer, of course, to the oldfactory sensations."

"Olfactory?" I said, not so much to correct him as to check my own understanding.

"*Old*-factory," he said. "A term of some technical brilliance." He coughed. "In any case I suffered de courts marshall for my efforts. Seems whale's oil, even in the small cask dimension, is a capital outlay accordin to de calm-troller."

"Who is he?"

"The calm-troller is the calm-troller, son. It couldn't be more specific. Down below is the calm-troller manual and all its various specifics what which we has to live and die by the book."

He showed me the flag. It was neatly folded on the locker top. He undogged an oval iron door and admitted a cascade of air and light. Out there was the flag gallery, and, sure enough, out there was the flagpole. No, we would be foolish to actually fly the flag except during inspections. Up here the wind was always strong enough to "reduce our nation's glorious heritage to a case of de-tatters in a matter of a few hours." He slammed shut the door and dogged it with additional resonance, then, dusting his hands, pulled at the folded flag on its shelf just enough to display the "first stages of the insipid tatters."

I couldn't help looking up through the hatch in the overhead. A narrow, open stairway circled up through the opening. Chanty was chuckling.

"You like that last one, eh?"

"That's the last one?"

"After that we runs out of ourselves. After that, the rest is all wild blue yonder."

I put my hand on the rail. "Well?"

"You better let me go first." He began up the short ladder. When his head was through the ceiling he stopped, and his voice echoed. "This, you know, is the lantern from the original tower. This is a very old room up here." He wouldn't go up, however.

"Oh," I said, "what happened to the original tower that held this part up?"

There was a mumbling from inside the lantern.

"It what?" I said.

His body all but plugged the hole, and when he was through there was a blast of light and a ringing that ran right through me.

Before I could identify the source of the sound, it had stopped, but the pain lingered, seeming to pick up energy from the iron and light of the tight chamber into which I slowly crept.

"Come on, come on," he said. "This is what we is all about. Son, meet the chariot."

"Chariot?"

He slapped the slowly spinning case. As it turned its lens toward me, I ducked, but he only laughed again.

"Ain't nothin in the day time. I just turned it on to give you the demonstration. Now, you hit that switch down by your heel there."

I looked back down the ladder. There was a switch on a box. It could have been a simple light switch in a rec room. I tapped it. Jumped.

Damn bell again.

When it stopped there was Chanty's laughter, no less resonant in the iron and glass.

The chariot, however, had stopped turning.

"That alarm bell goes on everytime sumthin happen up here. No ding-a-ling equals no rest for the weary. Now pay attention because this is what you got to do to keep somebody from knockin on de door with their bow."

The lamp chariot filled so much of the lantern or chamber that when Chanty motioned me to pass him for a better look at his demonstration we had to squeeze together. Pinned on the far side of the chamber from the hatch, I had my back to the glass, through which I did not quite dare glance. Before me Chanty was unbuckling the sides of the chariot.

Inside the aluminum casing, behind the concentric Fresnel lenses, reposed two bulbs, each the size of a small ham grinder. "It's hard to imagine that light carries—how many miles?"

"Fourteen miles. This is a first class Aid. It's done with this here Frenchman lens."

"Fresnel," I said, "Augustin Jean Fresnel, 1788–1827. He replaced the use of mirrors with the compound lens."

I could feel Chanty's eyes burning and I examined the casing of the chariot. In raised letters it said "Airport Beacon."

"You know how to replace a defective bulb, Monsieur Fray-knell?"

"No," I said. "I'm only a fan. A lighthouse fan."

"A fan, eh?" he snorted. "Well, Mr. Fan, you better learn how to change the bulb."

"All right," I said. "I'd be glad to learn how to change the bulb."

"*Glad!* Glad?" He shook his head and began to display the ingenious if somewhat unpredictable switching mechanism which caused one bulb to swing around on its holder to replace the other much like one of those old Fair Weather-Foul Weather barometers where the beautiful and ugly figures swing in and out of the little chalet. All this was accompanied by the jangling alarm bell and cursing by Chanty. "Trouble is it's hot, cause I turned it on to show you." He spat on his fingers.

"But isn't that always going to be the way when the bulb goes out?" I said.

"No it ain't." He sucked a finger. "Sometimes it goes the minute you turn it on. Just like any bulb. Don't you know about *any* bulb?"

"That's true," I said. "*Any bulb,* as you say, will usually blow when you turn it on. It's just hard to think of this as——"

"Well, it ain't no different. People get wrong ideas." Slapping the aluminum casing back together like a comic suit of jousting armor, he sighed. "As you can see, it ain't always foolproof. At least not to this here fool, meaning myself."

"If the bulbs weren't working," I said, "I don't see how you could fit that Aladdin's lamp into the casing of the chariot in order to take advantage of the lenses."

"I already told you that. This is the new system."

"Well, under the new system what do you do with the Aladdin's lamp?"

"You just hold it up here in your hand like Miss Liberty." He did a shockingly accurate imitation which he broke off with a giggle. "Now: *look-athis!*" He spun, and there was a red pane of glass in the window. No doubt it had been there all along, but his moves had made it seem to have just popped into place on the shore side of the lantern. "*Red sector*, baby. You gets back there in a deep-draft ship and you is in trouble. That's why you won't see no freighters or tankers that side ever. Or if you do, you must have been dozin at the switch."

I was somehow aware, without actually looking, of the sea—how it existed not only far below, but, by some optical fluke and despite our long climb—still above us. It stretched up to meet the sky, also very blue that day, so that the wind shaking the loose panes all around the chamber seemed also to be carrying us away as if we were in a big balloon. It was a relief when Chanty plucked a curved white object from the ceiling with his dark fingers.

"You think this is a magnolia blossom, Mr. Fan?"

"It does look like one," I said. "But I suspect it's paint."

There were several bare spaces in the curved, galvanized ceiling. "Now, this is the old part of the tower, remember."

"Yes," I said, "and I'm still curious as to what happened to the whole first six stories that used to support this final room."

"Ah, they was modified."

"Modified?"

"Substantially modified."

"Good lord, by what?"

"Before my time. I ain't been here since the inception, you know." He laughed. "I'm sorry if I sounds like I has."

"No, it's all right," I said. "I find it——"

Chanty held up his hand. He appreciated my *patronage*, as he put it, but I must understand he was far from the ideal man the Coast Guard would wish their new men to be indoctrinated by. He was not a good example. It was understood I was to remedy all this. For instance, he had not used lemon oil to clean the lens; he had not washed the outside of the lantern windows, which were often encrusted with salt, though over seventy feet above sea level; he had not properly scraped the "onions" between the window-panes of the watchstander's room; he had not oiled the spring in the watch-stander's chair; he had not provided his women with adequate emotional support during his "long absences at sea"; he had not countered the punch of the pimp with the proper "deploy"; he had not yet shown me the stove or the refrigerator or the engine room.

"O.K.," I said. "Then let's go down."

He grinned. "So the heights is getting to you?"

"I'm sure I'll get used to it."

"You ain't gonna tell me again you is Mr. Fray-knell, the light-house *fan?*"

A SULLEN NOISE

For two days and nights the storm raged and the keepers imprisoned on it gave up all hope of surviving. The structure trembled and swayed from the successive shocks of wind and sea. Of none too solid construction the building leaked like a sieve. The lantern had several of its panes broken so that it was a continuous struggle to keep the light going.

—John J. Floherty, *Sentries of the Sea*

DOWN SIX STORIES in the engine room, he explained that this was, of course, really "black gang territory," meaning Toy or whoever would replace him. Yes. Toy was going to be replaced soon, too, and so too was the *ha-ha-officer-in-charge*, the "notorious Blump." This announcement was accompanied by a long, black finger stabbing at the stenciling on the inverted sailor hat. "I wearz de-Blump hat at this moment because, you see, de-Blump ain't here, as usual, and dat make me, ol Chant, de Blump."

"I wondered about that," I said. "How your hat came to acquire his name on it."

"Name *and* rate. And that's because I got his job. You understand, I *do* his job. And that ain't all I do of his." A raw, red thing shot out from under the hat and it had been wagging in the air before I realized it was only his tongue.

"My God," I said, "it's as if you've no roots holding that thing in your face."

He demonstrated not only the length, but the marvelous control he had over the tip of his tongue.

"It's as if the end is a whole separate beastie," I said.

Writhing, it was gone into the fissure of his hairy lips. "Now," he said, "we shall proceed."

"I just want to know what I'm supposed to do as a lighthouse keeper."

"Lighthouse *keeper!*" He spat. "So now it's not Mr. Lighthouse *fan;* it's Mr. Lighthouse *keeper!*"

"Duties," I said. "Just duties."

"Son, you *do* have some sense of humor."

The first thing he showed me was the workbench. It was a massive gray

57

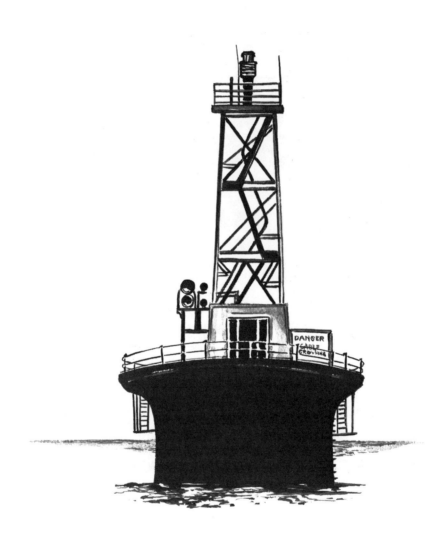

construction with built-in vises and a backboard upon which were carefully drawn silhouettes of every tool a householder could imagine, from cross-rip saws to carew cutters. Unfortunately there were no tools. On the bench itself lay a screwdriver and claw hammer.

"Very pretty art work," I said, "those silhouettes."

"Some will require a little touching up," he said, "the essence of a silhoutte being maintained in its crisp outlines."

The furnace was nothing more than a regular home oil burner. "It was a big, fat coal-burnin mutha when I arrived," he said, "but being an old coal heaver in the Navy before I came over to the Coast Guard, I had no trouble with your clinkers and green grates."

"The Navy, I take it, was after the Army," I said. "That is after your Anzio and Casino action that you spoke of earlier."

"At least when I pitched the shovel load into the fire down here, the deck didn't heave me in after. I seen a man go in that way once. When I was younger than you. Door slammed shut right after him. I didn't even know enough to open it up again." He stared off into space. There were no portholes on that side, for it was the part of the flaring base of the tower that faced the open sea, and the light came only from naked bulbs suspended from the overhead two stories up. "That may seem stupid to you, not to know enough to open that door after it slammed shut with my buddy in there."

"I don't imagine it had anything to do with knowledge."

"Oh, it don't huh?" He found my eyes in the gloom. "You don't think I have no knowledge?"

"That wasn't what I meant."

"You just be thankful you don't come down here in the middle of de cold night to play with this no more."

"I only meant——"

"I know what you meant. You can mean all you want to mean when you don't got to come down here in cold nights to stoke up, boy."

As we walked over a pair of manhole covers I wondered if they led to the famous "sisters," but thought better of dredging up that horror.

"Now, these," he said pointing to two big Buda diesels up on blocks, "these are the heart of the job." On this side of the flare there were portholes high up, so that the artificial light was ripened by the sky. Still, one wondered just how high the water was hitting outside. Although it was a mild day, the sea smacked with enough force to create a constant din among the concrete and iron. As a result there were times when I had to strain to catch what he said.

These diesels were compressors, he said. They "huffed up air," that went into the pair of silo-shaped tanks rising between the left-hand compressor and the workbench. They, like almost everything else down there, were gray, and they reached up into the dim, resonant light so that I could hardly make out their tops. The idea of filling these great lungs, even with the big compressors, seemed hopeless. Moreover, the thought of their being full was terrifying.

"Can these things blow up?"

"Just make sure the safety valve is workin."

The safety valve was a pretty enough thing, with a brass cocking lever, but unfortunately it was up on top of a tank of its own, which, while not anywhere near as big as the two silos, was still tall enough to put the valve beyond my reach.

"Does it ever get stuck?" I said.

"Just hit with de broom." He looked around. "Well, de broom ain't here just now."

There were other dangers. In engaging the compressor clutch, it was necessary to heed the compressor belt, which had demonstrated a "marked lunacy to react unfavorably." On these occasions it jumped off the drive wheel, and the operator was required to fetch a Phillips screwdriver, dismantle the belt-guard assembly, and reset the belt on the drive wheel, "in no case employing a sharp tool of any kind." Once the belt was back on the wheel, there was no guarantee it wouldn't fly off again, and the guard assembly, which had, of course, been properly reassembled, had to be disassembled all over again. To save valuable time it was necessary to wait until the belt engaged upon the wheel before going through the business of putting back the guard. "Only problem then is right here." Chanty indicated a left hook to the jaw. "Slap you upside de head."

"The belt comes off the wheel and hits you?"

"Don't laugh, boy. Many's a bout I done lost to dis here compressor drive belt."

"Knocked out?"

"Worsen. Knocked silly. And de whole time some big ship is bearin down up there outside de house." He pointed up beyond the silos. "Dats right where you come to expect de ship to come through."

"Wouldn't it hit the rip-rap first?"

"You seen them ships? You know how fast they go now days? You seen how much *rip rip rip* we got out there? Now you tell me what's gonna go rip-rap!"

"But don't they have radar?"

"What do you think de lighthouse for?"

"To tell them to keep off the rocks."

"But first it tell them cum-cum-cum. . . ." He hunched and beckoned. "Cum-eer, lil ol'super ship." He stood up straight. "What you call your

Landfall and Basic Harbor Approach. You see, they is lookin for you and you got to let them know where you is, precisely. And you know where you is precisely in that situation?"

"I'm not familiar with the precise coordinates."

"The precise co-ordin-ates is down on your hands and knees in de bottom of de well." He walked back of the compressor again. "Right down here, all precisely fingery with de grease, your nose in de slap-belt and yo ass in de air and you-know-who sniffin through de wall."

"There must——"

"Blow de horn, you say. Ha! Blow de horn yoseph. Ain't no peep outa no machine or no horn or *nothin*."

I stood there, emitting no peeps.

"You know why no peeps? You know why you is down on your knees with not even a whimper, boy?"

I gestured loosely toward the guard belt apparatus.

"Dat's it. Dat's it precisely. The disassembly situation is the situation, dat's why."

"That's quite a situation."

"Never mind smirkin at situations, boy."

Actually my face felt more like a grimace than a smirk. Nevertheless, my boot-camp training had given me a method for the instant modification of cheek bones and all the ancillary flesh which depended from them.

"You ever hear, boy, hear tell of the Elbow-of-Cross-Legend?"

"The Elbow-of-Cross-Ledge," I said, "yes. It fell over. A lighthouse."

He narrowed his eyes.

"It was a lighthouse," I stammered, "which fell over."

"*Fall* over? It didn't do no *fall* over. It was *knocked!*" He stuck out his lower lip and cocked his fist. "A ship is what knocked it. Bang!" The fist shot past my face, cooling the skin.

"Someone," I said, "Someone, I believe had fallen asleep on watch."

It wasn't until I saw his head snap back, much as if I'd just returned his blow, but with more accuracy, that I recognized the implications for him of what I'd just said. "That is," I stumbled on, "someone fell asleep on that lighthouse we were talking about, the Elbow-of-Cross Ledge Lighthouse. . . ."

He took a deep breath. "Let us pause here," he said, "to explain some things you may not have anticipated."

I assured him I had anticipated none of this. My mechanical experience previously had been confined to trying to keep the oil-change sticker from peeling off the inside of the car door. He smiled, a low chuckle capering across his lips.

"Excuse me," he said. "Now, the problem is you only use one compressor at a time. Got that? You use one compressor for a duration of four hours, then switch over, assuming, of course, the fog is still upon you. This allows the first compressor to cool off and also for you to fill the day tank." He pointed to a yellow tank labeled neatly:

DAY TANK

"These," he said, "draw down from the big tank up on the balcony, which in proper lighthouse phras'ology is pronounced *gallery*."

I said it all seemed logical so far.

"Overflow the day tanks," he said, "and dey drains down in de sisters."

So transfixed by his shift from almost BBC perfect English into his darkie bit, I almost missed the reference to the famous polluted daughters of the cellarage. I merely nodded wisely.

"Now I ain't even shown you the two hardest things: engaging the clutch and starting the compressor in the first place. I got to save the first place for the last, though, because if I did things in order you couldn't hear nuthin else I said."

Again I assured him of the reasonableness of his approach.

"*Reason?* Never mind reason. Never mind *reason!* What *you* gonna do, boy?" He was jumping up and down, waving the screwdriver in my face, his yellow eyes alive. "What you gonna *do* to make a noise let them know you is here?"

I found my eyes focusing on the point of the screwdriver. "That's not a Phillips screwdriver," I said.

"Phillips? Phillips? What Phillips got to do with it? Ain't no Phillips here to make no noise to let them know."

"Ok," I said. "You were the one who said it had to be a Phillips. I thought you were trying to see if I knew. Like they do in boot camp. Tricks."

"Tricks? Boot camp. Ha, this ain't no boot camp, boy! Dis herez de reeeeeeel world."

"I believe that," I said, though it helped to look away from his mad eyes and catalogue the workbench with its tool silhouettes, the big generator batteries, the day tanks stenciled "DAY TANK." "Since the generator isn't running and we still have power, I assume we are connected to land by some sort of cable and this is merely a standby."

"Never mind *connected to land*. That's only a fragile wire what jerks out sometime when everything gets to twitching in between."

"At that point, during the 'twitching,' as you say, we put on the generator."

"They think they's gonna make this automatic with that little wire, but what they don't know about is between here and there is a whole lot of twitching."

"We put the generator on then."

"Never mind *then*, I ask you how you gonna let them know you is here *now*."

"O.K., how do you let them know you're here now?"

"That," he said, "is de trick." He held the screwdriver aloft and, following it like a wand, stalked the right side of the generator, his bare feet slapping the concrete. "What you do, is you *arch-the-sullen-noise.*"

And with another lewd grin from under the inverted hat, his tongue wagging, he tapped the starting mechanism.

A stream of sparks flew from the area of the solenoid.

Balloons of them hung in the noisy air.

Some of them floated to the floor, where the grease received them with excited applause. Chanty squelched these small explosions with a deft series of bare-footed dance slaps. The overall din was up a hundredfold, and it filled the cavern.

"You see! You see!" he cried. "Dat's it: archin-the-sullen noise."

"What?"

"Dat's what I done."

"You done *what?*"

"I done made a sullen noise."

Nor was he yet through. He dashed over to the silo tanks, dropped to one knee, and reached way under, where a squeaking and a counterclockwise grimace indicated he was turning a valve.

We sprinted up the central cylinder—up-around, up-around.

Toy's face was at the window of the mess deck, like someone we were passing in a train. His lips were pursed, his eyes laughing and his head seeming to follow me as I yanked on the gray rail and pumped my knees.

Up-around, up-around past the bunk deck, up-around we burst into the storage deck, dove in dimness around to the seaward side which had its window blocked up so that the great fog trumpets might be seated against the tower.

Down on our knees, we lit matches because it was now that dark inside.

His hand danced.

Faucets spun.

Brass switches snapped. A gauge twitched.

A clicking commenced.

Then a gasp.

A wheeze.

A broken moan.

Then no noise at all, but just a tremendous shaking within my body cavity.

And six inches away from me, in dwindling match light, a pair of yellow eyes.

RIP-RAP

After its baptismal storm the damage was repaired, the structure strengthened and
the riprap around its base rearranged to more completely cushion the force of the
waves. The ocean would not be cheated, however, for a few years later it attacked
the lighthouse with unprecedented fury and battered it to bits.

                                   —John J. Floherty, *Sentries of the Sea*

HAVING BEEN INTRODUCED to the lantern and the foghorn, I
felt I could now relax, and since I'd not had breakfast and it was
nearly noon, maybe have something to eat. I even imagined that I
might have a good look at the view in some capacity that did not involve my
having to do anything about it. My hand was on the refrigerator, a bloated
Buick of a model.

"*No.*"

There was a hand upon my shoulder. The fingers were finding whatever
strings and sinews held up my arm.

"No?" I said. "No food?"

"So much for the more dramatic business," Chanty said. "now I'll show
you what you really do out here all day." He beckoned me around to a row of
lockers.

From the far side of the stairway, Toy yawned. "You'll be so bored in a
week you won't be able to pick up a wrench."

"From what I saw of the tool board below," I said, "there are no
wrenches *to* pick up."

"Hey, you stay the hell away from them." Toy had jumped up from the
famous chair and stood shaking in his rumpled chambray. "Those are *my*
tools."

"Now, now, boys," said Chanty. "Let's not have any fighting between
Divisions."

"*Divisions!*" said Toy. "Listen to him. Just because he's thinking of
going at last out to some real sea duty on a real ship———"

"I been on ships," said Chanty. "Been before you was born."

"Yeah, but you ain't been lately. You ain't been lately, and what you
remember ain't worth shit but to scare you. The fact is these lighthouses,
this here partic'lar Light, has made you *worthless* to go to sea."

"There's no reason why a lighthouse can't be run sailor fashion, Toy." Chanty opened one of the three closet-style lockers and began pulling out mops.

"*Useless,*" said Toy again. "This ain't the only place *I* been, you know. That ship I was on in Florida. A paw-fuckin-troll boat."

"A white elephant," mumbled Chanty.

"A *gun* boat, mister. And we had one of your Wickies come on board. One of them lifetime 'lighthouse keepers.' You woulda loved him: had the old U.S. Lighthouse Service uni-forms and all. The old cap. Like what a chief might wear but with U.S.L.H.S., got a pit-chur of a lighthouse on it. His coat got brass buttons on it just like a chief, but they sure didn't give him no chief's billet. They give him a first class and him with that hat with a handle on it and all them brass buttons and lighthouse pit-churs. You know what they told him to do?"

Chanty pursed his lips and rearranged the bouquet of mops.

"You know what they told that old fool to do? They told him to staythe-fuckoff the deck. Cause he was worsen useless. Only time he'd get to come up was sunset. They let him up at sunset. Figured he could handle that in his cap and buttons."

Chanty found that by fluffing the mop heads, amazingly subtle effects could be produced.

"Well, he must have been some use," I said. "He must have known how to——" I ended up offering Chanty's floral arrangement.

"They all just laughed at him," said Toy. "I tell you, they *howled.*"

"Well, I don't understand how such a thing was allowed to happen," I said. "I mean after all those years of faithful——"

"After all those years of faithful service they closed down his Light, that's what," said Toy. "Made it auto-fuckin-matic. Just like they're going to do here."

"They're going to make this automatic?" I looked at Chanty. His present project with the mop still had a few loose strands to work out. "You did say there was a plan."

"Hey, they got all the gear ready now," said Toy. "Them new pip-squeek horns up on the top gallery. They re-place the big trumpets stuck out on the side of the tower."

"Well, then what are we doing here?"

"Oh, it all ain't done yet. That's the good part, friend. Guess who gets to take down them big trumpets?"

"O.K.," said Chanty as he shoved a mop at me, "toot-toot, time to mas-ter some techniques here. Time to learn the tricks of the trade. Time to real-ize too much water on de deck causes a rupture in the linoleum, gets you do courts-marshall, time to——"

"Guess who was told to take the trumpets down, but didn't." Toy was advancing, his rumples flexing.

"Ain't no Gabriel," said Chanty, and he began poking at the floor with the swab. "Now, soap's your real enemy. Too much soap makes a buildup of de yellow film."

"You saw those officers coming out here so you turned off the horn, jumped in the chair and closed your big sleepy nigger-lids. The whole time you're chucklin' away under 'em, just knowin you was going to get offa here."

"Ain't true," said Chanty, and presented me with a mop. "I love de Harbor Refuge."

"You just wait," Toy nodded to me. "This is going to make you worthless to go to sea."

"Come on, sailor," Chanty whacked at my mop with his. "You know what this is?"

"A mop, that is, a *swab*."

He nodded and with a knowing wink took me by the sleeve and led me back around the stairwell toward the refrigerator. What he called my attention to, however, was a framed posting on the wall of the stairwell cylinder:

WATCH ORDERS AND STATION BILL

"As you can see, this is your *Bible*. It details all necessary drills, maintenances, evolutions, functions, and rescues, including escapes which your own billet might require." He tapped the frame with the mop handle.

Indeed, the drills, maintenance duties, evolutions, functions and rescues, even the escape routes and procedures *were* printed in type. The names of those who were to execute these duties, however, were smudged in with pencil, four names I'd never heard of. No Toy, no Chanty, no Blump even. *Kurd, BM1* was OnC, officer-in-charge, of this crew, personnel more phantom than Ahab's Parsees. "Is *Blump* a nickname?" I said. "Is *Toy* a nickname?"

"Evidently you do not understand the Watch Order and Station Bill procedure. We are a crew of four." He poked the mop at the strange names again. "Two from deck division, one a petty officer, the other a seaman or seaman apprentice. The petty officer is in charge. In our present case we have two boatswains on here, Blump 'n' me. He's first class. I'm second class. The reason for that is, though I got the experience on the Lights, they want a man whose record is well, a bit *cleaner*. If I was like some, I'd say it was because I was black, but that ain't it. I have been *unworthy of command*." His face sought the mop head for comfort.

From around behind the stairwell came a groan.

"Toy there got a point," said Chanty interpreting the groan. "That don't make Blump himself worthy." The mop agreed.

"He wanted you out here as a rated man so he could sneak off and leave you in charge," said Toy.

"Again young Toy here has a point," said Chanty. "We are supposed to have two weeks duty on, one off. During that time off we are at liberty to go ashore. The day of that occurence is called Boat Day, and it is on that day you go ashore for a week straight Compensatory Leave until the next Boat Day."

"Yeah, it's great if you're married," said Toy.

"Young Toy here has a tendency to mis-use his shore time. Frequently he is curtailed and, ah, frankly *returned*."

"I been on here six straight weeks," shouted Toy. "*Re-fuckin-stricted*."

"A restricted man he is," sighed Chanty. "I myself merely prefer to remain here during my so-called Liberty."

"That's because you're an asshole what can't cut it ashore. And Blump just eats that up with basket leave."

"Again, again, our young Toy is correct," sighed Chanty. "Alas, all too correct."

"Well, where are you on this billet?" I tapped the glass. "Where will I be?"

Chanty pointed to the seaman's billet, the last after officer-in-charge, engineman-in-charge, fireman. The name opposite the seaman's billet was *Friskis, Sn*. "I thought you've been here eight years," I said. "Don't you get your name on this after eight years?"

"It don't matter the names," he said. "Times change, names change. Some of these boys may be dead. The jobs they stay the same." He coughed. "Besides, these here screws gets rusted to the glass."

I had to duck back and forth to keep from seeing Chanty and myself reflected in the glass, Chanty and myself and, out the window, above the rollers of the washing machine, the sea.

When I was able to pierce the reflection, there were sentences, whole paragraphs concerning fogs, fires, lifeboats, and "station abandonment." To the right, in a little printed box, was what was required of each man. In each case, *fire, fog, lifeboat*, and *station abandonment*, each man was required to bring something. Friskis, Sn, was, in the matter of abandonment, to bring an ax.

"How long has this tower been up?" I said. "You mentioned an ear-lier——"

"You don't have to worry," Chanty said, "ain't noboddy gonna check on that ax. We ain't even *got* an ax."

"Well, I understand this is not the first tower on the site. You yourself pointed out that the lantern was from an earl——"

"That ain't important, that ax—abandonment, all that for-lorn stuff."

"Well——"

"Look, all you got to know, all you got to know to keep this tower standing is what's called *Daily Maintenance*." He shook the mop. "And that's what you got to do."

"There must be more than just that," I said. I rubbed the glass. "That and giving up, *abandonment* . . ."

"You got to flip on the light. In fog you got to beep the horn."

"I mean I noticed on the chart over at the Group Office, several '*ruined towers*.'"

"It says here Daily Maintenance." He was, however, rubbing the glass and squinting. "Dark, you turn on the light. Fog, you beep."

"One more thing," said Chanty. We were down in the basement again, his back on the greasy deck, shoulder deep under the two-story tank that was the right lung of the foghorn. "Not that this will comprise the termination of your learning experience aboard this unit"—His face revealed he'd found his valve, and there was a confirming hiss of relief from the lung. "I've left considerable for you to haunt and formulate on your own . . ." He wriggled farther under the tank. We both watched it sigh its last. With the compressor also off, there was only the thud and back-souse of the sea.

"You notice I've just eased the tank from its burden of the horn drill. Now, I should have done that right away when we shut off the timer switch up on the third deck. I should have eased the old lungs here." He tapped the tank that rose two stories up from his face.

"I'm still concerned about the safety valve business," I said.

"Fact is, son, you may not like all this huffin 'n' puffin and tootin——"

"I understand and accept the need in fog——"

"I ain't talkin about fog. I ain't always talkin about fog. There is some nights when the fog ain't around at all and the stars is up there and the wind is howlin and the seas get to smackin and shakin and that's when you want to come down here and put on a little horn toot." He looked out from under the tank and wrinkled his nose. "It help hold up de tower."

"There certainly is a lot to know."

"Listen, Sonny, what I'm going to show you now ain't even my responsibility."

"I was wondering where we hung up our wash."

He draped his arm on my shoulder, a look of what used to be called *low cunning* emerging from under the Blump hat. "But if I don't show you . . . no one else will."

"This, then, I take it is more in the nature of dirty laundry."

"Rip-rap," he winked. "You said before you was bankin on the rip-rap."

"Big pieces of stone employed to protect a breakwater or other marine installation."

He chortled garlic in my ear. "Come on, Mr. Rip."

Like an evil companion taking me into a saloon, he led me past the compressors and their treacherous day tanks, out over the defiled "sisters," and down a step to where a double door yawned light and unmuffled sea sound.

"You have here a way out," he said, "which unfortunately is also a way in."

I could see his point. The doors were made of boiler plate, but the one closest to the sea was badly warped. In the archway hung finger-long stalactites of rust. I touched it.

"I don't advise suckin on them," he said.

"And the sea is right out there?" The spiles of the landing stage stood like a forest beyond the door and there was light glancing among them. I stood watching the dots bounce. It was like a pinball game where the ball never died.

"In the winter you got to try to shut this thing." He gave the curled bottom of the door a soft kick with his toes, and seemed only mildly surprised it hurt.

"I imagine you'd have to shut it *before* winter." I drifted out the door. "In fact I imagine you'd almost have to shut it right now!"

The sea, however, hit the rocks, went straight up to my right where it hung above my head and then somehow when it fell, merely dropped upon the rocks.

"You don't want to shut it any sooner than you got to," he said. "You got to shut it soon enough as it is."

"Well, it doesn't open so much directly onto the sea, as onto the breakwater," I said, "and actually it's really quite warm this time of year, the sea."

"You got to shut it soon enough." He fingered the splayed edge of the door. The pilot boat I'd come out on was going alongside its mother ship, a converted Coast Guard cutter with a big stack. It served to remind me that I had, after all, come out on the sea, had, in fact, played with it all my life. Why was I peeking out now like an old lady?

"You were going to show me something?"

"If I don't no one else will."

The creosote odor from the pilings mingled with the seaweed and the open sea. I inhaled grandly.

This, then, was going to be fun.

Summer excursion at the seaside.

It didn't even faze me when he seemed to be walking right out into the ocean. That was merely an optical illusion caused by the sudden brightness of the wet white paint on the concrete base upon which he was walking.

And upon which I too, of course, was walking.

Below us to our left was the jumble of six-foot cubes that made the riprap. The sun was nearly overhead. Two stories up, the gallery flared out so that as we walked on the wet concrete our sounds made footprints in the shadows.

One of the shadows, however, was oddly shaped. I stopped and saw it was made up of two shadows: trumpet bells. I could not quite see what was actually casting these without leaning out so far I would fall to the rocks. "Are those the fog trumpets way up there that Toy said we'd have to take down?"

"Never mind trumpets way up high," he said, "what we got here now is gapin way down low."

At the southeast arc of the base, he stopped. I stood back of him a few feet while he knelt. The expanse of sea all around him was so compelling I took my eye from his activities, and when I looked again he seemed to be performing some kind of Muslem prayer. As I watched, however, he merely backed off the concrete, his head and black hands slipping off the concrete.

"Come on, Mr. Rip," he said, "down on your knees to de rip-rap."

I plucked the creases in my dungerees, more like an accountant about to sit down to a bean dinner than a devotee of some more savage rite. Nevertheless my knees got soaked, and I was reminded that, while the spray was not now falling on the base, it had done so not long before.

"Come on," he said, "wiggle yo lil'ol' butt on down here with Chant de Blump. Come see de sights. Ain't gonna bite."

My feet flailed out for the rocks below. My chest was pressing on the wet concrete, my face kissing it as he grabbed my hips. I shook on down and saw, just before the edge of the concrete shot past my face, the full height of the tower up beyond the overhanging gallery, saw even past the trumpets to the conical lantern sailing among noon-struck clouds.

"There now," he said releasing me, "if you think that was a tall fall, then how would you like to try it from up on de gal-a-ree?"

I performed a few knee bends, making sure not to move my feet, however. There were two or three tumbled blocks of rock behind me. One had the grooves from the quarry. The others had barnacles.

"Ain't back there," he said. "Look up front. You just tell me what you see."

I leaned against the concrete base.

"You stare all you want, you don't believe it, does you?"

"I'm not sure what I'm looking for." Again I turned around. It was hard to believe a wave wouldn't come rolling up from there.

"Never mind out there," he said.

"That's a hell of a long fetch out there," I said. Indeed, Cape May with its lighthouse and Admiral Hotel was enough up the bay so as not to be of use if a sea came rolling in from this particular angle. "A hell of a fetch out there, Chant."

"Never mind out there, I tells you. *Out there* takes care of itself."

"Well, then I don't get it," I said.

He clapped both hands on my temples and, grunting because he was losing his footing on the rocks, he shoved my nose into it, a huge crack.

My head and hands and elbows and at least his hands all seemed to be in the crack and it went on up, closing just under the top surface of the concrete base. A strange sobbing spread from the deepest part of the damp until it was all about my head.

"Talk about a *sullen noise*," I said withdrawing.

"You play Amos 'n' Andy all you want to," he said, "that crack ain't gonna talk back but only one way."

"Well, surely," I said, "surely someone knows about this."

"Surely you and *me* knows," he said.

"This is supposed to be our secret? Good Lord, what happens when you go?"

He put his head back so far when he laughed I thought he was going to topple down into the water.

"I appreciate your confidence," I said, "but I don't think it's exactly the proper basis for a friendship."

He steadied himself by holding onto my arm while I flailed for a fingerful of wet concrete. "Hey, don't worry, Rip. Don't carry it all around with you, inside you all the nights." He broke off to laugh at the huge joke of the night.

"Other people do know then?"

"Ain't noboddy has to do with this place, but knows."

"Blump?"

"Why you think he, shall we say, absences himself from this place?"

"I'd heard," I said and looked away, "that it had something to do with his wife."

"His wife, all right. You want to see his wife? I'll show you his wife."

Again I found my head inside the hole.

"Now take a good whiff."

The seaweed that had gotton caught in there was not as sweet as that which lay about on the freshly washing rocks. When I had coughed enough, he let me back out.

"Engineers," I said. "Construction experts——"

"Right you are," he said, and he leapt back up onto the base, dusted his hands. "You watch when you come around on this base you don't slip and maybe break a finger or little pinky toe or something."

It took me three jumps to scramble back onto the base. I stood up and took a step.

"Jesus!"

There I was on my butt, just as if I'd slipped on ice. I ran my hand along the concrete. It was that slick. I counted five waves hit below and recede. Chanty had gone inside. The *Steel Age*, or whatever, was yet on the horizon. My bottom and legs were thoroughly soaked, but unbroken. There was no reason to continue to sit there.

I hadn't been hurt. Not in the slightest.

ESCAPE ROPES

A new structure was begun immediately and finished in 1908. Although of more sturdy construction than the first, it, too, succumbed to the fury of the sea and was destroyed during a storm in 1921. It was then that the present light was begun. After five years of heartbreaking effort, punctuated here and there by tragedy, the new lighthouse was completed in 1926.

—John J. Floherty, *Sentries of the Sea*

ALTHOUGH I HAD listened to the chow order coming in over the radio at the lifeboat station the previous night and had picked up that very order myself at dawn—had been in fact lugging it about, worrying it up into the tower—it had not occurred to me how one actually ate in a lighthouse.

Naturally I assumed that my guide, who had told me the secrets of the tower's very bowels, would include an item somewhere about such daylight matters as lunch. Instead he had merely jabbed at the ceiling over the stove where the wood was charred and told me never to leave anything on the burner while attending to work aloft. With that he had gone to the china cabinet, removed what he assured me was a book of "genuine poetry," and taken both it and himself indeed aloft. I was left with the stove safely silent.

Under the T.V. bracket was what looked like a booth table at an all-nite truck stop. The sink was more salty with its long brass spigot, but the sink was a place for cleaning up *after* eating. The refrigerator, which along with the pantry around the far side of the tower and the electric stove located near the table all adumbrated a stage *before* eating. It would seem, I thought, but a simple matter to bring all this gear into conjunction with the food that I had transported. I could not, however, locate the carton. Perhaps, I thought, Chanty, while I was executing his instructions swabbing the deck, had simply put away the food.

In the refrigerator was a heeltap of mustard. That much I saw before my eyes began to water. Apparently there was an odor, for I backed away blinking and tasting. What could be parsed was a half-gallon of sour milk in a floppy cardboard upon which was pinned a note:

S-A-V-E

Somewhere in that mist also floated part of a head of lettuce gone black around the feathers, and a fish with its tail off, eyes looking past me to the

75

sea. There were also a few pieces of bread strangled in a plastic bag, two slices of salami arrested in their final death writhings, and a plastic pitcher of Kool-Aid.

"I don't understand," I said. "What happened to all the gourmet stuff I brought out?"

"Chanty's squirreled it."

"I thought what he took upstairs was poetry."

"Hey, everything with him ain't poetry," said Toy. "And you'd better knock out them boxes cause cockroaches comes aboard in them even though they gives us hard candy at Christmas."

"The cartons I brought out don't even seem to be around."

"You want to be around on mid-watch when the roaches start keeping you company. You want to be around in winter when it freezes over all the way out here and you got to catch the ducks for dinner by ripping 'em right out of their webs."

"I don't understand that."

"You don't understand ice? You don't understand hunger?"

"I guess what I don't understand is *webs*."

"The ducks got webs. Don't you know nuthin' about old mother nature?"

"Well, when does the food I brought out get eaten?"

"It's fuckinsquirreled, I told you."

"But there was supposed to be enough food not just for tonight, but for the whole week. 'You drop that in the water,' the guy told me, 'and you drop the week's chow.' "

"I don't think you get the idea about food out here, sailor."

"There is a different idea about food on a lighthouse?"

"Sure," said Toy, and he licked his lips. "We make money out of it."

"You make money out of food on a lighthouse?"

"What you think? We got a machine in the basement turns lettuce into green stuff?"

"That lettuce I spotted in the refrigerator could use a little green stuff," I said.

"Naw, we *save*. We save our food allowance. See, you get extra money to live on a lighthouse."

"Like combat pay?"

"Combat pay? Ain't nothin out here to combat. It's food money. So we save it."

"And don't buy food?"

"Aw, we make out. Didn't Chanty tell you about the pilots?"

"I rode out with the pilots. They meet the ocean-going ships and pilot them up the bay."

"We steal our food from the pilots."

I looked out the window to where the pilot ship was a smudge on the horizon.

"Don't worry," he said. "Chanty's got tonight's meal."

"Up there with him in bed."

"He *was* a fleet boxer, you know. That part is the truth."

"So you just let him eat all the food?"

"You think he's a real bully, eh?" Toy was curled up all inside himself in the chair, grinning away. "You see him as a real *slap-up-side-the head.*"

"No, I'm just hungry. I've been up since before dawn without anything to eat."

"Tonight."

"Tonight's a long time to wait to eat."

"Tonight is the goar-may. Chanty's Last Meal." He rubbed his hands.

"Then he is going?"

"Maybe he is. He ain't due for two weeks in Baltimore. That's where he's going, you know. To the hospital. For tests." He poked at his head. "You know what I mean? *Tests.*"

"Psychiatric tests?"

"Hey, you been with him alone. What do *you* think?"

There was a counter running between the sink and the stove. It was covered with the same linoleum that was on the floor. Under it was a radiator, over it a window looking down onto the landing stage and the breakwater's long run north. I spread the bread out on the linoleum and applied the watery mustard. The window was dirty, lots of dead flies trapped between the glass and the screen; and when I looked closer, trapped where the window ran down past the counterlevel, was a whole sandwich load of them.

I put the salami onto the mustard. There were places where the salami hung over onto the linoleum, places where the bread was bare except for the mustard that had sunk through the airy fibers in search of the linoleum.

"So what do you think of dear ol' Chant? I ain't heard no reply. You know he just may stay here the whole time. He just may stay here the whole two weeks, *instructing* you. Many times he's done that."

"What, instructed his replacement?"

"Stayed his free time out here."

"I don't care," I said.

On the landing stage were frayed lines, Irish pennants. A third of the way down the breakwater was a ruined beacon. I wondered if that was going to be mine to fix. Then I wondered what had wrecked it, stripped the slats from the stanchion, left the wire raw in the air. A gull hung above the wires.

It was time to eat the sandwich.

"Listen, buddy," said Toy, "if you think you're getting near the straight scoop on anything he's shown you, forget it. He just likes to bust your balls. A minute ago he snuck over here and told me he'd told you that you had to go all the way down to the north end of the breakwater to light the small beacon out there." Toy paused a moment to chew a few laughs. "Hey, you don't got to do that. It's fuckinautomatic."

"I'm not worried about the beacon on the far end. I am curious about the one right out there with its wires blowing in the breeze."

"That ain't nothin. That's a wreck. Did he tell you you got to deal with that one, too?"

"He told me no such thing," I said. "Just some stuff about making sullen noises in the basement."

Toy's laughter faded. "He's not kiddin about that one, sailor. Christ, we've tried to order that part for over two years. In the meanwhile we got to arch it."

"I don't understand why you've got to do that," I said. "I mean, here in this atomic age and us on this important aid to navigation."

"Them fuckers won't send the part. Do you see what they sent out in that other box with you today? Base Bayonne, shit. Fifty fids. Fifty-fuckin-fids." He pulled a handful out, like sharply tapered corona coronas made out of wood.

"They're for working rope," I said, "like a marlin spike. You open up the strands for splicing——"

"Yeah, yeah, only you see any *ropes* around this place? See even any need for *ropes?*"

"Well, I, a——"

"Ain't no ropes. Unless you count them es-cape ropes."

"*Escape* ropes?"

"They're a joke, I tell you."

"What are we supposed to be escaping *from?*" I said.

"From here. From here, you jerk. You think everybody finds a light-house to their liking?"

"Well, no, but——"

"Well, they don't. It ain't no cute little sailor suit thing, you know. It ain't no Shirley Temple movie."

"*Captain January,*" I said, "the salty old sea captain passes on his years of wisdom."

"Ain't nuthin *cute* about a lighthouse at all."

"Fine," I said. "What I meant was these escape ropes. What are we supposed to escape *to?*"

"That's the joke."

"Well, that's all I meant."

"They hang from the balcony rails, got knots in 'em and everything so you're supposed to be able to grab on real good. Leap out the window and swing on down in case of a fire or something."

"And you land on what?"

"Your back." He was grinning. "Them ropes is thoroughly rotten."

"Maybe the fids were sent so we could rig new ones."

"Sure, fifty fids when you only need one and no ropes when you need hundreds of feet. Sailor, them fids was sent to us so we could stickem-upourass. That's what them fuckers is telling us to do. Base Bayonne."

"Well, obviously some clerical error," I said. "I doubt if there is some malign design on the part of Base Bayonne. I doubt if there is some guy sitting up there scheming ways to humiliate the crew of this particular lighthouse."

"That's not what Chanty says." He began cleaning his fingernails with the fid.

"And you believe him?"

"Hey, he's got enemies. You can believe that. He's got real enemies."

"At home maybe. In the South Philly ghetto."

"Hey, everywhere. He's a man can *make* enemies."

"Well, he does seem creative, if that's what you mean, but I doubt if anyone has it in for this place. Like I said, a guy sitting there with this place in mind."

"You're right there, sailor. They don't have us in mind way out here. They could give a shit about us out here stuck on this pile. Only the Philadelphia pilots care. They give you a Christmas goose dinner. Them and the guy at the store with the Christmas free gift." He winked. "Play your cards right with them and you'll get cut in on it, too."

"You mean the hard ribbon candy?"

"Hey, a whole fuckinbox apiece." He winked, and his face lit up in what I could only assume was genuine anticipation of the Christmas free gift. I had a strange inspiration.

"Say, when you go about ordering that part for the generator, that starting mechanism, how do you do it?"

"It's no use, I tell you. They won't send no sullen noise."

"But is that how you order the solenoid? The *sullen noise?*"

He got a funny look on his face. "We give up on ordering it." Then, giving me a hard look, he added, "Whatsa matter, you don't like ribbon candy?"

"Ribbon candy's fine," I said. In truth, despite the window sill of dead flies, the dry bread, the stale milk, the baleful fish, the curled-up salami, I was still hungry.

"You fuckinaye ribbon candy's fine." He tossed the fid in the box and scooped out another one. "And so's the Christmas goose dinner."

"I just hope I don't have to wait until then to get a well-cooked meal."

"You cook?" He held up, upon the point of the new fid, a large offscouring from his thumb nail.

"Cream of Wheat, hash, and eggs."

"Then you got a long wait till a good dinner." He flicked the dirt away.

"What was this you said about tonight? Chanty's big meal?"

"He's just gonna burn it. He's gonna get boppin and weavin in the smoke and keep choppin it up and choppin it up until it ain't nothin but little, tiny scraps o' burnt, dry shit."

I sighed.

"You don't believe me."

"Listen," I said, "I should tell you something." I stood over him. He sat there with the fid in his fist.

"Yeah? Go ahead, sailor. Tell me all you know."

"Chanty showed me the crack."

Toy whacked the arm of the chair with the fid. "I knew he would. I *knew-he-would.*" His goatee flopped in a dry laugh.

"It was down in the base. Down under . . ." I walked to the window behind the office chair. "Down under here." From there all I had was the sea and the pilot boat moving a mile away.

"So he showed you The Famous Crack."

"Yes, he did."

"He measures it every day. Did he show you his notebook? He keeps a whole notebook of measurements, sheets and sheets of 'em."

"What he showed me was the thing itself. Right down there."

"He must have showed you his notebook. His *writings.*"

"I thought they were poems."

"*Poems?*" Toy came dancing toward me. "Did he recite you his *poems?*" His arms flew about and his tongue gave a rather short-armed imitation of Chanty's wagging routine.

"Actually it was more of a tour of his difficulties," I said and turned back to the window. "He was most generous in admitting his errors."

"Hah, that's what you're going to get the rest of your duty out here, sailor. You're going to be eating a whole *feast* of his mistakes."

"You know, I can get off here anytime," said Toy.

"The escape ropes?" I was staring out the window toward where the pilot boats were working, but I wasn't really focused.

"There's a thick folder on me. A folder this thick."

I looked around and over the back of the chair emerged two fingers squeezing air in the manner of salesmen describing expense-account steaks.

"*This thick*."

"You mean like the one they'd got on Chanty?"

"Don't worry. You'll have one, too. Before you get off here."

"Well, Chanty's had eighteen years," I said.

"I looked him up one night."

I turned toward the filing cabinet.

"That's right. Over there. The *full disclosure*. The total skinny on all the good juice."

"You mean you have access?"

"Hey, what do you think this is out here?"

The olive-drab metal bonked under my fingers. "What I'm interested in is the engineering reports."

"You don't got to break open the damn thing." His cigarette smoke was in my face.

"How high, for instance, is the water; how high does it get in winter? What years did the ice prevent going ashore? When was the present tower constructed? What happened to the previous structure?"

Out rolled the drawer on its well-oiled bearing. "Here." He handed me a thick folder. I looked around both sides of the cylinder. "Don't worry," he said, "that's mine."

I looked down at it: *Toy, Reginald Phelps, FN*. "What do I want this for?"

"It tells how I fucked up. It gives it a name."

I handed it back to him.

"What's the matter?" he said, "don't you want to get to know your shipmates?" He had a new cigarette and was smirking around it. "Besides, it says in there how I won the pistol championship." He shoved it back to me. "Be my guest."

I took it.

"Go on. Open it up. It ain't gonna bite you."

I let it expand in my hands. A Cape May Receiving Center note stated that Toy, Reginald P., FR, was excused from swim drill due to an ear infection. Another said Toy, R. P., FA, who had graduated from Fireman Recruit to Fireman Apprentice, was now ready to go on to Fireman. A third said Toy, R. P., FN, was to be charged six dollars and fourteen cents for a crescent wrench dropped overboard at Group Miami. I faked through a few more pages and handed it back. He was beaming.

"The story of my life," he said.

"Wild."

"You fuckinaye. And I got one at home too, as long as your arm: twenty-three muffler violations. And there's some other violations in there, too, at home."

"Where is your home?" I said.

"A long ways from here, sailor. Want to see Chanty's?"

"You have a photograph of Chanty's home?"

"I got something better." He tapped the drawer. "I got his folder."

"Where are the engineering reports?"

He pawed through and came up with a thin folder. "Look at this," he cried. "The fucker's been tampering with his folder." He gave it a shake. A single slip fell out. We could both read it as it lay on the floor. *Chantily, P.,* had left his pea coat to be cleaned in the Greenmeal Paris Cleaners. "Look at that," said Toy, "he's faked his fuckin' folder."

I laughed and told Toy it was all right that Chanty was not going to be exposed to my gaze.

"You know what the skinny on him is?"

"It really doesn't matter," I said. "In any case you already told me he was going to Baltimore and we know what that means." I honored the scandal with a lewd wink.

"The real skinny is: he's not even a real Negro." Toy nodded and produced a counter wink.

"What the hell difference does any of this make?"

"He's got a kind of Chinese man-Indian stuck in there somewhere."

"Stuck in where?" I made as if to search the drawer.

"He just plays nigger to throw you off his track."

"For God's sake, what *track?*" I tried shutting the drawer. Folders billowed up to resist me. "This is worse than escape ropes that let you escape to nowhere. What track?"

"Ah-ha, that's just it: he covers his tracks."

We looked for Blump's too, but that, of course, was not there. There was, however, a long account of how Friskis, SN, had suffered from migraines, and another, shorter report by Kurd BM1, OnC, requesting a new outside door to the engine room.

"You never told me what happened to the door that is down there now. Was that the old one, something dating back to this fellow Kurd?"

"Hell, no. That was brand new this spring. Chanty, he just got so excited it was spring he flung it open. Can't you just see it? Can't you see him: Grinning at the springtime? *Wham!* A sea wrinkled her right up, just hit all that steel and wrinkled her right up like you see her now. Wonder that coon wasn't wrinkled right up with the door. And the bitch is we ain't been able to budge her, to get that door shut since last April. Winter time you guys gonna have real fun when the sea comes in there and snatches out your furnace."

"I should think you'd do like Kurd, OnC, here, and request a new one."
I flopped the actual writing in front of him.

"You can't trust none of these things in here," he said, and, grabbing
the paper, dropped it in the drawer, which he slid shut. "You just wait until
tonight," he said. "You'll learn more about him then you want to know."

On the deck was another slip. An Ice Report form. "What's this?" I said.

That, too, he grabbed and, opening the drawer just enough, stuffed in.
"You don't ever want to *mess* with them."

"It said *Ice Report*."

There was a noise from the other side of the tower, but the cylinder
through which the staircase ran blocked us.

"You been up since early," said Toy. "Why don't you climb to your
bunk and sack out for a while?" He winked and pointed.

"Can I do that?" I said. "I mean he's up there."

Toy shook his head and pointed again to the other side of the tower.
"Baby, if you don't get some sleep, you're just never gonna make it through
this night."

"Why?" I said. "It doesn't look stormy out." Was that still the *Steel Age*
on the horizon, or a new one?

"Because tonight, baby, you got the watch."

"Oh," I said, "you mean *all* night."

Toy wasn't listening anymore. He was negotiating the drawer back into
the cabinet, his cigarette smoke covering the operation so economically that
even the click that announced the closure was muffled by his cough.

There was the sound of splashing water. Chanty was doing his hands at
the sink. Grunting, he began batting the long brass spigot about as he delivered an expanded lecture on water tanks. "You is at the mercy of the *Herb*,"
he said. "That's a buoy snatcher, or *tender*, in the more formal parlance.
Comes but once a month. *If* you is lucky. Then you got to watch out for the
skipper. Mr. Milkins. A treacherous man, my friends. She also carries a
plain old outright sunofabitch buoy-deck boatswain. Of course, all buoy-deck
boatswains is mean. They got to be. All them levers and lines and heavy
weights and chains. You wouldn't catch me, not old P. Chanty, being no
buoy-deck boatswain and maimin young men left and right. I had enough
maimin when I was fleet boxer." *Bam-Bam*, he slapped the spigot in a rapid
combination. "And this *Herb* snatcher, she got a buoy deck boatswain with a
mean dog, too. Chase you around the landin stage when you're at your business with de hose."

"This is a literal dog?" I said. "And a ship named *Herb*?"

"*Herb, Herb*, don't you know buoy snatchers of the river floating class is
named after your more delicate florals?"

"And the officer, the treacherous officer is——"

"Mr. Milkins."

"And wherein lies his treachery?"

Chanty went into another spasm of combinations upon the spigot.

"This Milkins's treachery?" I asked.

"You go to bed."

"I beg your pardon?"

He was facing me arms cocked. "Get your ass up in that bunk, up there." He cocked his head toward the door. "Nap time."

"Nap time?"

"It's all right," said Toy. "You got the mid-watch."

When I began the climb up into the echoing steel case, I listened for footsteps, but they all seemed to be mine.

On the bureau I was to use on the second deck I found a Bible and an athlete's plastic protective cup. The Bible seemed well thumbed. I did not inspect the cup beyond what was required to identify it. I lay down on the bunk and looked out the window. Blue. I tilted the venetian blinds. There was a slight knocking outside. I opened the blinds, and the knocking continued. Soft knuckles on the steel plate that formed the outside of the tower. I opened the window. A great freshness swept in. I stuck my head out.

Hello?

Something was at the window. At that height it could only have been a bird wing.

It was not. It was a rope, swaying in the empty space. There were tight knots every few feet. The line seemed to be attached somewhere well aloft. With my face to the window I could not find the point of origin, so that the line seemed, even more than the cargo lifting line that morning, to be suspended by heaven itself. The rope, however, was gray from the weather.

These, then, were the escape ropes.

Who knew how long they had actually been up there? Had, for instance, Friskis, SN, in the reign of Kurd, OnC, spliced and knotted them in full confidence that they would transport him past the spinning rails and decks to the safety of the rip-rap below? And before him? What of the rumors this was not the original tower? How had the keepers escaped from the predecessor? And what, to use a spooky term, had befallen that place?

As for escape, it seemed to me a better choice to eschew all knots and splices by leaping grandly from an upper balcony into the blue blanket of the sea.

BROTHERS IN DARKNESS

It would be difficult to conceive of a spot more lonely than Harbor of Refuge light station even on a calm day. On the seaward side of the two mile rock pile that connects it with the land, the ceaseless heaving of the ocean keeps it in a continuous state of frothy turbulence. The kelp covered boulders, slippery as blocks of ice, are as impassable as the back of a glacier. Thousands of whimpering sea birds make it a roosting place but they desert at the approach of a storm. In heavy weather when house-high waves crash against the barrier, the din and confusion is terrifying. A two mile smother of spray leaps a hundred feet in the air. It looks like a dancing forest of snow-covered firs. Then the isolation is complete. Help, if needed, would be as distant as if the light were on Mars.

—John J. Floherty, *Sentries of the Sea*

THE STRANGE NOISE had awakened me. It was not the knocking of the escape ropes, but a cough and chatter like asthmatic rats in the wainscoting. Toy had mentioned the menace of cockroaches. Was one of the unspoken failings of the place some family of more toothy tenants?

The noise seemed to be not so much at my ear, as I had first thought, but around the bend of the round room. The design of the tower gave each bunk a view only of the other bunk's end. I could see two big feet over there. Black ones. They were jumping and twitching. Were the rats eating the man in the bunk?

I crept down to the foot of my bed, put my knuckles on the rough blanket folded there.

The noise was coming out of his mouth.

At first I didn't recognize him. The Blump, Bml hat had fallen off. It lay like another head beside him on the pillow, and his hair, released from the hat, had exploded. With his cheek distorted by the pillow, his mouth slack, his features looked like Kid Gavilan in the famous photo in which Sugar Ray Robinson has just connected with a right cross.

"Oh, no you don't!" He was sitting straight up. "I seen you sneakin up over there. Many a wop tried to sneak up on the old lighthouse keeper, but it only happened once. The other day." He shook his head. "That's why I'm leavin. *Caught, the doomed Bismarck.* They got me. Dozing on duty. Now I really got to go to sea. You know where I'm goin?"

"No one's told me," I lied, and at once began to sweat, remembering he had been down below around the bend of the room when Toy had shut the filing cabinet.

87

"You sure no one's told you?" He began to crawl down his bunk toward the foot. I found myself creeping back on mine toward the head. "Hey, you come back here. Don't you go oozin on around from me. You got to learn how to live in de round room, boy. You can't go always oozin on back out of sight."

"I'm going to fold my blanket," I said.

"You know why no one told you the truth about me?"

"I'm used to folding everything from boot camp," I said.

"It's no one's business, that's why. That's why no one's told you. It ain't their business. But I'm going to tell you now." He moved over where he could reach the bureau between our bunks. He was able to rearrange the cup and the Bible. "I'm going to the lightship, that's where. The *Delaware Lightship*. You'll be able to hear me making the twenty hundred radio check. You got to make that yourself from here. All the Lights do. You hear them calling in at O-eight-hundred and again just toward the dark at twenty hundred. There's Ship John Shoal; there's Miah-Maul Shoal; there's Four-teen-Foot Bank; there's Brandywine Shoal; there's us; there's Five-Fathom Light Vessel, and then, way out there, the furthest out there in the dark is the Delaware. I know because I been on 'em all down to here. You see, my friend, you see what they been doin to me?"

"They're moving you out to sea."

"Ha, that's what they thinks, they doin, son. You know the beaver?"

"The furry animal with the flat tail."

"Never mind the flat tail. I'm workin on the other end. You know what he does when he's got the fleas? The real fleas?"

"Scratches," I said. "Or goes in the water."

"Fuck scratchin. It's in the water you go. But you got to know how. Do you know how? Do you know how to go in the real water when you got the real fleas?" He was standing over me jostling the Bible in one hand, the cup in the other.

"Head first," I offered.

"No, that's an in-correct response. I noticed on your orders when you come in here you is a graduate of one of our institutions of higher learning, and I been lookin through your books which I incidently feel are too conti-nental and abstract compared to my favorites—John Greenleaf Whittier; William Cullen Bryant; Ralph Waldo Emerson; and Alfred, Lord Tennyson; but that *head-first* response is an incorrect response."

"Well, in any case," I said, "Fresh reading material."

"Yes, yes," he said and stroked his goatee, "fresh reading material."

"O.K.," I said. "Then how *does* a beaver go overboard?"

"Now remember, this applies only to the fleas."

"The *real* fleas."

"When the real fleas is prevalent, yes." He closed his flat eyes. "Now when the real fleas is prevalent, the proper method for the beaver to go into the water is by taking a bite with his incissors out of his fur."

"He bites the fleas?"

"No, he do *not* bite the fleas. You ever try to bite a flea, son?"

I admitted I hadn't.

"Then you better pay closer attention. I said he bites *hisseph*."

"He bites himself?"

"Sure, but he got a plan. You got to watch the plan, boy, because it's the *plan* I'm talking about."

"O.K., the plan."

"The plan is to get some of hisseph up in his face, the fur part of hisseph and then holdin it up there in his teeth to reverse on down into the water in a slow and deliberate manner. He do this so the fleas can transport themsephs up along the flat tail quarters and the regular tail quarters and all the other private and inadmissable quarters what are hard to reach at if you is a stock-lee built animal such as d'beaveah."

"Chubby," I offered.

"Don't get cute on me, son. Ain't nothin cute in this plan. This is a real plan and I'm gonna show you why." He nodded. "And incidently d'beaveah is a no-flab animal." He flexed his biceps and sucked in his gut. "I want you to understand sumpin." He looked hard at me. "Under all that fancy fur is a *hard* animal. A hard animal with a plan."

"O.K.," I said. "So he's got a mouth full of flea-ridden fur."

"The rest is easy, son. He jus' commits the Grand Subsidence."

"And all the fleas are left sitting up there on the abandoned piece of beaver."

"Just like a bunch o bankers at a re-sort."

"Only somebody pulled the plug."

"D'beaveah pulled the plug."

"And now he's clean away."

"*Clean away.*" He was laughing, a rasp-and-yap affair that collapsed in a moment of its own Grand Subsidence.

"Well," I said, "the beaver is an interesting animal."

"Fuck d'beaveah," he said narrowing his eyes. "That's me." He thumbed his chest.

"You are the beaver?"

"What's a matter with you, boy? Ship John Shoal, Miah-Maul Shoal, Fourteen Foot Bank, Brandywine, Harbor of Refuge . . ." with each light station he moved his fist further away from his belly. "And now: the *Dela-*

ware Lightship. That's the furthest subsidence you can be and still be in d'pond, so to speak. Now, that's just where you want to be."

"That's all very interesting," I said.

"*All very interesting,* your ass," he said, "it's the God's *truth.* As for you: get some sleep so you can stay awake tonight."

With that he shoved Palgrave's *Golden Treasury* down the front of his trunks, straightened his Blump hat parallel to the deck, and flung open the door to the stairwell. As the door came toward him he slapped a left-right combination on both sides that rattled the knob and produced echoes in the well. In a moment I could see the closed door chatter on its hinges as the door down below on the mess deck opened and shut. There was a loud exchange of voices and then only the knocking of the escape rope.

The bell woke me. At first I thought it was a school bell and that snow would soon be shuddering off the roof. But out there was no schoolyard full of noisy children, but, my God—the sea.

And it was getting dim in the round room. Dim beyond what the venetian blinds had done. The simple furniture had grown husky with shadows. The blue tongue-in-groove walls soft as the sea.

My God, I am on a lighthouse!

The beam had already taken effect. This time when I peeped out the window I saw the light moving between sea and sky, just barely, but there it was. The sea was two big colors across the tide rip, and the sky one color over the town and another color higher up where the sun had been. The moving beam was like a ghost. No, a ghost's breath. And until I, alone in a strange tower, thought of it that way, it hardly seemed a thing to fear, this ghost's breath; and then as I chanted the phrase, the very literariness of it removed the terror that for an instant had been there, and I was left with my window sill, the knocking of the escape rope, and, out beyond, a great empty space.

The shore, however, was still there, the Coast Artillery towers like toilet-paper cores on end, the stacks of the fish factory. The factory was now a big empty box, so light it could be lifted by any passing sky hook. There was the lifeboat station with its red roof and Victorian cupola. The storm-warning tower was an oil rig. Clustered about the station were beach bungalows and bass fishermen's trailers—loaves among the dunes.

A long line of dark birds flew between me and the shore. The sea under them was now of many different patterns, not just the two I had seen. There were many shades, broken and shifting into one another across a contrapuntal base of tide rips. I watched how the colors swept down the bay and folded into one another and there in the fold, the colors tried to tuck the birds down into the purple pie. I pulled the blue spread tightly over me. A door banged. My nose was against the window. Below, on the balcony was Chanty.

He had the sailor hat on, upside down. Though it was evening he was still shirtless. I was glad he had the hat on. The spread on the next bunk was still mussed. That bunk which was to be mine. The one I was in was Blump's. Blump, whom I had not met. Blump, whose hat was below me upside down on Chanty's head. Blump, who would eventually come and *look me over.*

Chanty, however, had a frying pan. As I looked straight down on him, on his bare shoulders and bare feet, he waved the frying pan, and a fan of golden grease sailed downwind toward the sea. He stood there a moment, watching it home. He looked in the pan, shook out a few last drops. These, too, he watched. Then he pissed, and this too he observed, the full parabola of the fall. At the same time he held the frying pan back of his ear, scratching his neck with the handle, but rotating the handle so a final drop of grease would not fall on his bare shoulder blade.

Chanty paused before the stove. Toy and I sat at the Formica table six feet away.

"Now this is a very special meal," said Chanty, and though he bowed slightly, he showed no trace of his comic-darky accent. "You see the difference between me and the other niggers is I don't have to keep on. I can stop jiving any time I please."

"That's because you ain't a real nigger," said Toy, "just like you ain't a real lighthouse keeper and this ain't the real Coast Guard and you sure as hell ain't a real cook."

"It is my last lighthouse meal," continued Chanty. "Not just the meal on this Light before I go home on leave. Not just the last meal before I am transferred from this *particular* Light, as I was transferred from Ship John Shoal, Miah-Maul Shoal, Fourteen-Foot Bank and Brandywine Shoal, but my last Lighthouse for all time. I expect that once aboard the *Delaware Lightship* I shall live out my days of service in that capacity." The frying pan roared its applause.

"It's the onions make him cry," said Toy.

"And it's also a special day for you. too, Mr. Replacement, for it's your first meal aboard your first lighthouse."

"You're right there," I said. "I sure don't count that noon salami. By the way, what's all this having to get our food by swimming out to the pilot ship?"

"I would not advise swimming," said Chanty. He was beginning to disappear in the cloud around the stove.

"That's beacuse he can't swim a stroke," said Toy.

"All those lighthouses and all those years," I said, "and you don't swim?"

"Bad and treacherous undertows," coughed Chanty and he backed out of the cloud, fencing with his spatula.

"Don't start choppin everything up," shouted Toy. "Don't start choppin everything up *smallernsmaller.*"

In the other hand Chanty now had, not a cookbook, but the Palgrave's *Golden Treasury*, and in those little pauses where the careful cook steps back to reflect, to give his raw materials time to soak or simmer, he would purse lips over a line of golden verse.

" 'Sunset and evening star
And one clear call for me' "

"He's choppin things up smallernsmaller," whined Toy, and he bit on his plastic Kool-Aid glass.

Indeed, the air was so thick now it was inside the glass, the very liquid we gulped to clean our throats.

"I'm merely addin' to my personal anthology," he explained. "I got to finish before I leave without this book, what belong to Mr. Replacement, and gets to stay on d'lighthouse."

"You have a personal anthology?" I said.

"He's cutting things smallernsmaller," moaned Toy.

"Yes, I do. As a matter of fact. In my sea bag, in my locker, ever since I took up boxing in the World War. Then I was a boiler tender. It is my dream to take my savings to a job printer I know in Philadelphia and get all these personal poems printed up in an orderly, portable volume. Of course, as Toy here knows, I do have most of them committed to memory, the great moments of poetic vision."

"Smallernsmaller," sobbed Toy.

After supper, three courses of progressively greasier material splashed liberally with Toy's triumphant howls, I washed the dishes in the sink beneath the long brass spout and watched the beam grow strong against the stronger sky, like a great propeller whirling over our head. There were nights later when, standing midwatches, I grew sufficiently hysterical to see it as some perpetually gyrating lasso that continually swung above us but never found a target suitable for release. At other times the propeller image came back, and I felt that this whirling beam alone kept us from sinking in the sea.

Chanty asked me to make the radio check. I had had thirteen weeks of communication training. I knew how to rate classified documents and in what order to dispose of them. I knew the phonetic alphabet and innumerable FCC regulations. I knew a *reverse blank original* from a *NAVPERS delete*, but when he handed me the microphone I could only clear my throat.

"You got to learn this, son," he said, "or they'll think you've let the light go out."

"They'll hang your ass for sure," said Toy, "and in winter you got to make ice reports."

The radio crackled and a voice came to us: *This is Ship John Shoal Light, Ship John Shoal Light, over.*"

"Now, you just listen to get the idea," said Chanty, "as I was telling you. These are your brothers."

And they all came in slowly, speaking up in the night, one after the other to be acknowledged: *Ship John Shoal Light, Miah-Maul Shoal, Fourteen-Foot Bank, Brandywine Shoal Light, Five-Fathom Bank Light Vessel, Delaware Light Vessel.*

Each had a story, Chanty said. Old stories and "currently happening stories." Brandywine Shoal, for instance, was a station going back to the previous century, when it had replaced a lightship with a screw-pile platform and tower. When that tower's piles began to disintegrate, a new caisson tower similar to ours was built. The old tower remained, however, without its lantern. Only the other night the kid on watch up there had called out in the middle of the night that he had seen a light moving across the staging in the abandoned building. And there they were over ten miles from the shore on either side.

"You will perhaps have already observed that there is no designation of the Elbow-of-Cross Legend," said Chanty. "No voice."

"Then they never replaced that light after the ship knocked it over?"

"Oh, there is the base which remains. On the top they have placed a *skeletal* tower."

"But no people."

"No people."

"I wish they'd make this place automatic," said Toy. "Chanty, you'd better make that radio check and not just spend the night standin there with the mike in your hand like some Coon dee-jay what ain't connected up to nothin but other Coons."

"I was awaiting a proper entrance," he said. "You should have learned by now, Toy, not merely to blurt out your identity on top of a whole mess of others."

Hunching his shoulders, squinting his flat eyes, he blew his wierd voice down into the radio, while, deep in the big leather chair, Toy, wrapped in his foul-weather jacket, squirmed with delight.

"Ain't he a pile a shit, though?" he shouted and clapped his hands. "Ain't he just *bad* shit?"

"These," said Chanty holding the mike away from himself as if he were a recording star, "these . . . are your Brothers in Darkness."

"*Awful*," said Toy. "I'm so glad he's leavin tomorrow. Man, I can taste it, I *am* so glad."

A few hours before midnight Chanty sent me to bed again. He was most concerned I have enough rest before taking on the all important mid-watch. I climbed under the spread, listened to the escape-rope knock, peered out from time to time at the beam traveling through the stars, and sifted the water sounds: the bay water's gurgle as it folded into the tide rip and met the sea slapping in from the open Atlantic. The sun was bright in my face when I saw Chanty standing over me.

"I never got up," I said. "Jesus, I slept right through it."

He was again in disguise, this time in full-dress blues. The effect was stunning. His flyaway hair was plastered down, his goatee removed, the Fu Manchu mustache clipped, balanced, drawn into a pencil-thin Joe Louis. "On a ship you got to be an example as a petty officer." He flourished his sleeves, heavy with service stripes. "You got to *set* an example."

"But the mid-watch," I said, "what the hell happened to my mid-watch?"

"You see on a ship, which is where I am going, one has to get along with all the men. It ain't like on one of these shit pipes. You got to perform." He finished his tie with a roll of the wrist and then, almost in the same motion, shucked back his sleeves to reveal under the service longevity stripes, embroidered in the lining with care more elaborate than Hester Prynne, a whole panorama of sea goats, dragons and mermaids. He watched for my reaction but a moment, and as I shut my gaping mouth, he turned away to adjust his tie once again in the mirror over his bureau. "In summertime, of course," he said, "the dress uniform is whites. Blues, nevertheless, is always a legitimate option for travel as they are more durable."

"I still don't understand how that watch got stood."

"On a ship you got to observe the realities," he said and slowly buttoned away the sporting sea goats, dragons, and mermaids so that their scarlet, gold, emerald, and electric blue now frolicked in darkness along the blood-lines of his inner arms. "Don't get carried away with that stuff." He flicked the sleeve. "That's just nigger stuff." He hoisted a small, white seabag to his shoulder and opened the door.

"This, you'll observe is one of the older bags which I, as a veteran performer, am allowed to retain although officially obsolete. In it I have secreted what you and I alone know: my personal anthology of the world's finest poetry." Bowing, he shut the door behind him.

I ran to the bathroom window where I could see him down on the landing stage. He was waving his arms, capering, and shouting while the Coast Guard crew on the forty-footer below returned obscenities. He had evidently already lowered his sea bag.

Down in the galley Toy was standing in front of the stove, hands out, but undecided which knob to turn.

"Chanty's leaving," I said. "He's down there on the stage already."

Toy conducted the air above the burners.

"Who stood the mid-watch?" I said. "Is everything all right?" I could see out the window, down there past the spice rack set in the sill, could see Chanty going down over the edge of the stage. "He stood my watch for me, didn't he?"

"Sure he did," said Toy.

"Well, *you* sure didn't," I said, "and I sure didn't."

"That's for sure."

From outside came the siren on the forty-footer. I ran onto the balcony. The boat was easing away on the swell. Chanty was in the middle of the long cockpit. He was stalking the kid engineman, who was back-peddling around the engine box. At first I thought all of Chanty's moves were boxer's, but there was something in the dance of his forearms that was more elaborate than the most exotic combination of Gavilan or even Sugar Ray. He was rolling back his sleeves, exposing his sea goats in a frantic attempt to fascinate the engineman.

The helmsman merely stood on his raised platform and laughed, baseball hat on the back of his head. Uncharmed by the embroidery on Chanty's sleeve, the engineman continued to evade.

Chanty broke his rhythm and began to lunge, the sleeves now no longer an adjunct to his style, but mere encumbrance. He wasn't punching, but grabbing.

The kid engineman had something of his—a sheaf of paper—and pages, shards, and shreds were peeling off it. And as the poems of Chanty's personal anthology floated away, the light broad and full of sunshafts struck deep into the green sea.

Inside, Toy was still poised above the stove.

"They threw all Chanty's poems away," I said.

"I hope you know how to cook," he said.

The blinds were all the way up. The lines holding them were fastened to the scrannel pipes, to the TV bracket, and to the *Comptroller's Manual* shelf, fastened in great loops like butterflies. The sea light poured in.

"He didn't hit them or anything," I said. "Poems he's been collecting every year he's been moving down the bay on these lighthouses. Scattered to the winds. Lost."

"He never could tie knots," said Toy. "Everything he ever tried to raise out of a boat or lower down from the stage always got busted apart. *All-ways.*"

"Well, maybe that explains it," I said. "They didn't start out trying to pry into his gear. That World War Two sea bag of his just burst when it hit the cockpit. Then with everything all over the place it was like confetti, festive. What the hell, he even started dancing around, jiving around showing off his goats and dragons."

Toy turned toward me, his hands scratching at his unbuttoned shirt. He cleared his throat and in a new voice I'd never heard from him said, "The first thing we've got to do is to give this place a thor-ough cleaning."

When I went to make my new bunk, I found the mattress propped up for airing; the sheets had all been stripped. I turned the mattress over. When I looked on my new bureau the protective cup and the tattered Bible were still there, lush as symbols on the cover of a historical novel. And in the top drawer, way in the back, crumpled like a dirty magazine, the yellowed hat marked *Blump, BM1.*

IN WHICH SOME
ANCIENT & HONORABLE
METHODS ARE REVIVED

The loneliness and isolation of the station have left their mark from time to time on some of its keepers. The original light, never considered entirely safe, so frayed the nerves of its crews that many of them believed it to be haunted. Strange and ghostly visitations were seriously discussed and often considered omens to be heeded.
—John J. Floherty, *Sentries of the Sea*

ITH CHANTY GONE I was, of course, alone with Toy. He explained to me the military consequences. Neither of us was what he kept calling "a rated man," by which he meant that neither of us was qualified to be in charge of the Light. A more pragmatic point was that neither of us really knew what he was doing.

Blump was supposed to come out and at least straighten out the compensatory-leave rotation so that there would always be a rated man aboard. Toy would be on with him then, and I would be on with a third-class engineman named Teddy who was currently on leave. But peer as we would through the binoculars, we had only the bluff upon which Cape Henlopen Light had once stood, the stacks of the fish factory, the two coast artillery towers, and the red-roofed lifeboat station.

"Well," I said, "do we really expect to see him strolling the beach or swimming out to us?"

"Binoculars keeps him from sneakin up. Besides, they pass the time."

The pilot radio was the key, Toy explained. Blump had persuaded them to leave a set aboard, and through it, unbeknownst to them, he kept contact with the Harbor Refuge on a frequency not guarded by the Coast Guard at either Group Cape May or the Greenmeal Lifeboat Station.

"See, the pilots got all these boats working the bay, and they connect with the Maritime Reporting station up there on the bluff at Cape Henlopen where the lighthouse used to be. Only they figure that fucker's a mile out to sea by now."

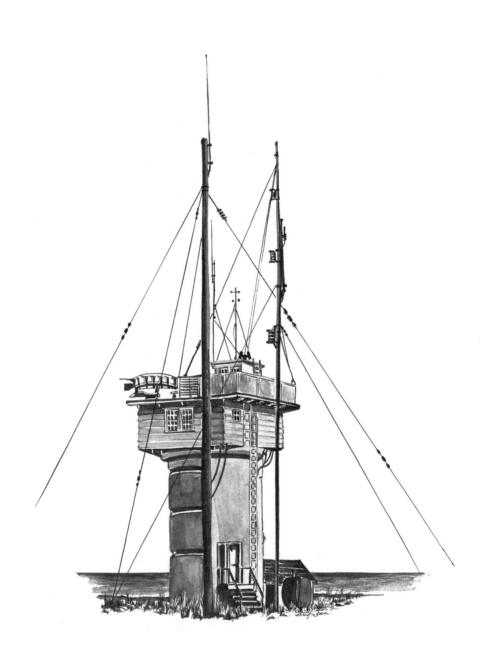

"The fallen lighthouse?" I panned from the high dune out over the sea. There were some rips, but the water was mainly flat.

"The place I'm talking about is nestled back of the dune."

I panned back up on land. There was a tower. Like the old Coast Artillery lookouts, the vertical section was built out of concrete, but unlike them it was capped with a white wooden shack that overhung the cylinder. A number of antennae poked up from the roof. There seemed to be plenty of windows. As I strained I could make out, trailing down into the dunes, several lines. "That's where the Maritime Reporting station man gets his mail," Toy said, "they put it in a sack and tug on the line."

"Doesn't he ever come down?"

"Either he don't never come or all them fuckers sound alike on the radio."

"How do they sound?"

"Farmer sound." He pointed at the radio, but did not turn it on. "If we don't got it on, Blump can't use us. He wants to know if officers are coming, then he'll hustle his ass out on the pilot boat."

"And they don't know how he's using them?"

"I don't think so. Maybe they just feel sorry for him."

"Why would they feel especially sorry for *him*?"

"He's one sad-lookin feller. You got to see him."

I looked through the binoculars but saw only Fats hanging in the door of the pilot boat peeling a banana.

My first mid-watch I turned on the pilot radio and heard what Toy had been talking about. The man in the Maritime Exchange tower did have a country accent, like a Maine man slowed way down. He would pick up the incoming ships and feed them to the mother ship *Philadelphia*. She in turn parceled out the work of boarding the pilots to one of her small boats. He also evidently passed on his shipping information to various interested parties. I tried to sort out the places and the duties. There seemed to be a quarantine station at Marcus Hook, immigration and customs men at Mantua Creek, dockmasters at Bombay Hook for Philadelphia and Reedy Point where the Chesapeake and Delaware Canal took ships bound down for Baltimore. I had never seen most of these places, so that hearing *quarantine*, *Bombay Hook*, and *Reedy Island* mixed in with names of ships from all over the world in that down-home voice coming at me alone in the middle of the night, a kind of poetry began to weave itself through the round tower.

Here, for instance, was the *Caruso Maru* from Japan laying over at Reedy Island waiting for the quarantine inspector, and I'd think of Kipling's old flotilla with its sick beneath the awnings, though no doubt the modern, efficient Japanese were merely waiting for a man with a rubber stamp. One night a freighter did come in with a man who had just died of what the pilots called "black fever," and the Coast Guard boat from Greenmeal was dispatched to bring him ashore. The next day I saw smoke on the beach and a black man dancing about a pyre. Later I found out it was merely the dead man's blankets being burnt by one of the lifeboat crew, but they did have to guard his body round the clock with .45's in their holsters until he was buried in "a sailor's grave" back of Greenmeal.

Other nights, Turkish submarines, Portland cement boats and Moravian tankers were all jabbering. Once, word came that the battleship *New Jersey* was going to come past on her way to becoming a museum up in Camden. The anticipation grew all night. You could hear it in the voices of the pilots and the man in the Maritime tower. She was being towed, and there was only one man aboard her! I had never seen a battleship except in movies. During the war my father had been on one for a short time and had told me about the thousands and thousands of men aboard. Why, he said, there was a whole bakery just to make her bread, and when her great guns fired the ovens flew open and the bread puffed out to cover the bakers.

At last she was passing. They had actually said our name, The Harbor Refuge Light. I jumped out of the chair. The man in the Maritime tower was calling us:

"*Hey, Refugees. Take a peek out your window there. You got a better view than me.*"

I thanked him and ran out the back door, around the gallery, and stood on the sea side, peering into the night. Was that it? By the lights it was the tow boat moving very slowly about a half mile off. I strained to see what that was aft. I had no idea how large an object to allow for or how far aft of the tow boat to look. In one of the last transmissions they had talked about shortening the tow line as they came inside the Capes. How short was short? And how big was big?

Ocean liners passing had floated glitter enough to light all of Greenmeal. Where were the lamps of the gunners and boatswains and navigators and damage-control men and commissarymen and yeomen and storekeepers? Where was the glow from the bakers' ovens? This was not wartime. There should have been a whole Greenmeal out there moving right to left.

Perhaps I was wrong. This was not the tow boat, but a trawler working a net. The window was open behind me, and I had left the radio up high. They were talking. Yes, they were passing "the lighthouse." I looked again and remembered the lone man who was on the battleship. I looked for a lone man's light, and there it was, moving high above the water. Around the bulb was a gray unlike the gray of the surrounding night, but where this gray became the night gray I could not exactly determine.

I ran in and got the binoculars. When I found the tiny light again I could see that it was but that one bulb stuck up under some overhanging mass and shining down to flood another mass. In between was a lighter gray that might have been a railing or bulwark. Was that a man behind the waist-high bulwark? Or was it merely an open door? It seemed to be a door, opened onto a gallery, an open door moving through the night.

The gallery rail was cold in my hands. The sea tapped the rip-rap below. There was another light, slightly smaller, it seemed, than the first, or maybe it seemed smaller because aft of this light I saw no iron gray, but only what I now knew was the gray of night.

Not all the night would be spent in these conversations with great ships. There were hours when all I had was a crackling, and suddenly the old down-homer would be on with the man on the *Philadelphia*'s bridge about getting lost in Baltimore or some other concern not strictly maritime, and therefore, considering the hour and the location, almost painfully touching:

"Yup, a body can surely get lost in all them streets."

"They wind about a good deal, don't they? In and out with all them cars and trucks."

"Yup, had a wife once in Balt-i-more."

"You had a what?"

"Wife. Had a wife, Cap. In Balt-i-more."

"You say you had a life in Balt-i-more?"

"Wife."

"Oh, wife."

"That's right, Cap."

"Tricky place, Baltimore."

Because they were run by young apprentices, the small pilot boats were more lively, often insulting each other with a rudeness that jolted me out of a dangerous doze, so that I would find myself blinking at some violent exchange that seemed to be chasing itself around the other side of the tower behind the stairwell. There were four of these boats, two working around the clock while the other two were being fueled or serviced. They were good boats, but being so hard driven they frequently had breakdowns or threatened them, so that I became as familiar with their intimate ills as a man overhearing pimps discussing their string: *Cape May*, she had a leaky stuffing box; *Brandywine* had her injectors gummed up; *Cape Henlopen*, "*Henny*," had her strainers clogged. As for *Delaware* she was O.K. as long as the fog didn't roll, for her radar was on the blink.

We knew not only the voices on the radio, but the sounds of the different engines, the high whine of the pilot boats' diesels, the deeper throb of the diesels on the forty-foot utility boats the Coast Guard dispatched from

Greenmeal or Cape May, the chug-chug of the menhaden fleet, the nag of
the rockfishermen's outboards.

One day Toy announced that it was time for one of these fishermen to
pay us his annual visit. It seemed that Swifty lived up in Pennsylvania and
had been coming to the Harbor of Refuge for fifteen or so years with a few
buddies to not only fish, but spend the night.

"Don't worry," said Toy. "He brings all the chow, including beer, and
does all the cooking and all the cleaning up."

Sure enough, Swifty arrived in his tin boat with two friends. As he
maneuvered in under the landing stage I could see he knew exactly what he
was doing. Toy, too, was drilled and sprang to a pair of davits I had never noticed, swinging them out from the staging. In a few moments we had the tin
boat derricked and safely slung up under our stage.

"So how do you like my davits?" He was a lean man in his mid-forties,
and he strode up to me and rubbed his hands in a way that let you know they
were his davits. "Navy surplus. Me and ol' Chant strung them up one night
some half-dozen years back. Inspectors never noticed them. My name's
Swifty." His hand was strong, and if his buddies seemed a bit puffy, he was
not.

Up in the tower he knew exactly where to go with his gear, unrolling his
air mattress and sleeping bag in the storage deck where the fog switches
were. "If you need any help with these," he said, "just let me know. Last
year one was stuck and I had to take the damn thing apart." Down on the
mess deck his stout crew was stocking the refrigerator.

"I think we can safely get rid of this sour milk," said one.

"Ah, maybe not," I said. "Chanty marked *save* on it."

"Oh," said the fisherman and he held out the carton until his eyes could
confirm the message. I, of course, still thought he'd toss it out, but he must
have thought I was serious, because he set it carefully back upon the shelf.
This left him eye to eye with the old fish. "How about this guy?"

"He goes," I said.

"You damn right," said the fisherman. "If we don't fill up this whole
shelf for you before we leave, may we never return."

"That old tomato there," I said.

"Well, we're not farmers . . ."

"O.K., give the tomato a reprieve, but for God's sake let's deep six that
damn lettuce."

"Right, deep sixing the lettuce." And out the back door it flew.

The meal that night was probably no more than many a family would
have ashore, but after Toy's cooking and mine, Swifty's stove work produced

a banquet. Because of their late arrival we had no fish that night. The steak and potatoes and broccoli spears served on our best United States Lighthouse Service china were washed down with Rolling Rock and stories about old times on "the Refuge," as our visitors called it.

Many of the stories, of course, were about Chanty, whose departure they lamented. They also shared what seemed to be the local revulsion for Blump. I was pleased, however, that they seemed quite affectionate toward the fourth member of the crew, the engineman, Teddy, who was still on liberty, able to enjoy an extra period because of Toy's restriction.

"Did Teddy sell his lawn mower yet?" asked Swifty.

"Now what would he want to go and *actually* do a thing like that for?" said Toy, and while the table erupted in laughter Toy's eyes darted from face to face, taking in his success.

"Teddy's got a power mower," one of the puffy fishermen explained to me. "He'll try to sell it to you every chance he gets, but don't ever take him up on it."

"But don't ever sell that boy short, either," said Swifty, and he poked his fork at me. "That kid keeps this Light functioning."

"I'm glad somebody does," I said.

"Don't worry," said the other puffy man, and then, as if to puff himself up even further, he leaned back and torched up a big cigar with a huge lighter. "We're here now and we got Swifty."

Swifty shrugged off the compliment. "Teddy's the boy. Just remember that."

Later when Swifty was down on the workbench assembling his fishing gear, I asked him about the history of the lighthouse. He said that it was true, there had been some big changes. When he'd first come out, for instance, there had been a different landing stage, one with some shacks on it. I said that I had thought the piles and planking looked awfully new. Swifty reminded me that "waterfront facilities" were subject to unusually severe stress. I asked him if he had seen the crack around on the open sea side.

"Ol' Chanty chasm, eh?" He adjusted the metal lip on his plug. "I figure to go deep tonight," he said. "So I'll just set this baby for a full dive."

That adjustment made, he marched out the cellar. As I followed I had the illusion he was going to take me around to the spot in question and give me his wisdom on the Chanty chasm, but he turned the other way and climbed down past the sewage outfall, where he found a flat rock to cast from. I watched him wing out a few, then, not prepared as was he for a night of fishing, I began to shake from the cold.

But Swifty is shaking too, shaking and cranking, and his rod's shaking and he's hollering. There's something jumping. Swifty bends and reaches out. Why he does not ooze on off the rip-rap I don't know. Up comes the splashing into his hand, and his arm jacks up and shakes, a very thick forearm, as if it is two forearms, and it is, two hunks of meat anyway, but one is the fish and the other is Swifty.

"Come here," he says. "Hurry up."

Teeter-tottering on the slippery rock, I reach him, slide into him, we both windmill to a halt.

"Here," he says. "Take him. Here, in the gill. The hook's already out of him."

I walk carefully back up over the rocks, my index finger hooked up in the raw gill. He must be twenty pounds, and he's still pulsing, so my finger is squeezed, and he flaps once or twice, so I gasp and totter down there in the dark, his flashing silver no light, but sheer panic; and I reach up for some staging, because I do not want him to dance me back down there, where he has all that darkness.

Inside, I found Toy at the table playing cards with one of the puffy men. Between them was a wall of empty Rolling Rock cans. I hovered over them a few moments, a full beer in my hand, feeling a bit nervous as when in college I'd spent nights before exams out watching my roommate play the pinball machine.

The puffy man kept trying to ignite his soggy cigar with that big flame thrower. "As a matter of fact, this is Al's own personal lighter. Not that the damn thing is any good."

"Thank God—it *doesn't* work," I said.

"O.K., Say-leer!" shouted Toy, and he jumped up, threw his cards down and stood hands on hips, face up in mine. "Let's get a little discipline around here."

"Hey, take it easy, Toy," said the puffy man. "Al will be down in a minute and we can——"

"Al won't be down," snarled Toy. "Al's asleep. Al's had a hard day getting prepared. What we need around here is some discipline."

"Al did the dishes before he went up," I said. "Swifty's down on the rip-rap doing what he came for."

"Rip-rap, rip-rap, you mean fuckin *rocks*." He turned to the puffy man who was crouched behind his cards. "You know what we call this jerk out here? We call him Mr. Rip-Rap. *Rip*, for short." He curled his lips to show just how delicious was this appellation. "You know why *wecallemRip?*"

"Take it easy, Toy," said the puffy man. "Al's coming down soon."

"You know *why* we call him *Rip?* Because that's all he thinks about and he don't even know what else we do here but look at holes."

I turned and started to walk away. The fact was, I noted, Al *hadn't* washed the dishes, at least finished washing them. My ears were tingling. My hands shook. Suds looked good.

"You want me to prove he don't know what goes on around here? I'll get the daily log. He don't even know how to fill in the daily log. I, an engineer, got to fill in the deck-ape log."

The suds were cold, and I had to drain some of them in order to fit in more hot water. Toy returned with the daily log and from about three feet away began firing:

On Mondays we had Signal Drill; Tuesday, Safety Lectures or as had been recently modified, Meetings of the Safety Committee; Wednesday was Officer-in-Charge's Report, or as had been recently modified, Leadership Discussion; Thursday was Boat Drill alternating weeks with Fire Drill, recently modified to Adjustment Evolution Phase One and Phase Two; Friday was Health Lecture, now a meeting of the Physical Fitness Committee; Saturday and Sunday were Holiday Routine, though this was rumored soon to be replaced by Recreational, Moral, and Cultural Opportunities.

"Good God," I said, "how do you know *how* to do all these things?"

He showed me the line you wrote it on.

There was also a weekly calendar of Maintenance Events: Monday, decks, shelves, ledges, drawers, crevices, and scrannel pipes; Tuesday, windows, venetian blinds; Wednesday, oven; Thursday, refrigerator; Friday, gurry bucket; Saturday and Sunday were again Holiday Routine, following the Saturday Officer-in-Charge's Inspection.

"When do we do the lemon-oil thing?" I said.

"Thursday is refrigerator."

"I mean the thing up on top of this place, the main light lens up there."

He looked at me. "Lemon oil is something we are *all* out of," he said.

"Well," I said, "I'm glad to be straightened out on all these matters. Now here's a towel, dry these fuckers."

He looked at me, then down at the daily log. "Here," he said, and handed me the book as I handed him the towel.

The alarm bell woke me up.

I probably shouldn't have gone to sleep with him like that, but I'd never seen Toy drunk and so didn't know what he'd do. Besides, when I went up, he was docilely drying the dishes, and Al had indeed come down, which, as the puffy partner had predicted, was a mollifying influence.

It was in fact Al who met me now at the door of the sleeping quarters.

"Toy's-taken-Swifty's-boat-and-the-lamp's-gone-out."

"You mean the——" I pointed straight up.

"Yeah, the you-know, the——"

As for Toy's defection, I let that pass, not really comprehending how he could have lowered the boat that had taken three of us to hoist evenly.

It was enough to keep yanking at the iron rail in the staircase. I must have been going up, because I did get there, but for most of the time it seemed all I was doing was yanking on the handrail and going around in circles. The bell was ringing the whole time, and all I seemed to have accomplished was to make it louder. Standing in the resounding watch room directly under the hatch that led up into the lantern, I was paralyzed by the din. Furious at the persistence of the alarm, I made fists and grimaced. Al tapped me. The other puffy was next to him. They both pointed up.

I went up.

It was loud there, but it was also dark.

Damn dark.

"Here," said Al and he thrust up his cigar lighter.

"Don't do that," said Puffy. "It may all ignite."

"They don't use whale oil no more," said Al. "I looked for a flashlight, but Swifty has the big one. The little one I forgot in my preparation. I couldn't find none that belonged to the station here."

I worked my fingers around to the bottom of the lighter. It was already hot. "That's because we don't have one," I said. "Can you believe that?"

"Maybe Toy knows where it is," said Al, "but he wanted to go ashore."

"Swell," I said, and groped for the buckles I'd remembered unhitched the sides of the chariot. The lighter did not get cooler, but it did throw enough illumination so that, among the lunging shadows, I got the buckles apart.

"Somebody's calling us on the radio," said Puffy. "I turned it up real loud so we could, you know, maintain the watch. I also left the door open, propped it."

I congratulated him and asked if he'd go down and answer the call. "If they're just reporting the light's out, roger them and tell them we are working on it."

Once inside the casing I could see the two bulbs. One had the little spring and bar across the middle dangling. The other looked intact. "The problem is, the automatic switching mechanism hasn't flipped the good bulb into place."

"I'll hold the lighter while you switch her over," said Al.

"Watch it, the damn thing's hot. As is this whole casing."

"It was the only lighter I got."

I took a breath and tried to remember just what Chanty had done that day to make the mechanism flip manually. Memories of arched sullennoises, South Philly pistol whippings, and yellow eyes was all I could come up with. The mechanism itself might as well have been a cuckoo clock made by a manic yodeler.

"Maybe there's a diagram," said Al.

"I'm sure there is. Somewhere." I poked about in the hot metal wheels. There was a gasp, but no click. As for the alarm, we had simply internalized it so that it no longer was a matter of the ear, but a jangling of the liver.

"They wanted to report the light out," said Puffy.

"Who did?" I said.

"Oh, a whole bunch of people. Cape May, Japs, pilots——"

"World War Two is fun," I said. "Have we been up here that long?"

"Here, hold this lighter awhile," said Al. "My fingers on both hands are charred."

Puffy poked the lighter at my nose.

"Not so close, please," I said.

"Maybe there's a diagram," said Puffy.

"Al's got it."

"I ain't got no diagram."

I was developing a cramp from leaning into the case, and the cramp had turned into a spasm, so I had to pull out for a moment.

"I'll just keep holding this lighter in here," said Puffy. "That way, what with these powerful French lenses maybe we can, you know, toss a little beam out there." The flickering threw his face into a mask, and the mask danced about the chariot in grotesque rhythms. The core of the light, however, remained steady. "A little beam out into the world."

To keep from dropping the hot lighter we took turns holding it in the chariot.

"This is more than the Aladdin's lamp could do," I said.

"Here's my fishing pliers," said Al, and we used them to grab the lighter. They were short and the reach awkward, so we still had to take turns.

It occurred to me at one point that if I took the replacement bulb out of its socket and simply switched places with the dead bulb we would accomplish the same thing, but for some reason the socket would not give up its prize, and I was afraid of shattering the bulb.

I did not look out. I could hear the slight trembling in the lantern panes, occasionally the crackling of the lighter's wick.

"This is the old part of the tower," said Al. "The original part."

"So I hear," I said. "But what I don't ever seem to hear is exactly what happened to that old tower. I mean if it simply fell over, what is this room doing back up here? This old room we're in right now."

"That's a good point," said Al.

The panes trembled. The wick crackled.

"In fact that's a very good point."

It was my turn to hold the flame. It seemed to be dwindling. We had been discussing the possibility that Al had more fluid in his bag.

"There's a boat coming," said Puffy. He could see lights.

"Oh, shit."

"Hey, it may be help, you know, aid."

"It's probably officers and us with a galley full of beer, unauthorized personnel and no engineman."

"Hey, it's the unauthorized personnel that's keeping this place lit," said Al. "It was the unauthorized personnel that had the light itself."

"I'll throw all the beer overboard," said Puffy.

"Don't hit the boat with it."

"I'll throw it on the ocean side."

"Save some of it, for Christsakes," said Al. "You know, hide it."

"Maybe I'd better just throw it all over."

"Maybe you'd better just get moving."

It was quiet for a moment, which I thought odd, as Puffy's descending footsteps should have been dripping all the way down the iron spiral. Then a voice from right under us in the watchroom said, "But maybe we should hide our own personal selves."

"Go!" I shouted.

He went.

Al and I stayed, holding the cigar lighter inside the airport beacon case up in the top of the lighthouse.

"Hey," said Al, "Just like the old days, wick and all."

It wasn't officers. It was Swifty coming back in his own boat. He did not bother with the davits, but tethered to the ladder and came right up all the way to us. He was hardly breathing deeply as he went to work on the changer with his fishing pliers. Presto, the light was fixed. After we helped him pull his boat up we held a post mortem around the table over steaming mugs of tea.

He had simply slipped off to do some bass fishing on his own, assuming that his partners were otherwise occupied. He had brought Toy back with him, however. Toy had been ashore, though how he had managed that without a ride from Swifty was unclear. Nor did it get clearer for Toy was, if not drunk, still at least much confused and apparently not a little chagrined. There was something about another bass boat that had been fishing near the rocks, something about a fight in the bar along the canal with some guy from the army base who'd insulted the lighthouse, something about some of the guys from the lifeboat station bailing him out and putting him aboard the pilot boat. From there it was clear. Swifty had been intercepted by the pilot boat and Toy transferred. When Toy and Swifty got to the Light they found Puffy heaving the beer, bottle by bottle, off the gallery.

"Full ones as well as empties," said Toy. "The crazy fucker."

"Who's crazy?" said Puffy, "at least I wasn't AWOL."

"You ain't been out here six straight weeks, either," said Toy, "in the prime of your youth."

"Now I know you're drunk," I said, "the *prime of your youth*. Worse than Chanty."

"Hey," said Al, "it's the prime of all our youth tonight. In all our years coming out here. I mean maybe we didn't catch no fish, but couldn't you see that light casting its beam out into the world?"

"Yeah," said Puffy, "you was out there, Swifty. You was out in the world. What did you see? Did you see the light?"

"All of a hundred yards."

"But you did see it," said Al. "And that's the whole point of this night: we did not let the light go out."

THE *HERB* IN SUMMER

One of the lightkeepers was a man of deep superstitions. The shapes of the surf leaping over the rocks, the cries of the sea fowl, the moaning of the wind around the lantern during the night watches all had their significance, to be pondered on carefully
in the hope of learning their occult meaning. One night, while he was winding the
clockwork mechanism, he was startled by a tapping on the glass of the lantern. To
the keeper it sounded as if the bony finger of a skeleton hand had knocked twice
sharply. A gust of cold air came up through the hatch from the watch-room. As he
looked up he saw a white bird outside the glass. It was not a gull nor a tern, neither
was it a dove nor any species he knew. It looked at him round eyed and pityingly.
The white flash of the revolving lens made its plumage sparkle like sunlit snow,
while the red flash gave it a ruddy color that suggested blood and violence. He could
see his own reflection in the glass against the darkness outside drawn in red and
ghostly white alternately. The bird remained motionless for a few moments and
then, giving a single tap on the window with its beak, flew off.

—John J. Floherty, *Sentries of the Sea*

SOMEWHERE IN Chanty's instructions had been a cadenza dedicated
to the buoy tender that was to service us monthly, filling our great
wooden water casks and the fuel-oil tank. Chanty had been sent to
court marshall at the hands of its skipper, I thought. Or was this the one
officer we could trust? Something, in any case, dramatic. And we were to do
dramatic things in return, for here was a ship coming to our very landing.
There would be, first of all, its side nuzzling the spiles and planks tied to our
tower.

Then there would be the machinery, levers, and gauges that controlled
booms and blocks which in turn managed sinkers and chains, all of this very
heavy on the deck, but capable of amazing quickness when something went
wrong.

The name of this ship was the *Herb*, and, like all of the class that worked
the rivers and bays, it was named, as Chanty had indicated, after flowers; the
larger ships were named for trees, such as the *Sassafras* from Cape May,
which worked off shore. There was naturally some rivalry between the two
ships, he'd explained, the whole shallow-water versus deep-water thing all
over again. The point was that we were not only the last stop on the *Herb*'s
run, but the place at which their territory overlapped that of "a real ship." As
a man himself migrating toward the open sea, Chanty had been sensitive to
the anxiety always felt by the small ship's crew as they steamed out to what

was for them, afterall, the edge of the world. "They will hand out abuse," he'd warned, "but it's only because they want to rush back up inside the Bay before they get caught out of their depth."

Nevertheless, it was with surprise one evening that I looked across the spice tray by the galley window and discovered, in addition to the garlic, celery salt, Wessen Oil, and Tabasco, the blooming booms and masts of what could only be the *Herb*.

I was glad that this had been one of the days we had decided to fly our flag, trusting the gentle winds not to be giving Old Glory a case of *"de-tat-ters."*

Toy was already down on the landing stage, dashing about as if in a play in which he were required to act the role of a man on fire. I tried to hear what he was saying through the window, but all the spice cans were dancing, and I realized a horn was blowing, the horn of the *Herb* no doubt, though the sound was so strong, even to one accustomed to sturdy blasts, as to have a life independent of any source at all.

Out on the balcony I could more clearly see the ship, her deck a mass of gear and her bridge above the turmoil slightly above our stage, like a box at the opera. In the late afternoon light of summer it was indeed all like a theater, and it was no wonder that Toy now shot an imploring arm up at me from stage center, a gesture straight out of a nineteenth-century melodrama.

His language, however, was something that no amount of leafing through last century's scripts would reveal. Nor, blashphemy and bodily functions aside, could I recognize what seemed to be the key twentieth-century term. *Toddler,* it sounded like. I was to bring the *toddler*. They needed the *toddler*. They needed the *toddler* immediately. What could I do from my balcony but implore those on the other balcony and him who strutted the stage below to accept my innocence in this matter of *toddler?* The evening azure received my gesture. In such a theater, especially with this kind of lighting, it was easy to see why Chanty had grown so histrionic.

If I were indeed in Chanty's shoes, or his lack of shoes, I would now run down the stairs to the landing stage and perform some outrageous court-marshallable act. As I descended, however, some of my lust for fame bounced away. The problem was that the lower I got, the bigger loomed the heavy rigging of the buoy tender. Furthermore, the faces along the bulwarks that had been merely in the pit, agape at the brilliant life above them in the boxes, were now on a level with me, eager to get at me with a growl. An actual dog barked.

"Well, where's it at, son?"

That not from the dog, but a boatswain with a bulldog face and the only man behind the bulwarks with a hat on. The rest looked like sullen youths hanging around. And wasn't it evening—*down on the corner*, et cetera? The dirt on their chambrays and jeans was not slum dirt, however, nor farm dirt, but sea muck, or at least bay bottom: caked slime made of worms and weed, neither quite worm nor weed. In this warm air, just before sunset, their clothes were as dry as they would get before the dew moved in to renew what the sun had undone.

It fascinated me, this business of dirt, for aside from galley scum, for a month I had seen no real dirt—that is soil, earth—and though I am no farmer, my hands itched for it and my nose craved news of it even if it need be dredged from the floor of the bay. I tried to recall what buoys there were between our Light and Brandywine, exactly what sea marks' sinkers and chains could have so plastered our guests, and could conclude only that there were none. That meant that the crew of the *Herb* must have been working some of the smaller aids inshore and upriver much of the day. I could see now the low freeboard she carried, especially where the saucy sheer took the gunwale down amidships and made her seem like a river steamer: a craft of backwaters, her hull an intimate of soft margins, her prow battened perhaps on lily pads, prop mellowed by spatterdock, her deck pungent with creek bottom.

It was strange too, to find myself not only a connoisseur of dirt, but a metaphysician of the working day; for as someone stuck in one place for weeks at a time, I was enraptured at the sight and even the smell of people who performed a set of tasks they began at one location at a particular hour and finished not only at another time, but at another location. This would be a day, then, which moved through both time and space, so that in late after-noon, say like this very moment, you could glance down at the muck that had dried on your sleeve and then look back up river over the stern and say, "Good, we have come this far. We have, after all, *progressed*."

"Get the toddler, for Chrissake," said Toy. "Don't just stand there dreamin."

A man in khaki came out on the ship's bridge. His hat was tilted way back, and his shirt and pants unpressed in the manner of World War Two skippers in charge of small boats on half-assed but lovable missions.

"Get us made fast, boys," he said. His hands played over the dumb compass which was set out on the wing for planting buoys, and his thoughts seemed to go out to Table Eleven of *Bowditch*, which dealt with Distance By Angle Between Object and the Horizon Beyond.

The distance between us and the captain was just about right for watch-ing a movie about one of the half-assed but lovable small-boat missions, and the wing of the bridge upon which our hero stood was high enough above us now to give his performance larger-than-life projection.

"Oh, for Christ sake," said Toy. "I'll get it—you go down on the rocks and make ready. But watch out. It's slipperier than eel shit below."

"Don't get hurt now, boys," said the skipper. His hands were still making passes over the dumb compass. If he could just get the right bearing on the pier, God knew what Half-Assed & Lovable stunt he might pull.

"You gotta go below," shouted the boom boatswain. He tugged on his baseball cap to demonstrate he had splattered upon its front not just the marl of the Delaware, but three sharp chevrons. And it was furthermore, a hat *square with the deck*, his goddamn deck. The skipper could be as jaunty as he pleased up there parading about in the evening air, away up with the spile tops trembling and the Wickies dancing, but down on deck where things counted, down where the boom was rooted and the slime still wet on the sinkers and stoppers, a man could crack his shin on any number of pad-eyes, sockets, wire splices, and shackles. He could sling his hand in a power vang or catch a crazy bone on a pelican hook. Down on deck, God damn, a man needed leadership.

"You got to get below, I tell you," he said again. "We ain't got but an hour of light." And damned if he wouldn't extend a little leadership up there to the lighthouse itself. He'd do that even if it were a big goddamn thing leaning over him that was supposed to be there doing that, and he was only a lousy boom boatswain on a lousy river snatcher. He'd do that even if he'd not come roaring in from the offshore lightships, the ocean-lighted whistle buoys and major flashing gongs, but instead come creeping down from nigger-creeks, a life of fiddling day beacons, cans, spar buoys and the minor nuns. "Come on now, you niggers," he bellowed. "This tide is like to sweep us all out to sea."

"Ain't no more niggers on here," shouted Toy.

"The hell you say."

"Oh, no, we got ourselves here a ruptured bugler."

"You got what?"

"We got somethin crazier than Chanty."

"Fuck that, boy. Get the crew moving. Whatever the hell it is."

"Yes, but don't get hurt," added the skipper. "We don't want to have to report any injuries here."

"For Christsakes, what the hell is he doing now?"

"See, see, I told you. Crazier than that nigger we had." And he came after me waving a two-by-four.

I made for the ladder down the stage onto the rocks, and Toy followed brandishing his weapon and shouting.

"O.K., I'm going," I said, "you don't have to swing at me with a stick."

There we were, in under the stage now in dimness and din, on planks over gurgles. Toy hollered about his bloody *toddle* and waved that stick while I stayed ahead of him tippy-toeing and teetering out onto frail under-pinnings, my own underpinnings frailest of all, and grateful my feet for the barnacles which cleated my soles to the eddying earth.

Leaning at last against a spile, against the other side of which was lean-ing the buoy tender's black iron, I caught my breath. Pale green light fil-tered down from the spaces between the planks above, and flashes of brighter light broke from between the hull and the pier as the ship smacked and eased.

Toy stalked me across the wet planks, using the stick for balance. I formulated a plan by which I'd grab the end of the stick and yank him forward past me into the water. As the stick came nearer I could see it would be easy to just grab it away.

"Here," he said. "Here's the *toddle*."

I almost dropped it.

"All you got to do is run it through the eye splice when the seaman hands you the line. Don't drop it, though. It's the only one we got, and without it she can't tie up."

"Oh, sure. The *toggle*." There it was in my hand! It was not going to subdue *me*, but control the great bulk at my back. "Naturally," I said, "a toggle."

As the eye splice came dangling down like a hangman's noose, I reached up.

"Don't get your hand between the ship and the piling," said Toy. "And hang on when he backs down on that spring line because the prop wash will carry you right outa yer fuckin shower shoes."

Taking the line, I reached around the spile. There were actually four of them driven together. It was like trying to hug an oak tree. I finally flipped the line so that it came whipping back around, allowing me to pass the stand-ing end through the eye and secure it with the two-by-four.

"There, you see why you needed the toddle now," said Toy.

I gave it a pat.

"Stand back," said Toy, "you never know exactly what this fucker Mr. Milkins will do next."

Indeed, someone was shouting. To my right, where the sheer of the hull took the bulkhead low, the boom boatswain appeared, cupping his hands. At his elbow the dog stood, paws on the bulkhead, also barking. When the boatswain saw that I was looking at him, he made a circling motion with his hand. It was clear he was used to hollering at dense lighthouse per-sonnel and there was no end to the repertoire in his dumb show. After all, hadn't he been commanding the boom all day with his fingertips? *Hoist*, *lower, drop, swing, faster, slower, easy, tip, tilt, tickle, release*. . . . Two bells rang, and with a roar the black wall slammed out all the light, so that when the splintering crash came, it was as if lightning had struck. I didn't know what had happened and stood clinging to Toy, the two of us somehow still on a submerged stringer, while the whole pier, from staging through cross supports, creaked and sobbed, fragile as a box kite. Where the lightning had seemed to strike was indeed a jagged white dangle.

"He broke the spile," said Toy. "He smashed one of our fuckinspiles to smitherins—for no reason at all."

A single bell rang out pure and gentle; there was a silence in which only the roiling waters of the prop wash caressed our toes, rolled up our ankles and, using our shins as a vine uses a pole, crept right up to our kneecaps before peeling back like a blossom and dropping. "My God," I thought, "Minot's Light, the Eddystone, this is exactly how it works, how even on mild days the tops of exposed towers get soaked, and it isn't even winter yet."

Although it usually seemed like a day's work, or at least enough to justify an afternoon, the climb to the upper balcony to take down the flag and throw the Main Light switch seemed as effortless as if I'd risen up the spiral staircase in a balloon. Once out on the balcony I could strut to the balustrade and, with but a wave of my straw hat, wipe the offending ship from the sea. Merely by extending my hand I could obliterate the entire buoy deck. A fingertip sufficed for the boatswain *and* his dog. It was, of course, proper that I be up there at that time, I reminded myself, for the sun was already low. Confused in this interruption by the buoy tender, we had almost neclected our real work and let the tower stand much too long into dusk unlit. Furthermore, there was this clear patriotism of halyards and buntings, stars and stripes coming now slowly in my arms just as the sun itself came slowly into the stacks of the fish factory.

"Attention to the colors," I shouted down.

One of the louts by the buoy boom saluted in the Italian manner. The boatswain himself bent over and coiled up the messenger line. The dog danced about its brown yelp. The skipper, however, out on his wing above them, squinted up at me and, recognizing a familiar flop of cloth, threw a sloppy highball and with the other hand pulled up his pants.

Toy was up in the beams of the engine room. "Where the hell you been in that faggy hat?"

"How the hell did *you* get up *there?* For that matter where the hell is that you're at?" I tried to trace his route: soda box, down spout, steam pipe, bottom barrel hoop, top chine: step, grab, straddle, chin, step, chin. Two stories of it, poised over concrete.

"Where the hell you been?"

"I've been tending to the normal round of duties," I said.

"To hell with the *normal round of duties*. Get me the hose."

"All right," I said, "but where is it?"

"If it was up your ass you'd know."

"Yes, but it's not, so where the hell is it?"

"Get the fuckin *Herb* hose, you fuckin ass-hole. What the hell do you think I'm doin up here, pullin my own hose?"

It was there in the doorway out onto the concrete base. One of the *Herb*'s crew had deigned to lug it up, but now had quit to stand in the door smoking. He seemed to be looking for a wall or door that was neither wonked nor round so that he could lounge in the manner to which he was, at that hour, accustomed.

"Hey, let me know when you're done," he said. "But hurry up. We got liberty ashore in Greenmeal tonight."

It was a big, black, heavy hose that kept wanting to ooze back down the base onto the rock and, for all I knew, back into the entrails of the *Herb*. I finally got enough of it in the door so that the weight was now in favor of keeping the damn thing inside the tower, at least for a moment.

"Jesus, will you hurry?" said Toy. "I'm gettin a nosebleed up here, and there's nothin but dead birds in the tank to keep me company."

Hauling up some additional slack, I began the climb toward him. The soda box started to waver. I put my free hand out for the downspout which ran from the eaves to the cistern in the old days when the fresh water had been collected off the roof. It occured to me the enormity of Chanty's recent error in poluting the cistern, an act that accounted for the casks being, now that I was up close, shockingly new. There had been no way to cleanse the deep cistern; it had been necessary to design an entirely new system, pre-fab it, ship it out and put it together, no doubt with a special crew from Base Gloucester. Had Chanty been aboard? Had he stood by watching them, occasionally fetching a barrel stave from the pile and taking their abuse, or had he sulked it out aloft in the watchtender's room putting thick paint on the mullions while muttering Tennyson? In any case it was clear that the old Wickies before him had not, as I was now doing, so roached their way up for water.

No sooner had I made my claim on the old cistern pipe, than it began to sway and I was prevented from falling only by whacking my elbow onto the steam pipe. Toy reached down for the nozzle, but there wasn't any more slack.

I shouted to the lout in the door, but, caught in two stories of concrete and iron, my voice came out pure caterwaul.

I tugged.

The soda box rocked.
The downspout swayed.
The steam pipe sweated.
My hat toppled.
And the nozzle erupted.
As did Toy.
And the water fell all over me.

"You bastards," shouted Toy. "You trying to blow me off my perch?"

"Point the nozzle down into the tank, will you?" I said. I might as well have been in the shower.

"Slack," he cried. "I need more slack."

"Slack," I cried. "More slack."

Slack-slack-slack, cried the cauterwaul and the lout joined in, carrying the great need out into the evening where it was passed aboard the *Herb* with her sweeping low sheer, her cabin ports lit in the dusk, making her more than ever a river steamer, now crouching behind the bay's last breakwater, her bridge wings only peeping over into the endless openness, while out of her belly tanks flowered her gift.

And the water that fell was, at last, ours.

ENTER BLUMP

During the dreary hours until sunrise when he put out the light the nervous keeper reviewed the bird's visit over and over. He knew it meant no good, but what it meant he could not fathom. He placed the cloth cover over the lens and drew the yellow shades to protect it from the rays of the sun, and again winding the clockwork mechanism, prepared to go below. When he reached the watch-room immediately under the light, he stepped through the door on to the gallery to see what the weather was like.

—John J. Floherty, *Sentries of the Sea*

B LUMP DID, of course, come that summer. In fact he came often. At least two or three times a week. The first time I saw him he stayed no longer than it required for the pilot boat to leave him flailing wildly at the iron ladder, streak out to the horizon to service a distant smudge, and return.

During this interim Blump, BMl did manage to haul himself up the ladder and across the landing stage. While I left a snickering Toy behind in the tower I descended to greet what was, after all, my immediate superior. Dressed in oversized chambray and dungarees, Blump looked, as Toy had suggested, the sole client of a drunken tent maker. Above this textile disaster worked a face full of antiphonal pouches and balconies, and eyes that could not be sought in the same place two phrases running.

"I'm on a diet, heh-heh," he said, and offered a hand that once might have been employed to shake, but now like spawning trout, merely promised a kind of mutual quivering in common waters.

"Chanty has been giving me a tour," I said and at once regretted it.

"Oh, no. Well, heh-heh, now we'll have to rectify all that." He stood at a loss as to how to rectify Chanty, his cheeks working in and out. "I got it," he said. "Have Toy show you." With that he looked up at the tower, looked down and with his eyes on his feet followed them up the stairs while I followed him.

Once inside he spent the whole time watching for the pilot boat with a pair of binoculars. Toy kept up a continual razzing at his back. When the pilot boat approached, Blump turned to me for the first time since we had come into the tower. "There's another man, you know: Teddy. Teddy, that's his name. He spells Toy here in the engine room and will be coming aboard shortly some time."

"*Some* time!" screamed Toy. "It's supposed to be on a *regular basis* which you, as the officer-in-charge, are supposed to set up."

"Heh-heh, well, I see my ride is here. Can't keep the boys waiting. It's bad enough to impose upon them in the first place."

On the way out, he grabbed the last bit of stale meat we had left and crammed it into one of the pulsing pockets located in his face. Toy screamed that we were supposed to have fresh food. Blump mumbled something about Teddy's bringing it. Toy accused Blump of not bringing the chow because he couldn't tie a proper sling knot to get it up onto the staging and Blump fled out the back door.

"Go ask him about your leave," said Toy. "Your kum-pen-sa-tory leave due *all* lighthouse personnel."

I found Blump still aboard. He was just out the back door, in fact. Big as life. Running his hand over the top of the rail. "Toy and Chanty relieved themselves out here."

"I beg your pardon."

"You can see for your own eyes," he said, "see just what it did to the maintenance job."

"You mean the paint?"

"You have to maintain an aid like this, you know. It doesn't just go around standing up by itself, you know."

"It might take more than mere paint."

"See that you scrape it all down to the bare iron here where they've been relieving themselves. Scrape it down to the bare iron, red lead it two coats, brown enamel it three, so that by the time I get back it will be smooth as a baby's behind."

"And when will that be?"

"That will be when you have done it properly." Shifting his cheek and almost looking at me, he added, "and stand up straight yourself. This is a prominent coastal aid."

"So," said Toy when I came back inside.

"I don't understand," I said.

"Sure you do. You're like everybody else out here. You just like to act a little."

Teddy also made his appearance, arriving in proper fashion on the lifeboat station's forty-foot steel-hulled utility boat. He even had the week's chow all trussed in a series of serviceable, if not eloquent, knots. I did not get a good look at him then, however, because Toy, at last freed from his six weeks' restriction, was stealing the show by chasing the engineman around the cockpit of the forty-footer, not as Chanty had, to recover his stolen poetry, but out of a more fundamental grab-assing. Later we learned that his flight had been short-lived. Racing his car as he had gunned the engines aboard the Light, he found himself stopped for speeding just outside of town. After the manner of some southern states, the authorities instantly fined him and hit him hard, so that to keep a roof over his head and three hot meals a day coming into his belly, he had had to spend his compensatory leave at the lifeboat station, where he was ordered to clean heads and wash all dishes.

As for Teddy, he seemed, as Swifty and the bass fishermen had suggested, not only a competent workman, but an easier person to get along with. From New Orleans, he was, however, slow of accent so that when he asked me without any preparation, except for Swifty's warning, if I wanted to buy his power mower I thought he was selling his parents.

"Thanks," I said, "but I have parents of my own."

"No, man, my paw-ma." And he pushed a phantom two-cycle around the gallery.

"Swifty and his buddies were out here," I said. "They said they missed you."

He stood there a moment, chunky and swarthy. "Oh, yeah, Swifty."

"Yes, well they are great admirers of yours."

"*Admirers?*"

"They say you're the man that keeps this place from falling over."

"No, I jus keep it so it can make its noise."

Later I tried to find out how he had come to acquire this power mower. He said he spent his compensatory leaves at the lifeboat station. Did they make him mow the lawn as they had made Toy clean the heads? No, there was no lawn to speak of, just saber grass sticking up out of sand in patches. Was it, then, some holdover from his New Orleans past? No, all they had had was a patio abutting a bayou upon which drifted a pirogue. This dug-out canoe had no motor, evidently, so that when the lawn-mower engine came up for sale, along, of course, with the rest of the lawn mower. . . . Then he was going to take just the engine back home and motorize the boat? No, that was all too far away.

"I see," I sighed, not really seeing at all.

"Then you want to buy it?"

"No, I didn't say that."

"You was interested, though?"

"Yes, I am interested. I mean I think you're owning a power mower when you—well, it's interesting."

"I had a lady interested in it once."

"Now there you go. I mean, a lady might have a, you know—*lawn.*"

He looked out the window at the long breakwater, but his lower lip did not, as the shadow from the tower grew, lengthen.

As for the balcony rail, I tried chipping it, but despite an exhaustive search of the tower from lantern to basement, found nothing more suitable for the job than the screw driver with which Chanty had *arched the sullennoise*. When I began using that, Teddy told me I'd better find something else. He did not scream at me as had Toy about "enginemen's tools." He merely pointed out that if, during the course of the chipping, I became excited, the screwdriver might easily bounce overboard. "What we got *then* if it gets foggy?" I argued that, unlike the magical days of Chanty, these were times when the screwdriver no longer flew about in sparks of glory. It merely stayed in my hand while I beat. He stood and watched me.

Every beat.

"Ok," I said, "but speaking of magic, why don't you simply order a new solenoid? After all, aren't you the leading man in the engineering division? Isn't it your responsibility to order that part and not Chanty's?"

He just stood there with his lower lip at last getting longer, so I surrendered the screwdriver, handle first.

"Surely you don't expect me, Chanty's successor, to order you engine parts."

"You ain't exactly Chanty's successor," he said and looked away.

"I got his billet. Hell, upstairs, in the back of my drawer I've even got the Blump hat."

"See, that's just it," he said facing me again. "Chanty, he wasn't just filling the seaman billet. He ran this place."

"He ran it all right," I said. "Including making out all the non-orders."

"Hey," said Teddy and he jabbed the air between us with the screwdriver. "Don't say bad things about him. Don't say bad things about Chant de Bump."

As for red lead and brown enamel, there were none, and Teddy advised me to close the lid on the paint locker before we lost that, too. There was, however, a small can of yellow paint and a thin "artist brush," as Teddy called it; taking his finger over the end of the great oil tank around the south side of the balcony, he found raised letters there which had been painted over in the same olive drab as the rest of the tank. We consulted the *Paint and Color Manual*, cross-checked it with the *Comptroller's Manual* and even called up Brandywine Shoal Light to confirm that yellow was a proper color with which to announce the purpose of such a tank. For the next few days, when not engaged in frying hamburgers, boiling Cream of Wheat or cleaning up after Teddy's two culinary maneuvers, (Western Sandwich and black Polish pancakes,) I carefully inscribed in yellow upon the raised letters:

FUEL TANK

When Blump came out one day, bringing the hang-dog Toy, he expressed delight in my initiative. I was a real artist with the brush. Even Chanty had not thought to paint *Fuel Tank* on the Fuel Tank. Saying nothing about the balcony rail or my posture, he departed on the first fishing boat that passed. Unfortunately, as Toy pointed out, he said nothing about my compensatory leave. Since Teddy had gone ashore on his proper schedule aboard the forty-footer, there were Toy and I again. "*Now* you're learning what Chanty went through."

A week went by. Blump had sent out some white paint and a note that I was to do the base of the tower. I was in the middle of the vast concrete wall, plastering the white onto the white in a kind of sea-drunken madness when a squadron of dragonflies began to mix themselves in with the sun-spots, dazzling my eyes. Soon all those eyes and mine were getting plastered together onto the white wall and only the occasional slop of the sea up through the rip-rap kept me sober. Another day we had a host of green ladybugs. The next day, mysteriously, they were all red.

Toward evening I would sometimes ride the pilot boats out among the porpoises as we all ran for the great ships coming in from the edge of the world. You could stretch your hand forth from the bow, and there would be a porpoise on each side maintaining its precise distance just ahead of the boat, the blue-gray flesh rolling just beneath your palm. On the change of the tide sometimes they would wake you with their snorting under the window. One night I woke ready to retch. Staggering to the bathroom, I saw a dancing sea of lights below and heard a rubbery singsong of bubbling shouts and cries. It was the menhaden fleet I'd seen that first dawn near the pilot deck, and they had now cornered a school the size of a Little League field. So compacted were the oily fish that their scent roiled up out of the waters to overwhelm me four stories high.

We were, of course, invaded by fog, though not so often, Toy and Teddy both assured me, as we would be come winter and early summer, if we got that far. Sometimes I'd wake up to the horn. My bunk was only a quarter of the way around the tower from where the trumpets projected merely one story above. I discovered why Blump had chosen the bunk at the head of the stairs, despite its lack of privacy. It was as far away as possible from the horns with the full core of the stairwell between its pillow and the strident bleat.

Not that Blump needed this insulation, for he never once spent the night aboard. As a result, when it was foggy those of us who had to stand the next watch would usually try to get some sleep by lying in this supposedly sumptuous bunk of Blump's. Toy, under the rather pathetic hope that Blump would one night actually have to roost with us, encouraged all to make nocturnal discharges in this bunk. Of course it was here, he claimed, that the pilot boys had put his sleeping hand in a pan of warm water, though Chanty, who had originally told me of the prank, had said the location had been Toy's own bunk. In any case it seemed to me a foolish thing to foul any nest one had to fall into and I never found anything untoward in Blump's sheets, though I must confess I did not look that hard.

There must have been times I slept when the horn was on, because I recall being awakened to take my watch. Often that was like rising up out of a well with the horn pushing me, its rhythm growing slower and slower as I surfaced, until the signal had assumed its normal spacing.

This strange speeding up of the horn during semiconsciousness was so marked that when Teddy woke me once I had a violent argument with him that the signal's characteristic had gone wild. We would be reported, I told him. We were violating our sacred niche in the *Light List* where we were assigned a precise noise to be uttered in a precise rhythm. If we allowed our horn to babble some other sort of nonsense no one would know who we were, and if they did not know who we were, they would not know where *they* were. Under this cascade of Confucian logic Teddy departed and it was only when I had reached the stove below and was well into boiling my Cream of Wheat that I realized the horn had settled down to its proper characteristic.

Later Teddy agreed with me that the horn did sometime seem to speed up if you were half awake. "Maybe it's like when you take a long trip in an automobile," he said, "and it's flat and just fields with nothing, so you count telephone poles to, anyhow, keep from gettin car sick, and the poles go by real fast because there's nothin in between 'em to look at, to, anyhow, hold them apart. That's like when you're half asleep and there's nothin in between the bleats to—hold 'em apart."

When Toy was aboard and it was foggy in the daytime, he would drag out the chess set that had belonged to Chanty and insist we play. Then the horn drove me crazy more than when I was trying to sleep; those times I'd really lose my temper and Toy would laugh and utterly vanquish me. Once, he offered to play me when the horn was not on, but so blitzed had I become by his fog game that I demurred. No doubt he could have beaten me in clear weather in the quiet of the Reform Club. He was, despite his surly inarticulateness and long listless stretches, a bright fellow. The foghorn then gave me cover, for I knew the only thing for which he respected me was what he assumed to be my superior intelligence in such abstract and useless endeavors as represented by board games.

There were times when I was alone on watch and had to start the fog compressor by myself. Since such an operation not only consumed fuel, woke sleeping mates, reached out to surrounding craft and even into the town itself, but involved the spectacular *arching-the-sullen-noise*, I was always reluctant to begin. Perhaps the wind would shift. Wasn't that really the Maritime Exchange tower I could see and not merely the mast of a moored sloop nearby? And those lights, were they not that of the town burning through and not the Menhaden fleet setting their nets? Once I had made the decision there was the whole business of keeping the din going. There were times after a few hours of what we charmingly called *running*, that the compressor tank would start to huff, the safety valve jacking away like a treading rooster whistling in obscene triumph. What did this mean? Was there going to be some *Natchez–Robert E. Lee* scene? And just where would be the best place to stand during an explosion? To flee to the upstairs might only put one more in line for the blast-off.

After four hours of running, the first compressor was to be stopped and the second thrown on line. Since it was always a question of whether they *would* start, here was a matter of leaving well enough alone. Most fogs at that time of year did not last more than four or five hours and one more hour on the engine certainly wouldn't hurt. There was also enough fuel in the day tank for maybe two more hours. More important, most fogs overlapped the watches, so the switching of compressors could always be left up to the new watch, which, in the case of my relief, would at least be an engineman. Nevertheless, there finally came a time when in the middle of the night I felt I must switch compressors. To have burned one out merely because I was afraid of the *sullen-noise* and the *slap-up-side-the-head* drive belt would never do.

In a shower of sparks I got the second compressor going, but when I eased the clutch in there was a terrible whacking. The belt had slipped off the drive. I had to shut the engine down, find a Phillips screwdriver, and take the guard off the belt. From above, the sound of the horn continued on the air built up, but the longer I worked, the fainter it became, so that by the time I'd almost gotten the belt pried back on the wheel for the third time, the sound from above was only a moan among doves. I glanced up at the spot in the wall Chanty had suggested as the most likely entrance for the cutwater of a super-ship. The belt slipped from my fingers.

Furiously I attacked the belt in an attempt to pry it back on. My effort probably more resembled an attack on a spastic adder. To use anything sharp, of course, risked nicking the belt, which would be tantamount to slicing it clean through. Somehow it had wrapped itself on the wheel again. I had only to replace the guard. Where, down in the dark, greasy niche behind the compressor, were all the screws? I fumbled and the guard clanged. I was on my knees, trying not to look up at the spot on the wall where the ship by now was as certainly due as a locomotive through the backwall of the station.

Coughs and sparks from the *sullen-noise*. When the engine was running smoothly I slowly, slowly eased the lever. It seemed about to catch. The guard rattled as the belt flew.

Everything had to be done all over again.

The only sound was my knocking about and the sea tapping the rip-rap. Perhaps the fog had cleared. I tiptoed to the back door and peered out. There was a faint swelling and shrinking above when the beam swung through. I could hardly see the end of the piles supporting the landing stage.

This time I decided not to replace the belt guard. I stood well clear of it when I engaged the clutch. Chanty must have been a fool to have been so close as to have gotten slapped. The clutch engaged in any case. The air built. The horn blew. The wall held. But there the belt ran on, unguarded. The next morning Toy just smiled. "Didn't you forget something, sailor?"

One morning when I was in the bathroom I heard a gentle cough just outside the open door.

"Hey, I saw . . . there was—"

"Yes?" I was shaving. The curtain blew across my bare back. It was the only curtain on the tower and there was a venetian blind hauled cock-billed behind it.

"See, I thought he had on them, anyway, *waders*." Teddy had moved past me to the window. "Right down there."

"Hip waders used by fishermen."

"Yeah. He was right down there by the landin'."

"I see." The razor irritated my skin as it always did in summer. "You saw someone this morning, someone when you were on watch."

"I was right here, taking a-a-anyway."

"Nevertheless a man on watch."

"And the thing is, see, he was taking a dump, too."

"He, however, was not on watch."

"I wouldn't have looked only I thought he had on waders, but it wasn't waders. It was all him but just a shirt and then while I was . . ."

"Maintaining the watch."

"Yeah, while I was watching and thinking it must be cheap, Jap pink waders, it comes out, what he was doing. It comes right out."

"Good Lord: An Embarrassing Moment."

"He was even standing up. Almost straight up in the boat."

"An unusual posture for an otherwise normal act."

"Yeah, it's normal all right, but it's a, anyway, *personal* movement."

"Of course."

"I think it is, anyway, important to have it."

"Yes."

"To have it as a personal movement."

"Well, do you think he was exhibiting himself to you? I mean you mentioned a boat. What kind of boat was it?"

"Small."

"No on-board facility then to, so to speak, *mask* the personal business."

"I thought it was waders. Cheap Jap ones."

"Then he was, so to speak, but a poor forkéd animal under God's own open sky, his vessel . . ." I checked the sea out the window, "his vessel heaving ever so gently on the ocean's broad and greasey bosom."

A slight cough from Teddy.

"Yes?" I was back at the mirror.

"We ain't got doors between our bunks upstairs here."

"True, Teddy, but on the other hand we do have one here in the bathroom, that is the *head*."

"Hey, I didn't mean to offend you. I thought you was just shaving."

"I am shaving." I proved it by scratching my face.

"I mean I think doors are important in a person's life. The only thing is, I thought it was waders."

Other less scatological fishermen came. I looked for Swifty, but never saw him. Mainly it was the party boats, which considered it enough to deposit their clients upon on our breakwater, where they would leave them until sunset when the skippers would return to retrieve their sportsmen. On weekends I counted up to fifty people milling about on our stones. Lugged along with them were all manner of impedimenta: sacks, pouches, bags, boxes, coats in all colors, yellow snorkel tanks, spears, rods, gaffs, nets and a whole catalogue of more peripheral accessories including radios, barbecue grills, refrigerators, and portable TVs. Starved for objects beyond our spartan equipment, hungry for something more than our diet of square, guano-covered rocks, I stood on the gallery to batten upon this feast.

Rarely, I actually descended to go among the visitors. They remained up beyond the ruined beacon, and although there were government signs forbidding their presence anywhere on the breakwater, I sensed that this part of the narrow structure was their territory. There was one party boat, however, the *Norma Bame*, which chugged confidently to our landing stage. One morning the skipper even shoved a few fresh planks at me under the tall pilings and we fell to nailing them down over the stringers for a catwalk.

"And this will help you, too, won't it?" he said.

"Sure," I said. "When the lighthouse tender comes."

"Sure," he said. "Us guys out here in the neighborhood got to stick together."

When he left I had a letter ready for him, but in the confusion of flopping fish and beer bags, he was off before I could get it aboard, and the tide was running so strong that he could not get back. I signaled for him to stand off a moment and ran up, got a tomato soup can, rinsed it, shoved the letter in and down on the new catwalk again, lobbed it out to him. The black mate reached out for it with a scoop net, but the can sailed over his head to land with a thump among the sodden sportsmen. They all backed away as if it were a bomb, and it rolled toward them slowly as the *Norma Bame* shimmied off a wave top and then . . . caught in a lull, everything—boat, passengers, can, message—all were suspended on a Sunday sea. *My God*, I thought, *I'll never get ashore again.*

Sometimes we got fishermen curious enough to come toward us from the ruined beacon, as if they might have wanted a tour of the tower itself. Usually they backed off at our approach, so I was suprised one day when a middle-aged man and woman in hooded sweatshirts and knee boots detached themselves from the crowd on the rocks, which included a fat man in hood dozing like a seal. Teddy, who I thought avoided tours, led them inside. In order not to embarrass him in his spiel, I kept away. Later he explained sheepishly that the man had slipped him a few bucks to use a bunk. "I made sure it was Blump's bunk," he said. "They wasn't married. That was the husband asleep on the rocks."

A more uplifting, if less profitable, incident occurred when a clan of Amish fished off our rocks. Not believing in reels, they employed hand lines, and when Toy started up the foghorn one clear day just so he could hear an engine race, one of the bearded gentlemen was so astonished at the noise that he flung away his winding frame and jumped overboard. We grabbed him with a boat hook, but his broad-brimmed black hat went skidding off around the breakwater, lost on the shockingly playful waters of Jehovah's Creation.

We swam on hot days ourselves when the pilot boat came alongside, and we used the low stern for a diving platform and trailed a line in case the tide got the better of us. The fat man, who loved knots, came out of the bandage-box cabin and tossed his cigarette butts onto the deck and said, "I see you ain't still tryin to pick them up."

"Hey," I'd say, "I'm perfecting the three-cornered Zulu trapeze knot to do the job."

And he'd say, "There ain't no such knot. Every knot I gave you maybe had a weird name, but it was a real knot in the world."

At which point Toy would splash me, and Johnny, the apprentice boy, would put down his soda and jump in on top of Toy.

As for stealing food from the mother ship, as Toy had at first suggested, we never did, though there were times when they'd send the boat over to us and bring us aboard for a meal, usually breakfasts of flapjacks, eggs, steak, coffee, and milk and juice served on a broad, gleaming table below the lights in their brass baskets. Waiting for a ride back to the Light, we'd voluptuate on deck under the awnings in the lee of the cowl-mouthed ventilators and listen to the pilots talk about the old days when there was a Maritime Exchange on the breakwater and the pilot boat had been a steamer, and before that when she was sail, and before that when there were no pilots, but pirates and Indians controlling the bay.

But there was for each day a night. At such times, when the party boats would all flee from us as the sun went down and their ever-diminishing lights spread toward the various destinations on the far rim, leaving between them and us and even between each of them the ever-increasing blackness, it seemed as if the universe itself were deserting across ever-chilling and silent distances.

It was then we were required to make our radio check, listening to all the Lights up and down the bay, and then, when they were all in, a booming voice would come yawning over the air:

"This is Dee-lah-ware Light-Vessel."

"Hot damn," Toy would say, "but the old Chant *do* sound sooooo gud."

LANDFALL

A coppery tinge suffused the sky to the east. "Red in the morning, the sailors' warning!" He muttered the age-old bit of sea doggerel to himself. A cargo steamer bound for Philadelphia was squaring away for the entrance to the bay. Great patches of red lead on her sides were intensified by the red morning sun. He thought of the bird and groped for an occult connection between the red of the bird and the red of the ship. The captain or whoever had the bridge changed the vessel's course to bring her close aboard the light. When but the length of a heaving line away the mate came on the port side and hailed the light through a megaphone. "Aboard the light there!" he bellowed. "A snorter's coming up the beach from Hatteras. Good luck!" That was all. The vessel went on her way, the splashing from her condenser exhaust being the only sound to break the stillness.

—John J. Floherty, *Sentries of the Sea*

TEDDY CAME back aboard, and Toy departed. Blump promised me a special deal which I could not follow, but I seemed to have no choice. He went back ashore and I went up to my bunk to sleep off the mid-watch. When I awoke I could hear Teddy below slamming in and out of the back screen door. I figured he'd had a bad liberty ashore at the station trying to sell his power mower. In not making him work when he spent his liberty there, they may have been doing him no favor. It left him vast areas of time in which to contemplate, there among sand and dune grass, his melancholy possession.

There was another possession of his, however, that was more mysterious than melancholy. I had not actually seen him lug it aboard and if I had perhaps I'd have just assumed it was some further absurdity from Base Bayonne, two dozen butter plates or gross of nuclear fall-out decals. But in my doze I heard him scuffling in his locker, nosing and butting some recalcitrant object or set of objects, driving this rummage further back, so it seemed, wedging it deep into the darkness of his lair. Once I was thoroughly awake I was tempted to look behind his locker door, but remembering what he had said about doors and the personal movements to be allowed behind them, I resisted. My curiosity nevertheless remained.

When I came down he was peering out the window on the seaward side, though no ship was passing. He gave me a pudgy little wave, but said nothing, not even about the power mower, let alone the mysterious gear in his locker. During supper, an hour when if there were just the two of us on the

131

lighthouse he inevitably brought up the mower, he did not even so much as
mutter about ease of blade adjustment. Strange as those discussions about his
mower had always been, I began to wish for their return. After all, even sur-
realism had through the years developed its own rules. But what of this thing
or these things panting up in his locker? It seemed clear he was not going to
admit them. This is worse than the crack, I thought. At least the crack is
below and it will not, when I climb to my bunk, be sleeping just around the
bend from me.

"Well," I said, "it looks like another night of watching the pilots climb
their ladders." Actually that had been good entertainment on these late summer misty evenings. When the small boats ran the pilots out to vessels at the
edge of invisibility, even without binoculars we could see the Jacob's ladder
unlink, apparently out of the sky, and watch the pilot climb up into a cloud
and vanish, leaving the ladder hanging for a moment ahead of the small boat.
As the boat backed down toward us, away from the invisible freighter, we'd
see the ladder snake up into the sky and disappear.

But I could not engage him in discussions of optical illusions or legends
of strange creatures rising from the sea. Nor did he even ask for the Slade's
pepper, though it was out of his reach and my cooking tasteless as usual. Finally I had to pass it to him. He jumped back as if he'd just seen a freighter
ripe from Zanzibar come thrusting through the window. I even turned
around myself, and there was nothing but the late summer sea and the pink
from the low sun. Since I had already switched on the beacon light there was
nothing to do but continue the meal. The camels on the Slade's pepper can
drooped slowly toward a distant oasis where lay dancing girls yet hidden by
the desert's hush. I had been on the light thirty straight days.

Though it was not my turn to wash up, I grabbed the towel, turned the
sink tap on, shook out soap. The sun had set, but there was still light from
the shore two miles to the west. There was also a tug on the towel, at the bottom, gently.

"Please," said Teddy, "please don't use the towel."

"It's O.K." I said. "I feel like doing the dishes."

"Don't use the towel." His voice was choked a little. "Please . . . just tonight. Don't . . . use the towel."

"Did you find something in *The Comptroller's Manual* about towel
abuse?"

"No, man, just for tonight."

"For Chrissake, Teddy, you sound like you've got some sort of *need*."

"That's it, man."

"Well," I said, "here she is." I let the towel go, not, I must admit,
without a certain faint regret. Smooth, only moderately damp and slightly
frayed with pale brown stripes on its border, it was a good towel.

"I'll just set these out to drain then."

"That's the idea, man," he said. *"Drain."*

"I suppose it is healthier," I said. "I'm sure *The Comptroller's Manual* has something on it. After all, a towel, no matter how clean, *is* dirty."

"Dirty is right," he said. He was smoothing the towel out across his legs. *My God*, I thought, *when you go in the service you're apt to be thrown together with all sorts of degenerates.*

"Well," I said, "since I've got the mid-watch, as soon as I finish setting these dishes out to drain I'll be going up." This in a loud voice, as if talking to someone else so Teddy could indiscreetly overhear me.

"That's all right, man, you can stay down and watch."

"No, I fully intended to let these drain more or less by themselves. I mean I kind of thought that was the point."

"I feel kind of like a de-generate all alone," he said.

"Teddy, you've got the towel, I mean——"

"You don't need a towel," he said, and to show his good faith he threw it on the drain board, smoothed out, dried out though it was. "We can just use the back of the chair."

"The back of the chair?"

"Sure, man." He trotted over to one of the leather chairs and dragged it around.

"I fully intended all along——"

"I'll be right down," he said, and it was he who went up. I used the privacy to wipe off a few plates.

When he came down he had a movie projector, the cord in his mouth to keep him from tripping over it, the reel under his arm. I immediately snapped out the towel and tried to dry it by breathing upon it.

"That's all right," he said, "we don't really need no towel." He set down the projector on the eating table and dragged the chair about.

"You're going to show a movie," I said at last. "On that new projector."

"What did you think I was going to do?" he said.

"I don't know," I said. "You had such a furtive air."

"I had air?" he said. "What do you mean I had air? I had this film I want to show."

"Obviously," I said. "I mean that's a perfectly normal thing to do, show a film. After all, aren't we American Fighting Men?" I helped him arrange the chair. "According to my father in World War Two, they lined up all the destroyers at Pearl and showed flicks off the fantails. You sat way up on a turret and had your pick of a dozen."

"This is a dirty film," he said.

"Well, World War Two was mainly for parents."

"With a girl."

"I think, being for parents, they kept the World War Two films pretty much to guns."

"This ain't got no guns. Just a girl." He pushed the chair around some more. I helped him, grunting a good deal to show there was, after all, a lot of hard work involved in things like this.

"If you don't want to see it, you don't have to," he said.

"That's all right," I said. "A lot of people might think there's no work involved."

We pushed the chair back and forth several times. "Since this is the very chair in which Chanty fell asleep on watch," I said, "it is in its own right, a famous scene."

"Hurry up," said Teddy and he struggled with the famous chair. "Hurry."

"For God's sake, Teddy," I said, "it's barely dark."

"Pull down the shades."

More to get away than comply, I stalked off around the tower undoing the goofy knots we'd rigged to hold up the venetian blinds. It was rather sad to have all our baroque bends and hitches unlink slackly, sadder still to have the sea at dusk turn into a mere clatter of unfolding metal.

"You know something?" he said.

"We've done enough work?"

"Work ain't got nothin to do with it. No matter how we arrange this, the curve of the lighthouse is going to make the distance so short the picture will be too small."

"That's it," I said, laughing hysterically. "This lighthouse we're on is curved."

"It's curved all right."

"Ah, how small do you think it actually will be?" I said. "This picture— the girl."

"About like a . . . a . . . magazine."

"Oh."

We both stood with our hands on our hips and pivoted slowly, scanning the interior, rather like early-warning radars.

"Well," I said, "let's try it. What can we lose?"

"It's going to come out like a magazine," he said.

"You must have known this."

"Sometimes you forget."

We tried it anyway, just the bulb on, no film, no frames passing through, no girl slipping out onto the leather chair back. The stark light itself was, as predicted, the size of a magazine. Slowly we withdrew the chair. The image grew, but assumed the distended proportions of a dirigible and then was onto the wall, flickering among the tongue and groove, the water pipes, scuttling all roaches. By then the famous chair was safely around the corner, and we had backed into the sink.

"You know it's too bad we don't have a great big drive-in movie screen," said Teddy. "A big drive-in screen for this girl."

"Some huge concrete abutment," I said. "The kind kids used to wipe themselves out on after the senior prom." I looked out the window. "My God, we do."

"Where's that?"

"Right here."

"Right here's a magazine."

"No sir. *Out*-side."

His eyes rolled. "*Out*-side." He made his lips into a soup-taster's pucker. "Ooooo, out*side*."

"Sure," I said. "*Out*side, out*side*. Healthy movies."

"I'll find some cord," he said. "Don't worry about your movie girl. We're gonna see her." His voice began down the spiral at the same rate his feet did, down around and then halfway became separated, floating as the steps sunk into the engine room. "We're gonna get your girl."

I carried the projector out, hugging it against the cool summer darkness.

I stood on the landing stage for some time with the projector under my arm, looking at the tower with its light going around and the fixed stars and the ships moving in from sea. It was a warm night, but I felt I might be better off with a jacket. Just as I was about to go in, Teddy emerged from the cellar trailing all kinds of cords. The plugs caught in the planks and rippled and knocked as he pulled them free.

"Yes, sir," he said, "just what the doctor ordered."

"Is the other end plugged in?"

"There ain't no use if it ain't," he said. He handed me the final plug and I inserted the prongs, gave them a wiggle and felt them merge softly with the projector's cord.

"Turn it on," he said with a grin.

I hesitated, watching his face light up instead.

"Go ahead," he said, and he reached over and did it himself. There was a hum and light bloomed in the iron and fled to the planks. "Point it up there," he said. "Go ahead." He took the nozzle himself and directed it. A great square of the tower leapt out at us.

"Wow!"

"We got to focus, man." He turned the nozzle and the corners sharpened.

"Shouldn't we, you know, set this damn thing down?" I said. It wasn't so much that it was getting heavy, as shaky. The tower was all a-twitch.

Teddy went in and got a kitchen chair and some spice cans for shims. He also brought the film. There was a large crackling from the tower. "I just thought I'd better keep the radio up high," he said, "Just to show we was still on watch."

"Of course," I said, "the film, though, the film."

"You know how to thread these?"

"Of course not, but let's get it into the projector."

"I think it's kind of pretty just that way," he said and he held up his fingers so they threw rabbit ears, obscenities and the usual tricks one sees in provincial movie houses during reel breakdowns.

"That's very funny, takes me back to when I was a kid," I said, "now thread."

"Oooooooooooo." He wiggled his fingers. A maniac jumped out of the third story of the tower, flew across and into the sea. "You want to see that again?" he said.

"Thread. you bastard."

"I can do a duck chasing a rabbit."

"If I thread I'll probably screw up the machine."

He began to thread. We sharpened the focus again. Numbers tumbled down the side of the tower. An odd buzzing, a flicker and there she was, fifty feet of her, doing a belly dance in a 1940 G-string with frills. Her bra was cut in triangles and had tassels.

"Ooooooooo." The maniac jumped out of the third story window and began assaulting her.

"Get your hand out of there, Teddy, I can't see."

"Ooooooooo."

"For Christ sake, Teddy, I didn't pay two bucks to see your hand."

"Oooooooooooo!" Teddy began dancing about, jarring the projector. The girl winked slowly and turned to us her bottom. It covered the second-story window, the sill hitting her just below the cheek.

"I suppose if you were up there all you'd get is a blinding light." I said.

Teddy continued to squeal and dance, cast nasty shadows, and jar the image. I steadied the projector, shoring up a box of Slade's pepper whose camels were threatening to gallop off after the girl. Suddenly we had a sound track.

"*Ahoy aboard the Harbor.*"

"My God, what's that? Too low for her."

"Must be the radio."

"*Ahoy aboard the Harbor Refuge Light.*"

We looked wildly about. The Slade fell out from under the projector and the nozzle canted, throwing the lady into a bizzare angle, leaving her head out somewhere in the night while her belly stretched and twitched across the tower.

"Maybe we ought to answer that," said Teddy.

I could see the pilot boat coming into view around the tower. She was about a half-mile off.

"I wonder if it's them," I said. "You've got the volume up so high I can't recognize the voice."

The call came again, and Teddy ran up into the tower. I watched the pilot boat for some telltale sign that it was talking to us. The girl continued to twitch, now almost upside down, her head in the sea, her bare legs wrapped around the top of the tower.

The projector was hanging by its cord, which Teddy had wisely tied to the chair. I picked it up and set it back, pointing the nozzle out at the pilot boat, but it was too far away. Evidently Teddy had turned the radio down, for I could hear none of the conversation. I put the girl back on the light-house. She shook her head and gratefully took off her bra. Her nipples were suction-cup arrowheads. She covered them with her hands and then let the tips peep through and smirked.

"Hey, man, you better cut that out," shouted Teddy. He was running down the steps. "Turn it off, turn it off." She put her thumb in her panties and yanked. A crease of flesh opened down the tower. "Turn it off, turn it off," he yelled.

"What's the matter?" I said. "We're just getting to the Part Men Like."

"No, man, nobody likes it. It's against the Federal Law." He cupped his hand over the nozzle and the tower went black as his fingers and face lit up in weird cracks. "The pilots, man, they said they'd had calls from ships." He killed the switch and we were in the dark, only the high beam above and the stars. "Ships from all over the world coming in to America, coming in from the wide open ocean and the first thing they see is a seventy-foot lady doing a dance."

"I suppose that would shake them up."

"They thought they was in New York with the Statue of Liberty."

"They must have a pretty funny notion of navigation."

"That's just it, man, when you been weeks at sea without nothing but numbers how you gonna know?"

"I think the pilots were just putting you on. Remember how they put that sea gull in old Henry's locker and used to leave each other off on ice cakes?"

"No, man, this is Federal."

"Let's switch her back up there. She's getting all turned in on herself there in the reel."

"No, man, that's a Federal Offense. They thought she was the Statue of Liberty and you can't go changing her characteristic."

"Oh, for heaven's sake, Teddy."

"You got to have permission from the District Commander Aids to Navigation, be published three times in the *Notice to Mariners*, and amended on to the *List of Lights*."

"But she doesn't look anything like the Statue of Liberty."

"That's the only other lady we could be."

"But we're not even where the Statue of Liberty's at."

"We're just supposed to be a plain old white tower with a bulb up top in Delaware, or Carolina, or wherever we're at, that's what," he said. "That's our characteristic."

"Well, I don't suppose there's any point in exposing this projector further to the ravages of the night sea air." I pulled the plug.

"Besides," he said, "it would give a pretty poor impression of America, don't you think?"

"I've already pulled the plug."

"I mean to have that be your first impression of America."

"I've pulled the plug."

PART TWO

Fall

LAUNDRY

The keeper began to descend the long spiral stair that led to the dwelling. His pace was slow; he was deep in thought. As he neared the bottom he stopped. His face lit up as the hidden meaning of the bird's message dawned on him. Willis, the assistant, ready to take over the watch, met him in the doorway between the tower to the dwelling. He saw that the keeper was upset and, sensing that he had something to say, returned with him to the kitchen.

——John J. Floherty, *Sentries of the Sea*

ALTHOUGH WE WERE careful of our fresh water, we knew that in the good weather there would be nothing to prevent the *Herb* from bringing more, and our casks were large, so we felt free to do our laundry like any householder. On Sunday, I wheeled the old machine out of the pantry and plugged its hose into the brass sink spigot, lay the exhaust back over into the enamel.

"You better tie that down," said Toy. "Chanty used to shoot that dirty water all over the deck."

So I tied the exhaust hose down into the sink drain and turned on the spigot.

My chambray shirts and dungarees were still new enough so that the water in the machine swirled a blue that would have been envied by Winslow Homer in his Caribbean period. When it came time to use the wringer I tried to remember how my mother had done it down in the basement when I was a kid. All I could recall were horrible tales of maimings.

"Go ahead," said Toy, "it's got a spring that can dislocate them rollers if you get your tit caught."

When the machine was done with all its gurgling, backeddying and yukkering, I bore the heavy, wet cloth out the back shack to the gallery.

"I know you like to be Chanty and go for the dramatic effect," said Toy, "but I advise you to use the line in the basement."

"You mean down there where all those greasy diesels are? I can see the necessity in winter, but as long as the weather holds like this it would seem a shame not to let the sea air blow through."

"It's the sea air I'm talkin about, son."

Toy howled and slapped his thigh. "You and Chanty . . . You and Chanty, and I'm gonna stand right here on this gallery and watch just what kind of a nigger rig you make."

"Then watch these clothes don't blow away," I said, "I forgot something inside."

I ran up to the second deck and dug out my *Coast Guardsman's Manual*. It was a volume I had not consulted since boot camp, where it proved useful only for answering multiple-choice questions such as: *What is the seaman's most valuable tool?* (An: His personal pocket knife. Warning: The seaman will not be allowed to carry his pocket knife while standing wheel watch, as even this small amount of iron may interfere with the compass.)

There, sure enough, among such items as "Overtaking a rum-runner," "Speaking over sound-powered phones," "Symptoms of and treatment of shock," and "Handling of frapping lines while lowering lifeboats at sea," I found: "Stopping clothes on the line." The entry that followed was rich as a fruitcake:

> Clothes should be secured on the clothesline by stops made fast to the eyelet holes in each piece of clothing. These stops may be bought from the supply officer. If two lines are used, all blue clothes must be on one line and all whites on the other. If one line only is used, all whites will be together above and the blues below. Clothes should be stopped on with corners lapping over so they cannot slip down and leave "holidays" (vacant spaces) along the line. . . .

From below came Toy's voice bewailing his boredom on the balcony among my wash, his accusations that I had stationed him there that I might the better practice secret and nasty vices.

"OK," I said below, "where the hell are the clothing stops and frapping lines?"

"You're just gonna lose yer whole sea bag this way, I tell you."

A cloth sack of wooden clothespins was in the pantry, and the sheer nostalgia of this item, so redolent of backyards, green cut lawns, and trees, swept my rock-bound mind away. In the paint locker was our one piece of dock line, more Irish pennant than Columbian warp. I tied one end to the escape rope and the other to the gallery rail. Carefully I gave each trouser and shirt the recommended "slight hand-stretching to remove wrinkles," and, plucking a wooden pin from the sack I held in my teeth, fastened the clothes to the line. The soft south-westerly of early autumn lifted the blue clothes against the blue backgrounds of sea and sky. All this, of course, was observed by Toy in choking merriment.

Although it was Sunday, I was in a rinsing mood, so I climbed to the lantern and washed down the windows. There was a good deal of salt crust up there, but the implications did not disturb me. I dreamed of my clothes below. Tankers outbound for Lake Maracaibo held down the far horizon. As my chamois rubbed across the glass, gulls carried their whiteness straight up until their climbing cries were lost in the squeek of the general brightness. I breathed deeply and knew that somewhere far beneath my feet every fiber of my denim and chambray would be breathing the same clear air.

Unfortunately when I went below later the improvised line was all that was breathing. The blue sea was still there and so too, the blue sky, but the blue clothes had simply, like the gulls, vanished into the background. If it were not for a few guilty clothes pins rolling in the gutter of the gallery, I should have thought that I'd never indulged at all in such a laundry orgy; or if I had done so, that I must have been so intoxicated as to have dashed to the rail with my moist armload—and in full enthusiasm with the well-washed world, heaved all into the mother-blueing sea.

To steady myself, I grabbed the rail in both hands. Yes, down there three stories below on the rocks lay a crumpled body or two. Slowly I backed down the necessary sequence of stairways and ladders, inched across the concrete base and by the sewage outfall, dropped onto the guano covered rip-rap. A couple of trousers and a shirt were still mine, all well soaked in crap.

"*Perfect*," said Toy, "a perfect case of Sunday nigger-rig." He pounded my shoulder. "Chanty'd be proud of ya."

We continued to live an idyllic life. Left alone most of the time, we were nevertheless in the midst of daily activity. Those who actually landed came on errands more comic than disruptive. A young officer arrived by way of the forty-footer one day to inquire into our Classified Document Disposal Procedure. Teddy and I offered him a cup of tea and listened patiently while he explained that ever since the Chinese Communists had snuck up on the *Pueblo* under cover of a jazz concert, it was necessary to know exactly what items were on hand and how best to destroy them.

To speed the disposal process and ensure that the most valuable papers were dealt with irretrievably, a precise grading system had been developed. Top Secret papers, for instance, were to be burned, but since the burn basket could only incinerate X number of pounds per minute, less vital documents were to be shredded. Since the shredder could only handle X number of items per minute, less secret items were merely to be jettisoned. The procedure, we admitted, was the epitome of the economics of destruction.

"Good," said the officer, and he licked his lips. The climb up the ladder had been a tough one for him, and the entrance to the tower itself a puzzle. "It's always so much better when the Unit grasps the reasoning behind the requested evolution."

"Only trouble is," said Teddy, "we ain't got none of them things."

"You mean you have not yet received your burn baskets, shredders and ——"

"Classified documents," I said. "We don't have anything here to hide."

"Oh," said the officer and he looked down at his clipboard. "No, I suppose not. This is a lighthouse, right?"

"Yessir."

"Well, then I'll leave you one of these Classified Disposal Stickers just in case. And . . . one of these."

The thing he put on the desk looked like one of those stickers canvassers leave when you've given to the Lung Association. "You never know," he said. "In war—that is, times of National Emergency, you may be asked to do many strange things out here." The sticker began:

I am an American Fighting Man

Another young officer on another day, after another tough climb, asked us for the inventory of our weapons. Teddy pointed out that Blump usually took care of those matters, but if the officer chose to, he could search the place. The officer said that this wasn't a *search*, but an inventory. We found him a fly-whipper, slightly tattered, its mesh sporadically by success besprent. He held it before him a full minute, a king into whose grasp had been thrust the scepter of a strange isle. When he left, we hung it back in the shack on a rusty nail and for days after genuflected in passing, for its success was now two-fold.

One night we were sitting around the table long after supper with only the main light on and a bulb burning way over by the desk. Suddenly the whole inside of the tower swelled up with light. It was as if something under us had exploded or was about to explode. We scuttled like roaches for a chair, a desk, anything to shield us. The room continued to fill. I put my hands over my ears, but the noise of the filling soaked right through.

"Let's run outside!" said Teddy.

We bolted to the shack, but *it* was out there, too—coming, in fact, from out there. And not from below, but above.

It was a blinding light, almost directly overhead, and it had forced its way down through our own great beam, outdueling us for supremacy of the night.

"It can't be an airplane," shouted Teddy. "I seen airplanes out here go by."

"Then it's one of those astronauts," I said.

"Maybe it's a shooting star. You get them this time of year."

"*Meteor Falls Harmlessly Into Sea,*" I said, "*Only Two Lighthouse Keepers Killed.*"

"Then we better run back inside."

We crouched behind the leather chairs and *bang*, out went the glow. Through the window we could see our beam once again flicking the stars.

"Had to be a plane," I said. "A big one to have a spot like that."

"I seen planes. Planes, especially big planes, especially big planes at night . . . they don't swoop, anyhow; they *go by*."

Blump came out one day with the television, positioned it up on the bracket as if he were an electronic technician, plugged it in, and watched *Exercise with Gloria*. He was sure that what had swooped on us had been a plane, advised us to confine our fantasies to the newly repaired television and then, when a pilot boat passed, flagged down a ride home.

One morning I woke to a great din of diesel. It did not sound like forty-footers. It did not even sound like a whole fleet of forty-footers. We had had a squadron of house flies the day before, so many that even the twice-blessed flywhipper had proved ineffectual, and we had not been able to open our mouths to eat without risking an unappetizing thickening of each morsel. Listening now, I thought, perhaps today's invasion was to be a swarm of basso-profundo bees.

What I saw out the window made me think I had the television set instead. A World War Two flick with John Wayne and company massing for an attack on Iwo. There must have been two dozen landing craft circling just off our pier. I saw no flags. Was this what the weapons officer had been warning us about? Was this what the security officer had feared? Had the mysterious blooming light been but a harbinger of this?

"Teddy?"

I opened the door to the lower deck and listened for him. I retreated to check his bunk. I called up the spiral staircase.

It was going to be necessary to go below.

At the back door was a soldier, his face blackened by battle grease. His rifle was slung over his shoulder. Our flywhipper was hanging in the shack not two feet from him. Our *American Fighting Man's Creed* sticker was on the window.

"Hey," he said, "where's the coke machine?"

"We don't have a coke machine."

"Then where the hell's the soda machine?"

"We don't have a soda machine."

"Then where the hell's the candy machine?"

"We don't have a candy machine."

"What the hell kind of a place is this, anyway?"

"It's a lighthouse."

"You mean it's a piece of shit."

I watched him slump on down the stairway to the landing stage, the camouflage bobbing in his helmet netting like petunias in a church lady's bonnet. Down there, rafted to the stage, must have been a half-dozen landing craft, and their occupants looked up at him. They had their rifles and bayonnets, but he had been their scout. His hands were as empty as when he'd left them. Theirs were full of up-jabbing fingers.

As the month passed, we discovered we had been a bit too prodigal of showers and laundering. The water from the brass spigot began to taste just a little casky. Toy accused me of consuming all the water through my need for flamboyant balcony displays and the subsequent need to rewash everything. Since the fiasco of the first Sunday laundering I had not, of course, persisted in such shows and had taken my few remaining clothes humbly to their line down by the furnace. Toy warned me not to experiment with that rope, because it was the very line by which we were going to have to tie the basement doors closed come the wilder weather. As it was, he said, maybe we should try and move the doors closed, as only the night before he had chased a bat or maybe only a gull up into the rafters with a crab net and it had vanished into the cask hatch somehow. "Just like it knew what it was doing."

I was tentatively tasting the water at the spigot. To stretch out my now meager wardrobe I was dressed in an inside-out sweatshirt, bathing trunks, and sockless shower shoes, so that when I heard the forty-footer roaring at the pier I panicked, thinking it was another officer. I rushed to the door, and there a fierce stare pierced the screen. No officer, no dog-face either, but a wild man without a hat. His work shirt was open to the navel, black body hair taking advantage of the air. He was tall, and he yanked the door out of my hand. My fingers stung from where the brass latch had been.

It was Farilla, the driver of the pick-up that had taken me to the pilot boat that first morning.

"What are you guys doing up here, anyway, sticking it up each other's ass?"

A shorter man, blond with regulation baseball hat and buttoned shirt, followed him. Down on the empty boat, the radio roared and cackled over the drumming of the two diesels. The boat did seem, however, to be tied up.

Toy slunk around the cylinder. "What do you say, Farilla?" he said. "You get seasick and decide to come ashore?"

"Them fucking niggers," said the big one with the body hair. "I hate them worse than ever. You got any water?"

"It's full of bat wings," I said.

"What?" He spun on me, looked me up and down, turned to Toy. "Who's this ass-hole?"

"That's the new man."

"How long's he been here? Christ, he was trying to lock me out."

"Don't mind him," said the other man. "Farilla's just plain obnoxious."

"I've already met him," I said.

"Obnoxious, hell, I'm thirsty. Where's the water?" He grabbed the brass sink spigot, twisted the knobs and looked wildly about. "Where's a fucking cup? Ain't you guys got nothin here?"

"There's cups there," said Toy.

"They're all fucking dirty," said Farilla. "You think I want to get trench mouth from you guys?"

"Then drink it out of the spigot," I said.

He looked at me again. "I don't get this guy. How long's he been here?"

"Longer than you have," said Toy.

"You know how long I been coming here? You know how long I been coming out to this Light?"

"I know how long you've been running that sink water," I said.

"Yah, Farilla, you want us to run out and stink?" said Toy.

"Listen, ya little guinea, you stink anyway." He stuck his finger under the tap. "Them damn niggers. I like it cold."

"We been up sixteen hours straight looking for them," said the other man, whose shirt said, "Cooper."

"It don't get any colder, Farilla," said Toy. "What do you think you're on, a ho-tel?"

"Shit, this is warm. Feel it." He snapped some at Toy. Then a handful so that it was all over the deck. "Shit, this is warm."

"That's because of the bats," I said.

"What is it with this guy?"

"There's bats in the water tank," said Toy.

"What do you mean there's bats?"

"Bats," I said. "That fly. They got in the hatch."

"Is that right?" He grabbed the drainboard and looked from Toy to Cooper. "Is he shitting me?" He even looked between the drainboard and the sink.

"How do I know?" said Cooper. "If you'll stop hogging the sink I'll taste it for you."

"I ain't touching it if it's bats," said Farilla. "Cooper and me. We got no coxswain. Just us two enginemen running this boat sixteen straight hours just to find dead niggers. What a screwed-up outfit."

"If it comes to that I been on here without liberty longer than I can count," I said, "And Toy, he's been here . . ."

Cooper finished his drink.

"How is it?" said Farilla.

"It's all right," said Cooper. "It ain't so bad. I ain't dead, am I?" Now with some leisure, he spoke in a soft rural mid-Atlantic accent.

"You sure?" said Farilla.

"I'm standing here ain't I?"

Farilla made a lunge at the sink. "Hey, what happened to the water?"

"I turned it off," said Cooper. "They only get water on these places once a month, you know."

"Ah, screw it," said Farilla, "I ain't drinking that shit."

We were all leaning on things in a semicircle around him.

"You lighthouse guys drink anything," he said.

"Come on," said Cooper, "we got to get down on the boat."

"Let em call."

"She ain't tied up so good."

"Screw it. Let her float off. *Bye-bye.*" He flopped toward the window and made a big lizzy wave. "Screw it. I wish the whole thing would sink. I wish this whole goddamn tower would fall over."

"Maybe it will," I said.

"Shit, don't count on it. Nothing ever sinks around here but niggers. Ain't you got any soda?"

"Why should we give you our soda?" said Toy. "You wasted half our month's water."

"That stuff tasted lousy."

"You never even drank it," said Toy.

"I could smell it."

"That was you," said Toy. "Your hairy chest. What a raunched-out chest."

"No, that was you, you greasy little runt."

"Come on, Farilla," said Cooper. "I done spend a year straight on one of these; I don't need no more time."

"You were on for a year straight?" I said.

"This is where you ought to be all the time, Cooper." said Farilla. "You ought to be right out here where you wouldn't be getting your pecker in a pickle." He turned to me, suddenly my confidant. "He knocked up his girl."

"Is that right?" said Toy. "That blond with the big tits?"

"Mary-Sue's a little late, that's all. Come on, Farilla."

"What were you doing on for a year straight?" I said.

"I was going around the corner last night in the Ford," said Farilla, "and I had a big piece of ice on the seat." He made the size with his big hands. "Christ, it slid out the door." The hands were left without the ice.

"You were lucky you didn't get written up."

"Aw."

"He was half out of uniform and all drunk."

"Why would a girl want to keep a guy's underwear?" Farilla said. "Jesus, what does she get out of that?" He was looking in the refrigerator.

"Your wife still in Jersey, Farilla?" said Toy.

"What's that to you?" said Farilla. "You want to screw her?" He slammed the refrigerator door.

"I never met her. Hell, I ain't met *no*body out here."

"What the hell, you got bat-water here. Gimme some soda, will ya?" He yanked open the refrigerator again. "Christ, I had this block of ice on the seat last night."

"Come on, Farilla," said Cooper.

"Was the girl married?" said Toy.

"Last night?" said Farilla yanking his head out.

"Any night," said Toy. "Christ, I haven't had nuthin in six weeks."

"You never had nuthin. You don't even have a soda."

"Goddamn Farilla's got wives he don't even use," said Toy.

"There's some milk there," I said.

"Where?"

"Come on, Farilla," said Cooper, "the boat's gonna drift away."

"With those engines going like that she just may charge off," I said.

Farilla grabbed the sour-cream carton and put it to his lips. When he spit, the trajectory was broken by the ceiling. "You fuckinbastard, I'll kill him." He stood about six feet away from me, his mouth twisted around the sour cream, his two hands crushing the wax carton so that the curds and juice ran out through his fingers, down his clothes. "You bat-shit punk."

"Can't you read?" said Toy. That said 'sour cream' right on it. Chanty left that."

"That does it," said Farilla. "Another nigger trick. Bat-shit here's probably a nigger, too." He looked at his curd covered hands. "They say you don't never know who's really a nigger."

"The milk is next to that," I said. "It says *milk* on it."

"I was on one of these for a year straight," said Cooper. He was looking at the ceiling. It was still dripping.

"Chanty nearly burned it down over there," I said.

"What the hell'd he leave that shit in there for?" Farilla walked over and put the carton in the sink, a sequence of gestures executed more elegantly than anything he'd probably do normally, a rolling of wrist and elbow, a lightness of step brought on by the curds capering down from his finger webs.

"Chanty did it just to piss you off," said Toy. "He knew you was coming."

Farilla washed his hands in the sink, an activity sufficiently complex to keep him occupied and relieve us from the need to entertain him. When he was done, he turned around and leaned back on the drainboard. "Where the hell is the old guy now anyway? Christ, he was one guy you could kid with." He laughed nervously. "They put him away, didn't they? Christ, he was one guy you could kid with."

"He's on the lightship," I said.

"I wish I was on a lightship," said Farilla.

"Go on, Farilla, you got it made in at that station," said Toy. "A different girl every night."

"I had this big cake of ice on the seat," he said. "Christ, does my mouth taste shitty. No kiddin, you guys, ain't you got any soda?"

"We got some of Chanty's old mouthwash," I said.

"Aw, come on, don't get me going, will ya? I been on that boat sixteen straight hours and the throttle broken on one for two hours when we thought we had *something*. I had to run her by hand. I thought I'd fry. All for them."

"If they got any sense they're already in South America anyway," said Cooper.

"You mean those guys that are overdue from Forestque?" I said.

"Six niggers," said Farilla. "In a fucking row boat. Figures."

"They're in South America," said Cooper. "Them nigras is smart."

"They ain't smart, they're just screwed up. Like Chanty."

"He wasn't an example of anything," I said.

"What do you know?" said Farilla. "He was a good shit. He was my buddy. He always gave me a soda."

"What were you doing on a light for a year straight?" I said to Cooper.

"The lucky bastard was in Alaska," said Farilla. "Up there they leave you alone."

"Sure, when he came back his wife was gone," said Toy.

"Except for the bills she left me to pay I don't regret it," said Cooper. "Like Farilla says, they leave you alone."

"You should have seen this redhead, Toy," said Farilla. "She had great big tits and chomped right down on me last night. Christ, I thought she was gonna tear it off. Her husband's in the army."

"You lying bastard."

"I'll show you the marks." He started to unbutton himself.

"Come on, Farilla," said Cooper. "The boat's gonna drift off."

"Where's Creel and Luntsky?" said Toy. "Christ, Creel's the best boat handler in the district. He can hold her right to the pier with no lines or nuthin."

"Creel's up in Baltimore," said Farilla.

"In the hospital?"

"He got wiped out again the other night and went into the wrong broad's house. Tried to get in bed with her. Shit, her husband was already right in there. He jumped up and punched ol' Creel out so bad he had to go to Baltimore. And you know what? That husband was an old guy. He was seventy-five years old. And so was his wife."

"That's two different stories, Farilla," said Cooper.

"What do you mean? What do you mean a *story?* It's the truth. He's in the hospital in Baltimore. Head's kicked in so bad he had to have his ID retaken so he could cash his check."

"I know it's true. I just meant it was two different times he got in trouble. It wasn't the old guy beat him up. That was last week he got in the wrong house. This week some other guys were waiting for him when he went to pick up his wife."

"He's got a wife?" I said.

"All these shore guys got more women than they know what to do with," said Toy.

"So what kinda women you got out here?" said Farilla. "Chanty always led me to believe it was Greek night out here every time the light went on."

"You don't need no women out here," said Toy.

"Oh, then the nigger spoke the truth."

"No, it's just you find you——" Toy faltered a moment, pawing at his clothes.

"Oh, I see. It's Mary and her five daughters?"

"Not much," said Toy. "You got to be out here to know."

"What is it then? Come on. It's got to be something. Porpoises? Seagulls?"

"That's just it," said Toy. "Out here you find after a while you can't even pick up a wrench."

"A wrench? Jesus, I like tools, but——" He spun on me. "How about you, bat-shit. What do you fuck out here?"

"It's like Toy said. After a while you just kind of——"

"That's right," said Cooper. "It's all a matter of habit. I know in that year I was on the lighthouse in——"

"I know what kind of habits you got, Cooper," said Farilla. "Hey, now I know where I seen this guy before. Luntsky and me took him down to the pilots one morning. Had to get up before dawn to take him someplace."

"Out here," I said, "you were supposed to take me out here, but the pilots brought me."

"Well, you're here aren't you? You probably been here since we left you. Don't you know how to get the hell off?"

"So how come Luntsky can't run the boat?" said Toy. "Ain't he always sayin he's not just a seaman, but a *boatswain-mate striker?* You see, Rip," he turned to me with an earnest face I'd not seen before. "That's why you shouldn't be out here. It ain't no good for your advancement. You can't strike for boatswain mate like Luntsky."

"Luntsky, that kid you see sometime on the forty-footer?" I felt a flush of jealousy, imagined myself at the helm of a steel boat punching out waves, cutting a swath.

"Yeah, Luntsky all right," said Farilla. "Some boatswain he'll make. Last week in that fog ass-hole Luntsky charges out to pick up a guy who fell down the hatch of some foreign freighter, some guy was messing around and got a little help if you ask me. Anyway he broke his back. Luntsky to the rescue."

"A most unfortunate occurrence," said Cooper.

"Luntsky is an unfortunate occurrence," said Farilla. "The little twerp gets lost in the fog. Lost in the fog. Can you imagine? He's out here cruising around with this poor bastard who's got a broken back, lyin there in the stretcher for three hours while Luntsky bombs the bay. Lost."

"Well, it weren't foggy when he went out," said Cooper. "It was clear as it is now. It didn't close in fog until they'd loaded the injured man on Luntsky's boat. Then pow, it socked right in."

"He shoulda taken reciprocal bearings," said Farilla. "Hell, even I know that, and I'm only a dumb wop mechanic. You don't catch me getting lost out here. I hate the fuckinwater too much to spend any more time out here than I have to."

"Well, that's why they got you runnin the boat instead of Luntsky," said Cooper. "They know you are gonna bring the boat back."

"Yeah, and shove it right up their ass, too. I hate boats."

"Then why did you join the Coast Guard?" I said.

"Because they promised to keep me close to home."

"You see that?" said Toy and he banged my arm. "You see that? Not everybody wants to be in this service to find a home. Not everybody thinks a place like this is a home."

"What have we got here?" said Farilla. "Another guy like Chanty? Another gung-ho lighthouse keeper?"

I just stood there.

"Come on, Farilla," said Cooper, "or you ain't ever gonna get home. They're probably calling you home right now."

"Let 'em call," he said. Then, grabbing a peach that was set to ripen on the window, he shoved Cooper on ahead of him out the back door. "Let's get the hell off this," he said. "Ten minutes on one of these drives me up the tree."

We watched them prepare to pull away. Farilla was at the controls, his shirt blowing in the wind, the levers in his fists feeding in fuel. They didn't even bother to untie the bow line, which was ours anyway, but took off full bore, snapping it like a rifle shot. In a moment they were into the tide rip, and at that speed it kicked high over the bow, covering them in a fine, white mist.

"If he always goes that fast," I said, "no wonder he can't find anything."

"Don't you worry, sailor," said Toy. "That's what you call *shore* duty."

THE *HERB* AT TEA

The keeper began at once to relate the incident of the bird's visit, interpolating many details to give it supernatural significance. He dwelt on the two taps on the window pane, and enlarged on the eerie change of plumage from white to red, and finally the single tap on the lantern before the bird disappeared. It was that tap that had bothered him during the night. When he had received the hurricane warning from the steamer the full import of the omen struck him. It was all as plain as day. The bird had come with a message from the spirits. If the two of them remained on the light only one would survive the coming storm. He ordered the assistant to take the boat and go ashore while there was still time. The young man bristled at the suggestion that he should leave his post.

—John J. Floherty, *Sentries of the Sea*

EVENING. WARM. Indian summer.

There was the garlic salt and the Wesson Oil and the buoy tender and the catsup. I wiped the counter around the spice rack and slipped the last two plates into the sink; I opened the brass spigot, and magically the hot water ushered forth. Now I could use as much as I wanted. At that very moment water was flowing into the great casks below. And since this was the last stop on the *Herb*'s run, there would be no point in her holding back; she could let her own tanks hollow if that's what it took.

As I ran the tap, I looked out the window and imagined the buoy tender lifting slowly, its plimsol blooming while our tower grew heavier and heavier . . .

To prevent this, I shut off the water and spread a thick layer of soap powder. Stirred it in with my finger, *a thorough preparation,* as Chanty would say. And the toggle business had gone well. Of course, the new planking contributed by the skipper of the party boat *Norma Bame* helped. The buoy tender itself had shattered no more spiles. The crew had held their snarling to a minimum, and the brown dog, which had resented our intrusion into its horizon last month, had jumped the bulwarks and come ashore. That is, if we were *ashore.* In any case he wagged his tail, and the lout who had merely leaned in the cellar door last time actually helped me lug the hose inside and up to Toy in the rafters. While resting a moment he had given me the story of the buoy tender's dog.

It seems the sour-faced boom boatswain had been driving through South Philadelphia on his way to the docks when he stopped at a light. The dog ran up to his car and kept jumping on the door. When the light changed, the boatswain pulled away, but at the next light the dog ran up to him again. Through some ten blocks of South Philadelphia the dog chased him, until, fearing for its life in the traffic, the boatswain opened the door and admitted the frantic creature. That had been a year ago, and the crew had even taken out an ad to trace the owner. I asked the seaman if the dog ever got under foot during one of the dangerous maneuvers on the bouy deck.

"Naw, you see that old boatswain, he may look tough, but he really loves that dog. He'll run right out there and scoop up the dog if there's any threat of trouble."

"That's nice," I said. "I was imagining several tons of concrete sinker sailing in low over that iron hull with about thirty yards of chain all in hot pursuit of a small, soft dog."

The seaman looked at me a moment, ran his hand through his hair and said, "Yeah, well you got to understand there's a lot of love on this boat."

Up at the sink I stuck my hands in the suds and thought about the dog which was back aboard the ship if I but wanted to step to my right and look out over the counter. Only that week my father had written that our dog had died. Although she was old and had mothered two litters, all the pups of which were yet alive with friends and uncles and aunts, it still seemed strange that dogs should only live a decade. And how did we now measure time? I was no longer in school waiting for promotions to the next class. To count the days until I got out of the service seemed madness when I could not, under Blump's system, even be sure of how long it would be before I got some time away from the Light. Better to think of watches and, for the longer unit, the visits from the *Herb*. The only problem with slowing time down that far was that geologic phenomena seemed to speed up: the rising of the oceans, the widening crack in the base.

"Make sure this place is all squared away," said Blump. "The skipper's coming up."

So immersed had I been in the metaphysics of suds, I had forgotten that Blump was honoring us with one of his rare visits. Somehow he had gotton wind ashore that the *Herb* was coming down the bay and had bribed a fisherman to bring him out by giving him a gallon of Coast Guard paint. Blump's politics were so famous, I looked forward to seeing him operate.

"Hey, Blump," I said. "How come the *Herb*'s skipper's coming up here? He didn't come up when just Toy and me were aboard last time."

"The skipper's coming up here for coffee."

"You mean we make it better than his own galley?"

"Don't be so touchy," said Blump. "Can't a man, can't one officer-in-charge, extend the amiabilities to another?" He rolled his hands over each other.

"One hand washes the other, eh?"

He looked down at the betraying flesh of his hands and stuck out his lower lip. "It's strictly social."

"Then he won't be up here prowling for discrepancies?"

"No, he won't be actually inspecting, but, you know, a trained officer's, ah, *trained* eye can't help but, you know, pick out things."

"Well, these dishes should be done," I said. "The counter's wiped. The table's clean." I shook the suds off the last plate. "So," I said, "*Duncan comes here tonight*."

"His name is Milkins. *Mister* Milkins to you." Then he laughed, his face a flummery of flesh. "To me, too, I guess."

"And what do you think this Mr. Milkins will say about the base of the tower?"

Since there was no sound at all from inside, I looked around to see if Blump hadn't merely padded off around the other side of the cylinder to his desk to consider shuffling his papers. He was, however, standing only a few feet away from me, stark still, and pointed at none of the three available windows, but at the sheer wall of the central cylinder. Its light-green paint held no object more interesting than a tiny run.

"He's not responsible for the crack," he informed the bulkhead. "That's strictly Base Bayonne stuff."

"I thought Base Bayonne was the supply unit and Base Gloucester, whence cometh the *Herb*, was the engineering port. In which case——"

"Just have the coffee ready," Blump instructed the wall, "and you won't have a thing to worry about, O.K.?"

"The coffee will cure the crack?"

"Just make sure the cup, his cup, is clean."

"I'll give him the one without the . . . *crack* in it." I set it sharply on the counter and Blump finally looked around.

His eyes, however, could not quite get up enough to meet that level, but slithered down the counter leg, flowed across the floor and under the table, where they fetched up in the rusting chromium claws with the gray swab strands. "You don't understand," he informed these damp remnants of cleaning frenzies gone by. "You just don't seem to understand that Mr. Milkins is a nice guy."

"I do," I said. "That's precisely why he should be interested in our welfare. In the welfare of the Light. Maybe that damn crack isn't a real problem. Then let's have someone qualified pronounce upon it, so we can forget the friggin thing."

"Mr. Milkins," said Blump, "Is a nice guy."

"Yes, but his personality aside, isn't his *job* to run a lighthouse tender, that tends the Light? In this case the crack."

"They don't call them 'lighthouse tenders' anymore," said Blump. "Boy, are you behind the times."

"Who's behind schedule?" Mr. Milkins, already inside the shanty, leaned back outside and tapped on the screen door to certify his manners. "I'm always reluctant to impose on the hospitality of you fellows, knowing how you try to *save on chow.*"

"Right this way, Sir," I said, only half realizing I had the dish towel across my arm like a *maître d'* and was falling into the Chanty syndrome again. "And a very fine autumn evening it is, Sir."

Seeing Blump slumped half around the cylinder at the table, the skipper pulled up by the counter to check his own posture in the sink mirror. His hat was cocked back. His khakis were mussed, but it did not look as if this condition had come about from any act which might in its jauntiness have strained the fabric. Rather the rumple had been the product of slouched hours, perhaps days—yes, friends, nights when in the loneliness of command each crease had only its neighbor to seek. A Sam Browne belt lunged across his shoulder to hook into his horizontal belt just in time to prevent his pants from falling. Nevertheless, the check in the mirror seemed to please him. He pranced. Perhaps jauntiness did indeed depend upon the horse by which you were transported and the *Herb* was your steam-snorting steed.

"I'll be cleaning out those flies in the sill there in just a moment, Sir," I said. "Soon as I gets yo coffee."

"Haven't I see you somewhere before, Boats?" He gave me the benefit of his scrutiny, working his frail blond mustache in and out of his mouth like a bottom feeder filtering an especially opaque medium. This mistaken assumption that I was a boatswain's mate served to pull Blump together at the table. I, however, was not yet quite ready to relinquish the honor.

"Perhaps you are thinking of my predecessor, Captain. That man had been Boats on here some six years, and before that two years up at Fourteen-Foot Bank and prior to that, I believe, a year at Ship John Shoal. It was he who discovered the crack here."

"Say, a regular Mr. Lighthouse, eh?"

"The crack in the base of the station, this light station, Sir."

"Ah, Sir," said Blump, literally rising to the occasion, "perhaps you'd prefer to sit down while you wait." He fought a chrome-and-plastic chair to a standstill. "Sit here while the *seaman* prepares adequately your coffee. At his preparing station." He made his jaw as square as the round flesh would allow, good and jut-square so that presumably I might get squared away. With a pale hand he once again offered the now-docile chair.

"All the comforts of home," said Mr. Milkins, and he awoke the chair again so that he had to fight it forward through windrows of swab hair, and his Sam Browne billowed and snapped.

"And how do you take your coffee these days, Sir?" said Blump, once again enthrowned in his own seat. "As usual?"

"Frankly I prefer tea," said Mr. Milkins. "As I have ever since convoy duty in the War. Now, what's this about somebody getting off a good crack?"

"Oh, is there a crack in the cup, Sir?" said Blump. "I thought we'd deep-sixed all that old Lighthouse Service junk."

"Tea cup, hell," I said from the stove.

"Yessir," said Mr. Milkins, "old World War Two ruined my gut for coffee, son. Nothing like convoy duty for coffee. Fortunately I was on a Limey ship eventually, and we, of course, quaffed tea."

"I'll bet you did have some interesting voyages, Sir," said Blump.

"By the way," said Mr. Milkins, "speaking of humorous voyages, wasn't that fellow you keep referring to, the fellow who was here all these years, the sort of resident genius, wasn't he a . . . frankly, a——"

"Frankly Negro, Sir," said Blump, "with some, heh, other things mixed in. A regular sea-pie. Or so he claimed."

"Well, he had been a cook, hadn't he? I recall some difficulties with his, ah, frankly, seamanship. That's the trouble with many of these Lights. They go around putting old cooks on them and call them boatswains. I, for instance, was a gunner in World War Two, switched to boatswain because there weren't that many warrant billets for gunners after the hostilities. This fellow, I think, went to boatswain because he was merely an inedible cook."

"Yes, well," said Blump and with effort clapped his hands solidly together. "All that's over now, Mr. Milkins. All water over the bridge, Sir. Now we have a totally modern facility."

"Chanty told me he was a boiler tender before," I said.

"Yes, well, I'm a steam man myself," said Mr. Milkins. "You probably noticed that. *Herb*'s one of the last hand-fed, coal burners in the district. Hell, probably in the whole Guard. There's *Hawthorne* up in New London, and they're getting ready to decommission her as soon as the new *Redwood* is viable."

"She ought to be some beauty," said Blump. "The *Redwood*, Sir."

"Frankly, we're O.K. as long as we don't push her. This, you know, is as far out to sea as we get." He darted a look past Blump out the window. "This is the end of the line for our class."

"If you'll pardon me for saying so, Sir," said Blump, "I never could, heh, figure out how you were able to recruit men to stoke those boilers."

"Chanty told me a buddy of his fell right into one," I said. "He told me that the day he showed me the crack. I'll be glad to take you down there right after tea, Sir."

Blump mumbled something about Chanty *not being* a boiler tender, but a former cook.

"Ha, no problem at all, my boy," said Mr. Milkins.

"Fine, sir," I said.

"No problem at all. Everybody who comes aboard, of course, wants to be a boatswain like you two fellows here, or a quartermaster—steer the ship." He demonstrated how one performed this task. "And all we've got to do is feed them to the boom boatswain or up on the bridge some flashing-light drill, keeping buoys on station, a little *HO Pub* 14, and they put their heads right down into their hands. 'Don't you have a job for us where we don't have to think, Captain?' I tell you, we never lack for coal heavers, m'boy. We just never lack for heavers."

"I heard a story once, Sir," said Blump, "about a fellow ended up heaving himself right into the boiler along with the coal. The door slammed right behind him and his watch mate was frozen from acting. Baked him like a big sea pie, Sir."

"That's Chanty's story," I said.

"Well, no, there's not that sort of danger," said Mr. Milkins. "Actually the main danger's out there: On That Buoy Deck."

"Speaking of dangers," I said putting the tea before him in the cup with the crack.

"Heh-heh," said Blump and he reached over and switched cups with the skipper. "Best china for guests." His eyes glared up at me out of their soft balconies.

"Danger everywhere in the Coast Guard," said Mr. Milkins. "A lot of people don't realize that. Why, in World War Two we lost more men per capita than any branch. I know. I was on the convoy patrol. Now, there was bitter type of duty."

Ah, I thought, it's here at last: the Half-Assed & Lovable Mission.

"Yes, sir, lads, I was a gunner in those days, gunners mate third to be exact, and they billeted me on a Limey ship for The Duration. That was a usual navy billet, I hope you realize: Armed Guard, but there I was: a shallow-water sailor stuck over the deep with a bunch of Limey blokes and a three-incher."

"*I say, old chap*," said Blump, and, looking about for *laffs*, he provided his own hearty snicker.

"A goddamn ammo ship it was, too. I was the only Yank. *That* was supposed to be because we'd lend-leased them a gun to go with me, or perhaps it was the other way around; they leased, lend-leased me to go with the gun." He leaned back, thumbing the Sam Brown belt as if it were a suspender.

"Pretty good," said Blump. "A lend-leased Yank, Sir."

"That is, the gun was supposed to be standard, good-old-made-in-the-U.S.-of-A. And it was, the Reading Textile Machine Works, right up in

Pennsylvania there." He spun around and groped for Pennsylvania on the bulkhead back of him. "Anyway, problem was the instruction manual——"

"Made in Japan," blurted Blump.

Mr. Milkins face fell, and his mustache filtered dust motes for a few beats. "Oh, no, son. You've got . . . I'm afraid you've got——"

"Made in Russia," offered Blump.

"That's it!" said Mr. Milkins and he slapped the table. "You see they thought it was one of the hundreds, thousands we were sending to Russia, but there it was stuck up on this Limey ammo ship. And the thing is that halfway through that model after a series of right-hand turns, there's a little pecker-head, if you'll excuse the expression, a little p.h. of a *left-hand knurled knob*. And me stuck on top of this floating ammo dump with a manual in that serrated alphabet they gotta use. You used to see it all over the lend-lease stuff set out on wharves, crazy-looking letters like you were doodling with a chisel, goddamn Chinese stuff almost. It probably said stuff like: *Danger High Explosives* or *This Side Up*. And I got to read it in a running sea that never quit."

"Sounds like sabotage, Sir," said Blump. "Infiltration of some kind."

"Hey, not that it mattered. The goddamn lens cap was frozen on the sight anyway. We were supposed to shoot stuff out of the sky *and* the sea with it."

"Well, Sir, wouldn't you get some backup help from your outriding escorts?" said Blump. "Your outriding escorts and plane cover, aerial cover."

"*Outriding escorts!* Hell, son, *we* were the ammo ship. Don't you understand?" He leaned forward on his sharp elbows and searched Blump's quivering face for solace.

"Yessir, *danger*, spelled with a very big *D*."

Mr. Milkins eased back, easing also air out of his nostrils. "Yes, well." He coughed. "Yes. Well, not only were we *loaded*, but we ran a good two knots below what the OTC had set as the formation minimum. Hell, son, *we* were the *outriding escort*."

"You mean you crossed all alone?" I said.

"Hey, Boats, you think *you* guys are alone out here on these isolated towers? Hey, Boats, *you don't know what lonesome is, til you get to herdin cows.*"

"But couldn't you at least get your gun fixed?"

"Come on now, Boats. Have you been out here on these Lights so long you forgot how the service works?"

"This is his first Light," said Blump. "A seaman apprentice."

"I've known others," I mumbled.

"The point is, boys, you both very well know how the old SOP works. You can't report stuff, you don't go around reporting stuff like that because it was supposed to be reported ASAP. If you don't report it ASAP, then it looks like *you are the breathless flower of springtime*. You get my drift?"

"You mean, Mr. Milkins, that it looks like *you* are the one who caused the trouble." Blump looked at me as if I'd just walked in the door.

"Right, son. Exactly right, or at least let the damn thing go all to hell in your care. Shit, fellows, if it's one thing this old service teaches a man is responsibility."

"With a capital *R*," said Blump. "And you know it, *whew!*"

"But couldn't you notice something like a frozen lens cap right away?" I said, "or at least that it was a Russian make?"

"Not a Russian make, son, right up here in Reading, Penn.," said Blump. "Hang in with the conversation."

"What do you think," said Mr. Milkins, "there's some guy in a furry hat doing a saber dance all around it?"

"Sure," said Blump, "Some guy, Sir, swilling vodka with a big woman, Sir."

"No——"

"The point is, Boats—and I'm sure you've observed this in your long experience on these light stations—you're given a job, and with it goes a barrel full of equipment which in turn, in many cases—granted you've been trained, and trained well I might add—in many cases you've simply never seen half the stuff before and *there's a war on, sailor*, so you blink your eye once, just once—don't forget you've been up half the night, the night seeing your sweetie off, maybe for the last time, *I'll be with you in ample bossum time . . ."*

"But, sir," I said, "I would think something big and, you know, *structural*——"

"Not at all, Boats, it could be the U.S. of A. love-of-your-life. . . ." He peered out the window past Blump into the first intimations of twilight. "In any case, you Go To Sea, baby. And That's The Way It Is." He knocked back the contents of his cup.

"Care for another, Sir?" I said.

"Excuse me, Sir," said Blump, "we'll be only too pleased to obtain you with another cup, but Seaman, shouldn't you be hustling up the old ladder here to provide the Main Light for the evening?"

"Have a cup of tea with us, first," said Mr. Milkins. "There's plenty of natural light left, and all you guys have to do is throw the switch, isn't it? I mean, I do as much with the porch light for the newspaper boy."

"There's a little more to it than that, Sir," said Blump.

"Oh, hey, I envy you guys out here. I mean let's be candid. This is no convoy patrol. Hell, this isn't even gate duty."

"There are nevertheless problems, Sir," I said.

"Yeah," said Blump, "like evidently Turning on the Main Light's a problem for some people."

"Well, frankly boys, I'm in for a change myself. Yessir, this is my last run. My last run aboard the old *Herb*, bless her coal-heavin belly. What was it Conrad said in a similar situation?"

"Something about the *lost festoons of Youth*."

"That's too bad, Sir," said Blump. "Are you up for retirement?"

"Not quite, son. Not quite. I'll be going ashore as CO of the Greenmeal Lifeboat Station."

"CO of Greenmeal?" said Blump. His face was a delicious pie of mixing emotions.

"I know. I know," said Mr. Milkins, "Usually a LBS doesn't call for a commissioned officer, but seeing as Greenmeal is so decidedly isolated way over here on this side of the Bay, GROUPCOM Cape May feels we require an officer of commissioned status out here on the beach."

"In case you need to marry anyone, eh?" Blump looked for an audience beneath the table.

"Well, documents, certain required procedures, reports, P.O.I.V.'s, that kind of gurry." Mr. Milkins extended his arms the better to shuck his cuffs, furl and otherwise subdue them. "But frankly, keep this under your hat, boys. Even my own crew doesn't know yet. You know how they'd lame-duck it."

"You can sure count on us, Sir," said Blump.

"And the *H*. herself is not much longer for this run, either, friends."

"What?" I said.

"Scuttlebut has her going to some banana republic as a gunboat. I've seen the work orders to plate her superstructure. It's wood now, you may have noticed. They're going to arm her with three-inchers."

"This time in English, right, Sir?" said Blump.

"Yes, and isn't that another one for Conrad, a what do you call it? I mean, here my ship finally gets a real three-incher and it's, as you say in English, and she's not my ship anymore. What do you call that if you're Conrad, Boats?"

"*Ineffable festoons of regret*."

"Right, and those wooden sash, the windows you see in her deck house, those and the big skylight over the engine room. Christ, she's really going to go to sea after all these years, and there's got to be some attention, some *thought* to Damage Control: Hell, right now what is she, bless her boilers, but a . . . *backwater antique*."

"And they'll put in diesels?" I said.

"Now *that* is something they may not do. Not out of homage to the Steamship Society of America, I assure you, but for strict economic reasons. Practical reasons."

"You bet," said Blump.

"With a steam boiler those monkey-fuckers down there in wherever can chuck in just all-kind-a-stuff. All kinds of crap goes in her gut. Hell, bunches of bananas, alligators——"

"A few jungle bunnies," said Blump.

"Well, it's either this banana republic or the Air Force gets her. I forget which."

"*Our* Air Force?" I said.

"Don't worry, Boats, you should see the new tender you'll be getting: all hydraulic, all up-to-date A-to-N, all steel, a collapsible boom. And you should see the steering apparatus control on these new snatchers, boys. Not a big dog of a wooden wheel that we got with spokes like something out of an oyster-cracker ad, but——"

"A chrome automobile wheel!"

"No, no, one step better, Boats. You're talking about the New Guard, the Coast Guard of the future R & D-wise: No wheel at all! Pascal's principle, son. All you need is a lever, one about *yea* long." He offered his little finger. "Can't you just see standing 'wheel' watches with nothing to fondle but that little clit?"

"No."

"Hey," said Blump. "Come on now, son. Did you ever have to stand wheel watches with one of those big, wooden dogs with spokes?"

"Sure."

"On an official U.S.C.G. WAGL, or in a cracker ad?" This time Blump found his audience across the table in Mr. Milkins.

"Got you there, Boats. Now what would Conrad term that?"

"I don't know," I said. "But when you are in at the Lifeboat Station as CO, will you then have some sort of say over the structural problems out here? I don't think I've ever fully understood the various overlapping relationships of responsibility involving us."

"It's simple," said Blump. "I'm your boss, son."

The various pouches played with each other across his face. My fists were clenched, and I wondered why Chanty had not long ago leveled this pale blob.

"I think," I said, "that Conrad would want me to light the lamp now."

"Atta boy," said Blump. "Pop up topside there and flick the switch."

On my way up the cylinder, I held the door off its suction just long enough to hear Blump say that, of course, Mr. Milkins was right about lighthouse duty, it was mainly for "niggers and other misfits," but more to the point, they would "soon all be automated."

From the upper balcony, however, the *Herb* seemed once again not only an exciting ship, but a beautiful one with her white superstructure and her complex rigging. As I peered down through her skylight into the glow of her boiler room, I thought about her being the last coal-fed working craft and how she must have been built not for the Coast Guard at all, but the old Lighthouse Service. She must have been coming to this place for maybe forty or even fifty years. If she could not save the tower, what could?

Surely, I thought, the relationship between these two things, lighthouse and tender, transcended the mere change of human commands, the petty concerns of the transient crews, the weakness of the present leadership. I would descend from the tower top with a message capable of changing a structural flaw into a bond that would outlast time and the sea's ravages! "Attention to the colors," I bellowed and took in the flag with all the resonance a pair of heel-clicking shower shoes could muster.

On the way down, as I was passing the sleeping quarters, I thought I saw the door knob revolve. I stopped, and my echo inside the cylinders stopped, but the shuffling inside continued. Well, it could have been Toy come up from the cellarage for no sensible reason, as the tender was still uttering forth her water. It could have been Blump retreating to his locker, a known armory of desperate amusements, in order to select for our guest's entertainment a game of Scrabble, Chinese checkers, or, all else failing, *Janes' Fighting Ships*. At the risk of catching him stooping neck-deep into this private act, I slipped the door open and eased inside the sleeping quarters.

There was no Blump hard by the door at his locker. There was no continuation of the earlier shuffling, either. There was only the sound of the watering below, various shouts and yelps, some more animal than others. The bathroom door was open. The blind, half up, was knocking on the window frame, reminding me the wind was north, the season autumn. The sink was dripping with its newfound fecundity, the drops a half-beat behind my pulse.

The simple thing would have been to charge the shuffling up to the venetian blind muffled by the door and go at once below to join the jolly fraternity. No doubt Blump would be there at the table gaily annotating Mr. Milkins's memoirs and predictions. Certainly he would not be up in this chamber cowering around on the seaward side of the cylinder in terror that he could no longer keep up his end with our guest.

If he were, however, would it be better to sneak off, leaving him unsure as to whether I had seen him or not? Wouldn't it be better to cough, or, even better, turn on the taps in the head, flush the toilet (that faucet drip in any case needed discipline regarding its new wealth)? And once having thus alerted Blump, I could then chug on around to where he would by then have accumulated enough excuses.

He could have been, say, removing the nude pin-up Teddy had above his bunk, stripping her who was already peeled from the bulkhead so that Mr. Milkins, should he chance to request a tour, would not by this brazen display be in any way disturbed.

There was a squeek from my bunk.

My bunk.

Goldilocks it surely would not be this time. I put aside my lust for spigots and the other mechanisms of the flush to charge full tilt around the cylinder, totally unheralded.

The young man on my bed sat up.

It was the *Herb* lout.

He formerly of buoy deck with but a mere tentative reaching out into our cellar with the hose that evening. He of the tender story of the boom boatswain's stray dog.

"Hey," he said, "you want to *mutual?*"

"What?"

"You want to, you know, *mutual off?*"

"I don't know what the hell you're talking about," I said, afraid I knew exactly what he was talking about.

"Our skipper says we can mutual any time we can get someone to do it with us and it doesn't take away from the performance of our job."

"Your skipper approves it?"

"He says he wants good morale."

"Your-skipper-who-is-down-below-here-on-this-lighthouse-now."

"Sure, I figure he's slipped in here to *check the place out*, why not me?"

"He's having a cup of coffee—that is, he's having *coffee* with our officer-in-charge. They're both having coffee."

"He drinks tea. He's a fruit cake. That's why I want to get off."

"He drinks tea and that makes you want to get off?"

"Look, port and starboard don't do me any good. What do you get here? Two weeks on and one off, right?"

"Look, I only came in here because I thought someone was trying to steal from our lockers. That is, in fact, my bunk."

"Oh." He stood up, reached back, and wiped at the spread, smoothing the embroidered anchor. "I was just checkin the place out."

"You'll find we're all very dull here, I'm afraid."

"You get a good bunk on a snatcher, too, but not as steady."

"We're all very dull here."

He fumbled in his chambray. "If you ever want to switch jobs, just let me know." What he pulled out was not a card, but a package of Camels. He held one out.

"No thanks," I said.

"Hey, don't knock a snatcher till you tried one."

"*Buoy* snatcher," I said. "Your ship, the *Herb*."

"Yeah, right down there at the wharf. See, you're a seaman and so am I. See, you could probably get along with the skipper. I heard you already talk to him."

"That was mainly Blump," I said. "Where were you, anyway? Lurking in the cylinder?"

"Hey, I don't *lurk*, you know. I got this girl. She lives way up in Pennsylvania where I come from, but port and starboard liberty don't do me no good to, you know, reach her. I need a week solid, like you guys get off. That's why I want to mutual."

"It sounded like . . . well, it sounded like an insurance policy."

"Why?" His eyes began moving like Blump's. "There something wrong with this place?"

"It was the word *mutual*."

"It's just the word they use. It's on the form, I think." Nevertheless he was opening a locker door, more as if he wanted to walk out than just check.

"The way down is over here."

"You sure this isn't a funny place after all?"

"It's a place just like any other."

"O.K." He walked to the right door and almost yanking it from its hinges stood in its opening. "And keep me in mind. My girl and I would appreciate it."

The smoke from his cigarette lingered in the sleeping quarters long after I heard the screen door down below slam.

When I returned they were still sitting around the Formica table, Blump propped on his elbows, holding the teacup to his face as if he were using it to drain his sinuses. The skipper dangled his cup off his thumb and fiddled the salt with the free hand.

"When I shoot coot, I always employ decoys," the skipper was saying.

"Oh, ya, me, too, Skipper," said Blump. "Decoys are the most accurate method."

I strolled around to the pantry. It was dim in there, and I began mechanically counting the canned goods.

"You know, Sir, it was a marked coincidence what you were saying earlier."

"Saying what, son? The war or coot shooting?"

"About your getting the transfer."

"Oh?"

"Sure, sir. You see I'm interested in a transfer, too."

"Ah."

"Not that you'd have anything to do with it as CO of *Herb*, Sir."

There was only the sound of the teacups being shuffled, the salt shaker falling, rolling, and being set right again.

"Well, son, transfers are basically Personnel Department work. You know, they have—procedures."

"I fully understand that, Mr. Milkins."

Despite this understanding, the salt fell over again and rolled even farther. When it was recovered and put back on station, however, it seemed to be set with such force that one had to fear for the very Formica.

"You see, sir, what I'd really like to accomplish career-wise is to be a commissary man. My old rating, Mr. Milkins."

"You mean you want to cook?"

"Yessir. You catch my drift exactly. At a lifeboat station. At Greenmeal, sir. It would be like you going back to gunnery."

The salt shaker did not move.

It was Blump who first spoke. "You were saying you fashioned your decoys from Clorox bottles, Sir."

"The real trick is the application of the lamp black, son. You've got to have just the right amount of white showing through to fool the coot."

Out on the balcony I almost tripped over the lout. He was holding onto the rail with both hands as if the stillness of the tower was acting upon him somehow like a merry-go-round. And why not, I thought, if at the heart of great whirling there often seems, under the strobe, to be but serene stillness, couldn't the reverse at least seem true at times?

"Hey, you see what I mean?" he said. "In there with him again. Eating it up. You'd like it aboard with him. He'd like you."

I wondered if I shouldn't tell him that his CO would soon be gone.

"You could be down there on that ship right now getting set for starboard watch liberty. That's tonight." He pointed toward the shore. "You see. The lights are coming on. There's a canal in there, right back of the beach and a bar with music and girls, right on the canal."

"I know."

"Well, if you been there, then you already know."

"I'll let you know."

"See, he don't like me."

Past him, down on the ship the few men on deck were moving slowly. The dog was playing, chasing a red ball the boom boatswain was tossing up against the bulwarks. The big skylight over the boilers was propped open, and up in the deck house the sash windows were thrown wide. In the pilot house was the big wooden wheel.

When it was time for the *Herb* to leave, I needed a flashlight to find my way around under the pier. The battery was dim, and the tide had come up so that the new catwalk I had to walk on was well covered. With the sun down it was also much colder than when we'd poked the toggle through an hour before. I could, however, hear the steam boilers working inside the black wall before me, and there was some light falling on my work from the big, brass portholes in the hull. I could hear someone calling the dog and smell the coffee on the galley stove and then the sharp smell of the coal smoke in the autumn night as the ship backed away, taking its portholes and galley smells and leaving just that acrid stinging in my nostrils and, in the dark, the taste of coal.

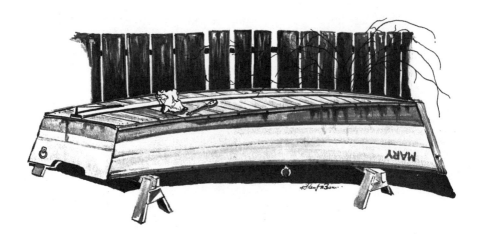

ICE & MARY

While they were talking a gust of rain struck the windows and the rising wind rumbled in the kitchen chimney. The keeper fumed, coaxed and argued; the assistant would not budge.

—John J. Floherty, *Sentries of the Sea*

B LUMP HAD finally signed my leave papers, and I'd come ashore on the same pilot boat he'd used to get out. The first few days I spent walking up and down the narrow main street of Greenmeal, standing before the multiplicity of merchandise in the Ben Franklin store, gorging my eyes upon displays of work gloves, balls of yarn, back-to-school pencil boxes, bicycle baskets, handkerchiefs, alarm clocks, shoe-lace packets, Scotch tape dispensers. Of golf caps, clothespins and umbrellas I could not get enough. Parched on the daily diet of blank blue sea rim, my eyes seemed never to have known such splendors as colored socks and package twine.

Later my parents came to visit me and rented a room in one of the seaside hotels in the more modern beach resort ten miles down the coast. While they exclaimed over the view, I sat with my back to it, gazing into the alley that held such finite delights as garbage cans against an old plank fence. We rented a skiff from the boat livery next to the lifeboat station and set out to visit my tower. The sea was calm, and my father handled the outboard as we came to the foot of the landing stage. I took the bow line up the ladder and made it fast. My father followed. We looked down and saw my mother hanging to the ladder like a starfish. "Go on," she said, "I've got a wide place here for my feet. I'm not as uncomfortable as I look." She let go with first one hand, then the other to show she need not actually hang on. I introduced my father to Toy and Blump. Toy actually looked him in the eye and grinned. Blump was as cordial as an ambassador and conducted the tour while I kept an eye on my mother. She waved from time to time to reaffirm her comfort. "A nice bunch," my father said on the way in. I did not ask him if he'd noticed the erosion at the tower's base.

It was early autumn after they had gone, toward the end of the time I had ashore. It was the hour when you begin to notice screen doors banging, the smell of flowers. There were voices from the bottom of the garden next to the place I'd rented, a murmuring and tapping. It was my neighbors, Hack & Rory, two old fellows foostering with their chalky, flat-iron skiff. It had been their custom three or four times a week to take this boat on a trailer to the launchway at the canal.

After all that time living in the middle of what was for the most part a blue saucer, I could not help envying their intricate and meandering cruising grounds. The canal, for instance, was part of the Inland Waterway, and it stole around in back of the barrier beach to connect with all manner of baroque shallows, like Mispillion River, Rehoboth Bay, Broadkill, Love Creek, and Indian River Inlet. There was no need for them to risk the weather out in the Harbor of Refuge, where, despite the breakwater, the sea could kick up badly for a boat like theirs. A few days earlier, while waiting at the lifeboat station for confirmation of my leave papers, I'd overheard a conversation bearing on men who dabbled in these modest waters. It had been a boarding-party meeting being held in the day room.

As he had predicted, Mr. Milkins had come ashore from the *Herb* to be the station CO. Apparently he had developed an esthetic sense that had been heightened in all his years aboard the buoy tender. "Now boys, I like to see a good-looking set of numbers on the bow of a boat. You don't see many good-looking bows these days running around, but fortunately we have the regulations on our side." He proceeded to ruffle the pages of the *Boarding Manual* until the rules for spacing between registration numbers came up. Bad spacing was a violation, he pointed out. Violations were to be "strictly adhered to."

It was strange to be on the edge of this conversation. After all, here was no diatribe about *chariots* and *sullen noises,* here was no warning about *day tanks* and *sisters,* no reminiscence of three-inch guns with left-hand knurled knobs, but the kind of stuff I'd grown up with, small recreation craft; I was drawn to the talk with growing indignation until I found myself standing in the door of the day room.

There were about five men in chambray sitting upright on the couches they usually lounged upon. I picked out Cooper and Luntsky and Creel. So well groomed was Farilla, however, so slicked, shined, and pruned was he, I stared at him before I recognized the disheveled visitor to our tower. It was as if an undertaker had gotten hold of him. The round chief, who had let me into the station the first night, was also there, and down by the television set, taking advantage of the habitual focus of the crew, leaned Mr. Milkins himself, complete with Sam Brown belt and hat at the full, lovable-mission jaunty tilt. From behind him came the light in off the sea beyond the dunes.

"Why Skipper," the chief was saying, "we write up these poor old guys around here and they'll be pouring in here hat in hand, scared to death.

Most of them live pretty close to the margin now, and they'll go under with a fine like that. Most of 'em have boats that ain't even worth that much. This whole coast once you get inside the Harbor of Refuge is pretty much backwater stuff."

"There seems to me, from my experience, Chief, to be plenty of water out there."

"Sure, there's water out there, Mr. Milkins, but that's not where most of the boats go that'll be hit by a strict en-forcement of these here reg'lations. I mean these fellas are sittin, like I said, in some backwater, and we come roarin' down on 'em in a big ol' forty boat with the radio squawkin and the bull horn bellerin and casting big shadows and throbbin's all over their fishin—why half the time they can't even remember their own names when we accost them."

"That's because they're usually drunk, Chief. Have you read the recent studies on casualties due to recent alcoholism?"

I must have coughed because Mr. Milkins shot a look my way. "Who is that man?" he said.

"He's lighthouse personnel, Sir," said the chief.

"Hey, Bat-shit," said Farilla.

"What's that?" said Mr. Milkins.

"I know him, skipper. He's ok," said Farilla. "He's lighthouse."

"Well, get him out of here," said Mr. Milkins. "Lighthouse personnel don't apply."

The chief got up and walked over to me, put his arm on my shoulder and led me through the dining hall. "You see, son, there's some people who don't really accept lighthouses as being part of the Coast Guard. It's like they are an embarrassment to them for some reason. I can't figure it out myself, because where I come from down Hat'ris way, we have the real Coast Guard, and that sure do include the lighthouse personnel." He winked, and said in a low voice, "Jus between you and me, son, you're going to have a new leader out to the ol' Harbor Refuge. Yes, sir, an Outer Banks boy coming to replace Blump and lead your station back to its former glory."

"Its former glory?"

"Sure, you ought to talk to some of the old timers around here. They'll tell you that station was the belle of the bay."

"Belle of the bay, that's very interesting," I said, "but it's not Creel who's coming out to recover from his confusions, is it?"

"You mean his contusions, son," laughed the chief. "No, Creel's a tough little bird and a hell of a boat handler, but what you are going to see is someone can whup Creel one hand tied."

The conversation that I could hear this afternoon, however, came from just beyond where my landlady's roses climbed the unpainted plank fence. That was the spot where our neighbors Hack and Rory kept their skiff, all right. Usually it was gunnel up on its trailer, ready to go. From my back porch I could see they now had rolled her over on two sawhorses. They seemed to be refastening her bottom.

The huge, horse-faced Hack held the brown paper bag of screws. A floppy white hat with green eyeshade cast a subaqueous tint across his big, loose mouth. From time to time he gave the little bag of screws a jiggle, then puckered the top. Little Rory, who wore a baseball cap, spectacles, and a bow tie, would reach into the puckered bag without taking his eye from the boat bottom, extract a single bronze screw and apply it to the newly tapped hole.

The screwdriver Rory used had a wooden handle as nicely worn as an old briar. Every once in a while he'd set the screwdriver down on the boat bottom and rub his hands together before reaching into the bag as if it were candy. Then you could see the screwdriver, how its handle looked. Rory himself could see the handle, too, because that's what he kept an eye on even when he was reaching for the bag after rubbing his hands. He could trust Hack to have the bag right there. It was never so far away he'd have had to lunge and flutter, or so close he'd bang elbows.

"Good afternoon," I said from my side of the roses. Safe in my civilian clothes, I could sneak a look to make sure their numbers were aligned properly and, later, work in a subtle warning that would keep at least these elderly boatmen of lower Delaware beyond Mr. Milkins's esthetic rage.

"It is that," said Hack, who since he was merely assisting, was the one who could talk. "A very pleasant afternoon for this time of year."

"Is it that unusual to have good weather here in the early autumn?" I said. Unfortunately I couldn't get a look at the numbers on the skiff because of the roses on my side. "Where I come from this is the best time."

"No, it is the best time here, too. I just meant it was a pleasant day that fit in well with this time of year."

From under Rory's baseball cap came a slight sound as of throat clearing. His eye continued, however, to be led by his hand.

"Well, it's a fine day to work outside on your boat now that the season is at an end." I plucked a withered rose or two to cover my espionage activity. Through the holes left by the departed roses I thought I caught a glimpse of a registration number on the skiff.

"We're not done with the summer yet," said Hack. "If I thought we were done with the season you can bet I wouldn't be standing here holding this bag. We're not fixing this boat up for next season. Not at our age. At our age you fix a boat up for the season you're in." He shook the bag toward me, tilting it, offering me a peek into this delicious little sack. I found myself passing through a gap in the fence, discarding my withered roses furtively as I advanced.

There, now revealed to me, however, was the bow of the skiff.

It wasn't that there were numbers improperly spaced on the boat. There were no numbers at all. What I had mistaken through the roses for proper registration was merely a name: *Mary*.

Startled, I found myself staring into the proffered bag of screws. "Those do look like proper bronze fastenings," I said.

"They are that," said Hack. "They are that indeed." He gave the bag a good shake in his enthusiasm, and this made Rory finally look up. Hack knew he owed his partner a quick explanation. "Rory, this is the young man from next door."

Rory, however, continued looking at Hack.

"The lad who's in the Coast Guard," said Hack, and he pointed at me past Rory with the hand that held the bag. "He's in the Coast Guard."

"Just the lighthouse," I said, "no boarding parties."

"Ain't nothin wrong with parties," said Hack.

"Ain't anybody on the lighthouse," said Rory and kept his eye on his tool. "Ain't been anybody on the lighthouse in years. It's all automatic."

"I'll have to remember that next time I turn on the light," I said in what I hoped would be taken as a tone more buoyant than severe.

"What lighthouse you talking about?" said Hack.

"Don't matter," said Rory before I could answer. "Them that ain't fallen over around here is all done automatic. That way they don't care if the rest fall over."

"Well, how many have fallen over?" I said.

"I give up countin."

"What lighthouse is the one you is, ah, actually on?" said Hack.

"Harbor of Refuge."

"Worst one," said Rory. He held up one of the screws. "You been chewin on this one, Hack? She's spavined as that old horse a yor."

"Pick another one then," said Hack. Turning to me, he added, "Li'l Rory here, he's some criti-cal."

"Yes," I said. "I like the Harbor of Refuge Light. I mean it may not be perfect, but——"

"Fell apart three times," said Rory. "Not countin losin her bell and at least twice the outbuildings right off her landin stage."

"Li'l Rory here, he some awful crit-i-cal," said Hack, and shook the brown bag.

"I'm not done with this one yet," said Rory, and he held up the screw for Hack to see, tapped it with his screwdriver. "I told you that game was at night."

"I'm not pushing you," said Hack. "We got all day. The summer's not gone yet."

"Of course we got all day," said Rory. "Then we'll have a drink and it will be time for the night radio game."

"He likes to listen to the night radio game," said Hack.

"Yes, well I was told she was once the pride of the bay."

"This boat here?" said Hack. "Ol' *Mary* here?"

"No," I said, "The Harbor of Refuge Light."

Rory continued working. It was necessary for him to do a certain amount of squinting. When the squinting was over I could pursue my inquiry into specifics of the disasters that had befallen the tower. There was a bee, however, who was careless with the roses and kept swinging out over the boat bottom on its approach pattern.

"He won't hurt you," said Hack.

"Of course he won't," said Rory. "I didn't think he would. You just got to stop jingling that sack."

"A bee stung my Mary once," said Hack. "Got her right in the ear with a load of blue ice. Went through my route so fast I couldn't find the tongs till we was done. Had to go back and do it all over slow. Ice, you know, takes a certain amount of time."

"How far out in the harbor does it freeze up?" I asked.

"Oh, we don't use harbor ice," said Hack.

"They don't use harbor ice," said Rory.

"No," I laughed, "I didn't think you did. I was just wondering how ice would effect my life out on the lighthouse this coming winter."

"Use pond ice," said Hack.

"The ice comes from the pond," said Rory without looking up.

"I understand that," I said, "but I've heard that when the harbor freezes over no supplies can get to the lighthouse."

No one said anything, and I wondered if they really knew about the lighthouse, the harbor, all that open sea out beyond. After all, they were canal fishermen and now, deep in this backyard of roses and hedges and bees, even the canal water was lost, the skiff a mere flower box.

"How you coming with that, Rory?" said Hack suddenly.

"I thought you weren't pushing me," said Rory. "Don't jiggle that sack prematurely."

"I wasn't jigglin' the sack. I was just telling about Mary bolting with the blue ice."

I decided to give up on the lighthouse in winter. In trying to assure them and maybe myself that I would not be on boarding duty, I had merely begun to frighten myself with thoughts of the coming season, my isolation in the bleak tower. "Mary sounds interesting," I said. "And where is Mary now?" I averted my gaze from the boat.

"Mary's dead," said Rory. He spit on the roses. It was not clear if that shot into the fading petals had anything to do with Mary's demise. In any case he wiped his lip with the screwdriver.

"*Of course* she's dead," said Hack and he let the green light play down through his visor. "I retired from ice."

"Mary, then, was your horse," I said stupidly. "Also the——"

"Also the name of his wife," said Rory, and not only did he not pat the boat's bottom or in any other way indicate he meant that *Mary*, but he actually lifted up his eyes from the skiff toward the roses.

"Rory himself here never had no wife," said Hack.

"Never had no horse, either," said Rory.

"Rory, he listens to the night radio game."

"You do, too," he said. "You listen, too."

"I got to," said Hack and he poked me with his elbow. "It's what goes on around here."

"Are you sure that you aren't thinking of Cape Henlopen Light?" I said toward Rory.

"Cape Henlopen only fell over once," he said. "Of course, it was burnt by the British, but that's going way back. I'm talking about in *my* lifetime."

"Well, then maybe you're thinking of Elbow-of-Cross Ledge," I said. "Knocked down by a ship, replaced by a skeletal tower."

"God damn it," said Rory, "let's go in and have a drink."

"I told you that bee wouldn't hurt you if you stood still," said Hack.

"Well, it's not the bee I need," said Rory. "I don't need no bee at all." Then he looked at me. "You come in, too."

We went in over the veranda and through the damp parlor. Down the street was a similar house where the widow kept the late husband's clothes all laid out on the chairs, and sometimes, in passing, your eye wandered in. That parlor had become for me the model for all the houses along the street, so I quickly passed through, noting only an upright piano upon which was a cathedral radio with silk across the vents.

Out in the kitchen the sun was coming in over a sink on enamel legs with a brass spout just like the one on the lighthouse.

"This is amazing," I said. "There is so much here that reminds me of the lighthouse."

Hack merely motioned me to the table. It was round and, unlike ours, covered with oilcloth. The chairs were wooden, painted thickly with green.

"This table, for instance," I said, "while not like our present table, is exactly as I'd imagine the earlier furniture to have been in the tower. These chairs are perfect."

"Perfect for what?" said Rory.

"He says this reminds him of the inside of the lighthouse before it fell down."

"Well, not exactly," I said. "I never was on it then, of course. But these tongue-in-groove walls——"

"That's Rory's humor all right," said Hack, "tongue-in-cheek."

Rory reached up to the tongue-in-groove cabinets. There was a Coca-Cola girl calendar for the present year and another one upon which was the sturdy-looking Cape Henlopen tower with its spacious keeper's house next to it like a regular house. Rory batted it with the back of his hand. "A mile out to sea, all that now." He tapped the tower, the house with its windows. "A mile out and God knows how far under." He reached in behind the picture and pulled out a squat bottle from which he uncreaked the cork. The sun danced through the sloshing liquor. He set three empty jelly jars on the oilcloth and tapped their rims with the bottle until each jar was filled half-way.

"Of course the keepers had time to get off," I said. "Erosion, afterall, is a leisurely affair."

"You want ice?" There was a bit of menace in the offer, or maybe that was only the sun off his spectacles in the otherwise darkening room.

"That's true," said Hack. "That old lighthouse took a long time to fall."

"And now the Harbor of Refuge," I said. "In all these disasters you were describing out in the yard—what happened to the keepers, then?"

"You want ice?"

"Ah, no thank you."

"Good."

"It's not we don't got ice," said Hack. "Hell, we got plenty of ice."

"We got *too much* ice," said Rory.

"It's just we don't use it," explained Hack.

"Maybe you want tap water," said Rory.

"A little," I said. I gave back the glass. He brought it up into the sunlight and splashed it. "As a matter of fact, I was told the Harbor of Refuge, in her day, mind you, was the belle of the bay."

"Had a bell," said Rory. "Don't know about *was a belle*."

"Then there *was* a bell."

"Ding-dong."

"Now don't be cynical, Rory," said Hack, "it was a lovely bell."

"It's a lovely bell under water," said Rory. "In fact there were two bells."

"That's right," said Hack. "The first never got set up before it was swept off the staging."

"How big were those bells? I mean we've got an alarm bell that'll———"

"Naw, not one of those jangling school bell things," said Rory. "It was a real bell, a real bell with a fine sound for the foggy air."

"Divers were used," said Hack. "Prowling all around after the storm they were. In the dark with their hands in the bottom of the harbor for them big bells. Never found 'em, either."

"And the woodwork of that place," said Rory. "Shiplap with palladian main entrance, carved pineapples on the gallery rails. She was an octagon."

"She was more than an octagon," said Hack, "she was, I tell you, a paragon. Like the lad says here: belle of the bay."

"Yes, that is true," said Rory, "but you have to understand, that one you're talking about, that was knocked all apart."

"About what year was that?" I said. "When the belle was kn———"

"Now what have they got out there? An iron cylinder stuck on the old base. No having a bell, no even being a belle. It's automatic."

"I had my days myself," said Hack, "Mary and me. Till she bolted."

"The bee it was," I said.

"My days," said Hack and he stared at his drink.

"What did *you* do?" I said to Rory. "Before you retired."

"I was independent," he said. He poured another drink.

"Ha, that's the joke, son," said Hack. "He was a lighthouse keeper."

I looked at Rory. His lips were pursed, but his eyes looked dead. "Is that true?" I said.

"I told you. I was independent."

"You were an independent lighthouse keeper?"

"I weren't in no Coast Guard."

"No, of course not," I said. "United States Lighthouse Service."

"He weren't quite that," said Hack. "He used to be like he says: independent. He substituted on lights, various lights. . . ." He waved his hand.

"Now he's going to ask me if I was on that Harbor Refuge everytime it fell apart."

"Well?" I said.

He took a long sip.

"Rory, he gets the night radio games," said Hack.

"Don't let em kid you," said Rory. "He was only ice man eight years before he retired."

"It weren't my fault ice went out," he said. "I worked hard, me and Mary. More than you ever on them lighthouses."

"Well," I said, "we're going to have to work hard when I get back. We're getting a new man up from Cape Hatteras who's going to set us to work so the tower will be O.K. for winter."

"Maybe he'll get that tower all fixed up safe like you want," said Hack. "Outer Bankers know about sea storms."

"I'll know soon," I said.

"*O the bee, the bee, the bee,*" said Rory in what was not quite clearly a song. The light danced off his spectacles.

"Listen here," said Hack, "did you bring in those screws?"

"I'm the one who put them away," said Rory. "But you were the one who was *supposed* to."

It was almost dark when I bumped back across the yard toward my house, and I knew that, lazy as Toy was, he'd managed to drag himself up all those gray-iron stairs inside the cylinder and scratch the switch on. The main light would be creeping out over the water to the beach and up over the canal and down into the backyards, so I stood swaying by the roses and the unpainted plank fence waiting for it until it came and touched the up-turned belly of Hank & Rory's skiff.

THE OLD BEAR & FLAP

So strong was his faith in the infallibility of omens, the keeper decided that if the assistant would not go ashore, he would. In his resolve there was neither fear nor neglect of duty. On the contrary he believed that his course insured the safety of both. The two taps on the glass obviously represented the two men in the light; the single tap as the bird flew off indicated quite clearly one of them would be lost. That was his belief and he would stick to it.

—John J. Floherty, *Sentries of the Sea*

IT WAS NINE in the morning when we idled alongside the landing stage. This time the Coast Guard had actually stooped to taking the lighthouse run, and I felt a bit more official as I went up the ladder and onto the landing stage where the early autumn sun was warm on the planks, and I felt warm, too, as I looked down on the wet rip-rap below. It had been silly to worry about coming back. After all, winter was a long way off. Autumn was the best time of year. Even if the porpoises of summer would no longer be around on the change of the tide, there were bound to be other creatures. Hack and Rory would, now that their skiff was refastened, have several more good weeks in the canal. All things did not die simply because it was fall.

And everything was clean and fresh in this October air. The far shore at Cape May—you could see the red roof of the convent, the white lighthouse, the old Admiral Hotel. Fourteen miles away, they looked newly scrubbed. The tanker standing in was brand new, launched, it seemed, that hour three miles off Five Fathom Shoal just for the occasion. Our own tower, the top of it, why, the salt had not dulled the patina so much as burnished the black iron work, whitewashed the steel plates, shined the lantern glass. Even down below, way down on the rip-rap where the water rinsed, those curious bits scattered all over the rocks were—*colorful*.

Since there was no one on the stage, I sent the chow line with the hook on the end down onto the deck of the forty-footer. Cooper was the duty engineman, and he took the line aft into the cockpit and rigged the sling. "This is the way we had to do it that year in Alaska," he said and gazed wistfully up at the tower. Creel held the boat in the current alongside the pier, tapping his clutch handles now and then, but leaving the throttles alone. His face was so historically battered by wind and ancient misunderstandings that the flesh had little room for the results of his most recent disaster, and in the

quiet triumph of his present maneuver had even taken on a benign snarl, if such a happy state could ever be assigned to so raw and beak-ridden a visage.

Cooper gave a jerk on the line and waved, and I hauled, timing the swing so the crate carried out from under the stage and came to me up on top. I moved the crate inboard, undid the knot, and sent the hook back down for the second load. When we were done, I waved, and the two crew men waved, and I got hold of the first crate and began carrying it up the wooden stairs toward the tower. It was amazing how simple all this was. Why had I ever thought it otherwise?

The stairs were easy after the iron ladder and the cardboard chow case rode easily against my cheek. A week's dinners. What were those curious things down below on the rip-rap? Those colorful things? All over they were. Scattered. Broken bottles? All kinds of colored bottles, apparently. As if each evening since I'd been gone, say just before turning on the main light at dusk, the crew had been into a methodical ransacking of the world's finest aperitifs—Russian officers celebrating the assassination of Rasputin by dashing their bottles and glasses into the fire.

That did not strike me as exactly Toy's style, but it was there, the evidence of whatever it was, and what a hell of a way to ease into winter, or at least it was the only way I could understand those bits of torn color all about me. They were up on the balcony ahead of me now. They were even on the top step, eye high as I climbed toward them so that I saw precisely just what it was, on this clear morning, I had been admiring—song birds.

All those bits of brightness scattered: warblers, vireos—was this, had this been an oriole? It was so pulped I could hardly tell. Around the back door that led through the shack into the tower was what might have been a scarlet tanager. In fact the whole gallery deck around the door was littered with bright scraps.

Inside, Toy was sitting in his usual chair. The rifle, which I'd never seen before, was propped against the leather arm, its mellow stock blending with the furniture.

"I thought they'd hit the lantern," I said. "A low flying stream of them seduced by the beacon."

He did not even smirk.

"That's the first time I've even seen song birds here," I said. "A month ago we had dragon flies one day, lady bugs the next. And gulls, of course. Always the damn gulls."

He was looking at the TV bracket which did, after all, now contain a TV. Gloria was exercising in her tights, deep knee bends.

"At first," I said, "I actually thought they were broken bottles."

He was looking at the TV and, indeed, his long black hair did require the attention of some sort of product.

"How did you hit that small a bird with a .22? Hit so damn many of them?" I walked over with the carton in my hands yet, setting it down only when I got to the table by him. Then I picked up the rifle, careful to keep my hand off the blueing so that in future times rust would not break through. I knew about such things, for I'd had a gun just like it when I was a kid. It was the kind of thing little boys had in World War Two. "I didn't know we had a rifle out here, Toy."

There were four deep windows I could have had from there and the sunlight was streaming in strong off the sea from all of them. I held the rifle up to the light.

"I mean, Toy, you had to get them all one by one, no?" Somehow I must have still thought it had not been the instrument. The barrel, however, was dirty and smelt strongly.

"I didn't think songbirds would ever come out here," I said.

He was looking at the TV.

"I just don't see how the fuck you did it," I said.

"It was easy," he said. "They were tired."

The name of the new boatswain mate in charge of the Light was Okrastone, and he came aboard one morning from a throbbing forty-footer just as I was emerging from the shack with the gurry bucket. He yelled up at me and shook his fist, but I could not understand him in the noise. Later I heard his accent as something between Cockney and Appalachian, and someone told me that the pure Hatteras was the language of Limehouse at the time of Shakespeare, but that it had been somewhat diluted by the building of a highway bridge after the Second World War. What I had now was just a bunch of chopped up syllables which he afterwards explained had only been a joke about the possibility that I might dump the garbage on his head. At the time I assumed he wanted me to help him, so I ran down the stairs to the landing stage and tossed over the hook and cargo line. He obliged by attaching his sea bag, but announced at the top of the ladder he'd "as lief carry it up the stage face on m'back."

"Oh," I said, "Well, we usually haul everything up on this."

He was a big man in foul-weather gear and he looked at the line in my hand, and I looked down at it, and it did seem a damn foolish rig.

"That's all right, son," he said. "We'll get to everything one at a time." He put his hands on his hips and looked up the bay to the north, and I looked up the bay, and indeed it was one dinky piece of backwater.

"That way is the open sea," I said, and we both craned a little to make sure that there wasn't something behind the tower we were missing, but gawk as we would, it was still a pretty flat-assed calm of a mill-pond ocean.

"As I said, son, we'll get to everything one at a time."

It did not seem the time, however, to suggest that there might be a flaw in the tower that these piddling waters might yet exploit.

Once inside the building, Okrastone seemed even bigger, and I realized that for all his ringmanship what Chanty had sported had not been a large body. Blump, too, though fat of face and soft of breast had not actually occupied that much space. As Okrastone paused by the sink, I found I had a major piloting decision to make as to which side to pass him on.

It was like that for the next few hours as he tried to settle in. He roamed and bumped about, alternately pulling the tower in about him like an overcoat and shrugging it off as a bad fit. His talk was of his last duty, a buoy tender that ran the Aleutian chain where there were long nights, cold weather, and long, cold seas.

As he grew into the tower he began to realize it was not something he had to wear, that it was a set of objects like any other; but he was often still nervous and talked of Alaska, and when he did he unconsciously rubbed his back up against the inner cylinder which held the staircase.

"You look like a bear," I said once.

"Never mind them *bars*," he said. "I know all about them *bars*. They were the ones made all the work for us. We got to climb up slipp'ry rocks to rapar all them rangers and day beacons what the bar done tor down just because he couldn't find no other *bar*."

"Good lord," I said, "and what would the bear have done had he found another bear?"

"Tor 'em right on down just like a day beacon. They ain't no cud'lah thing, y'know, but got lil ol' mean, *beady* eyes set close together and stink for a mile."

"Well, at least you could tell when they were coming."

"Don't you worry," he said and rubbed up against the cylinder. "I'll tell you when they're comin' on."

Fortunately my compensatory leave came up before anything came of Okrastone's restlessness and I took out some of the feelings of the season on my own quarters ashore, moving storm windows out from my landlady's basement and washing them as if I were up in the lantern, and even getting them hung. Hack & Rory watched from across the rose briars and wondered aloud how I was any good at all on a lighthouse where the climbing would be so much more spectacular. When I returned to the Light I felt then as if I'd somehow dealt with all the rituals necessary to see the winter in.

As the weather got worse and there was no outside work to do, nothing but house cleaning and government forms, Okrastone, however, grew more irritable.

"Winter's coming on, Boats," I said. "In winter bears hibernate, don't they?"

His blue eyes were not close together, but they did pop when he got excited, and he backed into the bulkhead, hunching and grunting. "Hibernate in winter? Bullshit, boy. Bars is beady-eyed and *mean*."

By then Toy had been transferred. He had gone off when I'd been ashore on leave—Okrastone at least saw to it we had our proper rotation. It was not as if Toy had really ceased being about, but more as if he had simply gotten less and less active until all his molecules had caved in on themselves, and he remained with us as a fluff of lint beneath Chanty's famous chair. His replacement was a different story.

Cy Flap, fireman apprentice, arrived dressed in full blues with his white cap rolled up to protect the rim from being soiled so that it looked as if he had, in Okrastone's words, "A Cot-dim kun-dum on his head." He also had the large manila envelope of orders in his hand, which he presented to Okrastone, who asked him if he also had a note from his mother authorizing him to spend the night on the Light.

"No, but as a matter of fact, my mom *is* sending a pie."

"She is?" said Okrastone and he actually took a step back. "Well, that's nice, son. Ain't nothin wrong with havin a mom and ain't nothin wrong with bein just out of boot camp, either. We got another feller just outa boot camp." He jerked a thumb at me and I was about to protest when Flap beat me to it.

"If you'd look in those orders, Boats, you'd see I wasn't just *out* of Cape May, I was *attached*."

Okrastone peeked into the envelope as if it were the promised Mom's pie. "*Attached*, eh?"

"Sure, Boats, attached. I was on the forty boats you see cruising all about this very bay."

"Well, I always say, boys, it's a good idea to be attached to sumthin."

This association of Flap's with the provincial seat of power was a fact that he managed to work into most of our early conversations. When I let him know finally that it was those very boats he would have to fear as they brought whatever officers would come to inspect us, he said, "Oh, don't worry, GroupCom and me are just like this," and he entwined his fingers.

"I can see that," said Okrastone, "that's why you is standin out here on this rock pile like the rest of us with our fingers up our ass."

It was perhaps a sign of Flap's affection for the literal that at that point he actually looked down at his hands.

Nevertheless Flap's smooth, pink face was as cheerful as Toy's sallow visage had been gloomy. There was a trace of Southern Mountain in his twang, and he admitted he was from West Virginia, but insisted he was not a hick because his father had a good business of his own and his ma was not only a good cook, but a "darn good housekeeper." He would, in fact, be glad to have us sample some of her recipes either through the mediation of his own talents or perhaps directly if we wished to accompany him back to West Virginia on our leave. This alternative both Okrastone and I quickly demonstrated to be impractical. His hospitality turned aside, he nevertheless remained buoyant. It was, in fact, a whole week before he stopped running in from the balcony after supper to inform us of the sunset's beauty.

"I dunno, Flap," Okrastone would say, "all that energy in a boy."

"A boy's supposed to have energy," said Flap. "A normal boy."

Okrastone would grunt, walk to the window, snap open a slat of the venetian blind and eyeball the slit.

"Yup, she's a-settin all right."

"That's just what I told you, Boats."

"But I do not hear the pitter-patter of little feet running up to turn on the light." He would let the slat go and turn back to us. "You see we got this little custom out here, Flap, everytime it gets kinder dark . . ."

One night alone on mid-watch I was sitting in his chair reflecting on how before his arrival it had been just *the office chair* and anybody sat on it who wanted to look out the south window and see the freighters dig into the rip off Overfalls Shoal. It had been merely a good place to eat a sandwich off the blotter and escape the thunder of the TV or the depressing slickness of the Formica table, which could produce, even without the aid of a congealed bottle of catsup, the effect of an all-night diner. Now, however, it was the officer-in-charge's chair, and it occurred to me that since we had not only the official chair, but the officer-in-charge to sit in it, we might well have in his office some documents having to do with his office: the maintenance of the Light. The moment seemed especially ripe because of the change-in-command reports that Okrastone was seen to be struggling over every day.

The fact that I had not myself brought to Okrastone's attention the crack in the base I charged up to sheer cowardice, but at times I balanced my loyalty to the old regime (skeleton in the closet) with my admiration for the competence of the new (father bear knows best). Furthermore, had I not offered Okrastone a tour of the grounds? No one else had. Blump was not present on the Light to hand over the keys, as it were. I was. Blump, in fact, according to Okrastone himself, had, when introduced to him at the lifeboat station, kept his hands buried in a sinkful of suds. And what had the veteran Outer Banker just off an Alaskan buoy tender said to me? "I do believe that I can find my way around on this station. As for any more stories from what that black boy told you about putting oil in his sisters and humpin with a sudden noise. . . ."

Not long after, I found myself in front of my bureau and on impulse opened the top drawer way in the back of which I'd allowed all these months the Blump hat to repose. It was, of course, still there. I fingered it, shook it out. As I leered in the mirror it hung on my dome like a bell:

> *Sunset and evening star,*
> *And one clear call for me!*

In any case, with the shrinking of the days it was easy for me to forget what went on down at the actual water's edge. We lived, after all, three stories above the sea, climbing an additional one to bed, and, whereas in summer we had not only welcomed but even cultivated contact with the water, that once-soft, blue stretch was now like a gray slum upon the edge of which we lived and against the presence of which we kept our blinds drawn.

This night, however, I went prowling in his desk, more in the spirit of a TV detective than a sailor fearing his ship would go down. I found a U.S.A.F.I. course Chanty had been taking in medieval history, a request for sick leave by my long-time predecessor Friskis, SN, and numerous requests for transfer by Toy. There was nothing about the structural difficulties of the tower past or present, and I just wondered where the history of such a place as this tower rightfully reposed. I had, in fact, exhausted every drawer but the top one, having long before been discouraged from sticking my hand in there by the windrows of candy wrappers therein secreted by Toy.

This time the flat drawer was clean.

Except for one sheet of paper:

Take Down The Fog Trumpets

FOG TRUMPET BLUES

As the keeper pushed off from the rocks a black squall, the advance guard of the approaching hurricane, struck. He rowed along under the lee of the breakwater while clouds of spray leaped over the top and drenched him. By the time he reached Lewes it was blowing a gale and the light was smothered in the murk of the storm. Willis meantime prepared for the gale, making everything snug that might go adrift in the blow. Although it was only midafternoon darkness had set in, making it necessary to climb to the lantern to start the light going.

—John J. Floherty, *Sentries of the Sea*

THEY WERE beautiful horns. Six feet long, cantilevered from the third deck, one pointed out to sea, the other up the bay. Flanged at the end into a trumpet bell, they looked like the sonorous sackbutts that serenade mariners from the corners of Elizabethan sea charts, horns that only the great four-corner winds could blow with cherub cheeks to hit double high C *fortissimo* in Gabriel's cloud-jamming band. They had nevertheless been rendered obsolete by a small set of gray automotive horns set well back inside the gallery. The idea was, as Chanty had said, that someday we were going to be automatic and that the big horns simply could not by mere machine be tamed.

"Boy," said Okrastone, and he smiled, "you know what we got to do before all the pretty weather goes? We got to take them horns down."

"Why?" I said, "what's wrong with just leaving them up there?"

"Them hooters don't work no more. We got them new little modern horns set back on the gallery."

"Just leave them up there. They look good."

"You mean like some kind of . . . *decoration?*"

"They were part of the main idea of this station."

"*Were,* boy. That's the key: *were.* Now they're just hooters without milk, and that's ugly. Besides, it's dangerous."

"Milkless hooters are dangerous?"

"They might rust and fall down. They hang out too far. They make you feel like they might some night up and tip the tower that way." He laughed. "I knew you'd like that one."

"Well, there *is* a danger in any work aloft like that," I said.

"Exactly, you want to climb up there come spring and chip and paint

them. That would take you two or three days you'd be at it, every spring you're out here. And I gather you plan to be here every spring for a while if we can convince you the place ain't going to fall over."

"Actually I think it's more likely the place will be made automatic. I mean isn't that what this castration of the horns is all about?"

"One fell swoop, son. Guaranteed to make your life pleasant out here in the long run, believe me. There's rust spots on them bells you can see from the deck right now."

"Well," I said, "when it comes to that, who's going to climb out there to take them down?"

"God damn, boy," he said, "a sailor's got to go to sea some time."

Meanwhile he had us sweeping and scrubbing, even painting window sills. In addition to keeping the removal of the horns hanging literally over us, he had us thinking about chipping down the whole tower. Ironically we were saved when the bad weather set in; raw mornings with northerlies that just kept building into late afternoon so that the whole tower hummed and the knotted escape ropes knocked against the steel walls and kept on banging inside your head as you tried to fall asleep before mid-watch.

"I don't know about those big old horns," I said. "They're kind of a tradition on this lighthouse."

"Tradition crap," said Okrastone. "Don't talk to me about tradition. I got twelve years."

"Well, you know, Boats, I was talking to some old salts ashore and they said this station was once the belle of the bay."

"The Coast Guard ain't no museum, son. We're runnin no belle of the bay, but an up to date Aid here. An Aid to Navigation."

"I'm not against aiding navigation," I said, "I'm just saying the Lighthouse Service has different traditions than the rest of the service."

"I got you there, boy," he said, "the buoy tenders like the one I was just on, they was part of the old Lighthouse Service." He gave me a big wink. "Now please do not talk to me about tradition. Why do you think they sent me out here? Just to be another Blump? Hell, I was sent out here to get this place squared away. Soon as I get here squared away I'm all lined up to make chief and go back down home to the lifeboat station there as officer-in-charge. You see, you got to keep in mind the big picture."

"Well, then there's something you ought to know about this place," I said, "and it isn't up on the gallery."

"The *hell* it ain't," he said, and gave me a little help locating the door.

Up we went onto the gallery, the wind banging the iron door against the iron tower, me dragging a big coil of manila. Aside from the escape ropes, the chow and clothes lines, and the ragged thing Farilla had carried off, it was the first piece of line I'd touched since I'd come aboard. "Where did you have this hidden?"

Okrastone just smiled. "Well, you look like a sailor finally." He even pulled in his own belly.

"Yes, usually I feel more like the Irish Washerwoman."

"We'll do some real sailing today." He looked over the rail like the captain of something outward bound. I in turn plucked at the strands, rolling them open to inspect for rot.

"That's a boy, check 'er all over." He actually locked hands behind his foul-weather jacket, hiking it up a bit awkwardly to do so, and paced off a few strides. "And we'll want a light line to put on you when you go out there."

"Where's that?" I was still examining the big rope. There was a good two hundred feet more I could play with.

"Down in the Boatswain's locker."

"Ok, I'll get it." Actually I had meant where was it I was supposed to climb out, but I was beginning to get an idea. I even stole a furtive glance at the horn bells, not quite able to take them and the sea seventy feet below with the same focus.

"That's Ok," he said, "I'll be glad to fetch it." He put his hand on my shoulder, and I could smell the coffee and cigarette, but up there in all that air, it wasn't like in the sleeping quarters, and I actually welcomed that little cloud of humanness that passed between us. "You're old dad is going to be taking good care of you today."

When he was gone I had the opportunity to look. The sea, of course, I assumed. I knew there was always much more of it up there and I knew I always was shocked by the effect of it no matter how hard I braced myself, so I just peeped over at the trumpets themselves. Still I had trouble with them, the way they swept off toward the horizon. Magnificence was one thing, vertigo another, and their silence was a blast into infinity.

I checked the brackets, which seemed strong enough with nobody out there. Except there were those rust stains running down from the bolts, running down three stories to the main gallery, with the guard rail looking like a good place to break your back. Or if you missed there were two more stories to the rocks, which you couldn't see because of the way that part of the tower flared like an ice-cream cone. And then there was, all else failing, the sea. Maybe, when you thought of it that way, the sea could save you after all.

But it wasn't Okrastone who came back with the safety rope. It was Flap and all smiles. I had forgotten to take him aside and pass on Toy's warning about where all this might lead, but then again, as I watched his beaming face, I knew that there would have been no way in which I could have corrupted him with even so healthy a notion as common sense. Flap was part of

Okrastone's new guard, and the days of Toy, Blump, and Chanty were gone. Only Teddy remained, and he was on liberty.

"Here we are," said this Flap, and damned if he hadn't already rigged the light line around him, turning it this way and that as if it were a bridal gown; and there was Okrastone right behind him, rubbing his hands.

"At last we're gonna do some real sailing," said Okrastone. "You all set?"

"Now what is it I'm supposed to do?" I said. The northerly had turned itself up a notch, ballooning our foul-weather jackets, running up my back. The guard rail was cold, and there were whitecaps as far as you could see. There were no ships in sight, no land that way either. On the passing wind alone the trumpet bells thrummed so you could feel them in your feet.

Flap still had the line around his waist and was pulling on it, testing it, beaming, still the maid in her bridal gown. "What do you think of it, Boats?"

"We're gonna *parbuckle*, boys," said Okrastone, and he spat into his hands. He hadn't bothered to shave. "You got those wrenches?"

"Sure do," said Flap. He got an arm free of the line and rattled his back pocket for us.

"Now what's the idea again?" I said. Various phrases from safety manuals loomed up: *work-party leaders should make sure all members of the work party understand the nature of the work; too late—there was no time to mouse the hook* [caption from a derrick disaster]; *boatswains should make sure no one is standing in the chain, voicelessly as Turkish mutes bowstring their victim* . . .

"The question is," said Flap undoing the loop from himself and getting mock-academic, "which of us is lighter?" He looked around for some place to deposit the rope.

"You just hold onto that a second, Flap," said Okrastone.

"O.K., Boats, I'll squeeze onto it all day if you like. I just thought you were anxious to get on with this 'sailing' business, whatever it is you guys have in mind."

"You got the tools," said Okrastone. "You're the one, Flap, what's going to have to undo those bolts."

"You mean *I* got to go out there?" A frown marred Flap's boyish face. "I'm twice as heavy as he is. Besides, I thought this *up-aloft* stuff was Deck Ape work."

"I wondered why you were so cheerful," I said.

"Tools, nuts, and bolts is engineman's stuff," said Okrastone.

"*Tools and nuts and bolts*," sang Flap, and, possibly not wanting to admit his cheer had been bogus, he completed the song with a little dance, butt out, fingers snapping.

"Christ," said Okrastone, "all you got to do is turn a few of them little tweakers there, Flap."

"Give the damn thing to me," I said.

"Just a minute," said Flap, almost as if scolding his own butt for the dance. "Let me take a look." He peered over the edge. "You know, Boats, you're right. Those nuts look pretty tricky. I mean they, the *bolts*, they go right through the tower. I imagine someone will have to go down inside and hold the other end. Who knows what might happen in there? Maybe I'd better go down and check. Like much of engineman's work, cursedly dark and hard to get at down in there if I recall."

Okrastone had his tongue in his cheek, but he didn't say anything, and indeed there wasn't much room as Flap babbled on.

"You have our seaman here turn those nuts from the outside," said Flap. "And I'll have to be down in that darn dark hole trying to make sense out of the other end."

"No, Flap," said Okrastone, "you're gonna do the horns *out*board."

I shrugged.

"O.K., I give up," said Flap, "but I still say I'm too young to die." He gave us his mom's pie smile.

"Really I'm suprised at you boys," said Okrastone setting his big hand on the rail, somehow making it look dumpling soft, like a dowager temporarily out of diamonds, but arm-weary nevertheless, setting her hand along the *Queen Mary*'s rail. He even went up on his toes a bit and wrinkled his nose, raised his eyebrows as he peered over. "Now if I were a young man, I'd skip right on out."

"I'm going to be twenty in a month," said Flap. "And that ain't a kid any more."

"Really, I'm very, very suprised," Okrastone wrinkled his pug even more.

"Toy told me steel workers from the base were going to do it," I said.

"Oh, now don't start quoting those niggers again."

"Was Toy Negro?" said Flap.

"Figure of speech," I said.

"No, he was a nigger all right," said Okrastone. "That Chanty, he converted them all."

"He was O.K.," I said. "What did he have to work with?"

"He had just what we got to work with," said Okrastone. "Him and that Blump. You ever take a look at this place?"

Flap and I shifted uneasily about, scanning unfamiliar areas.

"You boys ever really looked around here and see how screwed up this place is?" There was no twinkle in his eye.

"Well," I said, "for one, those twerpy little auto horns over there set on the deck to replace these trumpets."

"Well," said Flap, "except for some pretty poor painter's technique—runs, ripples, blisters, and holidays in the window sills, I'd have to say it's a lighthouse, and, by God, here it is still standing up under us pretty much, and at night it lights."

"There's a crack in the base," I said, "but it's been a home to me."

"God damn, boys, I say it's all nigger rig from one end to the other."

"Well, I don't mind," said Flap. "I ain't got nothing against it. At least it don't rock."

"God damn, that's just it. You boys never been no wheres. God damn thing." He banged his fist on the rail. "Just sits here."

"Well, it can always fall over," I said.

"No, it ain't gonna *fall over*," Okrastone said. "How come you always talking about it falling over, anyway, boy?"

"It's all those old books his mother sent him," said Flap, "Boy, I tried to read one last night. Not for me."

"They all fall over, eh?" Okrastone stared a hole in me. Big blue eyes, slightly thyroid.

"They only write about the ones that do," I said.

"Who writes? Who is this '*they*' what writes about falling-over lighthouses? They some kind of woman's temperance committee?"

"John J. Floherty," said Flap. "I swear to God. But don't look at me. It's his mother's book."

"Well, this Mr. John J. Floherty sounds like an Irishman to me," said Okrastone. "And like they say, 'an Irishman's just a nigger turned inside out.' Why don't your mom send pies like Flap's ma here? Them books you can't eat and they keeps you up worse than something what was the worse thing you ever did eat."

"Then you did read John J. Floherty's account of this place," I said.

A funny look started to creep across his face as if I'd caught him with his hand in one of Mother Flap's pies. "I started it, Bo, but I couldn't stay awake."

"I thought you said you couldn't get to sleep."

"I couldn't go to sleep; I was on watch, son. Now never mind all this lit'rary talk. We ain't gonna have the luck to fall over, so we might as well get back to work."

"Oh, hell," said Flap, "I thought we could keep you bullshitting till lunch."

"You can't fool the old bar," he said. "I knew what was up the whole time. Get them nuts off."

"Wait," I said, "shouldn't we rig the barnbuckle, or whatever?"

"Oh, now that might be a good idea after all," said Okrastone. "But it ain't 'barn-buckle', you fuckinfarmer; it's par-buckle."

I picked up the line and began coiling it. "O.K.," I said, "fit the safety line on me."

"Look," said Flap, "I got to go out there anyway, right?"

"You got to do the nuts."

"Right, so I might as well pass the barn-buckle or whatever you call it. No sense risking the two of us. And like he said, his mother's worried about him getting hurt on the lighthouse."

"No, I'll go." I pulled the line. He almost had it out of my hand. "Damn it, it's Deck Ape work."

"God damn," said Okrastone, "now you're arguing to go out there. A minute ago it was the other way."

"I don't quite see why we've got to do it in the first place," I said, "but seeing as how we are, I'm going to do my job."

"The danger's in climbing over the rail, as I see it," said Flap. He tried to look jowly. "If one man goes, we reduce the chances, and I've got to go to do my nuts-and-bolts thing, so I might as well do the rope thing, too. Even though, technically that's definitely Deck Force work."

Okrastone had by now turned his back to Flap and put his hand on my shoulder. "You run on down inside now, son, and twiddle them nuts from that end."

I made a wry face.

"Go on now." He lifted the safety rope gently from my hand. Flap reached out and put a wrench in its place.

Where I was it was dim and smelled of your old aunt's attic, but I could hear them hollering and banging out there in the wind. Once in a while the knock was for me, or so I thought: Okrastone rapping the wall to let me know it was time to shift my wrench to another bolt. I must have followed his intentions all right, because he didn't set up a barrage out there, just that tender pair of taps and I'd shift over. Finally the call came to emerge.

After the cramped dark, the high dizzy light staggered me. The wind was fierce. The two of them, pink and boisterous, were straining to hold the horn. It was out of sight below them, in a cradle formed by the par-buckle: the long line, its middle around a stanchion of the gallery rail, was passed double down the tower wall, under the disconnected horn and back up; the two ends came over the rail and each man held an end. The line was towing them and they were sliding reluctantly across the deck toward the rail.

"Woa, there," cried Flap.

"Don't let her get a run, Flap," said Okrastone. "And don't get ahead of me. Keep even with me or she'll flip out."

The line was new, full of needle-like fibers. The wind made our eyes blur.

You could look at the lines slipping over the rail or look at the immense sea. It was difficult, once we gave any line at all, to keep it from running away. When the horn was about halfway down the side of the tower, Okrastone dispatched Flap to the gallery below, where he was to pull outboard on a lighter line, possibly the old safety line, I figured. "Just give her a little steady pull, Flap, just like you got the old dog on a leash. We don't want that horn gettin a mind of her own and go knocking out all the winders on the way down."

"Right, Boats, dog-on-a-leash."

"Now don't stand under her, Flap."

"Right."

"Because she ain't no dog on a leash." ·

"Don't worry, Boats. I'm all set to run."

"He's a good boy," said Okrastone. Somehow we were almost stepping on each other. I smelled his coffee again.

"I would have gone out there."

"That's O.K. You just stay here and help your old dad. That's it now, don't let her get a run."

When we had it on the lower gallery we still needed to move it down on the landing stage so the buoy tender could pick it up, though God knew for what. It would have been much easier to have just bounced it into the sea where it could have joined the pair of fog bells from the days of former glory.

"That's O.K.," said Okrastone. "We can take her from here, me and Flap."

I had already started to rig a special hitch I'd been cooking up, a variation on the way Chanty had hauled up our food. I surrendered the line to Flap.

"You go in and get us some nice pea soup going," Okrastone said. "You know, that kind you do real good."

"Ya," said Flap making his new hitch to replace mine. "That pea soup oughta go real good about now."

"I thought you didn't like my pea soup, Flap."

"Hey, I could eat anything after this morning."

"You go ahead," said Okrastone. "Don't worry. We'll eat up your soup just like the three bars."

That afternoon, after I had done the dishes as quickly as I could, I put on my foul-weather jacket, but Okrastone said it was time for 'drills.' We tilted the blinds against the glare off the sea, and I made a joke about Chanty's spider webs. Okrastone laughed. "I guess he was some character, all right." Our 'drill' was a safety lecture, and Okrastone did not stand, as he usually did, by the cylinder, but eased himself into his office chair, put his feet up on the government forms, and, with a soft burp or two from the pea soup, told me again all about how you had to be careful of the 'bars' because they clawed down all the range markers when you were on a buoy tender in Alaska. I slumped down in the leather chair, still in my foul-weather jacket. After a while I unzipped it. Flap was upstairs sleeping off his mid-watch. The wind made the escape ropes knock on the walls.

It was a month before the other horn came down, and they did it when I was on liberty, just the two of them.

The horns lay on the landing stage. Without the lighthouse attached to them and the clouds sailing past their bells, they looked less like trumpets than cheerleader's megaphones, and the spray from the November seas covered them with ice.

SHIPWRECK

Just as the lens had begun to revolve an enormous sea charged up the rocks with a
roar that was louder than the storm. It struck the tower with the force of an avalanche and caused it to sway violently. The heavy Fresnal lens shuddered in its
bearings and the lamp flared fretfully and almost went out. It was the beginning of a
sustained attack. Sea after sea rushed the structure making it wince under each successive blow.

—John J. Floherty, *Sentries of the Sea*

MID-WATCH. Or shortly it will be when I am hailed out of bed by
harpy-footed enginemen. The light goes around. Well, it should.
That's what it's paid for. The weather behind the venetian blind
seems clear, and that is good, too. I let the blind slap back against the windowpane, the weather go back to whatever it wants to be. The door, however, sucks open. Ah, but it is only the lower one. I ease back on my pillow
and count the steps. It will be that many seconds before the top door opens,
before I am on watch, before the weather again must behave.

Something wrong . . . he's stopped. Going back down. The upper door
rattles the way it does only when the bottom one opens. And closes.

I look behind the blind again. Still clear. Good. I let the blind go. It
sways, and the slats form a J-shaped curve that floats away, flattens to kiss
the glass all along the back until the tail knocks up against the sill and the
door sucks, the steps begin again. . . .

"Say," says Teddy, "there's something rather interesting out here." He
is in the bathroom.

"What? An old rubber duck of Chanty's?"

"Naw, this is *out*-side the tower."

"Not that friend of your's in the cheap, Jap waders?"

"It's kind of interesting," he says. "A ship."

He is at the window, poking his finger through the slats, which kiss and
crumple against the pane.

"Right here." He spreads the slats; they buckle with a loud *bonk*. There
is our pier, and there, caught in our beam, is a ship, a huge ship somehow
back of the breakwater—this big ship, and she's leaning way over to one
side, bow on to us, listing to port. Very dramatically, she has steam or smoke
pouring out of the side. You can even see her faintly when our light is off her,

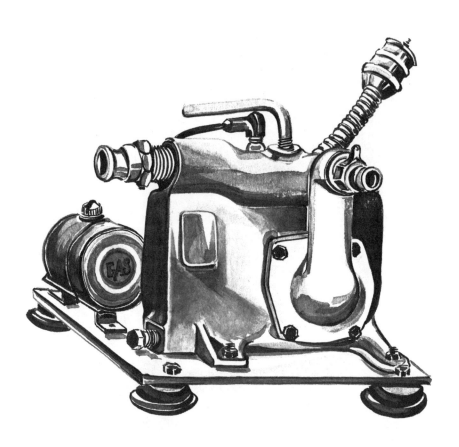

like an after-image that has just enough time to start to fade and then *bam*—
the beam is on her again, keeping her real.

"Now ain't that interesting?" he says.

"Jesus, Teddy. It's a sinking ship."

"I thought you'd go for that." He gives a flick of the venetian blinds,
fluttering them with his finger tips. The blind now hangs free and apparently
does not touch the glass. In any case you can't see out anymore. Not without
pushing him aside.

You can, however, hear.

"Listen, Teddy, their voices . . . their actual voices."

"Ah, you can't understand nuthin' they're saying."

"But how did they get back in there? Chanty said that if ever a big ship
got back in there——" The rest is unthinkable. And afterall, the Main Light
is on now.

"You can't understand nuthin' they say."

And he shuffles off to bed.

Now I crouch behind the blinds. Tap the slats. I can't hear anymore.
There is the ship, dark hull, lights in the superstructure. It is a little bigger
than my pillow. And the stuffing is coming out. But what if she isn't a picture, but a real ship there behind the glass and she blows and splinters, and
all the glass goes wall-eyed?

I go to the other side of the tower, around behind the cylinder.

In boot camp they had showed us the Halifax film three times. Two dy-
namite ships (for pedagogical purposes green arrow and red arrow) meeting
at the narrows (shaded area). The first flash brought everyone to the windows. Their eyes were wide open. They made the same mistake in navigation class, seamanship class, and orientation during the week following hand
salute with amputation.

Bang-bang!

The radio has shot me dead. But left a weak voice piping in the after-
heaven: "Coast *God*, Hello Coast *God*, this *Mannermore*."

I creep between the two leather chairs.

"Coast *God*, this is *Mannermore*, we're having a bit of difficulty. Can
you hear me?"

The radio crackles. I put my hand on the knob, expecting some big, au-
thoritative coast god to chime in. In any case, we are no doubt to be blamed.
Is it possible that a ship like that could have gotten into the mess it is in if it
had not been somehow our fault?

"I say Coast *God*, we're back of the lighthouse here and I'm afraid
there's water coming in and we can't quite seem to cope with it."

I count five and pick up the mike.

"*Mannermore*, this is Harbor Refuge Light."

"Yes, Light, come in. We're right back of you."

"*Mannermore/Harbor*, yes we noticed. What is all that steam?"

"*Harbor* Light/*Mannermore*, say again. There's a good deal of commotion aboard here, I'm afraid. We can't seem to locate any of your vessels."

"*Mannermore/Harbor*, suggested you try to raise Cape May."

"*Mannermore*, this is Cape May, we've been monitoring you but have been busy other freaks, please switch 2686."

Across frequencies we all race. Identities re-established, *Mannermore* says he's anchored on 'The Shears,' a sixteen-foot-deep spur off the back of our Light, and there he's settling to the bottom 'quite satisfactorily.' My God, I think, I didn't know it was only sixteen feet deep back there! "The Shears," and all that! And here comes this foreigner who knows more about my view than I do.

Cape May is sending boats. Our local lifeboat station is sending. Everybody's coming to the party. I race upstairs and tell Teddy. He rolls over and yawns.

"It's a goddam Limey ship, and it's sinking," I say, "right back of us. There's a bit of water he '*can't quite cope with*,' he says."

"Those Limies sure are queer."

"But he's sinking."

Reluctantly he gets up, heavy footed, follows me into the bathroom, our previous roles reversed. We stick our fingers in the slats, and there is the soft *bonk* as the slats buckle.

"I suppose we could always pull the sash cord," he says.

"She might blow up. Look at that steam."

There is a ripping sound and my eyes get bigger so that I feel the sleep cracking around my rims and then the ripping settles down into a rattle. "Anchor chain," I say. "Teddy, you can hear their voices and you can actually hear the anchor chain running out."

He yawns, lets go of the cord. "Ya, well, I'm going back to bed. Let me know if she blows up."

"Let you know?" I look out again. "Christ, the ship's only a football field away, and it's a big ship."

"Well, it's got to come all the way over from England," he says, but he is around the stairwell.

"Listen, you know about Halifax don't you?"

"Who?"

"Halifax, Nova Scotia. World War One. All the ships blew up and when people ran to the windows to see what the glow was, they were blinded. The whole bloody city was blinded."

"I'm going to sleep."

"Teddy, the beacon's been on all evening, right?"

"Hey," he says, "stop trying to figure out what foreign people say on the water at night."

Dawn at last. I have been running about, peeking through the blinds and talking on the telephone like an old lady. Except it is not merely neighborhood gossip, but a Maritime Disaster, and I am one of the Rescuing Agencies. They are using me to hold messages while the other units are busy on other frequencies. After all, I can see the ship, and I was her first contact. The lifeboat station has now begun to work her, sending out forty-footers with handy billies and five-gallon gas cans to run these pumps. There is a steady shuttle going on from the inlet with these five-gallon gas cans, which are somehow to counterbalance the sea pouring in through *Mannermore*'s wound.

The gash goes from below the water line almost to the first deck and is three or four feet wide at the top. The skipper says he has "free communication with the sea" which, announced in his laconic Limey voice, sounds if not Wordsworthian at least like a Sunday stroll through Kew Gardens, roses and duck ponds and at the end of the far arbor a public circulating library.

I have been straining through the dark to see the wound itself, but it has been obscured by the steam. Now at first light, as the ship begins to define its textures, I stand on the balcony, my shirt blowing slightly, and stare. The sunlight is making the hull seem rustier than I'm sure it is. She has two masts, as I thought: cargo booms. Her bow faces us, but just off center so that I can't see the wound. Now in the daylight, the list seems even spookier because the ship itself is defined so clearly. Even without the list it is a strange feeling I have as I sit watching her, simply because in six months of looking out this back door I have not seen a big ship in this area. It is as if one awoke one day in his rural cottage and saw an apartment house sprung full blown in his lettuce patch. Perhaps Adam felt this way when he rolled over and first saw Eve. One welcomes the company, the novelty, yet resents the intrusion, the mere physical shock to the spatial sense.

The large buoy tender *Sassafras* can now be seen working alongside. She came during breakfast, talking of collision mats as I made a few pancakes out of sympathy. How small she looks next to the great listing hulk she serves!

They have procured pumps from all the lifeboat stations along the coast, clear up to Atlantic City in the north and down to the Maryland border.

They have even gone into garages and boat sheds to get some models not seen slurping a bilge in decades.

Everything is very important. I expect to be interviewed, so I turn on the "entertainment" radio. All that happens is broken hearts and Elizabeth Taylor running off with Richard Burton. The announcer keeps talking about it. He has, by ten o'clock, whipped himself into a frenzy. Plays Eddie Fisher records in between diatribes: "Tonight We Love." "What Kind of Fool Am I?" This he plays several times. It is a question of whether he can last to the ten o'clock news.

We have lost the show. Nobody calls me anymore. It's all being handled by the *Sas*, which is, of course, *On Scene*. Greenmeal Lifeboat and *Sas* exchange gas cans and handy billy parts. Greenmeal and *Sas* do things with "personnel." I recognize some of the voices from the station, or at least I think I do: the chief I saw so long ago at the screen door, shaving in his underwear, fantastically garlanded in lather and moths. Or at least I imagine he would sound this way, because I've never heard him on radio. They must be working frequencies I can't pick up, because they refer to previous conversations I've not heard.

It occurs to me they have direct contact with each other.

They actually get on each other's vessels, pass things hand to hand, see faces, feel hands, shoulders.

Nor has Elizabeth returned to Eddie.

In all this scandal there is one piece of benign news. The Pilots are talking to the buoy tender and the words hang happily in the air:

"The other ship we hear is ok."

"Roger, it's a good thing for *Mannermore* she had the Harbor Refuge to hide behind after the collision."

I want to get Teddy and tell him all is forgiven, but I realize he knew all along he had done nothing. It is I who must be forgiven.

Teddy comes down at last, wants to know why I didn't wake him up on time, why I'm not anxious to go to bed, to my deserved rest. I show him the wreck, babble details, drop names (the captain of the *Mannermore* and I are old friends; the officer of the *Sas* does not appreciate me quite as he might.) At first I think it will take me eight hours to tell Teddy all that happened, but my words pile up like snow before a plow, billow and topple, are thrown to the side; and in less than a minute I am repeating myself, stammering into silence. He chews his lower lip, inhales, sighs . . . "Man, I'm gettin transferred." Scratches his oily forehead, squints out the window, and then walks over to the stove.

"I put in." He fiddles with the stove knobs.

"Chanty used to do that."

"Oh, no, he didn't never put in at all. They put him off."

"I meant fooster with the stove knobs. Of course he'd been a cook."

"They puts lots of cooks on lighthouses if they can't do it, so, anyhow, people can eat what they cook."

"So I'm told. But you weren't a cook."

"No."

"And I sure as hell wasn't."

"You do good Cream of Wheat."

I just look at him.

"I got to go anyway," He turns from the stove. "I had to put in."

"U-huh."

"So I got a lightship."

"Ok," I say, "so you're being transferred to a lightship."

"See, what you got to realize is that when you put in, they sometimes really, anyhow, do it."

"You were surprised?"

"Toy kept putting in, and nothing ever happened. So did Blump."

"You mean nothing happened until it happened."

He looks at me blankly.

"Do you see either of them around here?" I say.

"Sometimes I feel Chanty—sometimes I feel he's still here only maybe he's on leave or up asleep or on top of the balcony doin something weird with the flag."

"You didn't do it because of the crack?"

"*Crack?* I don't take no offense. I know it's hard for you out here."

"It's not hard for me out here. That's just the trouble, maybe. It's just that nobody seems to realize the whole thing's going to fall over. Nobody gives a damn."

"Hey, it's Ok. I don't take no offense."

"It's not you and it's not me. Damn it, Teddy, don't you understand. It's the . . . tower."

"You could put in." He looks at me with sad eyes. "You could put in, too."

"I don't want to put in for a transfer. I like it here. I always wanted to be on a lighthouse. I just want them to fix the damn thing. I'd think they'd *want* to fix it. It's supposed to be a fixed thing."

"Yeah," he sighs, "in this world a lighthouse *is* supposed to be a fixed thing. That's right."

"And something else," I say. "Do you realize this lighthouse was once considered the best thing going? It had fancy wooden sides and fancy windows and decorations on the gallery rail. It was known as the *Belle of the Bay.*"

He stands there scratching himself.

"Well?" I say.

"Hey, I put in."

Thinking of the old boot camp joke about pancakes being like collision mats, I decide to try my hand at a recipe from the *Amy Vanderbilt Cookbook*. Leaving out the more exotic ingredients, I produce some flapjacks that are actually edible.

"Hey," he says, "you made collision mats." He holds one high on his fork.

"Yes, I thought they were especially appropriate today."

"I never thought when I was in boot camp eating these here 'collision mats' we called them, I never thought we'd be having real ones out the window."

"Well, I thought it was high time we took some reality-oriented action to integrate ourselves with the ongoing external community and its problems."

He looks at the dripping pancake to see if it can receive this impact. "Yeah, well, supprised me was where you got the syrup."

"Chanty's secret store."

"Oh." He allows the pancake to ooze back onto the plate.

"You know what Chanty says is the great thing about being on a lighthouse compared to a ship like that one out the window, or even say a lightship?"

The posture of the pancake upon his plate requires his full concentration.

"Chanty says that at least on a lighthouse your mistakes are pretty much your own. On a ship, they tend to become diffuse."

"Say, there's something I want to ask you." His look is half on the pancake; what smile escapes up to me floats as crooked as the smirk of Toy.

"Yes?" Already I know it is not about the cooking. Neither is it about the shipwreck or for that matter, theories of relative responsibility on various Coast Guard units.

"I mean I got something to say." His smirk has hardened. It is even frightening. There is no help from collision mats real or metaphorical. It is a frightening gaze partly because it is clear that it frightens him as well. He is, nevertheless, bound that at last it is to come out.

"How long," he says, "I mean, look, how long you actually know this Chanty?"

"Well, I don't think it's the actual face-to-face time spent that counts, Teddy. You yourself were just saying that you yourself felt his presence, often."

Proud of myself, I indulge a look his way. He is not so proud of me. This makes him not so proud of himself. His gaze does not meet my benign brimming. "You yourself," I begin again, "you sense of Chanty's presence—"

"Naw," he says, "I just meant I keep finding things around here he did wrong."

"Well, in any case if you're going out to the *Delaware*, you'll have his . . . presence."

"I don't think so. I ain't heard him on the radio in a long time." The radio Teddy now fools with is the entertainment unit.

"Maybe he's above making radio checks. After all, he is a boatswain."

"Not really. He was a cook they made a boatswain real quick and stuck on a light." He twiddles the radio knobs.

"Then he's cooking aboard the ship. Granted lightships are not organized like weather cutters, do lightship cooks radio?"

"He can't cook in the first place."

"Well, damn it," I shout. "He still exists. Out there——"

But Teddy has found the Hollywood scandal again and sits back with a second cup of coffee, indeed entertained.

Upstairs on Okrastone's bunk I watch what is not yet entertainment. The steam has ceased coming from the ship. The Coast Guard boats bustle about. I finally take my own pillow and blanket and, with my face pressed to the window (I have fearlessly raised the blinds), go to sleep dreaming in that wide blue, suspended above the wreck, in free communication with everybody.

When I wake up, the sun is setting, and there is the ship, listing; yet in all that magnificence, the small boats are still needed to work her, though in these colors she might not be merely a malfunctioning motor vessel floundering off the Greenmeal fish factory, but something exotic steaming into a tropical harbor thick with bum boats and native cries.

Teddy is poking at supper. "Evidently Eddie Fisher's not going after them," he says.

I serve myself from the stove and join him.

"I notice your friend seems to be still in a bit of trouble," he says.

"You saw it first," I said. "Last night."

"Well, I never talked with him," he says and takes a forkful. "Though I heard him this afternoon, and you're right, his voice does sure sound *peculiar*. It must be the British in it. They is all screwed up in the mouth from marmalade." He chews up the word *British* and a small piece of green escapes from his lip. I worry about where he got a word like *peculiar*.

I wash the dishes and take out the garbage. The gulls don't seem to be interested in us tonight; in fact, they are nowhere around. Teddy has the television on: a war in the Near East, but no footage on the Taylor-Burton affair. We wonder if the radio announcer hadn't been stretching things a bit. "It's getting damn hard to know just what entertainment is," says Teddy. At nine o'clock on 2686 someone talks of a gas can. Around ten-thirty there is something about a pump freezing up. Teddy has gone to bed. I stand on the balcony, and it seems to me they are using high-intensity lights from the rigging. From time to time I hear the clank and spin of machinery. At eleven I pick up a book on shipwrecks. I recognize I am getting a bit edgy. I have trouble getting into the page:

For three days and three nights the gallant crew of *The Golden Eagle* clung desperately to the masts of their valiant ship which refused to succumb to that monstrous, raging storm . . .

At midnight I throw the book against the overhead and go out on the balcony. It seems to me the arrangement of lights has altered. Either they have moved them about, or the ship itself has swung, which means it has begun to lighten. I rush to the radio to hear confirmation of this. I want to hear the captain say he is officially floating. Occasionally there is a slight pop from the receiver. I pick up the shipwreck book and hold it, closed, in my lap. At one o'clock I bolt and run upstairs to bed.

I am almost asleep when I remember that to keep the show going, I have to wake Teddy.

"Hey," he says, "don't be offended because I put in."

Morning. I take a peek at the window, not even through it, not wanting to spoil anything. I dress quickly, but not frantically, doing all the buttons on the shirt and the fly, smoothing down the wrinkles, brushing my teeth, fingernailing the goo from my eye. I go below only when I'm presentable, for it is going to be like Christmas morning, and what finer present than this long-wished-for Event, which now, after thirty-six hours, I am ready to receive. I nod to Teddy, who is poking at his breakfast, and without further ado I swing through the screen door like a bridegroom coming into his chamber.

And there she is. Radiant in the fresh morning light. Turned to show us her wound, now patched with great mats, her masts almost in the perpendicular, the small boats busy about her. I watch for some time with a beautiful disinterest. The door behind me slams. Teddy drifts to the rail. I sense his nose twitching, his eyes winking into place. He pulls out a folder, taps it on the rail; a four-color pitch on his power mower.

"She's floating," I say.

He is moving closer with the pamphlet.

"You know, Teddy, I thought a dumb thing back there. I thought a dumb thing back there the other night when she was sinking."

"I know," he says, "you thought I let the Light go out."

"Well——"

"Here," he says, handing the brochure to me. "If I get transferred way out there you'll be the closest guy I know to land." I unfold it. There is a smiling father, just a bit stout, striding along a suburban lawn behind the mower while a boy and girl gambol in his wake.

She remains for the afternoon, however. Her departure is discussed on various frequencies. A helicopter appears and circles several times, even sweeps by us, and we can see the camera. There is a different disc jockey on the record show, and absolutely no Fisher records are played. We watch the evening news, and there are shots of Burton and Liz and the ship; and then, almost unrecognizable because of the overhead camera angle and the mobility given by the zoom lens, is our tower, rising up like a rocket, perfectly, shockingly round.

The announcer's copy is equally irrelevant. The times are wrong. No causes are given. Us he calls the "Cape Henlopen Light." He omits names, including even the *Sas* and its take-charge officer. About the latter my emotions are mixed, and in trying to straighten them out in conversation with Teddy he reminds me that life on ships maybe will not be all that bad. "You know, just 'cause you go to sea don't mean you *got* to sink," he says.

The next morning the *Mannermore* has not yet left, and we stand on the balcony with arms folded. That afternoon, when we are doing some long-postponed work in the engine room, we come out for a moment on the white concrete base and notice the blank space between us and shore.

"Well," he says, "I can't say I'm sorry to see that thing move away."

I agree that the affair has been dragged out rather too long. We look toward the open sea and agree it is the time of year to fasten the lower doors. It is difficult, because they have been badly warped and the hinge pins are rusty, but with much effort and a bruised finger or two we get them as tight as we can. With them shut, it is dark in the cellar, only the distant bulbs dangling from the overhead, and, with the fresh air cut off, the diesel smell, despite the afternoon's scouring, is quickly oppressive. We take down some shirts drying from the water-tank supports and use the clothesline to fasten the doors tight, tying one end around the furnace.

"If a great sea hits I suppose the line will break before it pulls the furnace out," I say. "Pulls our heat right out from our guts."

"I don't worry about that kind of thing," he says.

"Yeah, well you're not going to be here." I am shocked by my own tone. Hadn't I forgiven him last night?

"Hey, look Rip, I didn't worry when I was here. It's just what we do this time of year."

"Like putting away the picnic table and taking down the awnings."

"Yeah. That kind of thing."

"Still, even that lets you know."

"Let's you know what, Rip?"

"Winter."

"Hey, you don't got to sink—even in winter."

OVERDUE
BEACH PATROL

During the turmoil of an assaulting wave something in the tower snapped with a sharp report; a splintering noise followed. The tower lurched under the shock. The steel wire of the clock weight twanged. Several panes of glass in the lantern were shattered; the light went out. As Willis hurried to relight the lamp another big one struck.

—John J. Floherty, *Sentries of the Sea*

IT WAS A gusty day when I came down for breakfast and heard the forty-footer at the stage. It was not Boat Day. No one was due to arrive or depart. There had been an Overdue on the radio, but it was inconceivable that just because a citizen was missing on the Bay, Farilla or some other member of the boat crew would again bother to climb our long iron ladder to drink our sour milk and hector us on the impossibility of celibacy.

Okrastone was at the sink, pouring water into the coffee pot. It seemed an act that required his full attention.

"What's up?" I said.

"Why, I thought I'd just have time to make you a nice little cup o' coffee, Rip, but they done already sent the boat."

"Sent it? Sounds like it's already down there."

"Yes, as a matter of fact, I believe you're 100 percent correct on that one." He rubbed the brass spigot with his forefinger and largely succeeded in removing the green spot that had festered there overnight.

"I gather they have come for me."

"That's the correct analysis, son." He finally met my eyes. "As a matter of fact, they have."

"Who has?" I said. "Precisely *who?*" I could have looked past him out the window, but it seemed more urgent to study his face for evidence of a put-on. To protect my own face, I drew a smile. "I mean it's not my leave week. Hell, it isn't even Boat Day for any reason."

"Just for a while today." He found it necessary to add some water to the pot, and this, of course, required a steady gaze upon the subject at hand. "Something Mr. Milkins wants to see you about."

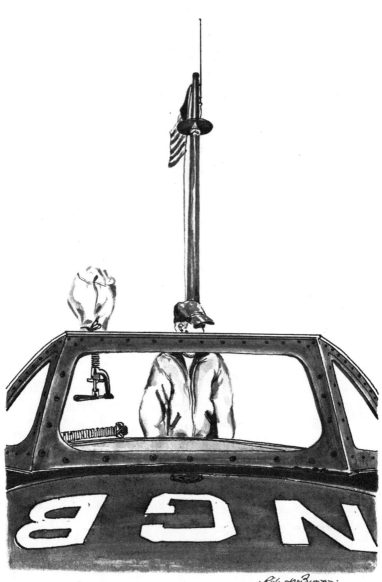

"Mr. Milkins now of the local lifeboat station? The old *Herb* CO? The Sam Browne belt and the seedy crumple to his hat?"

"That's the fellow, all right. He done got himself *transferred ashore*. Now any fellow that wrangled that can't be too seedy, son." He winked at me.

"But what's he got to do with us? With me? I thought we reported directly to the Group Commander across at Cape May. That the lifeboat station only provided taxi service out here, indifferent at that, and no supervision, or at least evaluation. As a matter of fact, the last time I was in there this same Milkins told me himself, in front of the whole crew, that lighthouse personnel didn't apply to his life."

"Watch all them big words when you go ashore, son."

He shut the spigot off, having not watched the flow himself and only too late seen some of our precious supply slip over the pot lip and down the drain into the sea. "Them *words* is exactly what ev'dently got you in this fuss. Something to do with the beach patrol."

"I never had anything to do with a beach patrol. What he got mad at was my listening in on a boarding party meeting. He's got this thing about what people write on their——"

"That's my point, son. It was this business about your writing."

"My writing?" By now I had given up watching him and was at the counter looking down past the spice tray out the window at the stage. The boat was hidden beneath the planks and spiles so that only the exhaust drifted out, gusting off over the tightly breaking sea.

"Something to do with bottles," said Okrastone, and I could hear the water sloshing in the pot behind my back. "You'd better hustle down to the stage there. Creel's a good boat handler, but it's a bit airy to hold her to the ladder."

I grabbed my foul-weather jacket, groped the pockets for my watch cap and gloves. It wasn't until I was all the way down on the landing stage and reaching for the iron ladder that I heard from him again.

"You should be in your blues," he shouted. "You should be dressed up in your blue suit."

I squinted back up at the tower. The sun was blasting around both sides of it so I could see Okrastone only as a drop of water poised upon the balcony. "Should I change now?"

Another voice was shouting at me from below. I turned and saw the top of the signal mast rising. "Come-on, say-leer," shouted Creel. His sharp face had been further honed by the wind until under his baseball cap his cheeks and nose made one bloody hatchet blade. "Jump on down," he shouted. "Jump on down if you don't want your ass in a sling."

I turned back toward the balcony and waved both arms like a wounded gull.

"O.K.," shouted Okrastone. "But don't say I never warned you."

Below the engine box of the forty boat heaved and fell, and the exhaust vanished on the wind as fast as human breath.

All the way in I clung to the rail back of the coxswain's platform and the flag cracked machine-gun fire over my head. Creel and his engineman stood close together on the platform with me, and our foul-weather jackets were continually bumping and nudging in the bounce of the sea. I gave up trying to arrange my clothes to look more formal and let myself imagine I was the third member of their crew and that we were off up the bay on some winter mission. It was, in any case, too difficult to talk in all that air, and the real reason for my presence hung in limbo.

It was not so at the Boat Haven pier. I always liked to arrive there. After the open water it was a pleasant nook of backwaters reaching up into the canal that ran through town, and the piles of clam shells behind the ramshackle wooden factory made the air, even in winter, seem solid. Sometimes there was even the singing of the black women who worked in the clam factory with their ample elbows on the warm wooden sills and the pint of Thunderbird right there as they tossed the shells out the window. Today, however, it was cold enough to keep the singing shut inside, and what I had was Luntsky with a pick-up truck. "Hey, is your ass in a sling." He had on a baseball cap, foul-weather jacket, and jeans. Like Creel, he got to drive.

"Yes, I understand the skipper wants to see me," I said. "Something about a beach patrol. It makes no sense."

"He's after your ass."

"But why? I have nothing to do with any beach patrol. I live on a rock pile without a grain of sand within damn near three miles."

"It ain't you personally. It's them *writing notes.*"

"*Writing notes?*"

"Sure. Don't you know you even do it?"

"Know what I write . . . notes?" All I could think of was Chanty's poems, how he had secretly hoarded them aboard the tower all those years and then lost them all when his seabag split and everyone had laughed.

"The ones in the bottles. We find them every day on beach patrol. We got to go on beach patrol now because some dumb bastard went out fishing and didn't come back and his old lady haunts the station. I mean she's got her fat ass in there everyday so the Old Man's got to turn us out onto the beach looking for that Overdue and that's when we find your fuckin bottles. We never find no body, just those fuckin notes. And the old man's getting reports about 'em all up and down this whole coast to Mary-fuckin-land."

A vague recollection came to me: some mid-watch *passacaglia* of a month before. It had been after we'd lashed the cellar doors against the coming of the winter—a bit of capering upon the gallery, some scribbling aloft in the trembling hand . . . It had happened more than once. "And they're in apple-juice bottles, right?"

"They're crazy notes. You'll see."

Along the banks of the canal, the townspeople got to carry their brown paper bags and crates or walk their dogs or even just stand in the shingled alleys in the lee and lean against the patches of the sun.

"You know, sailor, it's too bad you blew it."

"Blew what?"

Luntsky removed his hand from his beloved wheel to offer me the whole sun-rich and steady street. "Sure, scuttlebutt had it you and nigger Peal were going to trade duty."

"*Scuttlebutt?*" It was shocking to hear one of my father's World War Two navy terms in the mouth of Luntsky. Such an acquisition must have come from Mr. Milkins himself.

"Yeah, scuttlebutt, but you blew it with this fuck-up you been into."

"You mean Peal, the station yeoman?" I saw a pretty girl, her long blond hair alive with sunlight as she swished in under an awning.

"That's the very one."

"But how could a seaman mutual with a yeoman?"

"The new skipper, he's not all hung up on rates and ratings and that crap. He thought it made more sense to have a college man in his office and a nigger on the lighthouse."

At Greenmeal's only stoplight I got to look at the upside-down town in the canal.

The smell of cooking almost knocked me down the minute I opened the back door to the station. And there, a step inside, was Blump. He had on a T-shirt and white pants, his white hat rolled on the top of his head like a condom. "You'd better change into a coherent uniform," he said. "Or don't you even have a coherent uniform?"

"You mean like you got on?"

"Hey, it's not my ass that's in the sling, friend. I only got to be the cook here. You're the one that's got to face the music. I'm only looking out after you because I still got a warm heart out for lighthouse personnel, especially personnel which I had under my wing at one time, personally, so to speak."

"Well, there wasn't time," I said. "Creel had his hands full holding the boat to the ladder."

"That foul-weather jacket, for instance. It's not coherent. You should turn the collar down and un-zip it a uniform two inches from the neck. The proper head gear is the baseball cap worn with proper insignia appropriately."

"Watch cap is issue."

"Only on chilly nights, friend. Chilly maneuvers at sea and then only by O.D.'s command. Otherwise you could be anybody, because a watch cap's got no designation insignia. You could even be a BM1, like I used to be before I wised up and lucked out as cook here."

"Well, I'll have it in my hand, anyway."

"Oh, no, you're On Duty Reporting to the C.O. Therefore you wear your authorized head gear in order to present a proper hand salute." He put his arm around my shoulder so that I was once, again, so to speak, under his wing. "Gee, I'm sorry I didn't have time enough to instruct you in all these procedures when we were serving together out there on the Aid to Navigation, but I had hoped that the man they finally found to replace me had had at least *some* sea background."

I managed to cough a small hole in the close aroma, into which I slipped my praises of Okrastone.

"Well, he can't be all *that* right to just, throw you to the wolves in here." His eyes began shifting around in his pouchy face. "Your life ashore is a whole lot different than it is out there." He worked up a dry laugh and checked the passageway. "Here you got to cut the mustard, boy. Here, there's no hiding out." His eyes checked the back door.

"It's all right," I said. "Except for the smell of cooking, we seem to be alone." This, however, was not a thought which especially comforted me, caught as I was between going on to *face the music,* as he had said, and lingering in the passageway under his fetid and all too vafrous wing.

"The fact is," he said, "Teddy got his request for transfer *quashed.*" He licked his lips as if quashing were just the recipe for transfers. "No more guys gettin off before winter."

"Well, I'm sticking it through out there," I said. "As for Teddy's request to go to the lightship, I don't see what the hell business it is of yours anymore."

"The fact is," he said. "In here we've got a public relations function." Releasing me, he tiptoed down the passageway. Near the end he began mugging and pointing.

I approached. On tiptoe.

"*This is why your notes out there have taken on such serious proportions,*" he whispered.

"*Who is it?*" I said. "*The public relation?*"

"*Shhhh.*" More pointing. Extravagant mugging employing a malleable face. "*Bereaved.*"

"*The Overdue Widow?*"

Nods. A tug and a presentation:

The profile of a woman I might well have taken for Blump himself in drag had he not had hold of my collar. She was sitting at the bare mess table as if waiting for someone to clatter out the plates. On her head was a hat such as women used to wear to church, and her housedress might well have served as wallpaper in some peeling flat from which the heat had been denied in winter. It was, after its fashion, however, a *coherent uniform.* "She's been in here every day for a week waiting for her Overdue to wash up, or at least some word."

"What does she hope for if you do find his body?"

"She'll have to wait seven years otherwise. Insurance regulations."

"That doesn't seem fair."

"What's not fair, friend, is the finding of all those notes."

Blump handed me on to Yeoman Peal. As the secretary of the station he was the only man in dark blue uniform, and his black skin added to the dignity of the occasion. The last I had seen him he had been on the beach out front burning the blankets of the blackwater fever victim from the merchant ship. His eyes now looked no less *sepulchral*, as Chanty's poems would say. I wondered if I should allude to those works, for on days when I'd been in the station to have Yeoman Peal process my compensatory liberty papers Chanty had always been the binding joke between us. Afterall, I had Chanty's famous old billet and Peal was rumored to be the only other black man in the Group, possibly even the District. As the station crew conceived matters then, Chanty had split in two, leaving his job on the lighthouse to me and his skin to Peal, obviously to them a mismatch of body and vocation.

"Well," I said, "here I am again, your friendly old lighthouse keeper."

"And here am I," he said, "your friendly old yeoman."

That of course, was not quite how the joke went, but usually we had Luntsky or Farilla to help by making crude references to Chanty. I had, naturally, assumed that Peal and I had understood each other on the precise value of Chanty in the modern maritime world, that, in fact, it had been to celebrate this preservation of Chantyism that our little exchanges took place, meetings that to observers seemed designed merely to process my compensatory liberty papers. Nevertheless, now that the new CO was said to be thinking along Luntskyesque lines, now that there was a possibility that the lifeboat station office would be occupied by a white man and the lighthouse once again by a black, I was no longer able to meet Peal's eyes with the same old confidence. It was not the Luntsky logic that had seduced me, but there was no question that the rhetoric of the sun-warmed and stable streets of Greenmeal through which we'd just passed had done the work in betraying us.

Yeoman Peal nevertheless was talking to me, granted his *sotto voce* was more the convention of the mortician than that of the intimate sharer of essences, but there was the bereaved woman in the outer room. There was the matter of her husband's demise. The tragedy was, appropriately enough, the subject of my friend's murmuring. Something about the beach patrol. Of course yeomen, even in small lifeboat stations, did not usually go on beach patrol, but in this case the widow's pressure had necessitated certain exigencies. . . . In the fog, at the curl of a cuspid inlet, Yeoman Peal had found an upright jacket filled and pulsing with tidal sand. He had, in his solitude, been reluctant to approach. The jacket's lack of a head had not put him at ease, for he imagined the victim's skull was merely lolling on its stalk down hill.

"Now it's just a funny story," he intoned humorlessly, "but you should be out there all alone in the cold fog looking for a——"

"Body?" I offered.

"Yes," he said, "exactly. A body."

THE NOTE
IN THE BOTTLE

The tower leaned farther from the vertical and trembled; it seemed to slump on one side, the deck of the lantern sloping sharply. The light, the lens and the actuating clockwork were now out of commission.

—John J. Floherty, *Sentries of the Sea*

I T WAS INDEED the same Mr. Milkins who had so recently declared lighthouse personnel nonapplicable to the shorebound life, a fact I kept repeating to myself. Slouched behind his desk, he looked as if he'd washed ashore for the benefit of Yeoman Peal's beach patrol.

"Yes, son, come right in."

And it was a cheery room, for all the funereal gloom in the passageway, lots of white and blue paint, a small, dark-red rug under the light-blond pine desk. The desk itself held further testimonies to life, an array of gilded dime-store frames which, half-cocked for both visitor and occupant, revealed not daughters with tinted cheeks or even fluffy cats, but waterfowl. Nor were these birds, for all their desperate deaths, a display of morbidness, so cheerfully had the spreading fingers of their slayer fluttered life among the faltered pinions of their flight.

"Coots," explained Mr. Milkins. "Photographs of coots."

"Yessir," I said, "photographs."

"I get these coots by means of a system of decoyment in which I employ a common household trick." He leaned back farther in his chair, taxing the spring to its fullest and sighed. "Though not any more, I'm afraid. Not since they dragged me ashore in the middle of all these sand dunes; damn sand dunes." Leaning forward, he cupped a hand to confide. "I got every one of those coot, every one of those damn coot at sea." He winked. "At dusk." Having unburdened himself of this classified aspect of the affair, he allowed himself to lean back once again and expand upon the lyrical angle: "They stretch," he said, "long and low over the waves far out on the bay." Sensing he had perhaps gone too far, he coughed and rapped the desk. "The point being, of course, that no other right-thinking hunter would be out that far that time of year."

"They could well end up an Overdue," I said.

"And so you see there are some advantages to being stationed aboard a buoy tender." He looked about him, frowned, and added, "That is, if you are still stationed aboard . . . a buoy tender."

"Yessir," I said. "You told me last fall. When you came aboard our station, Sir. And I served you coffee, that is *tea*. That was, as you'd say Sir, *at dusk*."

He pursed his lips and looked me up and down. I clawed at my wool watch cap, hoping the gesture could be taken for anything from a salute to a doffing. He continued to stare, and I realized that I had never seen him with his own hat off before. His hair was sandy and thin. "It was cold this morning, sir, cold on the boat coming in, so I wore my watch cap."

"Yes, yes, of course," said Mr. Milkins. "*Wool*." And he shivered, more for the wool than the cold, for wool worn at dawn can attract dew and what we all know about wet wool would fill any man's trembling.

"I have, of course, a baseball-style cap in my locker out aboard the lighthouse, Sir."

"Oh, you play, do you?" said Mr. Milkins who was coming out of his woolies. "Maybe we should get you transferred in. I'm looking for a shortstop come spring. Are you a shortstop?" He licked his lips. "I'm a firm believer in getting your sport one way or another. What psychologists called *deferred payments*. If we can't bang a few coot at dusk anymore, well, sure as hell we'll get a few whacks in here. I'm going to launch this program as soon as we get on firmer ground." He waved a ruler out the window. "Right out there. A home run is into the sea. Either that or it's an out. I haven't decided yet. Haven't looked up the price of balls. Haven't for that matter tested the batters. You say you are a shortstop?"

I wondered where the yeoman position had gone to in all this. Perhaps I could be brought in without having to replace Peal. Perhaps it would be Luntsky who would go to the lighthouse and Peal and I could frisk ashore as keystone kids. "I suppose, sir, I could play short, but I must admit my usual position is outfield or first base."

"Ah, well we've got a load of outfielders who can play the primary bag. What we need is someone who can dig those soft, sandy grounders out of the sand and wing them accurately without a lot of sand spinning off of them." Mr. Milkins blinked his sand-spattered, first-baseman's eyes.

"I could *try* shortstop."

Visions of soft, sandy summer days, the pudding whack of the ball in the forearms, running back for towering drives hit toward the curling edge of the sea . . .

"A-hem," said Mr. Milkins, "Unfortunately I do have one additional matter here *written down.*" He adjusted his head and the paper until, presumably, they came into mutual focus. "This matter of——" He was looking at me as if he had never seen me before. "Now you are the one from——?"

"From the Harbor of Refuge, Sir." Cap now in hand, I felt like a temporarily reformed rummy selling pot-holders door to door. "That is the lighthouse, Sir." I poked a finger over my shoulder to indicate where I had last left that worthwhile institution.

Mr. Milkins, however, was going through, if such a phrase could describe anything Mr. Milkins did, *going through* a thick stack of papers. It was coming to me now with a growing sharpness. They were right. Okrastone, Luntsky, even Blump. I had, as they alleged, *written.* It had not merely been a dithyramb upon the balcony, but something actually said to someone else. In fairness, though, I thought, it had been said at night, and the night, especially when encountered alone and most especially at sea, should have its licensed moments.

But here was a house full of sunshine, and Okrastone, Luntsky, Farilla, Creel, Blump, Cooper, Peal, and now Mr. Milkins and a whole roster of hypothetical baseball players, God knew, a *league* all ready to play games in full daylight. What had such a world to do with a loner in desolate hours writing humped over already-folded sheets, mumbling, encoding baroque jokes to be forced down the necks of bottles, sealed and slipped into the dark void? Hadn't my mother warned me that men sometimes did awful things in bottles in alleys? *Twisted* things? But what better man to have sitting in judgment than the former skipper of the *Herb,* he who for so many years had run the string of towers, he who had seen the sun go down and the solitary lights come on, he who had himself flipped, God knew, how many bleach bottles into the cooty waters.

The papers he had, however, did not seem sufficiently maimed to have been mine.

"You know what these are?" he said.

"Those?" Had my scribbling somehow been transcribed for this meeting? Would it go against me if I denied that the words were mine merely because the setting for them had been wrung out, so to speak? "Not those particular sheets of paper, sir. No, sir."

He waved one in my face.

"An ice report, Sir?"

"Negative, son. These are *beach reports.*"

"I'm not familiar with beach duty, Sir, though Yeoman Peal and Seaman Luntsky have indicated to me that I am responsible for certain discrepancies in their recent investigations regarding the current bereaved and her Overdue." I caught my breath while he blinked. "For which I am sorry, Sir."

"We don't expect you to be familiar with beach patrols," he said, for the first time a slight tone of annoyance in his voice. "You are *strictly* lighthouse. Lighthouse Personnel. Not concerned with the overdue and presumed lost or drowned. Our boys out there in the fog and rain, day and night are the ones properly concerned. Even my own Yeoman, Yeoman Peal, has been pressed into this business. A most unusual ah——"

"Yes, Sir. He told me he was startled by some of the things he saw."

"It's hard to find good, competent yeomen," said Mr. Milkins. "Yeoman Peal is a good, competent yeoman."

"Yessir," I said. "But I believe what got to him, that is upset him was, sir, an optical illusion, not a piece of my writing. It was I believe, Sir——"

"Yeoman Peal perhaps more than any single sailor here is highly susceptible to ah, *writing*." Mr. Milkins moved the papers away from him. "A susceptibility, incidently, especially dangerous if one is to practice seriously the yeoman rating."

"He saw a jacket filled with sand, Sir. Sand and water so that it looked like a body in the tidal wash."

"You see that woman in the mess room?"

"The bereaved?"

"Did she look to you like a jacket filled with *tidal wash?*"

"Ah, no, Sir. That was not the image."

"I'll tell you what the image is, son. It's a poor public-relations image, a damn poor-public relations image, that's what it is."

He flung open his desk drawer. There was a rippling and popping of papers, not reports these, but little crumbled papers that had resisted smoothings—torn and sometime soggy papers that leapt out and attacked Mr. Milkins's wrists, forearms, knees—apparently, by his actions, even his ankles and toes. "Look at them," he cried. "What kind of an image?"

"A very messy one, Sir, and I know what they are and take full responsibility."

"We lost a cutter in World War Two just like this." He was grabbing at them as they made for the floor. "Damn kid's love letters got jammed in the handy billies. Damage Control was helpless. Water just kept rising. Bulkheads panting. Young lives lost when the Rottmer Releasing gear mal-functioned . . ." He disappeared for a moment behind his desk. "Fortunately," he said, surfacing red-faced and short of breath, "Fortunately, I believe we've managed to corner most of them, corner most of the damn things." He set his newest catch upon what was already heaped upon his blotter.

"I'm sorry, Sir. I had no idea I had drunk that much apple juice."

"Drunk?" He pulled his lips down across his teeth. "That's hardly an excuse."

"Not drunk, Sir. I never drink on duty. It was apple juice because of the water in the tanks."

"There's one under your foot, son," he said. "I could see it from the deck when I was down there. One had slipped out from under my command and gotten under your own personal foot."

I bent and picked it up:

H e l p !!!

I   am   a   prisoner

on   a

Chinese   Lighthouse

"Ah, this, Sir, was, er . . . just a joke." I held up the limp paper upon which the joke was written. He beckoned me to deliver it. I laid it down before him. He let his fingers dance upon the air a moment, drying them perhaps, before he had them glide down to their smoothing duties.

"Chinese?" he said looking up. "Why *Chinese?* Most of these—" he indicated the pile—"most of these are content to merely state the truth. Ah, that is the *fact*. The fact that your are stationed on an American lighthouse. The, ah——"

"Harbor of Refuge Lighthouse."

"Right, so what's this *Chinese* business?"

It was strange to be tried against the orthodoxy of my earlier heresies, so I stood there a moment, wool cap in hand.

"May we assume then, son, that it was, this one was, a joke?"

"Yessir. They *all* were jokes. I had these apple-juice bottles, you see, Sir, and——"

"You keep bringing up this business of having to drink apple juice."

"Yessir, instead of the water from the tanks. No offense, Sir, as the skipper—former skipper—of the tender which serviced our tanks, but the tanks themselves, not your water, Sir, that is, the water you and your men delivered, the *tanks*, the tanks that were already there when you came, they were full of gulls."

"You maintained gulls inside your water casks?"

"No Sir, they died in there."

"Why were you trying to, attempting to keep gulls in your casks? That's no place to house a bird, son."

"They weren't pets, Sir. They just flew in when the cellar doors were open. They got way up in the beams. That's a good, two-story cellar Sir, and they somehow got in under the hatch on the top of the tank and they couldn't get out."

He was standing by the window looking out at the fish factory. "You realize, of course, that you are charged with the monthly task, monthly, I believe it is, of cleaning your casks? The *Comptroller's Manual* is quite specific on the matter. Either that or it's the *Aids to Navigation Manual*."

"I don't recall that, Sir. It would mean *draining* them monthly, wouldn't it? And then hoping that the buoy tender could make it on time to resupply us."

"I don't recall us being more than a day late and then only so because of adverse conditions."

"Sir, I'm not blaming the *Herb*."

"First of all, son, it's not *the*, not *the Herb*. It's proper phras'ology to say '*Herb*.' 'Aboard *Herb*.'"

"Yessir, I, in fact enjoy visits from . . . *Herb*."

"You put a *the* in front of the name of a vessel and you know what you accomplish?"

"No, sir."

"You make it cute."

"Yessir."

"No vessel in the Coast Guard is cute."

"Yes, Sir. The, that is, *Herb* is well over a month late."

"Change of command may be responsible for that one, but I assure you there is nothing cute involved."

"I do recall Fireman Toy attempting to curtail the gulls by means of a crab net waved aloft," I said. "Of course that was when they were yet alive."

"Probably drove them, *herded* them right into the *hatches of the casks*."

"In any case, the jokes, Sir, the notes."

"What is it now? You want them back?"

"I would like to clear the matter up, Sir."

"Very well." He strode to the desk. "You say these are mere jokes. Try this one."

The paper he thrust into my hand had something to do with a crack in the base of the tower. I felt a chill come over me.

"And this one?" He placed another item about the crack. *Crack Reports*, they were called. He had others. One after another.

"Now," he said. "You tell me these items are not bad public relations."

"Well, you're right about these, Sir. They are not jokes, and they are, as you say, Sir, a poor way to handle the matter, but they are, Sir, the truth."

"The implication is that this disorder is fundamental, that it is, furthermore, *spreading*."

"Yessir. I measure it every day. I record my finding. I don't always send a note on it. In fact, very few times do I send a note on it."

"You measure the crack?"

"Yessir."

"Does your officer-in-charge, is he aware you are spending your time in this manner?"

"I'm under that impression, Sir."

"I see." He looked out the front window. The place was surrounded by dunes and snow fences. The lighthouse was out there somewhere. "I've spoken to your, to him, about these, these 'notes.' "

"Yessir. He told me."

"And you still persisted?"

"No, Sir. It's just that some of them take a while to . . . drift in."

"You mean there's to be more of them?" He faced me.

"I didn't count them, Sir."

"Yeoman Peal has them catalogued."

"Yessir. At this end he may."

"But you *have* stopped?"

"I've stopped putting notes in bottles, Sir. I haven't stopped recording what I find."

"Do you feel it is the duty of a mere seaman to *record?*"

"I hadn't thought of it, Sir, as anything to do with *duty* one way or another. You see, I think of the lighthouse, with all due respect, as where I happen to live."

"Well, you happen to live there because the Coast Guard allows you to live there."

"I am aware of that, Sir. For most men it is unpleasant duty."

"Son, there's is nothing to be ashamed of in working on a lighthouse. In the old days maybe when many of the keepers were, frankly, *defectives,* maybe yes. But not in the modern Coast Guard."

"The odd thing is, Sir, those old men had to deal with much more complex equipment: clock-drive lantern chariots that had to be timed and rewound on the mid-watch, coal furnaces that needed stoking, bell strikers, whale-oil lamps and wick trimming."

"Precisely my point. Now we have the modern Coast Guard. More to the point, we'll soon have a fully automated system of lights, even the isolated offshore ones like . . ."

"The Harbor of Refuge."

"Just before I left *Herb* we got a long-range report from Base Gloucester recommending that very station go on automatic with all due haste."

"Then that explains the crack."

"Not at all. We don't want a facility falling into the water with or without manned conditions."

"That's good to hear, Sir."

"You see the fact is, son . . ." he leaned forward and I drooped the better to catch his words, "Put that baby on automatic and we can watch her right from this room. Any trouble—horn off, light flickering, anything at all—we just pop a boat out of here with a team of trained troubleshooters."

"Then that means there is or will be a report on that crack?"

"Well, now son, you've got to realize that's the Engineering Department's job, not mine or for that matter, frankly, yours. In any case they won't be working on it before spring. I mean, let's face it, son." He rapped hard on the window. "You can't expect men to go out there, go out on an exposed position like that and try to accomplish anything in the winter."

"Ah——"

"Not that we haven't accomplished a great deal this afternoon, right here, son." He turned his back on the window and like a matador strode away, leaving the sea to paw frustratedly there where it stood.

"Yessir."

"Time for each man to get back on his own horse."

"Yessir."

"Get out there and scour those casks." He stood up.

"Yessir."

"And son . . ."

"Sir?"

"While you're at it, work on digging out those shortstop grounders."

On the way out I did get to tip my watch cap to the Bereaved, though her lewd smile was not quite what I expected.

THE BELLE OF THE BAY

Another sharp crack echoed as the tower lurched dangerously. Knowing there was nothing he could do now to maintain a light and that the tower might be carried away at any moment the assistant hurried down the long winding stairs. When he had reached the bottom he waded through several feet of water toward the kitchen.

—John J. Floherty, *Sentries of the Sea*

OF COURSE when I left Mr. Milkins's office I did not step immediately into a waiting gondola bound out for the lighthouse. Yeoman Peal informed me that there would be "a considerable wait." I could not, being yet officially on lighthouse duty, go into town either.

"We could find you a bucket of warm water and you could squeegee the baseboards," he said. "At least that way they wouldn't give you anything worse to do and you could work in the day room with the TV on. Just as long as you didn't actually sit down and watch it, but kind of, you know, let it go on over your shoulder. Some of those quiz shows are pretty educational."

"Hey, I could use a mess cook to help with this big noon meal, which, if you play your cards right, you may get to eat, too," said Blump. "By the way . . ." His cheeks began to work in and out. "How did you . . . *make out with the old man?*"

"O.K.," I said. "By the way, Blump, did you ever try to do anything about the crack in the base of the tower?"

"Crack?" his eyes shifted toward the window, but ran back before they actually went out over the dunes to the sea. "Hey, why do you think this sailor's in here serving warm meals?" With a pudgy bow he danced off stage.

"Pretty good," said Peal. "That's one way of getting rid of him. Just the same we have to find some work for you until the pickup comes to take you down to Boathaven."

"I was noticing those blue volumnes you have over there," I said. "United States Lighthouse Service Reports. I wonder if there is anything in there about the Harbor Refuge. I have a lurid account in a book about its having fallen over once."

"With the guys in it?"

"Yeah, they were in it," I said.

"Jesus," said Peal and he ran his hand along the spines of the blue books.

"How about letting me at those?" I said. "I could work in here and well, make it look like work."

Peal's eyes checked out the room. "We do have the chief's desk. He's home today because his little girl's sick, though he'll probably stop by in midafternoon."

"My boat should be ready by then."

"They'll be coming up from Boathaven for the noon meal, and you will be going back with them afterwards."

"O.K.," I said, "then I'd better get humping. There are a lot of books." I was already at the bindings.

"Oh, by the way, if you want Lighthouse Service stuff, you want these red ones," said Peal, and he dumped some on the chief's desk. "Those you got are Life Saving Service, shore stations like this damn thing."

The red volumes were slimmer and more scuffed than the blue ones. The bindings were weak in some cases, and the old foxed pages drifted out from their moorings. The fact that my hands were shaking did not help.

The first mention of the Light I found was in the 1901 Report of the Light-House Board:

Harbor of refuge, Delaware Bay, Delaware.—The act approved June 6, 1900, appropriated $30,000 for the erection of a light-house and fog-signal on the new breakwater. Plans and specifications for the structures are being prepared pending the completion of the breakwater.

There were two items listed under 1902. The first seemed reasonable enough until one computed the "average settlement" across the remaining fifty some years:

Harbor of Refuge Light, Delaware Bay, Delaware.—A line of bench marks or points of observation were established on top of the breakwater on March 4, 1902, preparatory to observing its settlement. On June 21 a line of check levels was run over these bench marks, which showed that there had been since March 4 an average settlement of the breakwater at the proposed building site of about 1½ inches. Preparations were begun for making an alternative design for the new light-house.

"Alternate design," indeed! On a blank bill of lading I figured that if the breakwater had continued to settle at that rate it would have by now gone down nine feet. And that without any building on it! The second item was the first record of any kind of light being actually mounted out there:

484. Harbor of Refuge Temporary Beacon, South End, Delaware Bay, Delaware.—A frame tower 30 feet high was erected near the southerly end of the breakwater, a 5-day lens lantern was mounted upon it, and the light was exhibited for the first time about January 1, 1902. Various repairs were made.

"Various repairs." Now what in hell did that mean?

The following year introduced the bell, which Toy and Rory had spoken of, and the foundations I had sat upon many a day:

501. Harbor of Refuge temporary beacon, south end, Delaware Bay, Delaware.—A wharf with boat-hoisting apparatus and a temporary fog-signal house and dwelling were built. A 700-pound bell was mounted, an old striking machine installed, and the signal was put into service on May 25, 1903. A new striking machine was purchased, and arrangements were made for casting a 2,000-pound bell. A railing was placed on the platform of the temporary light tower.

The next volume was out of order in the stack that Peal handed me, and it took me a few moments to fumble it free. So far so good. There was the breakwater. There was a light. There *was* a magnificent bell. The tower which I lived in, the tower which I could just see out over the dunes behind me, had not yet been built, but that was obviously to come. These things did not happen overnight. Temporary structures had to be erected in preliminary stages. Ah, here was 1904.

"You know I always wanted to go to sea," said Peal.

"What?"

"Sure, that's why I joined the Coast Guard. I wanted to learn to navigate. I want to take my own boat around the world when I get out."

I looked at his face, trying to regain my concentration on the book in my hand.

"Of course it would be a small boat," he said.

The 1904 entry on page 66 was a fat one, and my eye skidded across the small type three or four times before I could hold it. Then certain phrases jumped out, and I had trouble holding them down onto the page so I could follow the rest of the story. That is, if it were a *story*. The language of John J. Floherty was one thing, the language of reports another. I tried to imagine the clerk who wrote up this particular item. Had he merely composed from the various reports sent to him without any thought of what was coming out? There among items telling of the topographic survey and the bank sluice at Mispillion Creek, the fate of the iron lantern on the Mahon River station (its parts were properly marked, boxed and stored at the Edgemoor lighthouse depot), was:

501. Harbor of Refuge, entrance to Delaware Bay, Delaware.—The severe storm beginning on September 16, 1903, during which the wind was reported to have attained a velocity of 85 miles an hour, carried away the temporary frame light-tower, and washed from the wharf into the harbor a 2,000-pound fog-bell and a fog-bell striking machine which had recently been landed, and did much other minor damage. A diver was employed to search for the lost bell and striking machine, but failed to find either. The settlement of the breakwater at the site of the wharf caused by this storm was about 2 inches. A light galvanized steel tower was erected in the place of the lost wooden one, and new lens lanterns, lamps, etc., were furnished. A striking machine was purchased, a 2,000-pound fog-bell cast, a mounting design constructed, and the apparatus was installed on May 15, 1904, in place of the bell and old striking machine. Various repairs were made. An appropriation of $30,000 was made by the act approved on June 6, 1900, for completing this work. The preparation of a design and specifications for the proposed new brick light-house is in progress. Lines of check levels run over the bench marks established on top of the new breakwater showed that the settlement during the year averaged from nothing at the northerly end to about 5 inches at the southerly end, where the proposed new light-house is to be built.

The estimate of the cost of this work was made some six years ago. Since then there has been a large increase in the prices of labor and material. The experience of three years since the completion of the breakwater has proved that the site for this structure, which is at the exposed end of the breakwater, is an extremely dangerous one and subject to attacks of most violent seas. It is now found that it is impracticable to build a safe and suitable structure here for the sum appropriated. It is estimated that $20,000 more will be needed for this purpose, and the Board therefore recommends that an appropriation of this amount be made therefor.

"The only reason I got stuck in this office is because I'd made the mistake of going to a business college for two years. That constitutes an incredible education for an enlisted man in the Coast Guard. If they'd thought I was just another dumb nigger I could have at least been sent to sea where I could strike for quartermaster and learn navigation."

"Yes," I said fumbling a page. "Navigation."

I looked out the window, but could not hold my gaze: "carried away the . . . frame . . . washed from the wharf. . . ." so those were not the bell foundations I had sat upon. It had never been set up, but merely set upon the wharf. "A diver was employed to search for the lost bell and striking machine . . ." there in the old hard-hat diving days, feeling his way in 1904 down in the dark Delaware for the lost bell. Would not the underwater undulations lead to the bell? "Lost bell and striking machine." Did that mean there was no horn, then? And what precisely was a *striking machine*? Was it something other than a simple pendant knocker? Perhaps Yeoman Peal would know, Yeoman Peal who had known of lolling skulls below the tide, "but failed to find either."

"Say Peal," I said, "would a *striking machine* make a groovy sound or just a, you know, *machine* sound?"

"In college everyone thought I should be a musician."

"A musician!" I said and I waved the book. "Not music, Peal, the *sea*."

"Well, I did apprentice myself to a piano tuner to pay my way through school, but I had no rhythm, just an ear."

In my distraction I must have looked at him in what he took to be a literal manner, for he put both hands up to his lobes.

"Oh, yes," I said, "*ear*." But I was already back in the book, or rather the lighthouse.

Yet there was this, too: a striking machine was purchased, another bell cast, a mounting constructed, "and the apparatus was installed on May 15,

1904, in place of the bell and old striking machine." The bell is dead, long live the bell.

On the other hand, "The settlement of the breakwater at the site of the wharf caused by this storm was about 2 inches." Two inches in one storm!

As for that business about "extremely dangerous" and "subject to attacks of most violent seas," pure John J. Floherty. Was our clerk drunk? Or at least Irish? Did he that evening ride the trolley home with bells clanging subaqueously in his head and visions of most violent seas? And when he sat down to the table among his wife and children, did he tell them it was impractical to build a safe and suitable structure for the money appropriated?

The door to the CO's office opened, and Mr. Milkins emerged with several papers in his hand. He began to put them on the desk. "Oh, you're not the chief," he said.

"I told him he could use that desk until the chief got back," said Yeoman Peal.

Mr. Milkins let his pale-blue eyes fall upon the stack of Lighthouse Service reports. "Well, I'm always glad to see a sailor working on his education," he said. "You know, if you finish that course you're taking there, you probably will be able to be transferred off that rock pile."

Yeoman Peal simply took the papers from Mr. Milkins's hand, and the officer subsided back within his office.

The next three entries were less dramatic, but they did contain the first hints of what the structure that I lived on was to be made of:

Harbor of Refuge, Delaware Bay, Delaware.—Detailed drawings and specifications were prepared for a design of a concrete block and iron shell substructure. A design for a frame superstructure suitable for the above-mentioned substructure is nearly completed.

                                                                         1905

Harbor of Refuge, Delaware Bay, Delaware.—Plans are being made for the superstructure of the proposed light-house. An additional appropriation of $20,000 for the establishment of this light was made by the act approved on June 30, 1906.

                                                                         1906

514. Harbor of Refuge, Delaware Bay, Delaware.—Contract was made for furnishing the metal work for the substructure of the proposed light-house. The contractors began work in December, 1906, and practically completed it in May, 1907. In June, 1907, it was delivered upon the iron pier at Lewes, Del. Contract was made for constructing the concrete foundation of the proposed light-house. In June, 1907, the contractor commenced the work of excavating in the top of the breakwater. The War Department made no objection to the building of the light-house on the breakwater.

                                                                         1907

The business about the War Department was odd, since the year was what I had always considered a rather peaceful moment. There had been nothing before about a war department and the Lighthouse Service did not seem to be allied with such an organization or any other back of the 1907 book.

"Mere bureaucracy," said Peal when I showed him.

Harbor of Refuge, Delaware Bay.—Amount authorized, act April 30, 1900, $30,000; amount appropriated, act June 6, 1900, $30,000; limit of cost increased, act June 20, 1906, $50,000; amount appropriated, act June 30, 1906, $20,000. The foundation of this light-house was erected under separate contract from the superstructure and completed in October, 1907, at a cost of about $16,500. A contract for the erection of the superstructure was made in the sum of $14,800. In November, 1907, all the metal work was erected, and work was then discontinued until May 1, 1908, since which date about 40 per cent of the frame superstructure has been completed, including walls, cornices, tinning of balconies, stairways, concrete partitions, and lantern.

The 1908 report seemed straightforward enough, unless one read in between the lines about the work being discontinued between November and May. Perhaps the writer was becoming more used to the perils of the Harbor Refuge paragraphs, or maybe he had been reprimanded for his former indulgences. In any case, I liked the business of the cornices and stairways and especially the "tinning of the balconies." Behind me, rising from the sea in my mind, was a structure upon which someone could now live:

But as I read on it was not the building in which I actually did live:

Harbor of Refuge light-station, Delaware.—On November 20, 1908, a fourth-order, incandescent oil-vapor light, illuminating the entire horizon, and flashing white every 12 seconds, was established in the white, hexagonal, three-story frame structure, with lead-colored trimmings, resting on a brown cylindrical iron foundation, located on the southerly end of the Harbor of Refuge Breakwater, southwesterly side of the entrance to Delaware Bay. The foundation of this lighthouse, completed in 1907, consists of a concrete block 40 feet in diameter and 15 feet 6 inches high, resting upon the enrockment of the breakwater. The superstructure consists of a center column of iron, a basement 32 feet in diameter of two courses of iron plates, and an hexagonal frame superstructure from the basement to the lantern. The fog-signal is a first-class siren operated by compressed air.

The cheeriness of the writer's prose could not ease my fear. Afterall, this "hexagonal, three-story frame structure," was not at all the cylindrical, four-story iron tower in which I dwelt. And there to confirm the horror was a photograph on the next page of a dozen workmen in suspenders, derbies, top hats, and even boaters standing proudly on the lower balcony. Rising behind them was indeed a wooden structure complete with clapboards, squared-off corners, and a grand Greek Revival entranceway with fluted pilasters.

"The belle of the bay," I sighed. "There she is."

"What?" said Peal, "a steamboat? An old sidewheeler?"

I couldn't take my eyes off her. The lower balcony rail was a solid bulwark with scuppers running all around, but the two upper galleries sported rails of white wood which would make a veranda in Natchez jealous. The windows in the smaller top deck had elegant fan lights. I found myself thrashing at the venetian blinds.

"What's the matter?" said Yeoman Peal.

"Look at this." I extended the book, keeping my eyes between the slats, my eyes watering as I tried to pick out details on the white column beyond the dunes.

"Pretty interesting, eh?" said Peal. "You care for antiques?"

"Fuck antiques. Look at it. Now look out here."

"Time passes," said Peal. "Things change."

"Damn it, Peal," I said. "Don't you see it?" I waved the book at the window. "That tower fell down."

With index finger and thumb Peal poked open the slats. "There's quite a glare off the sea today."

"It fell down after they had built it specially not to fall down. After they had spent the extra sum. Here, these guys." I jabbed the workmen. "Look at em, Peal. Don't they look damn proud to have made that thing?"

"Maybe they were drunk."

"May be, but look at the woodwork. Damn fine stuff, eh? And then up there so high above the sea."

"Of course workmen dressed differently in those days. I mean everybody did."

"Peal, the craftsmanship was *better* and the tower fell down."

"Well, maybe the craftsmanship was better, but the technology certainly wasn't. Besides, where does it say it fell down?"

"It doesn't. Not yet. But I know it did, and that's what I've got to find."

"Well, you'd better hurry up," said Peal, "because Blump's going to be serving the noon meal soon, and the men will be coming from Boathaven to take you back out there, and these books can't leave the room."

"Jesus," I said, "I feel like a condemned man."

"Don't get so excited. I told you, the technology is better."

"Sure, like the even newer technology which built that Air Force tower just a little further out there. Old Shakey that fell over only a few years ago."

"Ah, the Air Force is full of shit. What do they know about sea towers?"

"More than they *did*," I said.

"Well, these books can't leave the room, so you'd better hurry."

"Say, son." The office door had opened behind me. "You won't get an education by looking out the window."

"Yessir," I said and sat down. "Just stretching, Sir."

"And you won't get an education by stretching, either." This time he picked up one of the books. "Nineteen-ten? Son, this material is woefully out of date."

CONTINUED INROADS
OF THE SEA

The rising water had put out the fire in the stove; the place was filled with the smell of steam and pungent gas. Water was coming in at half a dozen places, chairs and tables were afloat amid patches of slimy sea grass; the keeper's favorite corn cob pipe bobbed against the stovepipe.

—John J. Floherty, *Sentries of the Sea*

Fourth District

Harbor of Refuge, Delaware.—The act of June 6, 1900, appropriated $30,000 for establishing a light and fog-signal on the new breakwater, Harbor of Refuge, Delaware Bay. The act of June 30, 1906, appropriated an additional $20,000, authorized by the act of June 20, 1906. The light was reported in the Annual Report of the Light-House Board for the year 1909 (p. 19) as having been placed in operation. The fog-signal, a first-class compressed air siren, which was being installed at the close of that year, was placed in operation on October 4, 1909. The total cost of this project $49,940.84.

S O THERE it was. The first announcement of the Harbor of Refuge Light functioning as an actual lighthouse in which men lived. Under the entry for Harbor of Refuge Light, the *Light List* which I had seen out on the tower had 1901 as the date the station had been first lit, but that obviously referred only to the unmanned temporary structure. It had taken them almost ten years to get a habitable tower out there after the breakwater had been built. The next question was, how long had that wooden neoclassical tower remained safe?

"Boy," said Yeoman Peal, "I can smell that noon dish cooking. It won't be long now."

"Damn it," I said, "I'm only in 1910."

"You know, I enjoyed history in school myself," said Yeoman Peal, "but I do think I enjoy the noon meal more. Even if Blump is cook."

"Yes, well, I've got the first real Harbor Refuge Light right here."

This last item was under the strictly fiscal section of the book. What I had usually been finding the Light under was the part called "Progress of Special Works," a title that had delivered more detail I could visualize. Where, for instance, was the account of that "severe storm" which "seriously damaged" the Harbor of Refuge? I looked again at the small type, "severe

239

storms." Well, then, where was some sort of account of the severe storms? Or at least the serious damage?

The back door to the station slammed.

Shouts.

Insults for the cook.

"Yes," said Yeoman Peal to me, "the Boathaven crew is here."

"Damn."

"Here, let me help you. Exactly what are you looking for?"

Handing him the 1922 volume, I asked him merely to look up anything to do with Harbor of Refuge. I continued to thrash the 1921 volume for those severe storms.

"Here you go," he said and stuck 1922 "Progress of Special Works" under my nose:

FOURTH DISTRICT

Joe Flogger Shoal, Del.—Project completed; for description see page 41.

Aids to navigation, Delaware Bay entrance.—Appropriation, March 28, 1922, $138,000. Preliminary plans and estimates have been prepared and preparations made for active work in the coming fiscal year, at Brandywine Shoal, Harbor of Refuge, and Hen and Chickens Shoal. As appropriation is not available until July 1, 1922, no expenditures could be made.

"That all?"

"All for that year."

"Try next year."

The noise in the passageway outside was louder. Blump was trying to defend his cooking by pointing out its current public-relations function. I gave up the 1921 volume and reaching across Yeoman Peal's tightly buttoned cuff, grabbed 1924.

"Here," said Peal, "Nineteen twenty-three."

Aids to navigation, Delaware Bay entrance.—Appropriation, March 28, 1922, $138,000. Under this appropriation a contract was entered for riprap and breakwater protection to Brandywine Shoal Light Station in the estimated amount of $29,250. The work of transporting and placing stone was in progress at the close of the fiscal year. Detailed plans and estimates were prepared for the rebuilding of Harbor of Refuge Light Station, including the wharf and minor buildings. The date of completion is indefinite at present. Total expenditure to June 30, 1923, $12,302.

"Thanks, Peal." I handed him 1925 while reading 1924. My eyes were still rocketing around in the appropriation figures when Peal began mumbling phrases from what I soon saw was the same entry I was reading, his breath coming over my shoulder.

"Goodness," he was saying, "they had to rebuild it. Something really bad must have happened. Look at this, "continued inroads of the sea . . .

presaging its early destruction . . . should the old structure fall or become so unsafe as to endanger the lives of the keepers. . . ."

"That's Cape Henlopen," I said, "its shifting dune."

There was no getting around the fact that it was a bad neighborhood, however. And there was no getting around the fact that something nearly all consuming had happened to the lovely wooden structure with its palladian windows and Greek Revival door:

Proposals were invited for the construction of metal work for rebuilding Harbor of Refuge Light Station. The work of rebuilding the wharf at this staton is making favorable progress. Materials have been collected for the temporary tower which is to take the place of Harbor of Refuge Light during the rebuilding of the station.

In consequence of the continued inroads of the sea upon the site of Cape Henlopen Light Station, presaging its early destruction, a temporary skeleton steel tower was built at a safe location on the sand hill and fully equipped ready for lighting should the old structure fall or become so unsafe as to endanger the lives of the keepers in continuing to maintain the present light. The total cost of this item was $7,592.56.

Outside the office door it was ominously quiet. Peal cocked his head. Put a finger to his lips. Like the first drops of rain came the tinkling of silverware.

"Damn," said Peal. "Damn-damn. Here, let's each take one more."

In the 1925 volume I found:

Aids to navigation, Delaware Bay entrance.—See Annual Report, 1924, page 33. Appropriation March 28, 1922, $138,000, and allotment $29,600 from appropriation of February 27, 1925. A contract was made for the metal work for Harbor of Refuge Light Station and delivery of a portion of this material has been made. The rebuilding of the wharf was completed, except for such details as have been deferred until the work of erecting the light station can be started. The temporary tower and light which is to take the place of Harbor of Refuge Light during the rebuilding is ready for erection and the cement foundation is prepared to receive it. In consequence of the inroads of the sea, Cape Henlopen Light Station was discontinued on October 1, 1924, on which date the light on the temporary steel tower was substituted.

The fire at Edgemoor Depot, Del., destroyed materials and machinery purchased for work at Harbor of Refuge Station valued at $6,000. An additional appropriation or allotment will be necessary for replacing these. Total expenditure to June 30, 1925, $101,239.23.

The door to the inner office opened and Mr. Milkins stepped out. "The noon meal, gentlemen. The noon meal. Time to put away our work for a well-earned rest and fueling up."

Peal passed me his book. I gave him mine, "Note the fire which delayed," I said.

"Note the continued bad weather which hampered," said Peal.

Aids to navigation, Delaware Bay entrance.—See Annual Reports, 1924, page 33, and 1925, page 27. The metal work for the tower of Harbor of Refuge Light Station was completed and delivered to Edgemoor Depot during the fall of 1925. In the spring of 1926 a temporary light was erected on a skeleton steel tower near the site and the work of tearing down the old structure began. At the close of the fiscal year the concrete filling in base of tower was nearly completed and the lowest course of new structural cast-iron plates had been erected in place. Continued bad weather has hampered the transportation of materials from shore. It is anticipated that the house can be made habitable and the light exhibited on the structure before the coming winter, and the entire work completed in the spring of 1927. Total amount expended to June 30, 1926, $143,194.77.

"Come, come," said Mr. Milkins. "There is a time and place for everything."

All the way out to the Light on the forty-footer I kept staring at the tower as if I'd never seen it before. The icy wind was right in my face. Farilla had even hunkered down in the cutty. Luntsky, who for some reason had been trusted with the boat, was at the wheel, and possibly to cover his nervousness he kept shouting wind-torn phrases in my ear. He was running the boat so fast that the stern had buried enough to put the scuppers below the water, and the long cockpit was awash a few inches deep all the way up past the raised engine box. There was no place dry to stand except up on the cockswain's platform right next to him. I hung onto the grab bar, which had a fancy bit of whipping on it, and tried to catch that precise moment when the tower up ahead would cease being merely a column against the vast blue and become a building you could penetrate, actually live in, a house made habitable before the coming of winter.

"So what did the old man want from you?" said Luntsky.

"He wanted me to play shortstop."

"Fuck you," said Luntsky. "I play shortstop."

It was too late. I had missed the transition, and the building was already over our heads. Farilla peeped out of the cutty as if he expected the tower to fall on his skull. It was clear he'd been asleep. I grabbed the ladder as it sailed past, but before I could get it in both hands, the iron ripped out of my fingers.

The ladder was gone. Where was I?

I was awash alongside the engine box, stretched flat out, so that the water ran past my nose. My fingers ached for the ladder.

There was a clanging over my head and I thought the tower had fallen down. *Ah*, I thought, *the tinning of the balconies is complete.*

It was Farilla throwing open the covers to his diesels. His cursing hardly got through as the engines filled the air. I grabbed the gunnel and pulled myself up. We were not heading straight for the rocks anymore, but planing parallel to the breakwater. Seas were hitting the outside of it and slopping right on over to our side, where they poured as grandly as a waterfall. Aft of us the tower was getting smaller, but at least it yet stood.

We were at a place so far down the breakwater that I had not been there since midsummer, and then only after painful picking through gull droppings and over gaps. I tried to see if I recognized anything, but it all looked merely cold. With a shout Luntsky threw the helm over to port, and we rode up into the curve steeply enough to put me clattering onto the flopping engine hatches. When I looked up we were heading back for the tower. *My God*, I thought, *he's going to ram it*.

The stanchion back of the coxswain platform was still something I could trust. I had both hands around it, but was not yet up there on the wooden platform itself. Luntsky, of course, had never left it. Perhaps his grin was merely a grimace.

The engines cut out, and we sobbed and farted into a great silence, our wake following us and breaking against our stern, nudging us forward.

The lighthouse stood there calmly. No one had even come out onto the balcony, and the gulls were returning to the railing on the landing stage.

The sea continued to pour over the breakwater.

"Fuckin throttle cable," said Farilla. "Fuckinwinter forty boats. I hate 'em."

"Can you fix it, Tony-babe?" said Luntsky, and I suddenly realized he was barely twenty.

"Fuckinwinter," said Farilla. "What do they have it for?"

With our forward motion all but stopped, we now fell into the trough of the sea which, while milder than what was outside the breakwater, still packed a good push, so that the engine-hatch covers, now folded up like drying cormorant wings, began to rattle.

"Hey," said Luntsky, "you want to play shortstop? You can play shortstop."

"Fuck shortstop."

"Fuck winter," said Farilla. "Fuck boats." He turned and shook his pliers at the tower. "Fuck, you, too, you goddamn . . . you goddamn . . ."

"Lighthouse," I said.

"Ah. . . ." He gave it a wave with his tool and dove back into his realm.

"So," said Okrastone, handing me a mug of coffee, "I finally got this ready for you." He took his own cup back around the curve of the tower and eased his Papa Bear body into his office chair. "Sit down. Make yourself at home. This is your home."

I sat down in the big leather chair under the Helocrafter radio, the chair Chanty had so fatally fallen asleep in on watch. "I'm not going to write any more notes and put them in bottles," I said. "It seems to upset the beach patrol."

"Yes," he said, "the beach patrol is an important part of the Coast Guard, Bo. Down in Hatteras we really do a job on er. And that's a real beach, too. Up here, well . . . I'm sure the boys do their best, but——"

"And we discussed the crack in the tower here."

"You *are* going to make me fill out a mess of papers on that damn little ol' *crack,* ain't you?" He stuck a toothpick in his mouth.

"I found out there used to be another tower out here that fell down."

"Temporary spindle, boy. That's all that was."

"Yes, that went down, too. I'm talking about a regular wooden structure men lived in. Just like us. Except more beautiful. The old timers called her the belle of the bay."

"*Wooden* structure? Well there you go, son. Wood ain't no good for the sea. Hell, they don't even build boats out of it anymore. About all wood is good for is to pick your teeth." He demonstrated with the toothpick. "As for bein' beautiful, son, when them old seas get to goin they don't care nothin about beautiful."

"But even an iron structure which was undermined——"

"Undermined? Do you know how far this old girl goes down in the breakwater? Just like a tooth in your gum." He rolled up his cheek. "Roots, son. Roots are what this girl's got and what's going to save us."

An especially heavy wave hit and the coffee slid out of the top of my cup all over my hand.

"You ought to drink your coffee, son, afore you gets to spilling it all over like that."

"He also wants me to play shortstop on his team this spring."

"Hell, boy, if you want to go round in the sand pile playin ball in the daffodiles, that's fine with me."

"It wasn't my idea," I said.

"I'll be glad to write you out a transfer. Snuggle right in there as mess boy in the galley with ol' Mother Blump. Yessir, I hear he's on the look out for an *assistant.*"

"I had enough of him today."

"Hey, I thought you got along with him just fine. All the old happy gang what was out here."

"I wouldn't say Blump was really part of it."

"And that boy Luntsky, a seaman like yourself. I hear he's looking for a job on a lighthouse ever since he had that problem in the fog running an injured man in from a freighter."

"That was him today. Except I don't think it was his fault. Something mechanical."

"Well, word is he'd mutual with you."

Then I remembered something; Blump perturbative among his pots and pans: "Teddy's request for the lightship was quashed."

"I know all about that, my friend." He looked steadily at me. "In fact you might say I was *aware*."

"Oh."

"*Oh*."

I drank some coffee and instantly my stomach felt like the water casks full of gull wings. "Hey, Bo, like you say, this is my home."

He pulled out his tooth pick. It had enjoyed a rather bloody riot among his gums. "Home on the ol Harbor Refuge."

"That's right," I said.

"The belle of the bay, eh?"

"Yup."

I walked around to the north side of the room and looked out the window. Without thinking about it I found my eyes had wandered on up the breakwater to the point where Luntsky had finally gotten control of the boat. Looking down on the spot from a distance, I tried to recall what it had been like being out there only a few minutes before. One moment all that stone had been buried below us in the sea. The next instant it had been rising above us, throwing water and stinking like a breaching whale.

"A real pretty station, too, Bo?" His voice came to me from around the curve of the stairwell, and I realized that, without meaning to, I'd drifted off from him.

"Sure," I said, and I almost charged his desk. "Octagonal, with beautiful Greek reviv——"

"Whoops! Now there you go, boy. You can't be having things goin on like that around the water. Least wise not in these here parts, in this here country." He stared at the tooth pick, puzzled by its damp, red end.

"Well, at least Mr. Milkins did have one encouraging thing to say. He said *Herb* was coming soon, that the delay was only a matter of change-of-command and that they hadn't simply forgotton us. *There's* something to look forward to."

"You know what is even more en-couraging, Bo?" He leaned way back.

"What's that?"

"He done cured you of calling that damn ol' steam snatcher 'tha' *Herb*. A ship don't have no 'tha' in front of her. She's just plain *Sassafras* or just plain *Cherokee* or *Chincoteague* or *Bibb*. 'Tha *Herb*,' Cot dim, but didn't that always sound like some damn thing what ought to be in the tub with you and a *rubber* duck."

PART THREE

Winter

THE FEBRIFUGE
OF REFUGE

Outside and inside were a confusion of noise and water gone mad. Willis held on to
the door jamb to steady himself in the swirls that rushed through after each sea. The
tower went with a deafening roar; the west wall of the kitchen cracked, then opened
to the sea, the ceiling sagged like a slack canopy.

—John J. Floherty, *Sentries of the Sea*

IT CAME down the bay, out of the north, and it came rapidly, unless my
lack of sleep from standing mid-watch had caved in my sense of time. As
it approached in the dawn, almost as if under its own power, it altered
its angle slightly, but still maintained the sharp, classic crescent and the
purple color. From horn to horn it must have been a hundred yards, and
with the binoculars I could read into its deep, soft pile of indigo and madder.
It was the luminous *abrasc*—a Turkish carpet, loomed in the tents out of
richest wools, crafted with the complex yarns of battles between the birds of
appetite and the Tree of Life. Or perhaps I had been unduly influenced by
the passing of a Turkish submarine the day before. In any case, as the carpet
rushed the landing stage, I ran down to meet it. Halfway, as it cocked yet
again upon the tide, I stopped, fearful that some bizzare undulation would
lift the whole design into flight. But the object stayed low in the water, and
as it swept past, what had seemed lush with narrative, now, drained by shifting optic angles of its rich hue, turned out to be merely soggy.

Ice.

I had not been looking for ice. I had not, despite the cold, even been
thinking of ice. What I had been looking for was the lighthouse tender, for
we had not been serviced for over two months, and while our diesel supply
was holding out, the water coming from the brass spigot was spitting forth so
casky that there hardly seemed any point when making tea to add the distant
products of Ceylon when right beneath our feet we had mixings more exotic
than could be provided by the remotest slopes of Pidurutalagala.

Up the bay there was, however, no more ice to be seen, and when I
looked out to the open water, even what I had had was gone. The air didn't
seem that cold, and I couldn't understand why the ice should arrive at all, let
alone isolate itself in that ominous crescent form. As for the color, I could, of

course, charge that up, like so many problems, to sunrise. When, an hour later, Okrastone sat down to his last breakfast before going ashore on his week's leave, I broke the news.

He did not so much as hesitate before putting knife to egg. In fact, he sawed with elbow-flailing vigor. It was only when he had the sopping yolk secure upon his tines that he let the fork pause just outside his open mouth. "Well, Bo, I guess we're just going to have to dig out them ice report forms before I slip away today to the sunny South."

I watched the sunny yolk slip into his face. Not much remained upon his lip. "My God," I said, "I suppose that *was* it, wasn't it."

He blotted his lip with a paper napkin. "That was what, Bo?"

"What all that was about."

"What *what* was all about?" The steam rising from his cup offered him opportunity to be bewildered.

"The warp and weft," I said, "the Turkish carpet. Our future life, our Fate."

"Bo, I wouldn't trust no Turk if I was you." It was hard to know what was trustworthy in his eyes, because as soon as his face left the updraft of the cup, it had the rise off the still-steaming egg. "They use them rugs, you know, for every *kind* of thing."

"What I meant was winter."

"When I'm gone, just fill out them ice reports, boy." He swept up the last of the eggs with his toast and blotted his lips. "Just fill 'em right on out."

"Fine," I said, "and what if *Herb* isn't able to get through the ice to service us? We've already got a moratorium on showers, and as for that tea you're drinking—"

"I think it's all them seagull wings that Toy friend of yours herded into them tanks."

"Yes, well, you'll be pleased to know Mr. Milkins has picked up on your joke about Toy and the seagulls, but maybe you should know he doesn't realize it is a mere jest."

"Well, as you know, Mr. Milkins *is* the CO in to Greenmeal now, so old *Herb*, she got another skipper who maybe is a bit chary of coming all the way down her route. That Mr. Milkins, now, he's your old, odd duck who'd as lief take a tired boat like that and stick her nose out this time of year. Not every man will."

"Great, what are we supposed to do, drink gull-wing tea, crap out the window, and bathe in sea water?"

"You just be patient now. Old *Herb*, she'll know the way by herself."

The next morning snow had fallen.
It was along some parts of the rail, in patches on the balcony deck, in

the corners of the windows, and—the great marvel—down the breakwater, not just gull shit but snow, real snow lying deep but light, so that all the cracks were filled and on the landing stage was a puffy quilt.

Silence.

Teddy was still topside sleeping. When he had come back I had merely waved to him and gone up to bed and then he had gotten me up for my watch and gone to bed himself. With two on the tower, this routine, of course, was usual, but somehow in the warmer months there had always been someone else around, pilot boys, fishermen, porpoises. Now there was just this great silence. Not even the boff and push of the wind against the steel plates and the glass. Not even clouds in the blank blue sky, and the escape ropes hung hard as icicles.

I set the kettle going, even though the water out of the spigot choked forth in fetid flashes. I could not recall a day this still, not even in summer. There seemed to be no wave action at all, not only on the sea front, but below the back door where usually the current at least kicked up a fuss. The shore was white, too, whiter than the usual dirty sand, and I imagined how drift on drift had covered dune upon dune so that Cape Henlopen would now be drifting in this contrapuntal sumptuousness.

It was, of course, cold, and yet I did not feel it. In just my chambray and jeans, I strolled around to the out door thermometer. It was plastered. I rubbed it clear, my index finger leaping with the cold. I sucked it and shook my hand free, the whole while staring at the numbers on the thermometer:

Zero.

Cape May too, was etched in white. The lighthouse, the red-roofed nunnery and the Admiral Hotel, though altered, at least were right side up and still at home. Toy had told me about the grand mirages he had himself seen in which the Admiral Hotel, long boarded up, the nunnery and the automatic Cape May Light had appeared not only inverted but reborn out to sea over where the tide rip ran at a spot called Overfalls. There had been a lightship there in recent times, and it was this one Chanty had seen upside down in endless hallucinations, so that when it was replaced by *Delaware* five times farther out, it was natural for him to think he could, by peering eastward on days like this, see some semblance of her rig thrown up to him from below the curvature of the sea. Such visions made his final transfer homier, he insisted, though it was hard to find how you'd be at ease in a world you'd only known upside down. In any case, it was as likely he had seen her masts, even in refraction, as one could, by mere blinking, dredge up the fallen tower of Henlopen.

The actual, floating ships of the morning were also *placed*. There were some half-dozen freighters and tankers set out with the pilot craft, each hull sharp enough to cut your finger on. Yet their masts and booms, even the rigging, seen up close, must have been not at all lean, but fuzzy with ice and snow, freighted like the trees at home. No doubt the boatswains would have the crew turned to with mallets to knock away the ice. Chanty had stories of 'white elephants,' weather cutters with their antennae cracking, the great bed spring radars loaded tragically, sagging until all navigation was shed and the ships surged on blindly into blind seas.

Much of Chanty, of course, was rhetoric, and yet I wondered if this extraordinary day's visibility would not throw a mirage our way, one in which he himself paraded upon the deck of his *Delaware*—far out at sea, a prancing prince among the mallet swingers of the white woods. I began to dance.

And throw snowballs at gulls.

And drink from sculpture, quaffing the rococo additions to our gallery rails.

When I heard Teddy inside I ran around to throw a snowball at him and slipped, almost sliding under the rail. I sat there, clinging to the stanchion, laughing hysterically.

"Yeah," said Teddy, "I feel real lightheaded, too. It must be all this bad water we been drinkin."

The buoy tender came at three o'clock.

As simple as that. After two months, I looked up, and there it was, right outside the window, where it always was when you first saw it, looming up behind the Wesson Oil and garlic salt. Many times I had thought to have seen it out on the bay, that low-cut hull, the derrick on the foredeck, and the thick coal smoke; but it was either some coastal barge or nothing at all. You never saw it until it was too late, and it was already in your kitchen, catching the tower with its pants down, a hundred discrepancies and the tender's crew already angry at poor docking preparation. And yet, never did their skipper inspect us; never was there anything we could really do to help her moor but have the toggle ready.

Since it was cold and we felt righteously petulant at their long neglect of us, we stayed indoors and, ruminating on a month or more of boiled bat wings, watched them maneuver. There was still no wind, but the tide was running, and, going with it, *down* tide, they made three passes at the dock, each time rushing by with engine reversed. We pressed our noses to the window and jeered at this elementary folly. The skipper stood on the bridge wing and cupped his hands. We pressed pudgy obscene gestures to the glass, assured that he who was so stupid about docking down tide could not see through the glass. He went inside his bridge, however, and the radio crashed behind us.

"Harbor Refuge Light!"

"Oh, oh," said Teddy.

"Damn it," I said, "I knew I shouldn't have washed those windows."

"Harbor Refuge, anybody home? This is *Herb* with your water."

We capered about the cylinder, shouting at the radio.

It crashed again, and we howled. Teddy at last picked up the phone and, in what was a surprisingly effective parody of a TV newscaster, answered.

However, in spite of the fact that Teddy could answer our radio in not only a professional, but outright *commercial* fashion, the buoy tender said that since he could not make our dock, he was going on.

"I'll be back next month, boys."

Teddy's voice broke, "Hey, captain, what is we gonna do for water?"

The skipper said our tanks were ample.

"But you ain't been here in three months."

There was a pause.

"Maybe I should have said *sir*," Teddy said to me.

"Fuck him," I said. "It's his job to get us water."

Teddy asked him if he couldn't make it the next day.

He was sorry, he had to be up the bay.

"What the hell's up the bay?" I said. "We're *down* the bay and we're his job."

The skipper broke in. It was hard to believe he really couldn't hear us unless we chose to admit him with a casual click of our thumb. He wanted to know how much fuel we had. That much we knew exactly, because the tanks could be sounded and, in fact, by regulation had to be measured every week. Not only that, but they really had been checked, and, furthermore, Teddy had the figure on his tongue. It was a low number. This impressed the skipper, and he agreed to try the dock again. Water evidently was a luxury, but oil to pump up the fog compressors was something else.

Teddy suggested the skipper make his next pass into the tide, and I winced at the breach in decorum, and Teddy modified his statement so that it sounded like local knowledge passed on by tradition rather than a basic rule of boat handling announced by an engineman third to a warrant boatswain. I was amazed at how well Teddy was handling it all. I recalled incidents when I'd talked down to him. I now thought of actually buying the power mower.

Again we watched, this time from the slippery balcony, but it was no go. He did come against the tide, but if he slowed at all the current took his bow one way or the other. Our smugness began to wear off; not only was the skipper not so dumb, but he was not going to be able to get us juice. He told us over the radio that he had a malfunction somewhere and was apprehensive about knocking down the pier. We'd heard rumors he had done just that a month earlier at Brandywine, and with no tide; and there was, of course, the last time his more experienced predecessor had visited us and *he'd* even split our piling.

We returned to the balcony and stood looking down at him. He looked up at us from his wing. His cap, unlike Mr. Milkins's, was not summer jaunty, but set grim square for winter. A little low on the ears. Most of the crew was out of sight, but one or two shadowboxed about the derrick to keep warm. The boatswain and a surly third class stood by the gunwale. I did not see the dog.

"My God," said Teddy, "the prick is really going to leave."

I couldn't believe it. There they went. Our heads followed the ship as it steamed out to sea. The skipper had even gone inside. Well, it was cold, and we were back inside.

"I should have thrown that snowball at him," I said.

"Where'd you put it?" said Teddy.

"I suppose he expects us to gather the stuff off the breakwater and melt it. Gather snow and boil all drinking down."

"We just may have to," said Teddy. "We had to eat ducks once."

"And I didn't believe that story," I said.

"*Huh.*" He, pale as he was, had sounded just like Chanty.

We were about to begin preparations for the evening meal. I had the meat out, and Teddy was doing something with lettuce, saying that he felt a little better, that getting pissed off at the skipper had brought his appetite back. I wandered around to the bay side and without much thinking about it, looked out, and without thinking much further began a diatribe against officers, the incompetence of the Coast Guard, et cetera.

"Hell," said Teddy, "he's probably halfway back to Philadelphia and some broad, while here we are playing with our lettuce."

"They ought to make every guy on a buoy tender spend a year on one of these things," I said.

"Well, I had a chance to mutual onto that ship right there last summer, you know." He got a misty look on his face, as if it were still summer aboard *Herb*. We had not yet discussed what had happened to his request to go to the lightship, but I presumed Okrastone, if not Blump, had passed on the news that the transfer had been so deliciously quashed.

"Yeah, I had that offer, too," I said, "some creep up in the sleeping deck."

"Hey, it couldn't have been the same guy as offered me, you know."

"A guy I found sneaking around the sleeping deck," I said. "A real creep."

"See, you and me ain't the same rating. You ain't an engineman, like me."

"I know that," I said, not having thought of such distinctions.

"And I'm a petty officer, too. I'm an E-4. You is only a seaman, an E-3."

"Yes."

"I mean that's why what happened to you about that ship out there and what happened to me can't be the same."

"Right." I opened the refrigerator. It seemed warmer than what had been outside. "If you wanted to make that move, you had a chance this afternoon. Now they has done de-parted into the dying day. And we, friend, are once again alone."

"Don't make me nuthin," he said, "I got a, anyhow, *light* head."

"Christ," I said, "I wouldn't even want to give you chicken soup with our water boiled."

"Chanty had a receipt for this. Somethin his grandma gave him to put to flight the fever, he said. He called it the 'Febrifuge of Refuge.' "

"You mean this happened often? You got the flu or blackwater fever or—" I broke off, not wanting to scare him or for that matter scare myself for I was not feeling well, either. Would Peal end up burning *our* blankets on the beach? "You know if we were ashore we'd have a doctor look at us and he'd say, 'Yes, you've got *what's going around*,' and tell us to take two aspirin and go to bed. As it is, we don't even know if we *are* sick or just kind of giddy on the snow."

"Chanty, he was like a mother to us."

"Maybe there's something in that 1915 *Lighthouse Service Medical Handbook*." I opened the china cabinet and the gritty tan book fell out and hit my hand. Behind it was the disorderly row of squat brown bottles, labels sagging and indecipherable, contents of such viscosity as to resist, even when shaken near the ear, audibility. The *Medical Handbook* revealed: *breed in fresh water . . . quotidian . . . paroxysm . . . fever and ague . . . chills and shakes . . . yawns . . . spreads over whole body.* "Well," I said shutting the book, "it's a lucky thing those guys couldn't land our water today. I mean I'd hate to think of us having to go down there on those treacherous snow-covered rocks and trying to handle that heavy, wet hose. We'd be lucky if either of us got back. I mean it seems to me the essence of this disease is it makes you so you can't quite trust yourself, your limbs."

"Chanty knew what was in them bottles. Which was for which."

"Well, mother's gone and those lucky bastards on the tender are gone and here we are."

He pulled at the corner of the venetian blind as if he were going to look out, but he didn't. "I don't know, Rip, them guys didn't seem too happy out there on that buoy deck when we was out there on the balcony looking at them."

I snorted, shockingly like Chanty.

There was a tremendous retort, as if someone had lit off our horn, only an octave lower.

We looked at each other, and Teddy let the venetian blind go.

It didn't do any good. The blast came again.

"That can't be *our* horn," I said.

"Who else is around?"

Then we both got that wry look like Okrastone assumed when he either was putting someone on or just realized he had been put on.

"It couldn't be," said Teddy.

"Come to think of it, I didn't see them going up river."

"It's got to be."

"No," I said, "it couldn't be. What the hell's he been doing all this time? Has he been just lurking there in our blind spot back of the pantry, just backing and filling like some sort of pervert in a railway station men's room?"

Teddy looked at me mouth open and I put my hand to my head. It did seem hot. "Damn," I said, "it's just that now we do have to go down there."

"Hey, I'll go alone."

"The hell you will. You're worse than I. Feverish, I mean."

"I feel fine. Just light-headed."

We both stalked around the cylinder, each in an opposite direction, and met by the back door, both suprised at finding the other. There, too was *Herb*, or at least her stern, wedged between the refrigerator and the pantry, just over the washing machine. "Crap," I said, "what is he doing there anyway?"

We ran out onto the cold balcony. The skipper waved us down onto the rocks. For some reason he wasn't using the radio anymore. "Some malfunction, no doubt," I said.

"No doubt," said Teddy. "He just doesn't want anyone overhearing him mess it up again."

I leaned back into the shanty and grabbed a jacket. As I fumbled down the ladder to the landing stage I was pleased to discover it was my jacket, and the pockets were stocked with watch cap and the garden gloves I'd bought my last liberty in the Greenmeal Ben Franklin. Stepping from the landing stage down onto the rocks, I discovered the snow came up to the tops of my ankle-high buoy boots.

Fortunately most of the snow seemed to have shaken down, so that the gaps all around each big cube of rock were visible. Still, there might have been similar fissures, so I worked my way carefully out the thirty yards

toward the old bell foundation on the seaward end of the breakwater. There
was no wave action there, not even a surge, just the tide running, so that,
standing on the end of the breakwater, I had the illusion we were going out
to sea. I was out of breath, however, so I brushed off the snow and sat on one
of the old bell foundations. I knew, of course, that *Herb* was near at hand,
but because I had had to concentrate on my footing I had not yet looked up
to see exactly where she lay. A voice let me know.

He was standing on *Herb*'s stern, which loomed way above me. I could
just see his shoulders and head behind the gunnel and the head and
shoulders of the surly third class. I tried shouting up to them, but a skinny
kid appeared from the left and heaved me a messenger line, and I had to
drop to one knee to grab the monkey fist. From then on I had no time to
question what they were doing up there. All I heard were shouts to hustle
and a few warnings not to get hurt, the usual advice you get from boatswains.

By the time the messenger line was in, I was sweating, and my jacket
and face were covered with the sea water wrung from the line. My hands felt
like seal flippers. I began to heave on the big line and watched my hands as
they kept crossing over each other. What I was actually pulling on and
whether or not it was emerging from the water seemed less important than
the process of my hands flopping in this slow, spastic dance. If I thought anything about the nature of what was in my hands I assumed it was some sort of
lead mooring cable, and so it was with shock that I looked back over my
shoulder to find that what was landing behind me was my old friend of the
autumn: the water hose.

Another fifty feet were up, through my hands and behind me, and I had
been well cursed for each foot of it, before I realized that Teddy was not with
me. When I'd gone charging down on the rocks I'd been too busy to worry
about him, but now I became aware that I was the only one being yelled at.
What if the feverish Teddy had slipped back of me somewhere and simply
oozed on into the cold sea. I had once heard of a sailor standing guard duty
back home on a submarine who had done just that, oozed on over the side
and gone straight down through the water while standing up the whole
while. At least the divers found him at attention at the bottom of the harbor.
Well, I thought, at least he'll be able to ring the old Harbor of Refuge bell
down there. My, God, I thought, I'm not that well myself; what if I slip?

"Hey, Teddy!" As I paused, some of the hose took the opportunity to
run back the other way. When I got it stopped I decided I'd be damned if I'd
start hauling again until I knew where he was. Bracing the line with my
elbows and knees, I hovered above the slippery rock in a perilous squat,
peering furtively over my shoulder, torn between anger and fear. When the
boatswain shouted down again, I had a revelation of just how ludicrous must

have been my posture: some Komik Post Kard hunter caught in the piney wood, grunting his bowels out.

"God damn it Teddy. Where the hell are you?"

"Hey, Rip, but I'm sorry, man." There he was, back on the bell foundation, looking round and bronze in his foul weather gear. On such a day I half expected to find the old bell there itself, dredged up by Chantyesque mirage to give us respite with some angelus learned in its long-submerged life. "I wasn't thinking about getting transferred."

"What?"

"I was thinking of bringing my power mower out here."

"*What!*"

"So people who might be interested would, anyhow, see it."

"Just keep sitting there," I said.

The hose began to walk back into the sea and I grunted, which he must have misinterpreted, because he was at my elbow.

"Jesus, Teddy," I said, "I was mainly worried about you. I mean you've got the flu, right?"

"We got to get this line up."

"Not if it means getting hurt."

"I ain't hurt."

"Yeah, but you got the flu."

"I got the febrifuge, too. Or at least we used to."

"Christ," I said, "are you drunk?" What if he had gotten into some of those sticky brown bottles up in the China cabinet? What if his already light-headed mind had gone ballooning off on some magnificent febrifuge? "Teddy, you didn't get into any of Mother Chanty's polyphony? You didn't did you, Teddy?"

"Chanty ain't here," he said.

Light-headed or not Teddy still had his body and with that weight we could stop the hose, hold it right there at the edge of the rock, marshall our strength and get the hose coming back up the other way. Toward this end the sullen trio on the fantail of *Herb* continued to give us the chill-garbled wisdom of their years at sea, their words clattering in the stillness like ice scaled over ice.

Teddy said he'd hold the hose from going back if I'd run up the break-water with the slack, which I did, hoping, on the one hand, that he wouldn't get too much better, or on the other, truly challenge my heroics by actually passing out.

The cold air burned my lungs if I moved too fast. It was as if every cilium waving away down in there were getting scorched. I charged the base of the tower and for an instant in my dizziness saw the humming squadrons of the summer's dragonflies. On the top of the base somehow, I flopped about like a seal before I could rise to my feet. It was good to lean against the tower itself. It was not necessary to look at Teddy or the water, or the buoy tender.

To keep from inhaling too much of the raw air, I put my face inside my jacket, sipping at the world through the fur, which unfortunately soon stiffened into a crust.

Somehow I was inside the tower; the line was with me. Teddy had fortunately opened the big cellar doors from the inside, and, once in by the furnace, I began to sweat so that I was soaked as I climbed up onto the soda box. The spout and the steam pipe itself thudded with hot water under the wrapping.

With no flashlight, I could hardly see up on top of the tanks, the brilliance of the day now leaving me blind. There was a pain in the ends of my fingers, and I knew I'd found the raised lid of the hatch. Thumbing it open, I listened for it to flop back on its hinge. When it did, I poked in the hose and, with my drenched collar riding around my ears and my head itching from the wet wool of the watch cap, flexed my gloves and waited. Slowly my sight returned, and I saw the hatch properly back on its hinge, the hose in the hole.

It was disappointing then when Teddy staggered into the cellar, because I thought he would bring me some sort of news that, in spite of my catbird seat, would require me to move, remilling my damp surfaces into new and less comfortable creases. I decided to take the initiative. "O.K., Ted. I'm all braced up here. Have them sock it through."

He padded on out the door, and in a moment I could hear faint cries. He would be standing somewhere down by the old bell foundation, giving them a wave of triumph, and the guys on the fantail in turn would be passing that triumph on along the deck to the man on the valve, and soon the great gift of fresh water that *Herb* had brought to us all the way a hundred miles down the bay would begin to flow through my fingers into the tank. I began to doze.

Maybe Teddy had slipped away himself by now. Slipped down into the chill, bell-clear waters to do his duty with all submerged sonorities among the bronze-flanged depths.

"Anything yet?" He was down there, his hand against the furnace, his eyes squinting because he had just come in.

"Not yet," I said pleasantly.

"Give it a shake."

I did.

"Nothing?"

"Not a thing."

"Squeeze the end, try banging it out."

"Banging what out?" I said. It was warm and pleasant. Nothing needed banging. "Bang *What?*" I said.

"The ice."

I rapped the edge of the tank a few times. All this fiddling was really quite annoying. How much better just to sit there holding the hose with nothing coming out, no worries about overflowing or the pressure getting away from you, causing you to drop the hose——

"Can you feel where it starts?"

"What's that?"

"The ice."

I looked down the end of the hose, couldn't see anything.

"Feel it," he shouted. "Feel along the hose."

I did. It all seemed the same to me, all the way down as far as I could reach. "Seems all right to me."

That worked. He went out. A few drops fell into the tank. In a moment he was back. "Ok," he said, "let her down."

"I really don't like to complain," I said, "it's been so pleasant up here, but I know you and I are interested in more than five drops of water for the next month."

"Is that all you got?"

"It might have been six. It might even have been eight."

"Are you sure?"

"What the hell," I said, "make it twenty."

He went out and came in again while I continued to doze in the rafters, my jacket all hunched up so I felt furry and damp—a fine old rancid owl.

"Let it down," he said. "He's got another hose. This one's dead as a stick."

I let it drop, a black and broken bowel. Then, of course, I had to climb down.

By the time I got to the end of the breakwater again I had most of the stiffness worked out of me. I caught the messenger with one hand, flourishing the monkey fist, and began the haul. Teddy sat on the bell foundation, his head in his hands. My end of the hose got caught under a rock, and I had to let it back down three times and try to flip it clear. This seemed like fun and even drew a shout from the fantail. I thought of being Chanty, but it was too cold. When I got it up, my work began again.

By the time I tried to crawl into the tower, I could hardly put one leg in front of the other, and my lungs were on fire. The temperature had not come up all day. I crawled into the cellar, my pants soaked, my knees aching on the concrete. Somehow the variety of climbing up the soda box, the spout, and the steam pipe combined with its familiarity, and I was able to make it. I poked the hose in and waited with my eyes closed. I could almost feel the new sweat slide over the old layer, dried and frozen, feel them grating on each other. I tried to pretend I was the rancid owl, but I had too much pain.

After a while, Teddy appeared in the door again and I shook and banged the hose, felt it, milked maybe five or six quarts out of it before it too went dead. Without invitation I let it drop.

And then I dropped from steam pipe to spout to soda box to floor.

I got out in time to see the last ten yards of the hose go over the rock and into the sea. At this point, however, they stopped pulling on it.

"Coil up the messenger line so it don't get wet," shouted the boatswain's mate. "Coil it up careful, and make sure it gets back all the way up here."

I stood up and looked at him. A thick cloud of coal smoke was over my head. In the late, crisp light it hung as firmly as a roof.

"Come on," he shouted. "Throw back the line."

In my pocket was my knife. And what was a more valuable tool, as the beloved *Manual* itself would have it, than the *seaman's own personal pocket knife?* Holding my wet glove in my teeth, I reached into my pocket and pulled out this most valuable personal tool, opened it and cut the line.

Freed, the hose slid, then crashed back into the sea. It was for them now to haul it up. I folded the knife, stuck it back in my pocket, replaced my glove, and coiled up the messenger line. As I put it over my shoulder I could hear them holler for it, but the boatswain, if he was any good, could make another one before they docked. We were the last on their line anyway, and besides, I had always wanted a monkey's fist. After all, hadn't Chanty once said it was just like a human's brain?

We struggled through our meal: fried godknows, washed down with an armload of balcony snow boiled into tea. Teddy had to forsake the Formica almost immediately for the leather chair, his eyes glazed in fever so that he looked like Toy after six weeks of restriction. Because I was too tired to do anything else I did the dishes, eeking out the lees of the casks so that I wondered if it were not a cleaner thing to leave the plates in what was, after all, their familiar patina of edible grease. I stayed to watch a TV program because I simply did not dare to go upstairs.

I knew I had to get to sleep right away, and I was terrified of lying there powerless to do that, my exhaustion and aches and pains pressing down upon me, yet not snuffing me out. If only I could have taken a hot shower or had some booze, I thought. I watched another TV and then forced myself to the door.

"Don't worry," said Teddy, "I'll probably fall asleep down here and forget to call you."

"No," I said, "that's not right."

"A lot of things aren't right," he said.

"That wouldn't make this right." I opened the door and began the climb, hoping, of course, that he would fall asleep and not wake up until, say, three. It was almost two when he grabbed my toe. I had gone right off, thinking I had all that time, something I knew I couldn't have done if he were certain to come at twelve.

All this was clear as I limped down to cook my Cream of Wheat and look out into the clean night where the crystal ships washed themselves in the stars. It wasn't until five or so I started feeling heavy. The office seat did not shriek out from under me until almost first light. It was perhaps the third time I chinned myself up off the floor by grabbing radiator and window sill that I realized I was not in the cellar climbing the pipes to the casks. I remembered the monkey fist, found it in my jacket, a damp rope ball among wet garden gloves. Chanty's book of knots showed how to make a monkey fist. I looked from diagram to model, staring into the intricate coils, and the sun rinsed the far wall pink.

After I had turned out the main light, I undogged the door onto the flag gallery and stood in the iron archway, breathing deeply. There was snow on the deck, for the wind had not come up in the night, and down below there was clean snow yet on the breakwater, except at the very prow, where there were many intricate tracks, thrashings, and scars, as if a great brawl had used for its ground those stones between the old place of the bell and the sea.

CHRISTMAS EVE

Dear Mr. Floherty,

As you can see from the address, I live at the Harbor of Refuge Light Station, Greenmeal, Delaware. We have been reading your account of the destruction of the Light in your book *Sentries of the Sea*. I have been trying to determine from various sources, interviews with elderly locals, records aboard both here and the lifeboat station, exactly what happened. Please do not take this as an insult to your account, which is both fulsome and gruesome, but could you recall exactly what records you consulted in drawing up your exciting narration?

The question, as you might guess, is not one taken lightly out here. I have been accused of harboring a book of mere boys' tales.

> Yours,
> Rip Falorp, SN

DRUNK ON STRONG wind and an old man's raspy sea-shouts. Thank God the pilots had still not come for their radio and we could have their talk as they worked the oceangoing ships off our tower. Right now old Captain Trasker aboard the mother ship was herding his small boats about him for protection. Out the window I could see their lights diving and rising about a mile to the northeast. You'd think they'd have been back of us for protection on a night like this, but they preferred to fight it out in the open, even though the small boats were only some forty feet long. Of course they had to continue to meet the ships that came in, and that had to be done with plenty of sea room and to hell with the conditions. And to hell even with this stuff about the cold coming that the three merchant princes riding in out of the East had of it on another night nearly two thousand years ago.

"*Pilot Ship* Philadelphia *to the pilot boat* Cape Henlopen, *come in* Hen *and get yerself clucking over to my side here.*

"Philadelphia/Henlopen, *Captain Trasker . . . there's . . . a hell of a sea running . . . here.*"

"*Aw, come on,* Hen, *what do you think we've all got to sit on out here tonight?*"

"*Sure Cap, but you got some more under you than we do.*"

"*You'd better have the pilot aboard, you liddle-old-lady* Hen, *you-you, you liddle ollllll LADY* Hen.*"

"We got him, Cap."

"Then bring him right out. We got somebody standin in, and we can't send her up the bay naked on a night like this."

"Right, Cap'n."

"Cluck-cluck, you ol-lady Hen."

"Click-Click," They rogered by depressing the mike key and letting it crack static. And it was not only the method by which they acknowledged commands, but the captain's whimsy as well, so that as he danced through his growls, songs, puns, and stutters, they laughed back with their sharp clickings. One imagined the guffaws of lobsters to be composed of such castineting.

"You know, Teddy, when I make out these log entries I'm not even sure what the little symbols mean anymore. Take this little dinker about checking the main beacon and the aid to navigation, that little beacon down at the end of the breakwater." I pointed to the notebook where I had written:

0030: Checked main light & a/n.

"Yeah," said Teddy, "after a while if somebody came up to me in the street and said, 'hey, what's a lighthouse?' I think I'd give him a blank look."

"Say, speaking of people coming up to you in the street, I don't want to pry, Teddy, but what's been going on with you ashore lately?"

He gave me what I took to be a good imitation of the blank look people who came up to him in the street were getting lately.

"Oh, well," I said, "it's just a sleepy little town."

"Yeah but they got the "Christmas Free Gift." His eyes now were not dull. In fact I could not get him off the subject of this no doubt gritty box of gum-spiking, throat-scratching hard candy that the store will send us. That and the "Christmas goose dinner," which the pilot cook Wong apparently was going to serve us aboard the *Philadelphia*. That would be a treat, if it was to be anything like the few breakfasts I'd had aboard on my way out to the Light.

"Hey, ain't it strange," said Teddy, "how we're all one big family out here even though we hardly ever see each other's faces? And lookit now, them good warm friends who are going to serve us a good, warm Christmas goose dinner ain't nothin but tiny lights jumpin up and down out there in the night."

He stood at the window and sighed, having completed what surely must be one of the longest sentences he has ever uttered.

"I think I'll steal that for my Christmas card this year," I said.

"Steal what?" he said.

"Hey, have you ever actually seen Captain Trasker's face?" I ask. "Listening to him on a night like this is like having your back to a warm fire. I just wonder what he really looks like."

"I seen him."

"You did? What did he look like?"

"He just looked like anybody else."

"Then how did you know it was him?"

"His face——"

"Yes?"

"It had his voice coming out of it."

0100: Checked main light & a/n.

"Hey, you know what I can't help feelin'?" said Teddy.

"Homesick?"

"No, man. That wasn't what I was gonna say at all. I was gonna say I can't help feelin' a bit that maybe, well, you know, ol' Okie-ree-stone and maybe even ol' Flapper there don't feel a teeny-weener bit envious of us out here now."

"You mean because of the goose tomorrow?"

"Sure, you don't get a goose everywheres, you know."

0130: Checked Main Light & a/n

"Hey, Maritime."

"Yeh, Cap, go ahead."

"You busy? Keepin' your feet dry up there on that sand dune?"

"Couple of Jap reindeers standin in. I just called Reedy Island. Bombay Hook must be havin a nod."

"You sure you don't mean a nog?"

"A what, Cap?"

"Nog. Egg-nog. Christmas Eve, for Godsake."

"Oh, sure. Christmas Eve. That's what I said: Japanese reindeer."

"Click click."

"Click-click."

"Hey, Teddy, aren't you going to bed? I mean you got to get up tomorrow just like any other day."

"I never go to bed on Christmas Eve, man."

"You're not expecting the bearded gentleman?"

"I'm expecting a Christmas goose dinner."

"What time does he usually serve that?"

"Oh, not in the night time. In the day when the sun is out."

"But is there any special time? Like, say, noon? Or three in the afternoon? Sitting down to a big festive meal, you know, it can make a difference."

"I think it goes on all day. You know how they serve over there. They got so many to feed, and they can't all eat at once because they have to keep working the ship."

"Jesus, it's like a shark, isn't it? The damn thing can never stop, not even on Christmas. If it rests, it sinks."

"This here lighthouse got to keep going all the time too, or *everybody* sinks."

"Takes your breath away, doesn't it?" I said. "You know, sometimes I look out this north window here at the breakwater, and I imagine things."

"You don't have to look out no window, north or south, east or west."

"Do you ever imagine anything, say about that breakwater there?"

"Sure. I imagine sometimes it's a bunch of big blocks. You know. Like you can play with as a kid. Stack up and make a . . . make a garage out of."

"A garage?"

"Sure, you got to put your car somewhere, your things."

"Like the lawn mower, eh?"

"Hey, be nice now. You got to put the lawn mower away, too, you know. You got to take care of your things. Not just leave them outside. Not just leave the things you love out . . . there . . ."

"Do you ever imagine anything weirder?"

"Weirder than my things left outside?"

"Yeah, well, maybe weird things that happen to your things when they're, well . . . left out there."

"Sometimes I imagine the breakwater's a dragon. That its tail goes way off up there, and the north beacon light there is its spike on its tail like, you know, Chinese dragons have always got a spike in their tail what lights up a lot."

"Maybe that's where Chanty got that business about there being fifty men on a Chinese lighthouse."

"No, sir, he got that from a doctor when he broke his thumb in a fight. The doctor that fixed his thumb found out Chanty was on a lighthouse and said that when he was a doctor in China, along the coast there, you know?"

"Yes, the China Coast."

"Well, they got lighthouses over there, too, you know."

"I think you told me this story before."

"Yeah, well, they still got to have fifty men on a lighthouse."

"I don't see that that follows."

"Because they're Chinamen, and they got to do a lot of work just to keep them paper towers up in the air." He did a little dance, raising his knees high. "It's like a bicycle on them. You got to keep pedaling."

"Or the lighthouse falls over?"

"They do it from down in the cellar."

"According to Chanty——"

"According to Chanty's doctor who set his thumb and actually was in the real part of China."

"The Chinese Coast."

"That's it."

0200: Checked main light & a/n.

"*Cap'n Trasker, this is* Brandywine, *we were right alongside and reaching out to get* Hellenic Hero, *but we had no boatnook . . . our fingers bruised with rust . . .*

"*Go over lay alongside the Light, alongside the Harbor Refuge Light. You ain't gonna be able to lay alongside me in this wind.*"

"*Click-click.*"

"Hey, we're gonna have some up-close company on Christmas Eve, after all," said Teddy.

He went to each windward window, set his hands on the sill of the deep reveal, and thrust his head in. "Yup, here they come," he said, then switched windows to follow their progress around the tower and into our lee. When they were behind our back door he shouted around the curve of the tower to me. "Hey, come on out back here and wave to 'em. Wave a warm Christmas Eve."

"Are you crazy? You'll be swept right off that balcony."

"Not me. I can wave and hold on."

"They think we're in distress."

"They know me. They know I wave on Christmas Eve."

0230: Checked main light and a/n.

"*Howzzz she holdin, Johnny?*"

"*She's pumpin pretty good, Capn' Trasker, but she's still got a lotta water.*"

"*Well, now boys, keep an eye right on her. And check them strainers.*"

"*Click-click.*"

"You know, we was listenin to the radio one night, me and Chanty, just like this, only it was Christmas Eve."

"This *is* Christmas Eve, Teddy."

"Yeah, I know, but it was Christmas Eve we was listenin to. You know, the music. What they call them Christmas carols. *Hark* and *Silence* and *Little Towns.*"

"The eloquence of simple melody."

"That's it."

"You mean you would rather I turn down the pilot's radio and dial in the entertainment radio for something more appropriate on this festal night?"

"No, that wouldn't be no good at all."

"Oh, I see. Or rather I don't see."

"Like I was saying, Chanty and me did that one night, heard all them tunes playing, the simple eloquent melodies, like you said."

"And it made you sad? It made you just too damn sad to think of being stuck out here away from your loved ones at home?"

"No, that weren't it, you see."

"The discrepancy between the image of Christmas goodfellowship as projected by the culture and the raw actuality of life as it's lived in the outposts by those who protect that very culture."

"No, it wasn't any of them things."

"I see. That is, I don——"

"The thing was, the radio wasn't even plugged in."

"The entertainment radio. The radio to which you were listening, upon which you heard the simple, eloquent——"

"Them melodies wasn't coming from any place. I know. I looked down, right here at this kitchen table, I looked down and the radio was right in the middle of the two of us, on the table like it was a big meal we was eating."

"Like a Christmas cooked goose."

"Yeah, only it wasn't plugged in."

"Obviously a portable Christmas cooked goose."

"No, it was a regular plug-it-in radio. The plug was right down there by my feet not plugged in."

"Some radios allow the option of cord or battery."

"You don't understand this radio. It was a strictly plug-it-in radio. One of them old kind with the wooden cabinet what comes up like a church and has silk cloth in the winder-ways in the front where the music comes out. It was left over from the Wickie days."

"Perhaps Chanty was merely humming. You know, scootched down over here on this side of the big radio, but humming suggestive tones upon which your holiday-hungry mind composed complete triads, progressions, the full pomp of Christmas anthem."

"No, this was actual music, man."

"Which somehow was not, either in you nor in him, nor in the radio, *actually* there."

"Hey, we was just sittin there. Just us in this room, out here."

"One of the Unsolved Acoustical Mysteries of the North Atlantic."

"Hey, I didn't say nuthin."

"What an interesting way to spend Christmas Eve."

"Like I said, I just sat here. I didn't say nuthin."

0300: Checked main light & a/n.

"Say, this 'Christmas free gift,' " I said.

"Every year they send it out."

"Now, the store does, right? The store we buy our provisions from?"

"Well, it ain't nothin really but candy."

"*Hard* candy."

"Them kind what comes all bent up in ribbons with the red stripes in 'em."

"Some are shaped like . . . *canes?*"

"No, not too many of them kind. Just, you know, them ribbon kind."

"I see. And when, exactly when are we to expect this cargo?"

"To tell you the truth, I think it should have been here by now." He let his hands explore the deep reveal.

"And how was it to . . . arrive?"

"It could come with the week's groceries on the forty-footer from the station. Or it could come special by way of the pilot boats."

"There is a guy up north who plays Santa and visits by airplane. Helicopter now, I guess. Edward Rowe Snow."

"Yeah, well, this ain't up North. This is . . . this is . . ." He continued to gaze out the window. "This is here."

0330: Timed Main Light & a/n.

"*Is that thing you got stuck in your prop able to be got out by reversing her?*"

"*No, sir, Cap'n Trasker. We done tried that.*"

"*Is she vibrating?*"

"*Ain't vibrating, but she's pretty bad.*"

"*Well, hang on till we get the* Brandywine's *bilge pumped out.*"

"*We'll try, Cap'n, but this sea's really up.*"

"*You do that, boys. Don't get your toesies wet.*"

"Hey, Teddy, where is that radio now? The old one with the cathedral cabinet you just spoke of."

"It ain't what you call 'aboard' now."

"What happened: Blump take it home to his wife for an antique?"

"No, man, it sorta went over the side."

"You threw it away? Those things are beautiful and nowadays considered indeed antiques."

"It could make you kinda nervous, though."

"So you just chucked it over the rail?"

"Chanty said he didn't mind."

"Was this the very same night you heard the ghostly melodies of Christmas past?"

"Well, we didn't do it *right* away."

0400: Check main light & a/n.

"*How is he now?*"

"*He's O.K., Cap'n Trasker. I think he's gonna be O.K.*"

"*He didn't get crushed in there or anything?*"

"He's pretty wet and shaking, but we got some dry stuff in here."

"But was he crushed when the two hulls came together?"

"No, Sir, he says he wasn't crushed or anything."

"I don't see how he wasn't crushed. I saw the two hulls come together after he went in between."

"It was 'cause he didn't have no life-preserver on, Cap'n. He says he just sorta' pushed himself down under the roll of the bilge when the two boats came together. We fished him out on the back roll, real quick."

"You must have been quick."

"If he'd a had a life preserver on he couldn't a done that."

"You boys want some hot coffee?"

"We sure would, Cap'n, but I don't think we'd better risk coming alongside a you again."

"O.K., boys, maybe not for a while."

"Not for awhile."

0430: Checked Main Light & a/n

"Teddy, I don't mean to dwell on this rather barren subject of the Christmas hard candy, but who exactly is giving it to us?"

"It comes from the store."

"And is paid for by the store?"

"You know, you got a point there. Like it's some kind of *bribe?*" His eyes lit up. This was good candy, indeed.

"Well, let's just say an *inducement.*"

"No, it ain't any of that," he said, fading. "I forgot to tell you it comes from the town."

"Greenmeal, Delaware?"

"Yeah, I think that's it." He wandered toward the back door. "That one out there. The one we see sometimes. When it ain't foggy or nothin." He cleaned the window with his sleeve. "I can see it now. That is, the lights. They send it. From in there."

"Is there a committee or what? A committee of concerned citizens? Or do they put out boxes in the banks and Ben Franklin Store? *Remember the Lighthouse Keepers this Yule: Keep a Light Burning in the Hearts of those who keep One burning for You.*"

"You're beginning to sound like Philo Chanty, man. Don't do it."

"Or the Church: the Church collectors, in narrow canisters will clink out for our bleak Light: *Relief for those whose Souls are Beacons.*"

"From the town in there, that's all. That town, right there. Them lights."

"Do you think any of them would notice if they looked out tomorrow and saw just ocean here?"

"You mean people in there? Over across the . . . in there?"

"It would make a good story, wouldn't it? Level sea at dawn . . . bodies of the keepers discovered by Yeoman Peal."

"Hey, please, Rip, don't start that again. I mean you ain't going to put any more notes in the bottles, is you?" I get nervous every time you go out on the balcony at night."

"I wasn't aware I harped so on it. It must be like my grandfather about communists."

"Yo grandpa was a communist?"

"I think the idea was supposed to be he was against them. In any case he spent a lot of time thinking about them."

"That's the trouble with thinking."

"What is?"

"It makes you get a lot of time."

0500: Checked main light & a/n.

"*Hey, Sand dune. What happened to those Japanese reindeer?*"

"*Got 'em just off the* Delaware Lightship, *Cap.*"

"*What ever happened to that crazy guy was on the Harbor Refuge? Didn't he go out there to the lightship?*"

"*I know who you mean, Cap. One of the Exchange boys said he was riding the train back to the home office and this fellow was on the train in his sailor suit. All slicked down, don't you know. He'd cornered some old lady across the aisle and was readin poetry at her.*"

"*Doin' what to her, you say?*"

"*Poetry.*"

"*Oh, yeah, poetry.*"

"Well, there you go, Teddy, you see it doesn't matter whether I begin to sound like him or not."

"Maybe they was talkin about somebody else."

"Why didn't you want to think it was him? You were just talking about him and you with that weird radio bit. You were willing enough to bring his name up when you had that gull-wing fever. You said his Febrifuge had cured you."

"What cures one thing don't always cure everything, you know. Like that crack business. Always about that crack down in the tower. He got me to thinkin about it, and then he left and I stopped thinkin about it, and then somehow, even though he ain't ever really here no more, he gets *you* to thinking about it."

"Me?"

"I know it's Christmas Eve and that's maybe why you shouldn't want to bring it up."

"No, Chanty is more to me than that. As far as that business goes, that crack business, well, I often just plain forget about it. I do sometimes, you know. For whole days at a time. Even those notes you were worrying about. Most of that was just fun."

"It was?"

"Sure, you know, here we are on a goddamn lighthouse. Did you ever think of that? And now, as you say, it's Christmas Eve and here we are on a lighthouse."

"It don't seem nothin to write home about."

"Write home?"

"Yeah, I got a home, you know. At, you know, *home*."

"Well, wouldn't they like to know you are on a lighthouse?"

"I told them I was on a Life Saving Station."

I sighed. "Well, what the hell, it's Christmas Eve, right?"

"Sure, you don't got to think of things on Christmas Eve."

"And who knows, maybe somebody will wash overboard and we can save them right out here."

"Christmas Eve you don't got to think about anything."

0530: Checked main light & a/n. Secured cellar door.

It had blown open with a sound like the furnace exploding. Funny thing was it didn't wake Teddy, who had finally gone to sleep, his arms stretched out on the Formica table. I guess I assumed he would join me down there in the basement, but he never did.

I had to tiptoe out onto the slick concrete of the base to recover the end of the door. While I was out there a wave hung way up over my head, and I had to dance back inside.

The wave hit the door and slammed it shut again, and while I worked a clothesline into the handle I kept seeing that wave overhead, poised there in the swing of the beam, and even when I got the door all tied down to the frame of the water casks and had done what I could and was climbing back up the stairs I saw that wave.

It was Teddy, however, who had vanished. I knew someone should have vanished in all that. It took me a moment to figure it out. In the corner of my eye, out the window, the *Philadelphia* was much closer, hung on a wave, sickening and sliding down a wild, white nightwave, its lights like a falling Christmas tree: *red over white, pilot at night* or was it *white over red, pilot ahead?* I'd have to look it up in Bowditch, because there was no way I could look out the window long enough to see for myself.

Teddy, of course, was in his bunk, having slipped away while I was below nearly slipping away. I was not angry. He was probably half asleep in his climb and should have been in bed long before. Nevertheless, I am now alone. The pilot's radio merely crackles. Their lights out there help some, would help more if I could watch. *Red over white; fishing at night*. Therefore it's *white over red, pilot ahead*. My solution is totally logical, verbal. I still cannot check the simple fact out the window.

0600: Checked main light & a/n.

Dare I think of Christmases past? Of the eves when my father would round up a bunch of uncles and neighborhood kids who played brass, and we'd go out through the cold night bleating *Silent Night* in four parts? The trick was to keep our spit from freezing in the valves. Keep our mouthpieces safe in our fists except when playing, so that the metal would not stick to our lips. Sometimes we were as many as a dozen, and we'd practice for weeks before. Each night after supper the bell would ring, and some of the crew would come puffing in, instrument case in hand. Sometimes some new person would bring music, usually sheets and sheets of it. "Enough for a whole bloody opera," my father would say. He did the arrangements by humming them or showing the fingering or writing them down with numbers for the valves instead of the notes. "I can only read violin music," he'd say. The uncles and their friends knew the barbershop chords anyway. *Hark the Herald Angels Sing, Joy to the World* and *Jingle Bells*. One night the Jewish boy from up the street arrived with a clarinet and sheet music for *Oh, Come All Ye Faithful*. We did it complete with the *pp* on the first "Oh, come let us adore Him," rising to the *fff* on the third one, when my uncle on the trombone would stride down the entire scale to the cellar note itself. It was enough even when played outdoors to keep you warm the whole night.

0630: Checked main light & a/n. Door continued to hold.

Tonight, even the stars seemed to be having no easier time than the pilot boats in holding their cold positions.

"*Click-click.*"

THE CHRISTMAS COOKED (WILD) GOOSE

> Willis watched the dwelling disappear bit by bit in a smother of white water. He
> also saw that in each corner of what had been a house a heavy stanchion stood
> defiant to the sea. The short passageway to the tower was still intact behind him; a
> spare heaving line still hung from a peg. The darkness of approaching night made
> the phosphorescence of the sea water splotches of green fire. As he watched the
> stanchions he appraised their strength and saw one after another give way to the
> sea, that is, all but one, a sturdy timber pock-marked by small knots. It was the only
> stable thing in sight. Slipping his arm through the loops of the heaving line he made
> his way gingerly to the standing timber and lashed himself to it with the skill of a
> sailor. As long as the stanchion held he was safe from being swept away.
>
> —John J. Floherty, *Sentries of the Sea*

AND NOW IT was Christmas Day, white foam everywhere with sea
birds ripping off the wave tops. I was trying to keep awake, not only
because it was my duty, but to see that exact moment when
Christmas Eve darkness modulates into Christmas Morn. It is an instant
which even the most childish expectation had never kept me alert enough
for in the past. Here was my chance to observe this day of days being born
clear of all tinsel and crowds, clear even of love. Perhaps that was too scary.
Again I missed it, the office chair sliding out from under me too late, or
perhaps my crawl up off the floor too slow, for by the time my hand hauled
my face to the deep reveal, our beacon had melted into the first light of the
east.

0700: Secured main light.

And there they were: the three ships sailing in, white as crystals. Although I had been watching them for six months, listening to them all night,
there was a moment when, with the full light of morning on their frozen
superstructures I did not recognize them: *Philadelphia* and her two boats,
Cape Henlopen and *Brandywine*, the embodiment of the voices I'd but
heard in the night.

"Good morning, gentlemen. Merry Christmas."

"Good morning, Captain Trasker. Yes, Merry Christmas."

"How is everyone? Did you get our fellow dry and warm?"

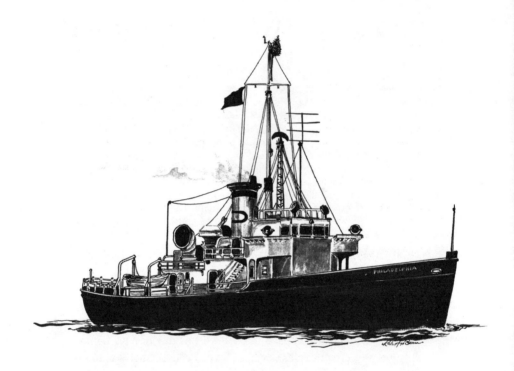

"He's feeling better, now, Cap'n. Just damn glad he wasn't wearing a life preserver."

"Well, he was supposed to be wearing one. Supposed to wear one always."

"We know. That's the scary part."

"Click-click."

"Click-click."

"Say, boys."

"Go ahead, Cap."

"She's settled down enough now, don't you think? Why don't you sneak in alongside me and have some nice, hot Chinaman breakfast? Get yourselves some rickshaw soup."

"Ah so!"

The mother ship went into a turn, heading into the leftover slop from last night's gale. The two small boats also turned, but they bounced as they came sideways on the soft-cresting seas. It had been hard to tell what was gull and what spume until now, but with *Philadelphia* hove-to, the flocks were assembling from all across the horizon to focus just above her fantail. I could just see, or imagined I saw, Wong, or more likely his mess cook standing there in white, the center of the universe.

I put a kettle of water on the stove and, at the risk of duplicating one of Chanty's famous errors, went aloft to put up the flag. The iron door in the watch keeper's room boomed open as I stepped out onto the upper balcony, and it came back to me how I was almost swept away the night before while closing the cellar door.

It would be fun to see the pilot boys and find out just what happened to their man last night. I thought it must have been Fats Davenport, he of the chow-sling knots, who was the one who fell between the hull of *Henlopen* and *Philadelphia*. In any case it would be interesting to swap near-disaster yarns over Wong's Christmas goose. The flag went up smartly. I saluted, my shirt filled with fresh morning air. The pilot fleet was almost under me now, and I could see down onto their decks. There was a small boat on either side of the mother ship, and the mess cook, an old fellow, was indeed leaning over the fantail smoking a cigarette while the gulls rose and fell between him and me in expectation that they too would participate in the mother ship's Christmas bounty. I waved, but the mess cook did not look up at me through his jabbering flock. The door clanged behind me as I dogged it shut.

Teddy was standing by the kettle as I re-entered the galley. "Hey, I can smell that old Christmas goose anytime *Philadelphia* gets upwind."

"That kettle didn't run out of water, did it?" I asked. "I don't want to pull a Chanty and burn the tower half down."

"Hey, Merry Christmas."

"Merry Christmas, Teddy."

"And you know what?"

"What?"

"It's just going to get better and better. I tell you I can sniff that goose."

I told him all about what had happened with the pilots since he'd been asleep. He shivered at the part when Fats Davenport fell between the hulls and had to shove himself deeper into the sea to keep from being crushed. He told me Toy's story again about the mess cook, how the old fellow had come aboard in the dark just before first light and opened his locker to face the sea gull the apprentices had put in there as a joke, how it had flown past him, its feathers in his face, its white panic wide across his apron.

"Well, boys will be boys," I said.

"You want to hear another one?"

"You mean because it's Christmas."

"Yeah, we ain't got no presents for each other. All we got is stories. I got to use the pilots, because I guess Chanty done told you all the stories about this place."

"No, I'm sure there are some left."

"Well, I saw this myself. With my own eyes."

"Go ahead."

"I'm not sure how to do it."

"What's the matter? You said you saw it with your own eyes."

"I did, but I'm not sure if it's supposed to be funny."

"*Supposed* to be?"

"Yeah, ain't a story, a story you tell, supposed to be funny?"

"Well, why don't you just tell what happened and we'll worry about what it's supposed to be when you're done?"

"O.K., but then it might not be a Christmas story."

"Then we'll make it a Halloween story, or whatever."

"You know that old guy?"

"The same one that got the gull in his locker?"

"Yeah, that's the guy."

"Nice old fella. Hard working. Down on his luck. Always gave me a piece of pie. In fact he's here right now. That is, he's outside on his deck."

"Yeah. He was on deck once, having a smoke. The guys had tied a line to one of the garbage cans below. But see, he didn't know. He thought it was a real line attached to something he should help out with. It was attached only to the garbage can in the galley, though, see. They got him to help out up on deck, pulling. He thought it was an important line, that they needed help."

"Nice fella."

"Yeah. So he pulled on it. And they all got excuses to take off. They got on the small boats and went away. One by one, saying they had calls to go do important ships, and so that made it even more important for him to hang in there and pull."

"Faithful servant."

"Yeah. Pretty soon he's all alone and there's this awful noise. It was like a drum solo or something. I heard it."

"And where were you exactly in all this?"

"I didn't tell him to do nothin. I was just there."

"Just where?"

"You know them big ventilators with the funny hoods on them?"

"Cowl-mouthed ventilators."

"Yeah. There's one by the ladder coming up from the galley. That's where I was. Kinda hiding, anyway."

"And up came the clanging can."

"And Wong the cook right behind. He had a meat cleaver. He had been going along after it, trying to straighten up the mess it was making as it got dragged through his galley. It raised holy hell. Eggs, milk, dishes—whatever was in its way. In the can's way."

"So did anyone explain it wasn't really the old guy's fault?"

"It was pretty funny to see all that going on and know what was going on."

"So what did Wong do?"

"See, it made me feel pretty funny to be crouching there."

"Behind the cowl-mouthed ventilator?"

"Yeah, you know that big hood thing."

"I can see it from here, aft of the stack."

"Yeah, that's where I was."

"You call that a *cowl-mouthed ventilator*."

"Oh, I didn't know the name for it."

"*Cowl-mouthed ventilator*."

"O.K."

After I did the breakfast dishes I decided to go up to sleep a while before the famous meal, which Teddy still maintained was to be served sometime in the early afternoon. The idea was that they would come over and get first one of us, then the other so that there would always be somebody on duty. If the weather had really moderated they might bring us both together. While that would leave no one on the Light, who would care more in the dead of winter than the pilots themselves, and they could put us back at the first sign of trouble. They also monitored the Coast Guard frequency so could cover for us on any official calls. Besides, we would only be a few hundred yards away. And it was, after all, Christmas. The prospect of leaving the Light abandoned even under such carefully controlled conditions still gave us a bit of a thrill, like letting your bare foot stray out from under the covers on a cold night, and we passed back and forth various contingencies, more for the sake of flirting with the cold than any practical requirement. Then, as a final adjustment, while my hand was already on the knob of the door leading upwards to sleep, Teddy added yet another item of Toy's:

"You know, last year when there was all that ice out here, them pilot boys put one guy off on a big cake of it and said they'd be right back, to, you know, get him, but they let him float out to sea for hours. Then they got him back."

"Why are you telling me this?" I asked.

"Then another time they came up here and when Toy was in his bunk, they done slipped his hand in an outstretched pan o'warm water . . . ?"

"Yes?"

"That made him pee the bed. In his own sleep."

"Ah-huh."

"But that was in the summer time."

"Teddy, why are you telling me these stories now?"

"Well, I knew you was going up to bed after being on watch all night and I could see you was upset by what they did to the old mess cook so I didn't want you to think them pilot boys was just plain mean."

"You wanted me to see they were more broadly humorous in their intent."

"Well, I knew you was going to use them to get you over to that Christmas goose dinner."

"I see." Yawning, I opened the door to go up.

"Hey, you know what I can't help feelin?" said Teddy.

"Homesick?"

"Hey, how come you always put in *homesick*?"

"You're not going to tell me you're feeling sorry for Okrastone and Flap again because they won't be going over for the Christmas cooked goose?"

"Sure, you don't get a goose cooked everywheres, you know."

When I woke, I knew by the slant of light coming through the inshore windows onto the pale-blue tongue-in-groove bulkhead that it was already late afternoon. I ran to the window around on the open sea curve and looked down for the pilot ship. She wasn't there, and it was only when I let my eyes float way out to the horizon that I saw her working a smudge. At least the sea had moderated.

When I opened the door into the galley I half-expected Teddy not to be there. After all, the day was well gone, and he should have been out on the horizon eating his goose.

"You've been and come back already?" I said.

He was running water over his outstretched finger.

"Geese are greasy," I said, "or so I've heard."

"No, man, they ain't that greasy. I was only going to make some Kool-Aid."

"But you did go?"

"No. Not yet." He continued to stare at his finger. "Actually, I done cut this a bit. Was slicing up a tomato."

"The mother ship is awful far out," I said. "I saw her working the horizon from upstairs."

"From down here, you can't hardly see her at all." The water continued its slow but prodigal run over his finger. "That's why I was cutting the tomato."

"That tomato, you realize, has been with us a while. I recall Farilla trying to lunch on it well over two months ago. In fact I think it was part of Chanty's legacy. You might say it is one of the traditional fixtures."

"You remember that Aladdin's lamp up in the watch keeper's locker?"

"Blump stole it."

"Did he tell you?"

"Who else? I'm only mad I didn't take it myself."

He looked worried. "I'll put it back."

"It's all right," I said, "I didn't want that tomato. Not to eat anyway."

"Hey, we got Kool-Aid, too."

Teddy had gone up for a nap. I was to call him when they came. The plate holding his bleeding tomato sat on the counter. Beyond it I could see the tide was way out, a winter low tide with the northerly keeping it out there so extra sections of rock were visible along the breakwater, the sea purulent along the raw edge like pyorrhea.

To seaward, *Philadelphia* was visible from this deck, now, but I had simply never in six months seen her work ships so far away. Even her boats running from the dock in Greenmeal cut far in toward the Cape and away from us, so that I could make out only their silver wakes. The buildings on the shore were involved in some strange winter optical illusion and seemed stretched to four times their normal height. The Cape Henlopen cliffs looked ominous. The old light that stood up there, the one they said was now a mile out to sea, it must be a broken column, not one hunk of tower—a scattering of masonry across the ocean floor. Our old bell, both of them, were down there, too. Were they ringing on Christmas Day?

The pilot's radio hardly even cracked static, so they must have been working so smoothly they didn't need it. I had already checked it a number of times to make sure it was on and turned up enough. So strange after last night, when talk seemed important. Of course, I could have turned on the T.V.

Tonight I would be lying awake waiting for mid-watch, staring at the ceiling, watching the blinds blow inward in that slim *J* posture, listening to the escape ropes knock upon the outside plates, the chariot moan in the lantern, thinking of the main beam swinging around and around overhead that damn frantic lasso that mounted its strength with each circle, but never finally let go.

Maybe Wong's goose would make me drowsy. The stuffing, Toy said, was *"sumptuous."* Yes, his word, his face for once grown fat and joyful round the word like a carnal monk's. I could exchange last night's storm yarn with Fats. I tried to recall what it was that had happened to me. I knew what happened to him. I could tell him something about the big wave poised above my head. With what they go through, however, this would mean nothing to them. I could try stories about their pranks: the seagull locked away in a white panic for the rummy's eye-opener. Someone no doubt would say they were eating it for dinner, that the Christmas goose is really a gull. The mother ship was so far away. It hardly seemed possible they would be able to make two runs. That means Teddy and I would have to go together, abandoning the Light at dusk, a crucial hour even if we switched on the main light before we left. And then there was the radio check at eight o'clock. We could have made it from the bridge of the *Philadelphia*. We might have even met Captain Trasker that way. It would all be all right because they would have taken care of us. The pilots were our friends.

Why did Rory insist this tower was shut up? Who else thought this? Surely the pilots didn't. But the day would come when it would be, and then on Christmas this room would still be here, the windows boarded up and the furniture probably gone, but this room would still be right here, and it would still be Christmas, and the pilot ship would be out there, and so, too, of course, would be the sea.

The low tide ashore must have been leaving plenty of mud around the Boathaven docks. I wondered how the big black women who whacked the clams asunder and made such an opera with their Thunderbird and open windows would be doing today at home. It was hard to imagine they could top their daily festival.

And Hack and Rory? Would they, in the midst of their drinking round the green kitchen table, peek out the window and see by the withered rose bushes the upturned bottom of their boat and wish that it were all another day?

At home now we would have been at my grandfather's house. Milling about the Victorian parlor, all the relatives would have dodged contact with the paintings of bright-eyed saints and dim seascapes, but the best water picture was one of no water at all. It was a huge sepia photograph of the outside of the Coliseum that hung on the landing. My uncle would always take me up there and, *sotto voce*, say, "You know there's water on the other side of that. Sure, they filled it with water just like a big bath and then had a naval battle while they sat around in their shirtsleeves up in the seats above high water and watched."

Looking down the breakwater, I saw that the northerly had continued to keep the tide back, so that the extra steps of rock visible suggested the seats in a great outdoor theater. Gulls huddled in the lee, and where the wall made its angle they were thickest. From half a mile away in the late afternoon sun that turned the rocks sepia, the birds were my uncle's shirt-sleeved Romans in the Coliseum waiting for their triremes.

1600: Turned on main light.

There was still plenty of sunlight, but it would go fast this time of year, and I was afraid I might doze off before they came. When I was up there in the lantern, everything seemed so quiet, and yet how could it be more silent than any other day? And the sea below seemed empty, too, though the pilots were out there a mile or so, and two freighters were in sight. The flag was even flapping. When I took it down and shut the door, I thought I would scream, it was so still. The shrill alarm bell that tests itself a moment when we turn on the beacon was a welcome blast as it echoed in the iron.

1630: Checked & timed main light & a/n. Weather: Wind—NW at Force three; Bar—29.05; Dry Bulb—29; Weather Symbol—b; Vis—10 nautical miles or more; Sea Water Temp—45; Height of sea—three feet.

Does that make sense?

What the hell did I know about it, anyway?

Perhaps they did have Christmas dinner at night. Roistering in the mead hall with the gull flying in one porthole and out the other in order to please Sir Thomas Browne. And my uncle at the whiskey and the basso profundo:

> *The bell in the light-house*
> *Is ring-ing*
> *Ding-dong*
> *Ding-dong*

And then another uncle takes his arm and, clapping Auntie's hat on, parades about:

> *Oh, we do like to be beside the seaside*
> *Oh, we do like to be beside the sea*

Where the brass band plays:
Tiddelty-om-pom-pom.

I was afraid to go on the balcony with the flashlight to check the dry
bulb. The other night I was standing out there reading the gauge at 0400. I
had not talked to a soul since six the previous evening, when suddenly there
was a hand on my shoulder. I turned. Something with feathers and sinews
under the feathers thrust against my face. I could feel the whole curve of it,
the tension as it tried to open out. "Jesus Christ!" And I ran into the tower.
An hour later I could still feel the wing upon my neck and cheek, that vibrating curve, and the grip was still printed in my shoulder. What was it Baude-
laire said about cultivating his eccentricity until one day he'd felt the wing of
madness passing over him? Metaphor? On a lighthouse all metaphors collapse. "On this rock . . . ," "a sea of doubts . . . ," "a beacon unto. . . ."

Time out for clam chowder. I didn't like to play adultery to Wong's
goose, but if I didn't eat something today I would fall on my face. As it was, I
was so lightheaded from fasting I don't think I could have trusted myself on
the iron ladder down to the boat. Besides, the ship was still way out there,
and I was sure by staying on the small boat's deck I'd have a roaring appetite
for Wong.

I would, however, leave Teddy's tomato alone.

I wondered if he still felt sorry for Okrastone and Flap.

The Thunderbird-clam ladies must have really been into it ashore,
while Hank & Rory, without a night baseball game, must have been growing
drowsy.

And the uncle on the trombone swung by, narrowly missing my grand-
mother's nose, and my grandfather tilted back his head and poured a glis-
sando of cigar smoke at the roof.

1700: Checked main light & a/n.

Red light on the army dock. 17:30 . . . I had so much confidence in the
sea air and Wong's cooking that I had another bowl of chowder. It's funny
how on Christmas the air always seems different. I'd thought it was the
people and their decorations. Out here . . .

The mother ship had her lights on and seemed a bit closer.

Not that her closeness mattered. If she had been a length away she'd
still have to send a boat or push out a plank or something. Though if she had
been that close, I suppose I could have at least waved or been out on the balcony, played my bugle—something so they might look over and remember.
We could, of course, have used the radio, but that hardly seemed . . . One
thing, now that it was dusk, both Teddy and I would not be tempted like Toy
and Chanty to go over and have "the high old time" together. In any case, I
was not all that sure I wanted to sit there under those yellow galley bulbs

without Teddy, just me hunched over a remnant of goose while the old pilots grumbled in their gravy and Wong leered and the bulbs sputtered through their wire baskets.

When I looked up, however, it was Teddy who was looking at me. Odd I hadn't heard him descend.

"So . . ." I say. The ball, afterall, was in his court.

"Sometimes they don't come," he said.

It didn't hit me, however, until I saw him walk over to the counter, lift that tomato from the saucer, and commence to suck it.

FLAP'S MEAL:
ITS CONCEPTION,
PREPARATION,
INGESTION, AND
ULTIMATE APOTHEOSIS

Mr. Rip Falorp
Harbor of Refuge Light,
Greenmeal, Delaware.

Dear Mr. Falorp,

Due to a post office error your letter has just reached me.

I am glad to know you have read one of the forty books I have had published.

Regarding the destruction of Harbor of Refuge Light I first heard the story while visiting Execution Light in Long Island Sound. I later checked with Coast Guard Headquarters in Washington.

Considering the number of books I have written during the course of which I have interviewed well over 400 people, it is, of course impossible for me to remember the details of the hundreds of stories I have heard

I am sure if you write the Commandant of the U.S. Coast Guard in Washington and mention what you found in SENTRIES OF THE SEA, you will receive the information you desire.

With best wishes, I am

Yours truly,
John J. Floherty

TEDDY AND I had just about convinced ourselves that the same winter seas that had apparently kept us from dining with the pilots on Christmas would also prevent the Coast Guard from making the next Boat Day, which would return Flap and Okrastone while relieving Teddy. He was looking out the back door, his lip as long as when I'd told him

Bethlehem was not a port, when he cried out he saw them coming. I stood with him in the shanty. Leaning against the doorjamb, we were two sourdoughs peering into the whiteness. Carefully he showed me how to separate the white of the waves from that of the oncoming hull.

"My God," I said, "I thought that was a fountain."

"No, man, it's my liberty."

Then, of course, he apologized for rubbing it in that I had one more week before I went ashore. I assured him it was nothing for him to worry about, and I meant it. When the boat actually arrived and I watched his thick back descend the ladder toward the rolling cockpit, I felt as if a hunk of me had just dropped out. Okrastone's wind-red face rising to take Teddy's place did not make me feel better, and Flap's rosy moon filled me with despair.

"Hey, don't pull no long face on account of that goose," shouted Okrastone. "We got the skinnie on that bird."

I assured him I was no longer concerned with Wong's Christmas cooked goose, while he and Flap, to my inward amusement, stomped about under the guise of getting warm while they tried to adjust themselves once again to the inside of the tower.

"Yessir, Bo, that ol' Wong—from what we heard to the station—he got drunk and beat the shit right outa that goose with the carving knife. Ain't that right, Flap?"

"That's what I heard." Flap gave it all the fist-raising cheer he could. "That's exactly what I heard, Boats."

"That's all very well and good," I said, "except Wong is a known non-drinker, and, besides, what the hell would the boys at the station know about what goes on aboard the *Philadelphia?*"

Okrastone shot a glance at Flap, who let his own eyes fall to the linoleum. When he looked up, however, he not only had an answer; he had a program. "We cannot let this winter business get us down, gentlemen."

And so it came to pass that Flap prepared his leading supper: spaghetti with a rich meat sauce. He had ordered the "special fixings" two weeks ago, making several emendations in the list he broadcast to the lifeboat station. Throughout that night, and for that matter several times during the following days, various lighthouses called to have him repeat some of the items. Brandywine Shoal Light went so far as to debate the use of pre-grated cheese, claiming that one should grate his own. This led to a sleepless mid-watch for Flap, and when I came down to relieve him the next morning he hung around mysteriously, prowling in the wire spice basket and thumbing the Amy Vanderbilt cookbook, his usually smooth brow lashed with thought, his formerly barren lips awash with the windrows of enthusiasm. Finally he bolted to the radio, switched the station tower watch to the informal frequency, and ordered a pound of Stilton cheese and a grater. He even stayed up until he got a confirmation from Walker's which took another hour of agony, Flap circling the cylinder slowly, like a donkey round a sugar-cane mill. The message came through at exactly 1000:

No Stilton cheese. No grater. Suggest pre-grated Parmesan. Walker out.

Ship John Shoal Light had monitored and informed us they had a grater, slightly rusty, which they could send down on Boat Day. Flap rogered and decided he'd go with that, all else failing. Miah-Maul Shoal Light offered a quarter pound of some kind of cheese that "has been here since before anyone was here," which led me to wonder if it had gone back to the days when Chanty had sat upon that particular tower steaming in his fries, like the priests of the early beacons burning their faggots. Fourteen-Foot Bank Light also offered an undetermined size of what they too considered an exotic cheese. From Elbow-of-Cross Ledge Light, knocked cock-eyed and automatic by the supership, came, of course, silence, though the way things were going it did seem possible that some old recipe, some ancient wisp of cookery, like the aroma it had once long ago produced, might yet come to us, borne upon the all-contributing air. The Group Commander had nothing to offer, nor did we expect anything. We waited to see if Delaware Lightship would contribute. Maybe Chanty's voice would once again come surging into the tower to warm us. From the open ocean, however, emerged no recipe but silence.

And so, on Boat Day, from all over the hundred-mile bay came streaming watercraft laden with rich and rare gifts for Flap's meal.

When the grater arrived by the hand of a grizzled boatswain, Flap spent the afternoon scraping it, plucking the rust from out of the puckers with a rusty ice pick. The cheeses he unwrapped and sniffed, and after cleaning his nostrils with balcony air as a wine taster would blot his tongue upon a dry biscuit, he returned to his work until he was satisfied with the intensity of his ingredients. He then measured all the pieces and cut them into weights relative to the nuance he had worked out. The spaghetti itself was soaked in water, which was kept at a particular temperature by the frequent infusion of water from the teakettle. The meat was rolled, pummeled, fondled, titivated, and benumbed at noon by thumbs specially anointed in the fat of milk. There were several other steps, transitions, and manuvers which I was not able to observe directly as I was sponging the lantern windows, high in a sway above the scaling gulls.

The sun went down; the alarm jingled in the dusky cylinder; the smell of spaghetti filled the tower with a warm blanket. Okrastone and I stood out on the balcony and made our *Volare* of the twilight wind. When we opened the door, the evening meal enveloped us.

. . . *Afterwards*, leaving the dirty dishes in the sink, Okrastone and I repaired to the leather chairs, superimposing our stuffed condition upon the already-bloated upholstery. "My word," he said at last. For my part, I reached a fat palm upward toward the T.V. knob and, seeing it was a hopeless journey, let myself fall back upon myself. No pair of dolphins in full suspiration about our summer tower could have blown a more meaty wind that hour than we two, deep enchaired upon our linoleum sea.

And then, almost in perfect antiphon, came from the regions of the sink a burp, *basso profundo*.

"What was that?" asked Okrastone. His chin swung clear of his chest.

"Must have been a porpoise," I said.

"Too late," said Okrastone. "Dead winter."

"And that smell," I said. It was not at all pleasant, nor even the kind of unpleasant smells porpoises sometimes, upon the evening zephyr, decant. "Did you do that, Boats?"

"No, Bo, I been strictly staying with the burp."

"So have I," I said, slightly outraged. After all, if others could, why couldn't . . . *others?*

I went to the sink, and there, among the sauce-splattered crockery, floated what I at first took to be a very veteran Brillo pad. It had that kind of loose structure, the various mats hanging together in a suspension of pure habit, that same kind of rusty color. And then, to my horror, up from the plates and forks came another burp, followed by the fragments of a further fibrous and, alas, none-too-foreign body, a portion of which kissed the tines of an already well-sauced fork and shuddered into a dozen shards. Some sank. At that precise moment, as if on cue, the cylinder door sucked open and re-entered the creator, himself—Flap, himself, triumphantly completing himself, his buckling.

"Oh, boy," he said, "I feel much better now."

Okrastone was standing, hands on hips, watching the sink. I looked from the sink to Flap. Flap tucked the end of his belt into the loop, blotted his hands, and, looking at Okrastone, placed his hands on his hips. "Don't you all feel better?" he said.

"I can't say I do, Flap," said Okrastone, "yet again I ain't done my shit in the sink yet."

It took Okrastone no time to conclude what had happened. The drain pipe that took our waste overboard had become plugged up by ice. I suppose I knew there was such a pipe. The Amish gentleman who had fallen overboard while fishing from the rocks last summer had been somewhat involved in that plumbing but I'd been distracted from its role in the event by the more overwhelming factor of the fog horn that I'd assumed had been the main cause of that pious man's downfall. That Okrastone was able to put his finger right on the seat of our present problem, so to speak, dazzled me. Who knew what other interior windings, structural nuances and other engineering aspects of our life he had under his benign control? For the moment we were to move down to the workshop to assemble our equipment.

The heavy diesel smell in the cellar was a welcome relief. All three of us searched frantically for a blowtorch.

"I could swear Toy was burning song birds with it one day," I said.

"I saw it once myself," said Flap.

"There's one on the inventory," said Okrastone.

Under the work bench my fingers at last made contact with its gritty belly. I pulled it out and, turning to them, extended it at full length, the votive lamp which was to deliver us from the oppression of the evil genie.

There followed a lengthy discussion and search for the proper fuel. Gasoline was mentioned, admired to the edge of awe, at which point it was abandoned for kerosene. What we actually found, however, was gasoline, a pint or so in the bottom of an outboard can.

"Where the hell did this come from, Flap?" Okrastone held the gas can aloft and glared at Flap as if it were something he had fouled the nest with.

"I never saw it before, Boats."

"Ain't these compartments under your jurisdiction?"

"Sure. Sure, Boats, mine and Teddy's."

"Teddy?" Lacking Teddy's presence, Okrastone now turned on me and I hung my head.

"I do remember it," I said. "Blump ran out and got it one day off the breakwater. A fisherman had it up there for some compressor rig he was diving with. The guy got drunk and went off and left it. Or something like that. Toy told me."

"Jesus, Boats," said Flap, "it was hidden away up in back of the workbench there."

"All the more dangerous, Flap. That's what we got to watch out for on here. What's hidden away."

"I'm sorry, Boats. I can see it was my fault."

"Well, I ain't sayin it's your fault." He sighed and set the gasoline can on the bench. "It will be good to get rid of this gas, anyway," said Okrastone. "You don't want this kind of thing out here." He went on to add his own version of the Stanard Rocks disaster—"You know, them poor boys out there in that blizzard had nothin to keep their hands warm but their own lighthouse tower burnin up."

"Well, that's certainly not the idea here," said Flap.

The gasoline was poured into the torch. Flap held the torch, Okrastone the gas can; I stood by with a rag. Okrastone put the top on the torch tank. I wiped up the drip. Then we paraded out the cellar door, each with our piece of equipment, walking carefully in the dark around the concrete base, which was covered with pane ice. The waste drain ran out from this base on the landward side and into the sea, or just about 180 degrees around from where the crack was. In the swoop of the light we saw it was low tide, a bit of a shock, for with winter we had lost track of those rhythms, too.

The cast iron pipe stuck straight out from the concrete base of the tower about a foot before turning down in an elbow another dozen feet toward the water. From the end of the pipe hung an amber beard of ice.

Flap gave the torch a swirl. The gasoline sloshed inside the brass belly. Okrastone held a packet of matches.

"Maybe we can just kick that ice away," I said.

"You want to climb down there, Bo?" Okrastone, however, had not yet selected from the packet which match was to do the job.

"It does look a little slippery," I admitted.

"Let's just cut the pipe up here," said Flap. "Breaking the ice won't do any good, because it will just do it all over again." He gave the belly another slosh, as if somehow that would get things going without the risk of the match.

"Well, next time we can at least have the dishes out of the sink," I said.

"Don't worry about those dishes," said Flap. "I'll take care of those, but I must say it's a pretty poor way to arrange the plumbing." He formed a healthy chuckle and shook the gas.

"These goddamn old stations," said Okrastone. There must have been at least twenty matches to choose from.

"Well, we could always be on Tilamook in Oregon," I said. "A guy I knew claimed all they had was a chute into the sea and in a westerly, even though they were seventy feet high, they'd get green water up the sphincter."

"Well, we ain't on Til'muck, we're out on the ol' Harbor Refuge, and I'm freezing to death," said Okrastone. "Here," he said to Flap, and he gave him the matches, "Light that damn machine off, Flap."

Sputterings and various forms of false ignitions followed. At last a pale flame danced upon the crisp air. Flap lunged, and the flame lunged at the pipe. It bounced off, curling back upon his fist.

"Don't get no back-suck with that thing, Flap."

"Don't worry," said Flap. "We had enough of that kind of thing tonight."

"You ain't just singing a song on that." Okrastone laughed and put his hand on Flap's shoulder. "Give her hell, Flap, boy."

"You bet, Boats."

And then so close was his face to Flap's, so suddenly low was his tone I almost could not hear him. *"Go for that solder at the knuckle now. Hit her there where she's joined. This torch ain't got the heat of an acetylene, so you ain't gonna just blow through anywheres."*

"You bet, Boats."

"Only, Flap," he said loudly, "Don't get no back-suck."

"Right!"

I stood by with a rag. For a moment I was tempted to dash around the base and take a peek at the crack. It had been weeks since I'd taken one of my readings and the whole while the sea had been getting heavier with winter. Such an excursion, however, would have produced a shout from Okrastone for not only deserting the present project, but risking my life on the seaward side. In any case, even in the lee, we lasted maybe twenty minutes in the cold. The tower, in spite of its odor, was welcome warmth.

The next morning, however, it was intolerable in every reach of the tower. I spent half an hour going about to all the decks, borne continually upward by the gas, working open every window I could: the lyric sash of the sleeping deck, well oiled by memories of warm summer eves; the lonely, damp windows of the empty third deck; the two windows of the watch-stander's deck, their mullions brittle with height. Finally I went to the crawl door in the lantern itself, upon whose catwalk I circled, and there among the white, airy drippings of the gulls, I observed far below the daylight performance of that tableau with which we, poor hoarders of darkness, had ended the night: Flap holding the torch to the pipe, Okrastone just behind him, hand on Flap's shoulder.

It was too cold to stay long and I had to go down through the increasingly bitter layers of what was now, thanks to my window opening, a Venice-like odor of water, sewage, and cold. For lunch we ate the excess of the famous meal, cold meat balls. I tried to sleep off my mid-watch that afternoon, but it was too cold, the kind of winter it can only be inside an unheated building on the water. I went out into the healthier cold and stood next to Okrastone and Flap and watched the torch eat into the solder at the knuckle of the cast iron pipe.

"You see why we got to do it this way," said Okrastone. "Now Flap here, he's not just one of these grease monkeys outa boot camp what would try to just blow that flame all over the cast iron. He's got her right on the jugular."

"It's going to be a question of the gasoline's holding out," said Flap.

And so that very fuel which had intimidated us the night before, that careless product of Blump's thievery and hoarding, we now fluttered about, coddling and coaching, cheering on in its struggle against the pipe knuckle.

Both Okrastone and I offered to spell Flap, but he would not give it up. We had long ago run out of nasty parallels and even all jokes remotely scatological. The freighters standing off from the far corners of the ocean interested us not, nor the birds in their screaming drafts. For us there were no horizons, no Venezuelas or Venices, no atmospheres or ornithology. The universe was upon the torch tip.

At five o'clock, in the long slants of the winter light, there came from the pipe a sound, for already the geyser of tumbling brown and amber was gushing with the full weight of the tower easing its plumbing.

We stood back in awe, Flap with the torch still going, its tiny flame faithfully if randomly nipping at the air, Okrastone with the gas can, me with my rag. We did not dare look at each other lest we lose the geyser, but out of the corners of our eyes we let each other know where we were.

At last the marvelous fountain sobbed to a dribble. There was nothing to do but get a bucket and slosh down the immediate rocks.

"There," said Flap, "now I really do feel better."

"That was some meal, Flap," said Okrastone. "Let's go inside and cook ourselves up a supper."

"Christ, yes," I said. "Nothing like a day in the open to give you an appetite."

THE STORM:
THE FIRST DAY

Hours passed as countless waves rolled over him. He was buoyed by the knowledge that the post to which he was lashed held firm. The salt water bit into the spots where the ropes had chafed the skin from his back and chest.

He experienced loneliness on the light for the first time since it was built. The little town of Lewes with its snug homes and bright streets, although just across the bay, might have been ten thousand miles away. The familiar ten second flash of Overfalls lightship was more distant than Orion. The gaunt platform on which he stood had, but yesterday, been inside the house he called his home; the flashing radiance of the light that had never failed since it was built gave way to an inky void. It was hard for him to realize that there was any other world but the one of noise and wet confusion that overwhelmed him. The dawn was a sullen gray that barely dissipated the blackness. A shift in the wind made the seas more confused. Breathing became more difficult for Willis since the waves had lost their rhythm and now drove on the rocks without definite direction or regularity. He and the stake to which he was bound were all that were left standing. A shrill cry from a storm-swept petrel came from somewhere overhead. It reminded him of the white bird on the lantern and the keeper's forebodings. It seemed there was something to the omen after all; if the keeper had remained one of them surely would have been swept away.

—John J. Floherty, *Sentries of the Sea*

MARCH 5TH. Clear and surprisingly warm.

Okrastone a bit restless. Pacing about, peering out windows, lowering his head toward the middle of them as if to butt squarely the glass. Hands on hips.

After lunch we began painting the sleeping quarters. He and Flap took one side and I the other. They had the outside of the curve to make the time work out even.

Not that it was supposed to be a race.

We used the pale-blue, water-base paint, and it went on quite easily, my brush just the right width for the vertical tongue-and-groove sheathing. I hummed and chanted to myself: *O the pale pleasures of water blue going on good bristle, spreading on tongue & groove.*

"Watch her there, Bo," said Okrastone.

"What's the matter?" I had to turn around on my knees to see him because he was that far behind.

"Getting a little sloppy," he said. He grimaced at his knees.

"Where?" I said.

"Thought I saw a few spatters fly."

"Not here," I said. Then I noticed it, almost under my pants. I killed it with a knee.

"Ooops," said Flap. He shook his head and bent to touch the floor with his index finger.

"That won't do her," said Okrastone. "Better get a rag."

We finished up about the same time. "You go down to the pier, Bo, and put all this gear away now. Button her down real good."

"Righto."

I trotted down the long stairs onto the pier, and just aft of where the boat was lashed, I put the paint in the yellow, galvanized boxes bolted to the landing stage. To make sure the lids were tight, I tapped them in evenly all around with my jackknife handle. While I was doing the last one I felt some big drops fall. At first I thought it was more paint spatter, the way drops leap up from the rim when you compress the lid. It was not only rain, but sea, spray from the sea. I looked over the edge. It was still a long way to the water. To the east the sea and sky looked like one of those summer thunder skies, when you have the smell of wet copper screening, cut lawns, relief from humidity.

Except there was no screening.

And there were no lawns.

The atmosphere was closing in, and yet there still seemed to be such an awful lot of sea.

Perhaps it seemed like so much because it was quite dark out; I expected it to be night and at night the sea or at least the outer half of it usually seems to go away, so that at night I would not be aware there was so much of it.

Now in the darkness there was all of it.

Or the hint of what all of it might be, all of an ocean stacked up there behind what you could see. Pushing it. Leaning on it and getting ready to push. Able to.

A bird flew low through the middle distance, and in the baffling light, though he was now closer, I lost him. Often there were ships out there this time of day, but now there was only the strange light and the hole in it where the bird had vanished.

I looked back at the boat. It was a homey enough craft that had been shipped out one time after Okrastone had arrived and I had been on leave. At first I had been excited by it. Much like a Maine-built rowboat my father'd towed behind his old Friendship sloop, it brought back memories of my boyhood, but Okrastone had so rigidly corseted it with a strongback and some of his new line that it was clear this was one vessel that would never go to sea again, and I had ceased to think of it as anything but another piece of gear we would someday have to paint. Now for the first time since the early days of the boat's arrival, I put my hand on it and felt the wood of the gunnel, much as a man who has been accustomed to stepping over his old sleepy dog will one day stop in his busy rounds and stoop to pet his old friend.

When I came back up into the tower it seemed strangely dark in there, too.

They had the lights on, but since it was still day, the electricity didn't make it any brighter. Rather, the bulbs seemed to contain their light all within themselves, casting no shadows.

Flap and Okrastone were laughing about something. I heard my name. Then they saw me.

"What's the matter?" I said, "did I leave spatters?"

"Boy, we were just sayin it's a good thing old Bo got up here," said Flap. He was looking out the window.

"I'll wipe it up," I said. "Any spatters I'm responsible for, I'll get."

"Not that you won't," said Flap. He still insisted on the window.

"A big hat full o' spray washed down the pier, Bo. Just as you finished patting that old boat and started up the stairs. It was com'kul the way it snuck up there behind you unbeknownst."

"I had glanced out that way," I said. "There was a bird coming toward me, but I lost him."

"Yes, boys," said Okrastone. "She's scuffin up."

"You know there's a story about storm petrels."

"Oh, oh," said Okrastone, "here we go: Chanty time again."

"You don't believe in storm petrels?"

"I believe in storm petrels all right. What I don't believe in is Chanty time."

"Well, forget Chanty."

"Already have, Bo."

"Do you know where they nest, the storm petrels?"

"Between the waves. They nests between the waves, Bo. That's right where your stormies nest."

"They may ride in the troughs of waves, may even, so to speak roost there, but they nest in ruined towers."

"Oh, brother," said Flap.

"Damn it," said Okrastone. "I knew you was gonna sneak him back in here."

"Ruined towers on the bleak off-shore islands of Scotland. They hide in the cracks of dry walls made in prehistoric times."

"These are them ruined towers what was built by crazy monks to go look at the sea side?"

"Well, they weren't ruined when they built them, Boats."

"And the monks, they does dances to the sunrise on their tippy-toes holding hands." Okrastone gave a demonstration. Considering it was getting dark and not sunrise, considering no one held his hand, considering he was not yet on the tower's top, it was an impressive performance. "And then the little birds fly out to cross the mighty ocean to pay us a visit."

"White rump flashing in the curling trough, feet dancing on the water, yes."

"According to Chanty time."

"Well . . ."

"Or something John J. Flow-hearse done write. Something out of a book."

"You know, Boats, sometimes things," said Flap, "sometimes things from life gets into books."

"Not the way they happens, Flap. Not the way they really happens."

"Well, sure, Boats," said Flap, "I mean Scotland, say, for instance, now that's a bit of a stretcher if you wanted to fly as a small bird, granted a sea bird. If what was sighted here was a storm petrel in fact, I assume it was from one of our own personal ruined stations closer to our nation itself."

"Oh, don't worry none about things like that, Flap," said Okrastone. "Any body can ex-plain that. It is just a real strange wind we got blowing right now. We got a fetch coming in all the way from the mid-At-lantic, even though winds don't usually blow that way."

"I'm not trying to reverse the cosmos here," I said. "It's most likely I didn't see a storm petrel at all. After all, it could have been most any damn thing."

"That's right," said Okrastone and he poked at the blind slats. "You see them robins and finches darting all alone, darting low between the waves, white rump flashing, feet dancing, you see that *all the time*."

"Then you saw it, too."

"I saw it." He batted the slat shut. "That don't mean it got to be no Flow-hearse. That don't mean it got to be no *ruined tower*."

I went to the window. The landing stage was dark with dampness except when another wave hit, and then the wood was renewed with silver before it drained back again to dark.

"Hey," I said, "I was just down there. Never mind all that stuff about ruined Scottish monks. *I* was just down *there*."

They both laughed.

"You sure were a funny sight."

"Funniest sight I seen in a long whiles, Bo."

During dinner the wind began to get at us. It was not that we felt the drafts, though the venetian blinds were in constant agitation. It was more that we seem to have been sought out by invisible currents and isolated in unfocused eddies of irritation. This condition was made more visible by our not eating together at the Formica table. Flap, who had taken to bringing a new puzzle aboard from each liberty, had now replaced his earlier cows and Alps with something more suitable, a lighthouse in a storm. In honor of this appropriatness Okrastone had given him permission to leave the puzzle on the dining table until it was solved. So there we were: Okrastone at his desk, as if filling not his face, but a government form; I by the sink as if ready to wash my plate ere I had dined from it; Flap hovering over the puzzle itself, his well-sauced fingers rummaging among the cardboard waves.

"Kind of a buffet," I said.

"Buffet all right," said Okrastone from around the cylinder. "Don't get them waves all gooey, Flap."

"Don't worry about the waves," said Flap and he sucked his fingers.

I stood by the drainboard and noted that those first freak waves that had, in their comic fashion, soused the pier that afternoon were now the rule. It was dark, but the planks lit up with the bouncing spray.

"Boy, if I were out there now, I'd get soaked," I laughed. I needed, however, a little extra Kool-Aid to get the bread down.

Of course it was dark, but that was all right now, I thought, because in winter you got used to eating supper when it was dark out. I tried to remember if we had had dark during supper the night before. After all, it was March, and we had come through the worst of winter.

"Yes, supper is a bit later tonight on account of our working," I said.

"What are you mumbling about, Bo?" The voice came from around the cylinder.

"It's kind of fun to eat a late buffet," I said. "And what with this wind, it makes for a kind of change."

"We've had wind before," said Okrastone. He was bringing his dinner around to the sink. "We had wind before," he said. There was a lot of meat left on his plate.

Flap turned in early, early even considering he had the mid-watch. "Boy," he said, "am I pooped." As he reached for the doorknob there was a heavy detonation, and his fingers fell short. "That was a big one," he said and laughed. This time he made sure he grabbed the knob before it got away.

Okrastone stayed up with me until an hour or so before midnight. With some kind of mischievous delight I suggested we work the puzzle. "When Flap wakes up we'll have a complete *Lighthouse in the Storm*," I said.

The puzzle tower, a stark white cliché, had been completed, and so, too, had the more distant waves. Immediately around the tower, however, was a yawning void of Formica and sauce.

"Come on, Boats," I said, "*The Lighthouse in the Storm*."

"No thanks, Bo," he said. "I got work to do." He sat at his desk and looked out the window. Perhaps from where he sat he did have some of the darkness to study, but all I could see was his face, chewing slowly, an act which he justified occasionally by driving a cardboard matchpack deep into his gums.

I fiddled with the waves at the base of the tower.

"I thought you didn't like puzzles, Bo," he said. "I thought you said they was kid stuff." He had done a good job on the match pack, soaked. Licked his lips.

"This one seems more real," I said. "Those others were cows in puddles, water wheels."

"It don't matter what it's of," he said. "Some old bossy or a ship or a lighthouse, some boat in a storm. It's the figuring out that does her."

"Then come over here and help me with the waves," I said.

"I tol you, Bo, I got work." He continued staring out the window. Both of his hands were on the window sill. The fingers were on top and the thumbs under the sill lip, pressing up.

A banging below. For a moment everything had been chattering, the puzzle pieces only held down by the dinner sauce. Then we located it.

"Down below."

"Right. It's down below."

"Maybe you'd better step down and check, Bo."

"I'll step down and check."

It was, of course, the engine-room doors. That afternoon, because, as Okrastone had put it, "it's such a pretty day," we had opened them, and, more out of hope than laziness, had left them wide in their summer position, their sheer weight holding them out on the concrete base.

In the cellar there was the expected din. I kept assuring myself that all that noise was no more than I expected, any reasonable man might expect. The doors were still open, and I wondered if it really could have been they that had made such twanging. After all, here was no flimsy back-door slatter, but the stuff of which boilers were made. I waited to see, nevertheless, if the doors would make their move. It would not be the kind of move anyone would want to be caught in. A sea hit. I heard the thud against the side of the base, and then, after a decent interval, the gentle sprinkling along the top of the base. The doors were as mute as I.

I walked toward them and stepped through onto the concrete base. It was, as I expected, slick with spray. As the main light swung out to sea, I saw a dark shape coming toward me. It broke in the light. I started back to the doors, but I slipped and there was a bang and I continued sliding past the doorway and on around to the lee side where the wave zipped off the concrete down onto the rocks, abandoning me prone on the base as if I were a walrus awakening to find the flats had ebbed.

"Ho, ho, ho," I said and got up carefully.

Around by the doors I had my first moment of panic.

They were both closed. I pawed the edges, finding one sufficiently twisted to give me a grip, and I pried it open and tiptoed inside. There was a two-foot step up onto the engine-room floor, so there was no water up there yet, though the entrance well was slick with oil and water. I dragged the door behind me and, wiping my feet on a swab, stalked across the floor. I had no sooner arrived at the top of the stairs into the living deck when I heard the doors boom open again.

"*My word*, son." said Okrastone, "didn't they teach you how to close doors in that bugle school? And look at you. What a sight. Look like you done fell down into that crack you're always mumblin' about."

"I went sliding," I said. "On top. It was fun."

He came down with me this time, adjusting his belt.

"Another notch or two on that belt and you'll be eligible for chief," I said.

At the bottom of the stairs, when we opened the door into the engine room, the noise was as bad as before. Out through the doors we saw the pilot boat, or rather its lights, lurch past. It took both of us to haul in the doors. He shouted something to me over the din. When they were shut, it was not so much quieter as a different kind of noise, not the raw howl and splash but the moan and sock mixed into vibrations—that echoed.

I took the clothesline and lashed the handles to the old barrel frame. He frowned, shook his shoulders and motioned toward the inner door. As we rose away from the din he said, "I notice you had that clothesline rigged up like that, Bo, but that ain't the right way to do it."

"Do it any way you want," I said. "That's just the old way."

"We'll see," he said. "By the way, when you were out there before, slippitty-sliding around——"

"It was fun," I said. "Though I don't recommend it."

"Well, you didn't happen to see anything of that old crack, did you now, Bo?"

"No," I said. "The wave took me to the lee side."

"Oh, yes, of course," he said, "the lee side."

Upstairs, he turned on the TV, but it was jumping. He turned on the pilot radio. It was the first time I'd ever known him to use this civilian operation. Captain Trasker was bellowing, and Okrastone did not cut him off, though he did ease the captain down a decibel or two. "Well, tomorrow," said Okrastone, "tomorrow, Bo, we'll sure give her hell."

He glanced at the puzzle, picked up a white piece with a vicious curl in it, and without looking directly at either the piece or the puzzle, tossed the piece on the table and walked back to his desk.

With only a half hour to go I stayed down in my damp clothes. I'd even forgotten how I'd gotten them wet and was too tired to climb up to the sleeping quarters twice. When I did go, Flap mumbled, said he'd been listening to the storm, how was it? I told him it was a good howler but the visibility was still O.K. Captain Trasker was giving it hell, telling the pilot boys not to get their "tosies" wet, et cetera. Flap laughed at the Trasker story. I was glad to get to bed. I actually looked forward to a night of such wind, without fog, without the horn.

I had gone off to sleep for what was probably an hour, but seemed like only minutes, when I felt somebody shake my bunk. I paid no attention until it happened again. Opened one eye and looked over at Okrastone, but he had gotten back into his bunk. Dropped off again, but the bed shook me awake. Again by the time I'd gotten an eye open Okrastone had gotten back to his bunk. I formed a mild protest upon my lips and dozed. The next time I sat straight up the instant it happened. Okrastone was just rolling over and grunting something. It seemed mighty strange that he'd be up to such an elfish trick. Perhaps the old guy was merely getting back at me for having said below that puzzles were childish. How did one measure the mirth that was in those who commanded you?

I called out, "O.K., Boats, enough's enough," and lay back again. I had just begun to go off when the door burst open and Flap came running in. At the same time the room was lit and I could see he had a swab and bucket. "God damn it, Flap," I said, "this is one hell of a time to begin cleaning up the deck."

"Look-at-it; look-at-it," he shouted in a high-pitched voice. Although Flap had suddenly become a nut on cleaning things up, he seemed awfully sloppy. He had water an inch or two deep all over the place, under my bed, everywhere. "Don't put so much water on the deck, Flap," I said.

Okrastone was sitting up, rubbing his eyes and scratching himself. No doubt it had been his instructions to swab the deck in the middle of the night. Like the afternoon's painting and the oft-threatened tower chipping, this was obviously part of the new spring festival that was going to make an end of winter. Me, I was tired of cleaning up the damn lighthouse. "If you've got to clean, at least turn off the goddamn light," I said.

"I can't see if I turn it out," said Flap.

"Oh, for Christsake, what the hell are you cleaning the damn place in the middle of the goddamn night for anyway?"

"Look-at-it; look-at-it," he said. He then tried to open the window. I noticed he was at the same time trying to insert a large floppy piece of rubber—an object that could have only come from the engine room—into the frame. Just as he had his head under the venetian blind there was a crash, and water poured over his shoulders. It was as if I were looking at the back of one of those performers in carnivals who have whole buckets thrown at them. It certainly seemed a poor time for Flap to put on such an act. Though it did puzzle me whom he could have had working with him, throwing those bucket loads, I was also worried about Flap dragging up the rubber mat from the engine compartment. Who knew what sort of greasy thing he would next decide belonged in our bedroom?

"Come on, Bo," said Okrastone, "we might as well join in."

While there certainly was a lot going on inside the tower, there seemed to be a fair amount going on outside as well, and a good amount of the outside was trying to happen inside.

"Look out for the glass, Bo," said Flap. He was leering at his hand. It was bloody.

"Glass?" I said. I was sitting up on the bunk and blinking, making, I thought excellent progress. "Glass?"

"All over," he said.

"That's odd," I said.

Nevertheless I put my feet onto the floor, or what I hoped was still the floor, for my toes were fading down through very cold water, water cold enough to have been composed entirely of broken glass. "You're right," I said to Flap. I felt that admitting this was the least I could do.

We got the mat in the window, though it was hardly a good fit, Flap's frequent and frantic shearing work aside. Once the bendy old thing was jammed up and in, we slammed what remained of the window which was supposed to hold it, though just exactly what the window was by now composed of, we weren't sure. In any case, for a moment the mat held; no water came in. Everything seemed settled. I yawned, stretched, and, scratching my underwear, headed back through the shards of sea water to bed.

"Get all this water cleaned up, Bo," said Okrastone.

"You really weren't playing a joke on my bed," I said. I had seen the damn thing walk each time a sea had hit. Blankets, pillow, and all of the private rumplings.

Okrastone was putting on his sneakers and had a morning cigarette going. For all I knew he would soon utter his morning fart, and then, no matter how distant was the natural dawn, our day would have already been irrevocably ushered in. "How bad is it below, Flap?" he said.

Flap wiped his hands on his soggy jeans. "Oh, well, you know me, Boats," he said. And then he did tell about the storm, how he'd been sitting there on watch in the famous chair, getting a bit nervous at the way the puzzle pieces kept walking out of gear and then back in. The TV had gone off without his touching it, and there were just those puzzle pieces until Cape May came on with a weather advisory. The message said to expect "high winds" and heavy seas of "unusual intensity." Just as he'd rogered the message, and the group office was very careful to get everyone in the lighthouse chain to speak up, the radio exploded.

"It what?" said Okrastone.

"I looked up and saw this steady stream coming down on it, down on the radio."

"A stream?" I said. "Sure it was a stream," said Flap. "It came from up here. From the window there."

"When did you cut your hand?" I said.

"When the sea broke the window here."

"It did?" I said.

"You're damn right it did," said Flap. "What do you think's going on?"

"The whole sea?" I said.

"Well, maybe not the *whole* sea——"

"Come on, boys," said Okrastone, "ain't no time to bicker." He buttoned up his dungarees, grabbed a shirt, and they went below. I stood in the middle of the floor in my underwear and began to mop. "I'm not bickering," I said out loud. "I just want to know what the hell's going on."

As I squished about I was struck again with how cold the water was. I had my sneakers on, so I wasn't worried or in any way confused by the glass but the water was still awfully cold. At first this only annoyed me as it meant I had to interrupt my bailing to blow on my hands, put them under my arm, then when that zone was exhausted, between my legs. Eventually I'd worn out all my warm places and it became increasingly difficult to bring my hands back after wringing out the swab, and I began to grow bitter—after all, here I was doing my best to give this water, which had left the majesty of the sea to splatter and drool on my bedroom floor, give it at least the dignity of a bucket burial in the shower, and it was responding by stinging, then numbing the very fingers of funereal friendship.

With the second bucket I poured down the drain, a thought came over me as the water slid over a butter-sized bit of soap, swirled into that pipe made sweet by summers and shampoos—a thought chill as the iron bucket in my hand: *this now going down the drain, this is what we have all around us. This is what we may become.*

Such thoughts, I reflected, are bound to change a man's pace, one way or the other. I decided it was going to be the other. I trotted round to the window. The mat still seemed to be holding, though it was sweating tropically. There were, of course, other windows on that side, and the two sills over there were filling, hiccoughing, and spilling gaily. The broken window, I calculated, was directly over the famous crack and was no doubt head on to the fetch. I emptied the bucket in the shower without particular attention to the pattern or nostalgia of the swirl, and returned, skidding on broken glass, but holding my balance. The mat was running with sweat.

Several more buckets, and I seemed to be gaining. A few more and I had it pretty well under control, only a few damp spots, the kind that would horrify housekeepers on television ads but certainly would not send any mariners to their supermarkets. The broken glass I gathered and put in a wastebasket that had, in that first rush, been carried around to the lee side. I ripped apart Teddy's bunk, which, being directly beneath the window, had become soaked. It was too bad he wasn't aboard this week, I thought. He'd certainly have more interesting things to say than the others.

As matters were, it simply wasn't all that interesting. At this rate, if the great ship did go down, I'd not be singing "Nearer My God To Thee," but the "Irish Washerwoman," and at that not lyrically, but grayly, as befitted my gray and darling bucket.

I wrung out the mop.

Finally I had to go below, not that there wasn't more work to do: more wringing the sill slop into the bucket, more staring after the bouncing drops as they hit in the bucket, more trotting off to the shower to empty the bucket, trotting back to fill up the bucket. To hell with the bucket! I felt it was my right to . . . well, get out and see people. After all, who knew but that even then my companions, my mates might be pinned behind the officer's desk, their ribs stove in, but lungs still rising and falling in desperate breath.

Dramatically enough for my moment's needs, every piece of furniture was rearranged. Surely at last, after so many acts of comedy, tragedy, betrayal, and buoyant humor, we were being evicted. And, of course, I thought the sea had done it. But alas, it had been merely Flap under the petty officer's direction, who'd lugged, no doubt grinning, the whole lot to leeward. There was the famous leather chair and its less famous brother piled on top of each other in most infamous fashion. There was the desk, once proud bastion of red tape and infinite evasion, slid on the residue of mullion drippings, shoved to the very jaws of the pantry. Scattered saucepans, buckets, and the larger table vessels, once rich with steam and the pride of major meals, now lay about quarter-filled with tepid liquids gathered from the blotting of kleenex, the dipping of wash cloths, the puckering of sponges. And more water dripped from the overhead and slopped from the sills of windward windows.

Surely someone had not paid a bill.

Okrastone asked me how went the fight aloft. I told him. He wanted to know if that were the case, how was it water was still leaking in. We tilted our necks, and beads ran wildly about the overhead; there was one groove which had not even the decency to bubble before dropping, but steadily peed.

"Well," I said, "I never said it was all over with."

He and I mounted the stairs and went not for my deck, but the third. And damned if, behind that dish-toweled door, there wasn't water coming in. We climbed on up and checked the main light, which was still bravely squeaking. It was odd, but that sound which had so unnerved me when I'd first heard it in summer, a sound like a strangling seagull, now comforted me.

There was, however, some water sweating through the panes, and they rattled and wobbled in their unputtied state, so that they let in water around the edges which we tested by licking, though it wasn't raining, or didn't seem to be. But who the hell could know the difference in the continual drench? As soon as we tasted the drops from the windows we knew. Old black iron and salt. Seventy-two feet above the surface of the sea. We looked at each other. Our hands cupped to our face. All around us our reflections in the panes, so that we looked like a huddle of men about some ancient ritual. Our fingers caught now in our lips. Tasting salt.

And the swaying up there was very strong, so that in a way, were we glad for the familiarity of so common a day's table need as salt. And the taste of our hands. And as we rode through the black sky, so close to each other in the cramp of the squealing lantern, we were also grateful for the sight of each other's erupted follicles, scaling epidermis, and other skin imperfections.

"Let's just hope she don't short out," he said.

"How would that happen?" I asked. "A short out?"

"If she leans too much, she might snap something."

"And what might that be that she'd snap?"

"She'd snap the shore cable."

"Ah."

Below it was much better as far as the motion went, though Flap, who had not been aloft, could not appreciate such distinctions. To him, there amidst the first deck's spinning of saucepans, the reproach of removed furniture, there was careering enough. "Wow," he said, and latched onto his belt. "Let's go to the engine room," as if it were some place for a good peaceful puke.

Much better as far as the motion went, though the din was up as if to compensate. No question of speaking. Hard even to hold a thought. *Two stories high is this engine room*, I kept saying to myself, *two stories high and with roots that go deep*. In spite of my incantations the engineroom seemed but a resonating box in which to creep and slosh one's life out and I longed, as an old man will grow wistful for his fiftieth year, I longed for the lovely world of the middle decks where a man might sway with dignity.

In any case, the water was up six inches over the floor, that same floor we had painted with advice—proper quotation of the *Paint & Color Manual* from all of our brothers in darkness; that same deck on which Chanty had with bare feet slapped out the *sullen-noise* sparks; that same deck I'd limped over with frozen hose; found another time the belly beneath the workbench, the belly of the blowtorch which had generously freed us from the tyranny of Flap's sink-stopping meal. It was also a floor normally six inches above the entrance way, which was normally eighteen inches above the concrete base, which was normally chin high above the breakwater, which was normally scalp tall above the sea. In short, normally, a most normal floor. And these were not *waves* that were in our cellar, but what you might call, in such a storm as this, *mean low water*, or if that would not please a hydrographer's heart, *the level from which other things leapt*.

The compressors, however, were up another eighteen inches on concrete blocks, glowering like sphinxes, as if they'd seen such rising and falling before. Okrastone, out of homage or God knows, for it had been undeniably fogless above, determined to start one of them. Perhaps in all that howl and din he wanted some of the noise to be our own.

"You go on up," he shouted. "Turn on them horn switches."

"Go *up?*" I shouted. And by now I thought I'd found a home.

He made his thumb rise and I recalled that on those ice-spewed and bear-haunted decks of Alaskan buoy tenders, he had, after all, been the boatswain who determined just what sat on deck and what went up.

So I went up.

And stopped off to gain some sense of myself. I bailed a bit in what to me was still where it all had started.

The sleeping quarters. Where I continued bailing.

There was plenty of work to do, and I was doing it when Okrastone broke in. He had to wait a minute to catch his breath, and I took the time while he huffed up a speech to strangle the swab slowly, thoroughly into the bucket.

"You didn't turn them switches on yet?" he said.

"Oh," I said. "Oh, no." I dropped the swab and started for the door. I thought he was going to shout something about how the tower would explode with all that compression being built up below and no horns switched open to emit the hysterical breath.

Instead he came with me and putting his hand on my shoulder said, "I know you think it's silly to have the horns going when we can see the Greenmeal lights, but this way everybody'll know we're still here—even if the light goes."

"Well," I said, "if the whole thing goes at least we won't have to chip her down this spring."

"That's a good boy," he said, "keep your sense of humor."

I hadn't intended it for humor. I still felt that it was one thing to fall over inside a tower and quite another to go aloft on the outside of that tower to sway on a gantline, to flail with a chipping hammer as the tower wall sailed past.

It was necessary that I hustle to catch up with him as he pumped his legs up around the spiral staircase to the room of switches and valves. It was gloomy in there, but there was bailing though the swaying was worse. Somehow the water seemed colder there, too, and as I reached under the springs of the mattressless pipe berths to cull the spray, I thought, *a man lost in this sea . . . less than three minutes.* If only I could get the technique for wringing out the sponge before it got to my hands. I shoved them down inside my pants after each try. "My," said Okrastone, "but I'll wager that makes for a cold set of stones."

It did.

Okrastone threw the switches and went below. They clicked on after him, the pressure needles twitching, jumping just before each scream of the horn. Well, ashore they will know us.

If only I could get a technique for wringing out before it gets to me.

Well, by morning . . .

THE STORM: THE SECOND DAY

Early in the afternoon a break came in the storm; the wind subsided and the sea lost its fury. A patch of blue appeared in the east.

The keeper, watching every little shift in the weather from the dock at Lewes, stamped impatiently. The breakwater was still a two mile stretch of roaring white. He noticed, however, that the seas rolled over its outer end without their usual explosive crash against the lighthouse.

—John J. Floherty, *Sentries of the Sea*

MORNING DID NOT come. Time did pass, measured by dripping, erased by swaying; and somewhere in the swaying came a cold light out of the east. In that light I could see my sponge change color and the water in the bucket change, and when the water ran off the pane for a moment I saw out into such a mass of water as I'd not thought possible.

I don't know why there should have seemed to be so much of it. I certainly could see no farther than usual, and there were no landmarks out that way to be now covered. But there it was: *volume*.

The sea would yawn away from us, retreating to build a wall all along its backswing. Up and up went the wall, but that was O.K., because the wall at that point seemed to be moving away from us. We knew better, of course, knew that it was building back there, gathering itself for the onrush, yet it was better to forget that, to kid ourselves a bit rather than watch that grayness gathering and know that each foot up it went, each ton along the crest that was added, each increase in the thrust was meant for us.

And there it would halt.

Hang.

The windowpane had grown opaque. That thin glass was protected, so it seemed, by the wave itself. (Who knew what lay *behind* the wave?) And now, with the pane grown solid, we were defended from the sight of the wave, and it just seemed to hang out there somewhere. That the tower shook, the bunks walked, and the water wept over the sill meant nothing; the wave itself had not yet broken.

311

And when the pane had cleared for the moment, there seemed to be no sea at all, only a gray hole getting deeper, so that whereas a moment before we seemed helplessly squat, unable to lift our chins up to breathe, now we were tall enough to be flying. Or since we could not fly, to be perhaps falling.

As I worked I thought, from time to time, that I must really follow one of these waves, one of the larger ones, all the way through its cycle. I really must do that, I thought, for my children will want to know exactly what it felt like when one of the big ones hit. I could not, of course, spare the time at the moment, but surely there would be a wave I could be saving for them, some great graybeard curling just now out beyond the capes, making itself worthy of such posterity, an immortal mound of bleak fury gathering itself unto itself, assembling all its awesome tons to come charging down the fetch. Yes, that would be a fine wave for me to put in trust. For the moment I kept my head low over the galvanized bucket and once, as I stared into that handful of thin gray sea water—for that's what it was, not washerwoman water, but water from the actual sea outside—once with a punch it jumped right up, that two inches of water, and my head snapped back just shy of the wet hit.

I'd grown so used to thinking that our breakwater made us more than a mere pinnacle in the void that when I went below and looked north over the Formica of the dining-area table and I saw that there was nothing but gray, no brown—that is, no rock, nothing but sea—I grabbed onto a chair. Rooted there I stood, my fingers pinching the plastic chair-back while the breakwater slowly uncovered. In that withdrawal, the table, even the chair rattled, and sea water seemed to be running out of everywhere, sucked down, trying any way at all to get down, make it down through the big, square rocks; take them, if necessary, for the cracks between weren't opening fast enough for this water that had to get down, that had to be down just as far down as possible—drained, dead, and gone before the fresh load whacked.

The spices were in the sink, tipped, some wet and wrecked, stepped on, cheap cottages after a tidal wave. I looked out over the linoleum counter, out over the sandwich of dead flies, and saw that the flies seemed not dead but busy regrouping and bumping about in a grand flotilla, afloat upon a sill full of sea water. Out below them I could barely find the landing stage. It was awash, tilted. It might have been a raft canting past rather than our only hope for escape.

As I watched, the wave retreated and I could get an idea of what had once been. I could then figure out what was left, for it was so altered that at first I had no precise idea of what I was looking at, as in an old photograph one will hardly recognize the house he is living in. Especially strange was the fact that the last dozen planks were missing from the stage, those planks

and the spiles, too, so that everything remaining seemed, until I realized
what had happened, foreshortened.

The yellow paint locker in which the afternoon before I'd so carefully
tapped home the lids of the pale bedroom blue with the butt of my jacknife,
was gone. Another such locker closer to us was twisted from most of its bolts
and hanging over the edge. The railings and the stairway down to the stage
were smashed into flopping splinters. The boat was full of water, and as soon
as the stern line let go, it was sure to be off after the paint cans.

I thought about those spiles and looked at the ones that remained. They
were four in a single unit, each individual a good eighteen inches in diameter, and had been wrapped in two-inch cable. And, of course, they had been
on the lee side of the breakwater. No storm since I had been on the light had
come within twenty vertical feet of where the water now lay. As for the
waves . . .

Okrastone drew a chair up to the counter and joined me. So far as I
knew he had never sat there before, nor had any man, as the counter was a
working area and such sitting as he was now doing was naturally done out at
the Formica table. That was, of course, around more toward the open sea.
The look on his face was of great sadness. Sadder than the first day back from
liberty, sadder even than when I'd worn him down about the crack. For a
moment, he seemed about to turn on me and give me some sort of grudging
hell about my whining prediction, some admission that all that Floherty
business was indeed the way things were, and while there would have been
a time when I might have wanted that confirmation it was not now, and that
not because of anything to do with engineering or even our safety. I stood
awaiting his announcement braced as I had learned to prepare for the shock
of the seas. There were five waves before he spoke.

"What a goddamn mess," he said.

The visibility cleared a bit, and we could see down the whole length of
the buried breakwater, and though there was more light in the air, there
seemed to be even more sea. We now had enough of the breakwater to see
why the tower was chattering, see down the whole length of the buried
stones, watch them fold and unfold, feel the pull as it retreated, a pull that
seemed on twine attached to our balls.

We were not alone, however. Two destroyers lay behind us, less than a
mile back, rolling and pitching, narrow, gray reptiles with sharp faces, ships
we'd never seen near us before. I thought of what my father'd said about the
Japanese typhoons at the end of World War Two and how designs like these
had rolled and in some cases kept on rolling. Behind them, though, was the
pilot's mother ship, riding up and down, and it was comforting too, to think

that our breakwater was still, though buried, making a harbor for some-body's refuge.

We continued to bail, switching our duties to various decks not only for variety and to give each other a break on the excessive sway of the upper floors, but so that, as Okrastone put it, "We have a fresh eye now and then in each trouble spot."

I noticed the Bufferin supply was getting low.

Flap fried up some ham steak and, without anyone's asking him, he sim-ply swept the puzzle into its box, and we sat down at the Formica table and ate the ham. Okrastone got up and made eggs. I did some coffee, and when we'd eaten I tried to throw the garbage out the back door, which was, after all, in the lee. It all came back in my face. The other two laughed.

"But goddamn it," I said, "I ain't no piss-to-windward sailor; that's the *lee*."

"Ain't no lee these days," said Okrastone.

The sun broke, and the grayness turned to a blinding white and blue, blinding because so much more white than blue. It was not just whitecaps, but thick with white all the way out to where I'd never seen it white at all before. Back the other way, we could see what must have been Greenmeal. With binoculars we tried to find buildings, towers, anything to confirm that this was indeed Greenmeal, for our usual marks seemed so altered that we could not at first find our way about. And then, oddly enough, everything looked exactly the same. Apparently the only thing that had changed was the level of water lying between us and the shore, water which we now realized was not only a space between, but a plane over which we saw, determining, in a sense, what at the far end we did see. And now, looking over the backs of unprecedented waves, our eyes followed a piece of sunlight that was skid-ding and dipping, torn and at the beach, blown back. It was a wonder we had anything less than Arabia. Excitedly we passed the binoculars back and forth, each man finding something new: the inner breakwater underwater; the inlet wider; a house missing here; one shifted there.

We tried the radio, but it was still dead, and all we could get was the en-tertainment radio. They spoke, between melodic heartbreaks, of great losses all up and down the Atlantic. A lightship was sinking somewhere. It didn't seem to concern the announcer exactly where, but he did think we all should know she was sinking. A seagoing tug was rushing to her aid. It was named the *Cherokee*.

"Hot damn," said Okrastone, proud as an old Yale grad.

But the seas were too steep, and his old ship could only stand by.

"Then that could be the Delaware Lightship?" I said. "With Chanty?"

"I knew you'd figure some way to get that boy into our storm here," said Okrastone.

"Well, I'm glad Teddy's not out there," said Flap. "Not that they couldn't use his help."

"Oh, no," said Okrastone, "we wouldn't let our Teddy go way out there."

"Well, I'm glad he's not in here, either," said Flap. "Not that we couldn't use his help."

"Oh, I imagine he's turning to in there with the boys at the station. They probably got that canal right up to their back door. I know that was the way it was down to Hat'rus. The biggest problem, they always come across from the back door." He walked over to the stove and switched off the burner that had, until the last sea, been directly under the coffee pot.

Rainbows came past us all afternoon, and we lived without sleep in a swaying crystal. Fountains were everywhere, and so were sounds, shocks, bubbles, sonorous showers, and perpetual sprayings.

"Look at it," I said.

"A cot damn mess, that's what it is," said Okrastone.

We had expected it to let up by midafternoon, but only the sunlight lessened. Gloom rolled in through our geysers, but the wind picked up. It was sure we would be in for another night of it.

I decided I would try to sleep in the pantry. "I'm going up to the second deck and bring my mattress down," I announced.

"O.K., Bo, but take a peek around up there for me."

It was not only colder up there, colder than even the blizzards had made it, but the bed was still walking on each sea. I stood there a moment, like a man at midnight coming upon a pantry so thick with roaches that everything moves at him. "That's my bed," I said to my bed. It walked off anyhow.

I wondered if my bureau would support me in the sea. Of course I'd lighten it by emptying the drawers. As it was they jiggled in and out, offering me glimpses of their contents. Those were my socks just peeping out and there a bell-bottom. There, too——was that the Blump hat? Who knew what clothes a man ought to pack for drifting ashore? And books, what books should I take? There were lists for those going to spend time on desert islands and lighthouse, but what about lists for those leaving the lighthouse by bureau drawer? Now there was a syllabus to give a man pause.

Below in the pantry, it was much simpler. The cans that kept coming out from the topmost shelves and peeping down at me, old Jolly Green

Giants and assorted beady-eyed peas, smirking jellies and such, I merely moved to low, anonymous corners.

"Nice and snug in there, Bo?" said Okrastone.

"I know this is a bit of a scandal," I said, "broad daylight and horizontal in the pantry."

"It's all right if it's snug," he said.

Since it was my mid-watch I heard them bailing all evening. By being in the pantry I could keep my eyes shielded from the overhead glare my mates found so necessary for their slurping and tinking.

They did not talk much, but they did, of course, from time to time, speak. Usually it seemed to have to do with moving something. They seemed to spend a great deal of time moving a chair. Was it the Famous Chair? It was certainly on this day, gathering fame. And where was old Famous himself now? Here I was in the most sacred of all his sacred spots, his pantry. Old Mother Famous Chanty. Was he out on *Delaware?* or had he finally succumbed to deeper waters in Baltimore? Neither thought bore much looking into. And what of his other sacred spots right here? The whole place was a symphony of sullen noises. As for the famous crack . . . wasn't that what they were talking about just now? Wasn't that what Flap & Okrastone were whispering about? Wasn't that what their sponges were hissing? Ah, better the salubrious food of gossip than the gap itself. Yes, we were safe as long as we had yet our famous places.

After a few spasms of unconsciousness, which I let pass as sleep, I felt a lump larger than any Jolly Green Giant, and discovered Okrastone rapping at my back. In a moment Flap was tugging my shoe. I rose to let him stare at my favorite can of chicken chow mein.

There didn't seem to be much *new* water coming in, and what was already there, I figured, after the manner of sullen firemen in Chanty's boiler-watch stories, belonged to the watch that had left it. I tried reading, alternating a memoir of Joyce Cary's sailing off Ireland (but not too far off) with an even less suitable letter from a boot camp buddy now stationed in Nashville, Tennessee, patrolling a reservoir. This placid duty had convinced him that what both he and I needed (he referred to my "sedentary lighthouse duty"), was "a long open ocean voyage" in a catamaran canoe of his own design. One of us, to avoid getting on each other's nerves, was to be in each hull.

"I know that much is controversy and false romanticism concerning the sea," he wrote, "but I assure you I respect as well as admire her august & awesome majesty. Any boat you and I would embark on would be double-planked and adequately caulked."

Unfortunately, we had run out of Bufferin. There was some aspirin somewhere back in the medicine cabinet, but I recalled becoming sick as a child from such bitter and crumbling aids, and there seemed to be no mother to hold my head over a willing basin now. I tried to go back to Joyce Cary's Irish Sea, but though his publishers promised a "beguiling lyric through the calm seas of childhood," I found his linotypers and compositors had most assuredly played him false. They had made and composed all his lines in the manner of raveling scrolls. And then I saw what it was. It wasn't at all drunken and print-fingered men of Dublin setting a page of prose, but the gooseneck migrating upon the bulkhead. The lamp, neck and all, was bloody bobbing for eels. And lively ones at that, no mud dwellers as you'd expect in March.

I reached up to steady the lamp. "There, there." But my hand jumped with the gooseneck, and by God, so did the bracket, and when I looked about for other signs, matters of familiarity such as venetian blinds, the Heliocrafter radio, and the bracket holding over my head the commercial delights of the entire eastern seaboard—well, none of it was keeping still.

"Damn," I said. "There's nothing to do but bail."

And there, like a craven shirking his duty, crept the castered chair of the officer-in-charge, creeping on around the tower and coming a-thud somewhere up on the shores of the china cabinet.

A great surge of duty passed through me. I must, thought I, aloft to check what drippings have occurred in the upper precincts.

For the first time then since, in fading daylight, I'd seen my bed go mincing about, my intimate drawers waltz in and out, I attempted the upper decks. I opened the door to the cylinder and there still was the stairway. Good, thought I, we are still attached.

And I went up, rather smugly, lurching only occasionally against the iron walls. That, I thought, could be from lack of proper sleep.

I found the sleeping deck exactly where I had left it: precisely between the first and third deck. The only thing missing was the pin-up over Teddy's bunk. How long had that been down? Was it there when Flap had come to fix the broken window? Had he in his rage with the rubber mat flailed and stripped her from the sweaty bulkhead? Or had she gone at an earlier hour? Hadn't we just painted that wall? She must have been removed for that occasion, put carefully behind a locker door. Or had she simply deserted us upon some previous insult, perhaps months before?

I began reaching in under Teddy's mattress springs, not for her, but in pursuit of the coldest water that wasn't yet ice.

At which precise moment, as when someone sticks his thumb in a socket, something electrical happened. Or rather unhappened. We were, without quite feeling that sense of descent I'd once anticipated at the phrase, *plunged into darkness*. This is very interesting, I thought, how a cliché can be revived: "plunged into darkness." Very interesting and very *dark*, very much *plunged*.

I awaited the bubbles.

Cold sponge in my hand, no sense left but for the moment of swaying, yet very much in a specific place, sandwiched in under bedsprings with intermittent pangs of hide-and-seek and French comedy, but mainly just ho-hum:

plunged into darkness.

I waited for something to happen, a ripping or toppling, something to shove me as once a mainsail boom had done when gybing just as we'd entered a peaceful harbor at sunset and I had gone flying out at the end of the shove until I'd found myself in water. Or once when in football I'd gone to tackle a half-back and found myself looking up through watery faces. But there was only the sound of the wind at the windows and the crashing of the sea which now in the darkness seemed more in phase with the movements of the tower. And what were those movements? I tried to figure them out. Was it, for instance, squirming? How had the reports gone that detailed the demise of the Air Force Tower? What were those signals the keepers had sent from Minot's Light? What had happened just before the Eddystone went *souse?* What, for that matter had happened on the old Harbor of Refuge? Yes, John J. Floherty aside, what had really happened inside that tower? Had it felt like this?

Then wasn't this the time for the ultimate note in the bottle?

And what would one say?

I am terrified?

But was I?

It began to feel like a Sunday afternoon when caught in a walking doze one found himself in some odd part of the tower, say the storage deck where the seaward windows were blocked. But I knew I was but three steps from my bunk. I could just get in it and lie down, take a little snooze until the tower decided what the hell it really wanted to do.

I took those three steps. And reached. It was not quite there. And then it was there, just at my finger tips and just as I was closing my fingers over the iron head pipe, it was not there. But, of course, it was there when I took another step. Then I had the bastard. And I held it and it didn't go away. Now it wasn't going anywhere at all. Not now that I had a hold of it.

Unless, of course, the whole tower was going somewhere. Would that be like a carnival ride? I tried to remember what my father'd told me about what to do if a Ferris wheel began to collapse. Do you scramble back up, keep scrambling back around up like a squirrel on a wheel? Or do you run on down, outrunning the fall like a skier outracing his avalanche so that you arrive in a glory of extended arms while the disaster sighs to a death harmlessly stretched out just behind your heels.

There was one thing I was not going to do.

I was not going to stand there in the dark all alone holding onto my bed.

Not outrunning anything then, but merely shuffling through the sleeping chamber, scuffing the damp wood, pausing thoughtfully in the lurches, listening for the escape ropes which I did not hear knocking, though the venetian blinds were at work, I found the door leading into the central cylinder. It was for the moment, like a triumph in hide and seek.

So, I would go down, though down might be but a gagging drain; it would as likely be, if real disaster had struck, that down would be a hole up into the raw sky.

I went below, groping the rail, feeling along the incredibly smooth inner tubing. I could hear steps and shouts. *Good*, I thought, *we're still attached*.

They were down there in the cylinder, too. Awakened somehow by the darkness, they too had crept into the tube, the one place in the whole tower where never even a star's light had peeked.

Voices.

Ah, voices.

Down below. Where the waves were trying to go so badly this afternoon, where they were struggling to flee their rainbows, bury themselves, ashamed of such splendid colorings, afraid of the beauty they'd made. Down. Everything goes down. And that is even why the waves themselves mount so high. To go down. And the tower which, after all, towers. Well, it too can, as local examples might prove, come down.

I, too, went down.

And I did not think of it as a matter of giving up, but joining what everyone—seas, towers, and mates—were all doing. And there at what I took to be bottom, because there were no more ways to go down that my feet could fathom, I came to a door.

Behind which lurked light.

Which parsed into shadows and light and what we'd have to give up as darkness. The light was battery operated, hand held, hand that of a large enough shadow to be boatswain mate first. Other shadows included a man from Lever, West Virginia, who was carrying or perhaps being carried by a battery, itself from Detroit and large enough to drive auxiliary power.

Flap seemed to be losing his grip on the battery, so I pushed through the door. My intention was to take the hand light from Okrastone, liberating him to step forward to help Flap. There was so much noise when I opened the door that I could only tap Okrastone on the shoulder. It all seemed obvious enough, and soon the world would be restored to light.

What I met, however, was increasing pressure from the door on my arm. With what was left of my hand around the door I tapped Okrastone again. This time my wrist was almost cut off in the door. I shouted, but Okrastone had tremendous back thrust—the same back thrust I'd witnessed in better light scratching his Aleutian bear back. This wrist of mine was now all of me that was still on the other side of the door.

I pushed against the door with all my might.

The door had a whole chain of Aleutian bears, all brought up on the succulent battens and lanterns of range beacons.

Somehow, I got my hand free. There was a small crack left in the door and into this, without risking lips, I howled, "To hell with you then."

And began back up the stairs. The same stairs I'd just come down. To help. And do good. For humanity. And Detroit, which God knew could use all the help it could get. And the bears, too. Definitely an endangered species. "To hell with you then!" and even in the din, I heard a faint echo.

About halfway up, the door sucked open and admitted the fierce intonings of the bottom two stories of our battered concrete. And in that, too, were some of Okrastone's sounds.

"Bo?" A voice all concussion and no articulation, the difficulty compounded by his having selected as my nickname one explosive syllable indistinguishable from a grunt of the sea.

My arm, the wrist he had jammed, ached.

"Bo?" That was he, not the sea, summoning me. Though I'd never heard the loneliness in his voice. I felt it float past up into the darkness above my head, and though I tried to trace it with the hand-held flashlight, it bubbled upward, bouncing here and there off the smooth sides, slipping up the treads and railing of the cylinder. There was no hope of finding that forlorn voice somewhere high and lanternward where yet there might be a whole chorus of bubbling air.

The voice came from below, and, I already felt, too far below.

"*Bo!*"

"Yes?" Was that my voice snittering off aloft? Of what possible use could the body be which housed such thin acoustics when it came to outgrowling the cellar-surging sea?

"Come on down here and hold this light, Bo."

I did, and when Okrastone had grabbed the other end of the big Detroit battery, they hunched it up into place by the compressor, slapped home the terminals, and after a few more moves had the whole two-story basement lit up like Old Home Week. There were the great wooden water casks in which we'd fished for gulls and bats on summer eves. There was the workbench from which we'd fetched the brass-bellied gas torch to cut loose Flap's famous meal. There were the steel doors still slamming out the sea. And not one of us was dead.

In fact we trooped up and had coffee.

"That was you the first time, wasn't it?" said Okrastone. He was grinning and winking over a mug. "That was really you what tapped my shoulder?" He pointed to which shoulder.

"Who the hell did you think it was?" I said. I flexed my hand, allowed the juices to again run through my wrist.

"Well, you maybe shouldn't oughter do things like that," he said.

"Things like what? Try to help you out?"

"Things like down there in the dark, kinda . . . *reach through.*" He screwed up his face. "*You know, reach through and tap a body on the shoulder.*"

"Just who the hell did you think I was?" I said.

"Last I knew," said Okrastone, "you was up on the third deck."

"Maybe the next safety meeting we could work our Emergency Blackout Communications Systems," said Flap.

"I just don't see who the hell you thought I was," I said.

"Well," said Okrastone, "it ain't no good for a body what's already in the bottom to have his shoulder tapped."

It was now quite clear outside: Greenmeal was bright, and the lights that shone from whatever houses were left looked as if they'd been polished. The destroyers and the pilot ship did not roll or plunge so much as wallow, for the breakwater was helping them a little more now, though it was still covered by every wave. All that stone seemed alive, trembling like an exposed nerve. And there was our landing stage, even a bit more ridiculous than an hour before as the water dropped away, leaving the planks without an apparent excuse for their flopping. To the east it was still all white, even when our light was not swinging over the waves.

"It's real clear," said Flap. "Want me to secure that horn?"

"I know it's clear," said Okrastone. "We'll leave that horn on just the same."

Its hollow bleat.

THE STORM:
THE THIRD DAY

Within an hour or so the wind and sea had moderated enough to put out in a fisher-man's power boat. Hugging the lee of the breakwater the craft was buried in a cloud of spray that mounted from the windward side of the barrier. The keeper stood drenched on the forward deck shielding his eyes with his hands as he tried to pene-trate the curtain of mist. He did not falter in his belief that they would find his assis-tant alive, although his common sense as a man-of-the-sea told him otherwise.
—John J. Floherty, *Sentries of the Sea*

THE NEXT DAY there was no getting around it: the sun was shining, Greenmeal stood clear to leeward, and through the spray to wind-ward was Cape May. Okrastone turned the horn off himself.

Ordinarily he would have dispatched either Flap or me on this mission which, afterall, involved much hiking. We had slept two at a time, as we had the night before, in with the cranberries and peas, using the potato sacks as pillows. As soon as the sun rose Okrastone told me to gather all the blankets and take them up "where they belong." Nothing, not even the torn landing stage, the shattered boat, the trembling of the tower itself seemed to incur his displeasure quite like the sight of those blankets spread among the groceries. I bent to pick them up and he, like a married man fleeing a whorehouse at first light, slipped into the cylinder.

When I was up on the sleeping deck folding the blankets, I heard his steps in the cylinder, and then they were going across the deck above, slowly, as if trying to avoid telltale squeaks. There was a shudder in the compressed-air pipes; the hissing stopped. There were no more clicks, and the last horn bleat trailed away, for not only the pressure, but the timing which gave that pressure shape had been drained so that the final sound was not a signal, but a moan.

Flap invited me to see his engine room. The water had gone down, leaving only a ring. He made a joke about bathtubs to help him adjust to what had happened. We each grabbed a broom and swept the stains in the direction of the big doors. Fortunately there was still enough din all about us so that there was no talk of actually opening those doors and whisking our residue into the sea's face.

We did, however, go from the galley out the shanty door where yet here and there were egg shells and coffee grounds, shrapnel from my defeat of the previous afternoon. Today there was enough of a lee for us to trek the long six feet across the wet balcony to the rail, a firm substance at last in our hands.

"We're like a bunch of Cot-dim goonie birds up here," bellowed Okrastone.

Our three chambray shirts indeed busked and flackered away from our bodies, straining the tucks and seams. Our hair stung our faces. Our knees we kept bent, elbows and knees locked. Our teeth slid when not bouncing. Runoff water from the spray hitting the windward side cruised around our heels and slickered out past our shoe tips and on over the edge where it peed down on the rocks below.

The pilots slid and bounced, coming toward us in one of their small boats, or at least from time to time one boat seemed to be coming. It would tilt, gag, and be gone to come up in a place you wouldn't have expected, so that it was possible there were several boats coming toward us, hidden in the wave curl like Hokusai's fishermen so that you seemed to have only one visible at any moment.

"Cot-damn," shouted Okrastone. "They're gonna think we're goonie birds."

The pilot boat got up on top of a wave and ran the ridge, wobbling as the hillside spilled and took the ridge away with it. Fats Davenport in a T-shirt held onto the grab rail at the cabin's back door and cupped his hand to his face. Okrastone cupped his hand and contributed to the wind's volume. The boat teetered, and Fats, sliding door, and cabin were gone down the back side of the wave. In a moment Fats seemed to be climbing it again, following the mast top, but not necessarily supported by the deck. He waved as if to show off this stunt. Okrastone's new trick, however, was more disturbing.

It consisted of his waving his arms about in a manner that suggested a man with a terrible nervous disorder attempting to bless himself. Standing so close to him, I could feel the strange twitching currents as his arms jerked. Was this the man I'd been living with these last months, the man under whose command we'd come through three days and nights of storm?

As if the gestures weren't disturbing enough, to his more forgivable grunts, he added strange little cries and from his pursed lips ballooned chortles never heard on land or sea.

The third time Fats made his appearance, he came running downhill straight toward us, riding the stern of the boat so that he would not only catch up, but with a little more hallooing, pass by his own mast and bow. Okrastone, on the other hand, had enough material in his act to continue the

same performance. Somehow the boat cornered before the stern caught up
with the bow and, skidding under the dangling planks of our stage, galloped
away parallel with the breakwater, the fat driver urging the lagging stern on
with his free arm. In a moment they were climbing a hill at the top of which
crumbled the mother ship.

"What the hell was all that about?" shouted Flap.

"That was sema-phore," said Okrastone.

"What did you say to them?" I said.

"It was improvised," said Okrastone.

That night, I could not really sleep. We had all more or less agreed,
without saying anything about it, not to drag the blankets down again. In
fact, I saw Flap watching Okrastone restack the cans up on the higher
shelves which meant that anyone spreading his bedding in the pantry would
risk a good canning, for the tower was still shaking on each hit and withdrawal. There were only the two still moments: the first when the sea was
preparing to pull back over the sensitive breakwater, and the other just
before the new wave hit. The way the tower moved on the impact was quite
different from its movement on the withdrawal, a distinction I had not really
appreciated until I lay on my back up on the second deck and in the darkness
could feel everything transmitted through the pipes and springs of my metal
bed.

I wondered if perhaps I should go down into the engine room, get some
of those wrenches Flap & Toy so liked to brandish, and give everything a
good solid tightening. I also wondered if it would be preferable for the tower
to tip over on the impact or the withdrawal, and which way it would fall—
that is, which way my bed would slide in each condition. It was quite possible, for instance, for the tower to tip back into the open ocean if hit low. On
the other hand, if the bottom were sucked by the withdrawing wave, the top
could pitch forward into the "harbor." There was, of course, always a question of the whole thing merely unraveling: plates, rivets, stairway all going
wong. I tried to imagine whether this sudden expulsion would be preferable
to a more modest immersion still wrapped in the tower. I took up again the
question of the buoyancy of my bureau drawers.

I decided to take a pee, as if this temporary extension of my body would
act as some sort of plumb line which would, if not correct, at least measure
the tower's deviation from the vertical. Okrastone, however, was already on
the pot. He was smoking a cigarette and looking toward the window, occasionally farting and flicking his ashes into his underwear. The sea was still
running over the breakwater, and every third shock some would whack the
landing stage, causing the remaining planks to go white and fly up like piano

keys. Okrastone blew smoke. We talked in low tones, and quietly, serenely, like a father and son grown old through bitter disputes into a kind of mellowness; we stayed there, as if in our park of darkness, he on the bench, me lounging against something of wood, and we made bets about which wave would finish the landing stage.

"It will take a few safety lectures to set this place straight again," I said.
"I imagine."
"If there's no landing stage it will be tricky for anyone to—well—*land*."
"Or get off, Bo. Or get off."

I watched until my head began to nod and I'd blink my eyes free from the running foam, the flying piano keys, the cigarette smoke, everything hurrying into the dark harbor. I jerked my head from the window and padded back toward bed.

"See you in the morning."
"See you in the morning."

I think I did sleep some. Must have. In the morning, again like a child waking up to find what was under the Christmas tree, I ran to the window on the lee side, and there, an unexpected gift: the landing stage just as I'd left it.

Late that afternoon, the sea had dropped, leaving a swell that cracked over the breakwater but did not run across continuously. The destroyers got up steam. The lead ship listed to starboard as if she'd grown that way through the storm in a kind of Greenmeal tropism. Cold and gray, she led the other narrow ship close to our balcony. There were a few men walking about on their bridge. It seemed strange to think such iron could house men in blue wool uniforms, and they even seemed big enough to control the ship, which with its narrow angles and low bridge canopy seemed to cramp more than dominate them. They waved to us, little blue arms waving. A claxon went off, three whoops that at first seemed but an attempt on their part to further torture their storm-battered iron. When I realized it was a cheer, I felt good and thought of my father in World War Two and waved back. Okrastone's knuckles, however, fluttered along the rail.

"*Fuck you, Coast Guard*, that's what they're saying," he said.
"Come on, Boats," I said, "we were all in this together."
"Not them," he said, "they was on something that could float."

Inside he walked around with a coffee cup in his hand. His face was full of spots that wouldn't quite float. His eyebrows were ragged, and I realized that as part of his morning routine, he usually must have combed them. "I want to ask you something, Bo," he said.

Flap sat in the famous chair, hands in lap as if they were not his own to do anything with; nor was, for that matter, the lap itself.

"What do you want to ask me?" I said.

"Was you scared?"

I laughed and was grateful, if surprised, that I had gotten out such a robust laugh. I tried to keep it going, as a man tapping a gas well will urge on the silliest of fumes in hopes that something marketable will finally be uttered, but I could feel the bottom and there was going to be nothing more, so I got something out before I went dry. "I guess," I said, "I was aware of the possibilities."

"I was, too," he said, and I wondered what I'd meant.

I looked at Flap, but Okrastone must have already asked him for he sat there with his hands in his lap like a mother with a new child.

The next day brought more sunshine and a good deal less wind. I emptied the garbage, and the egg shells spiraled down from the balcony. The sea was still up enough to carry them off from the rip-rap around the base where they would have normally fallen if I had thrown from the rail. There was, of course, no question of my going down onto the landing stage, where I usually tapped the bucket on the spile. I did look that way, however, and there seemed to be about half of it left. The section of paint locker that had been held by one bolt was lying diagonally across the planking, and the boat was parallel to it. We spent the day inside mopping and rearranging the furniture as if we'd just moved in. The great quantities of light pouring in off the yet high sea kept us excited like fish in a tank.

When the sun was lower, about the time "American Bandstand" would have been on if we had had any television that worked, a Coast Guard forty-footer emerged out of the running seas under the westering sun. Its pilot house windows were heavily bandaged against the steep seas. In the long cockpit, his hand on the hump under which throbbed the diesels, was, of all people, Blump. In his hand hung a black, doctor's kit no boatswain would be caught dead with. The man at the wheel caught a swell that was moving at a freak angle and put the boat alongside our ladder, or what was left of it. There was nothing for Blump to do but grab the rung as the deck rolled away from him and with it, of course, the whole boat. There he was.

"Well, lookie that," chuckled Okrastone, "the man who got himself transferred off here so he wouldn't be aboard when the old girl fell over into the sea."

"I can still refuse," Blump shouted. At whom it wasn't clear. The boat had already slid off a length. "It's the electrical technician's right to refuse a jeopardizing landing."

"Will you listen to that?" said Okrastone. "He's going to be what puts us back in touch with the world."

The boat made another pass, though it looked more as if it were trying to goose Blump up the ladder than obey his inclination to be plucked off and taken home. We were around on the balcony far enough to see back toward the stage and the ladder as the boat's aerial and flags made their move toward the trembling buttocks of Blump. His head vanished in through the rungs so that there was only this absurd white-clothed body clinging, as it seemed, to nothing.

"It's still my right to refuse," came a voice from under what was left of the stage.

"What's he doing here, anyway?" said Flap. "I thought he was a cook now."

"Come on up, son," said Okrastone. "Come on back to your old home."

"They must have not been able to eat his food," I said.

Blump pulled his head out of the rungs. He opened his mouth. The flags and antenna came at him again. I looked away. Greenmeal sparkled in the morning sun. When I heard the exhaust break free, I knew the boat had rolled off. Blump had starfished the ladder, but still seemed alive.

"We was just wondering if the stage was all right, and we'd be interested in what you got to say about it," shouted Okrastone.

"I can still refuse landing," said Blump. The boat was a good three lengths off and sliding down the back of a wave that, in falling away from the landing stage, had taken all the water, so that Blump looked down onto what was definitely land. "I can," he said, "I still can."

But he began to climb. And he still had the doctor kit.

"I don't get it," said Flap. "Do they think you went crazy, Boats?"

"There was that dance he did yesterday," I said. "The mad-man's semaphore."

"Let 'em come," said Okrastone.

Blump was crawling across the stage, dragging the kit, which from time to time caught between the planks.

Inside the tower, Blump opened up his bag. He was now, he explained, not an actual electronic technician, but still technically a cook, though he was "phasing out" that end of his career, and the storm with its widespread damage and subsequent drain on an already understaffed rating in an undermanned service had resulted in his being pressed into service at a station with which he was, after all, already familiar.

We stood there looking at him until Okrastone pointed out that indeed Blump did have a "war" in his hand.

"Well, no," said Blump, "it's not quite a war, but something like *emergency powers*."

"Not *war*," I said, "*wire*." I reached out and gave the damn thing a tweak.

"It's still emergency powers," said Blump, and he pulled the wire back from me.

"Well," said Flap, "how do you like the old place?"

"First the radio," said Blump, "*then* the sea stories. I've got to get off here before dark." And taking the wire, he pivoted slowly until we steered him toward the radio. "Oh," he said, "these places are round, aren't they?"

Once at the radio, Blump rolled up his sleeves and went to it. He disconnected something. I helped him wiggle the heavy set off its shelf, and we lugged it over to the Formica table as Flap hastily wiped breakfast and lunch from under our grunts. In a matter of minutes, Blump had replaced the jellies and crumbs with a sumptuous repast of tubes, condensers, and a whole salad of wires. "I've been taking a course," he explained.

"I knew you were interested in old lamps," I said, "but I thought you specialized in the nonelectric, whale-oil type."

Blump's eyes rocketed at the reference to the missing Aladdin's lamp, but Okrastone, who did not pick up the allusion, got him off the hook by saying he'd heard about Blump's cooking. "You know the boys in a station will talk, Blumper."

"Well, you know how it is," said Blump. "One thing leads to another when you get interested."

"I heard about your cooking," said Okrastone again.

"Well, I've got to get on with this," said Blump. "They won't come back for me in these seas after dark."

"It does get dark out here," said Okrastone. "Most every night."

"Heh-heh."

Blump proved both his electronic skill and fear of the dark by rapidly replacing several items, his pudgy fingers probing and twisting the strands of yellow, red, green, blue. "This is all a code, you know," he said.

Okrastone walked by with a full coffee cup. "Them are sure pretty *wars*, Blump."

"Gee," said Flap, "maybe I should go into that. I wouldn't have to get my fingernails dirty, and I'd be home every night."

"I can see," said Blump without looking up, "that you guys really buy that old story about there being a crack undermining everything out here."

"When did I say that?" said Flap. "All I said was it would be nice to be home every night. I mean this spending the night stuff out here gets old."

"So, there *are* some people out here who believe that story just the same." He squirmed round to deal me his smirk.

"Hey, we're still standing aren't we?" I said.

"Sure, but just think how big and juicy that crack must be right now." His lower lip trembled while air passed rapidly back and forth over it. "Just think how big 'n' juicy."

"Blump," said Okrastone, "shut up."

Blump turned back to the radio. "Hey, I'm all done here." He buttoned it up, fluttering his wrists professionally. He nodded to me and I grabbed an end. We lugged it back to the shelf. As soon as we were somewhat shielded from Okrastone, Blump winked at me. "Don't let me get you about that crack, son. It's just standard service humor."

When he had connected the radio, he gave the mike a brace of snappy clicks, and, in a new voice, suitably modulated for radio, summoned the Greenmeal Lifeboat Station and several other shore units up and down the coast, some of which had obscure call letters and voices also modulated beyond the usual adolescent croak and whine of seamen standing tower watches. It was definitely the big time.

Moreover, it looked like the forty boat would be back to pick him up well before dark. Greenmeal Lifeboat Station radioed us, however, that the boat had been diverted to tow a wreck. Blump demanded the present location of the boat. Of course he didn't call it a boat, but a "unit." The *unit* was three miles off Cape May or almost a dozen miles to windward of us.

"Three miles with a good two hours of light," said Blump. Just the same, he wanted to check, and I handed him the binoculars, the new ones Okrastone had gotten to replace those Blump had taken, and he trotted around the balcony on the shore side until he came to the fuel tank, where he wedged himself between the big olive-drab curve and the rail, the better to peep out toward the already-darkening east. After a while he handed me the glasses. The white boat was barely visible between slabs of gray, and behind it from time to time showed a large, red, rectangular surface, which looked like one of the boxcars off the fish-factory siding. Beyond it more slabs of gray and a gray sky.

When we came in, Flap said that he'd heard Luntsky tell the station he'd gotten the tow cable wrapped around his wheel. There would be no ride home tonight. Blump's face fell, then his shoulders slid down inside his starched shirt so that the stiff planes broke into bevels, sagged to bags, collapsed into lumps. He was as he had been when he'd been in charge of the tower, that man whose clothes had been designed, as Toy had said, by the inebriated maker of portable desert habitations, and it all lay there, a heap in the famous chair.

"Welcome home, Blump," I said.

He stared at the TV bracket.

During supper he revived a bit and began telling us the promised sea stories, what had gone on ashore. The boys at the Indian River station just down the coast from Greenmeal had been flooded out. Their little Victorian station built in 1880 had been filled right up to the long, red eaves, and in the trailer park among the dunes the propane tanks had floated off and all night the trailers had rolled and banged into each other while one boy from the lifeboat station held the hands of two old bass men as they stood tiptoe on a sunken roof. Just those points of contact, their finger tips and toes and all the rest a cold, black rushing.

"Are we supposed to believe that?" said Okrastone.

"Hotels fell down," said Blump. He bunched his face like a newscaster.

Okrastone made his fart-detecting face and caught my eye.

"You know that line of hotels around the corner of the Bay?" said Blump. "Those big fancy ones all along Rehoboth Beach? The ones with all the modern conveniences?"

"Yes," I said at last to stop him. "My folks stayed in one when they came down here."

"Well, it's a good thing they weren't in one last night."

"How about Bo's folks here?" I said, "they *live* on Hatteras."

"Now don't go putting my folks in any place Blump's going to tell us about," said Okrastone. "It no doubt was bad enough for them with just the old ocean snuffling round."

"A salesman told me," said Blump, "that he was in one of those hotels." He began to laugh.

"Oh, oh, here comes a traveling salesman joke from Blump," said Flap. "I can see why you wanted your folks left out, Bo."

"Well, it's not that kind of salesman joke, son," said Blump. "In fact it's not a joke at all, but rather a Humorous Actual Incident."

Okrastone belched, rose and following his gases, strode to the sink. His coffee cup required the most meticulous attention.

"Well, if nobody wants to hear this—" said Blump.

"If nobody wants to hear it, you're just going to go on with it anyway, Blump," said Okrastone.

"I don't see why you guys out here who were so isolated during this recent storm, don't want to hear about what really went on in the world around you."

"Ok," I said. "Tell us what really went on around us."

"The hotels all fell down." He looked tragically into his cup. "I mean it. They all collapsed. Like a deck of cards, the partitions and outside walls, one after the other. All of them."

"Is that right?" said Okrastone and he actually looked over at Blump. "All them big pretty places where the summer people go?"

"Anybody killed?" said Flap. "Those were big, swell places."

"Fortunately they weren't occupied, except by a few folks like this salesman." He rubbed his hands, having at last gotton his foot in the door. "I used to be a salesman myself, when I was out of the service between enlistments. Boy, I tell you, it's rough On the Outside. Anyway—"

"What did you sell, Blump?" said Okrastone.

"Notions," he said. "But that's not the point. The point is this guy was drinking too much the night before and when the phone in the room woke him up and they told him to get out an hour before check-out time he was angry. He thought the noise in the corridor was the maid with the vacuum. When he was shaving they called him again. He thought his razor was shaking because he was hung over. He told them he still had half an hour to check-out. The third time they called him they begged for him to open the door into the corridor. It wasn't the maid out there. It was the wind. The whole end of the building was gone. The corridor, it was just kind of hanging there. He was on the top story."

"And he told you this himself?" I said.

"When you are stationed at a life saving unit you become involved in this sort of thing."

"Well," said Okrastone and he gave his cup a final shake, "I'm certainly glad you finally did get in-volved in the Coast Guard now you been in near a dozen years, including time-off for peddling notions."

"Hey, I suppose that you guys think this thing out here, this business you went through out here was the only adventure anyone was having. That this was going to be the Official Coast Guard Adventure."

"This was just the o-fficial Coast Guard Mess, Blump, that's all it was," said Okrastone. "A lot of mess and no damn sleep."

"And not much to eat, either," said Flap.

"I don't know, Blump," I said, "I'm kind of with you. I'm going to see it gets nominated as at least one of the official adventures."

"That's just because you've only been in a year," said Blump.

"I told you I was with you, Blump," I said, "I even liked your traveling salesman story. Hell, I liked the guys tip-toe on the Indian River trailer, too. Let's have them all."

Blump chewed his spoon. "I suppose you'll want to hear about Chanty, too."

"Oh, Jeeze," said Okrastone. "And here I thought we done flushed all that old stuff clean from this place."

"Well, it ain't much of a story," said Blump. "Not when you think of what kind of story he usually makes."

"He didn't hold hands with everybody out on that lightship of his, now?" said Okrastone, "He didn't get them all to hold hands and go *tippy-top, tippy-toe?*" His eyes were dancing, and he puckered his lips to manage the little tune.

"No, nuthing like that I'm sure," snickered Blump. "Just, you know, hanging on, I guess."

"No dancing, eh?" said Okrastone. "Just hanging on. You sure?"

"Maybe," said Blump. "I mean how would I really know what he did out there?"

"But I thought you was going to tell us just that," said Okrastone. "You already give us one song and dance here."

"Other people, too," said Blump. "Just remember that, other people can sing and dance."

He spent the evening laying out *The Lighthouse In The Storm*.

Flap and Okrastone slept. I did the dishes and made the eight o'clock radio check. It was good to hear the old voices: Ship John Shoal, Miah-Maul, Fourteen-Foot Bank, Brandywine, with Greenmeal answering up each time; and then a deep voice thirty miles out to sea. *"This is Delaware."*

"You know who that was?" I said to Blump.

"I know," he said. "Everybody thought he'd sunk."

"Well, he didn't. None of us did."

"You know there's a piece missing from this puzzle," he said, and he held up the ones on either side.

Upstairs I was pushing my bureau drawers back in, confident that this night they would not come walking forth. I pushed down the balled socks in the top drawer. Perhaps something was jammed back there. Of course, the Blump hat. Hadn't I seen it in the middle of the storm? And wouldn't it be a good joke to put it on now and prance about below intoning the appropriate Chantyisms? Wasn't it amazing how some things just worked out? Blump maybe could not find all the pieces to the puzzle, but I had the hat. Blump maybe had run off with the Aladin's lamp, but I had what was infinitely more magical, the very talisman that had gotten us through the storm: the *Blump de Chant hat!*

Except the thing in the back of my drawer was not it. A hat all right. I white, sailor hat. One of mine. What I had seen in the height of the storm had been merely my own hat.

Socks, shirts, bell-bottoms flew as I searched the drawers, all of them.

The door opened just as I was putting everything back.

"That's what I like to see," said Okrastone, "a shipmate setting his gear in sea-going order."

I stood there with my own hat in my hand. "This is my own hat," I said.

"Yes, sir," said Okrastone, and there was just the faintest twinkle in his eye. "Sea-going order."

PART FOUR

Spring

OUR LADY
OF THE HARBOR

As the fishing boat neared the end of the breakwater the spray had thinned enough to discern the hazy outline of the rock pile that had once been the base of the lighthouse. A skiff was lowered and soon the keeper and one of the crew were clambering up the boulders. On arriving at the level area on which the building had stood, they saw the limp figure of Willis supported by the rope lashed under his arms. He was unconscious. Sea water ran from his dangling arms. His head, dropped forward on his breast, lolled from side to side as the post swayed. The keeper quickly cast off the heaving line that supported Willis and with the aid of the boatman lowered him down along the boulders to the skiff.

—John J. Floherty, *Sentries of the Sea*

O KRASTONE SNIFFED THE air, pushed a hand each side of the shelter door as if to stretch the opening, and leaned out, his feet still safe within the tower. He leaned right out and wrinkled his nose.

"I'm afraid today's gonna do her, boys."

Flap and I wedged into the doorway beside him and tried to see out, smell what he had smelled.

"Look at her, all right," said Papa Bear, "smell her up good, boys. She's a *pretty day*."

"Yes, there's finally more sun than wind or sea," I said.

"Yes, sure is pretty," agreed Flap. He let his lungs collapse.

"Winter here ain't nothing compared to Alaska, though," said Okrastone.

"I thought you said it was better up there," I said.

"Oh, *it* was better, but the weather was a good deal worse."

"Well, good day to clean up the engine room," said Flap. Clapped hands.

"Engine room, hell, Flap," said Okrastone. "Today's gonna be *the* day."

"Damn good day for me to clean the lantern," I said. "I got the proper

337

lemon oil and what with the new addition to our red sector since the storm—"

"It ain't gonna be that kinda day," interrupted Okrastone. "It's going to be the day when . . ."

We were out of the shelter then and onto the balcony, and as we blinked in the roofless light, down on the landing stage gleamed the remaining yellow paint locker.

Halfway down the stairs to the landing stage, I realized I had the gurry bucket in my hand, having spirited it out from under the seductive sink.

"Never mind all that *housewife*, Bo," shouted Okrastone.

"Ya," shouted Flap, "let's see you produce those chipping hammers out of that paint locker down there."

"I know where they are," I said. "Exactly where they are. You forget. I was the last man down here when the drops began to fall."

"Ain't no drops now, Bo," said Okrastone. "Nothing but clearzabell old sunshine streamin down on the healthful body."

Walking carefully out onto the stage, I managed to get as far as the boat. It was half full of silt. The fetch that had carried that dirt had been at least fourteen miles to the nearest land. The stem, which was still lashed to a spile, had been ripped right out of the boat so that the planking which had once rounded up into the rabbet in the sea-kindly bow had lost this curve and now hung open and toothy like the face of a dead rat. It occurred to me I had not really been counting on floating out of my bunk onto a bureau drawer to shore, but making through surf and storm in this very boat.

A step beyond the boat and I began to bounce on what remained of the stage. This brought cries from my mates who assumed I was still goofing off in some kind of dance. Without looking out on the stage any farther than I had to, I plucked the snap shackle that held the hasp on the paint locker.

Fwang, the box top leapt. Inside reeked of thinner, and even out there suspended, as my knees and shoulder blades told me, suspended over the cold sea, the thinner made my head spin.

"Don't spend the day out there," shouted Okrastone.

"Do you see them?" asked Flap. "See any hammers?"

I poked around in the dizzying rags. There were wire brushes, shards of sandpaper, a can of the bedroom blue we'd used the day of the storm.

"Do you see them?"

"Just a minute." I sat back on my heels and tried to get some of the fresh air.

"Cot-damn it's gonna get into darkness before you make ready."

"If they're not out there, just say so," said Flap. "I got my own work to do."

I lifted a rag, and there were three wooden handles; I pulled the handles from under the rags, and there came three iron heads, sharp as the skulls of *Archaeopteryx*.

When I got back to the balcony, however, Flap was not there. Okrastone, who had been intent upon the hammers, seemed to have just noticed this absence and was looking about under the fuel tank and over the balcony rail, as if Flap had been either less chubby or a good deal more desperate than any of us had realized.

"*Cot*-damn, and just as we were all ready to break her loose."

"He seemed to be more interested in inside things," I said.

"I know where he is all right," said Okrastone, and he boomed through the screen door into the tower. "I know he went down in that hole o his. I know down in that stinky ol black hole." Okrastone clawed the cylinder door and filled the interior with his knowledge. "Flap, you come out of that stinky hole, boy." He listened to his sound drain. Then, much softer, in a voice that on the way down would not clog the future way back up, but would itself float and so doing carry anyone who could still be lifted into our new weather, Okrastone said, "Spring is here."

Nevertheless, I was glad when Okrastone told me to knock off the chipping and get lunch. It was almost two, and the three of us had been beating in tremendous fury since nine-thirty. Flap, who had started with the only pair of safety goggles, had gotten so steamed up, he'd shucked them. I had dark glasses and was glad I did because several chips struck the lenses. Even so, two had somehow managed to creep around and find a sharp bath in the pink rim of my left eye. My forehead was peppered, my hair weighted and itching as with dandruff. Okrastone used neither glasses nor goggles, and though his face was now the realization of a junior prom-er's nightmare, his eyes were still bright.

I made tomato soup and sandwiches out of a variety of luncheon meat. While the soup made its move from paste to bubbles, I washed the breakfast dishes. The breakfast egg was now quite stubborn, so I filled the pan with warm water and let the plates glide. It was something I knew I should have done that morning, but I'd figured that since the dishes weren't going to get me out of chipping, the least the chipping could do for me was to get me out of the dishes.

When I called my mates to lunch, they accelerated their banging, and the whole tower rang in time, resounding to the very shore, so that it seemed now as if everyone in Greenmeal town were a-building. And they kept it up a good while, seeing if they could stay with each other. Through the back window I saw chips shoot past them, covering the balcony with red and white. Some flew over the rail. I grinned and could feel my pocked face break. Standing in the back door, I felt like an old mama watching her boys. The harbor was calm, the sky as blue as their chambray shirts.

"Do you think they can hear us in town?" said Flap.

"I imagine."

"They'll think we're knocking her down. They'll think we been cooped up so long we flipped our lids."

"They'll think we gone insane out of our minds."

"Hey," I said, "soup's on."

There was a marked lift in the beat.

A pause—Greenmeal echoing.

Two hammers clanged on the deck.

The screen door banged.

Spoons clicked against bowls, teeth.

"Tomato soup," said Flap. "You sure got a thing out for tomato soup, Bo."

"Eat it up, son," said Okrastone. "Put har on your balls."

Slurping and the detonating of crackers. Lip prints appeared on the white bread.

"Got to get back before we stiffen up," said Okrastone. The table recoiled and his dishes shot up into his hands, went westward toward the waters of the sink.

"I'm already stiff," I said.

"That's because you been in here doing pussy work." Okrastone's fingers flexed, and the soup bowl arched end over end. Soapy water flew. The spoon bounced off the back of the sink, leaving a red splatter. The sandwich plate slid into the pan where the lukewarm breakfast juices murmured and lurked.

"Well, somebody had to," I said, "or you wouldn't be heaving all that crockery around right now."

"Heave her right overboard," said Okrastone, and he wiped his hands on his pants.

"How come you got this thing about tomato soup?" said Flap. He had it all over his face.

"Never mind now," said Okrastone. He was adjusting his belt in the shelter. "Like he say, somebody got to stoke the ol' boiler."

"Ya, but tomato soup." Flap smirked it.

"Fire them dishes right overboard, Bo, and grab a paint brush. We got to get this old girl covered up before dark. Can't leave her out there shivering all night."

Against regulations, Okrastone had hoarded the red lead away in the engine room, so in spite of the storm's losses out on the staging, we still each had a brimming full gallon. Red lead it was that went on outside things—on bulwarks and booms; range lights and davits; decks, braces, bridges, and stanchions. No pastel rubber base to do up bedrooms, but lead base to sling on the weather side of stuff you could break your fist upon. And you didn't get off your mistakes by rinsing in bathrooms, either. In Alaska, Okrastone said, after work the painting crew rinsed their skin clean by leaping into the fuel tanks. He did not explain how each body squeezed through the fill pipe.

"Never mind all them petty questions, boys. Get those buckets shook up."

Flap stood on the balcony out in the sun, eyes closed, and with his paint can between his hands like a concertina, shook out a few twist steps. You could hear it gurgle against his belly.

"Come on, boy, don't dance with it. Let's get this girl covered up."

We had chipped a bald spot to the height of the window lintels and as wide as the shelter to the fuel tank—that is, the southwest quadrant, or what inside would be from the back door, around past the refrigerator and washing machine to the pantry. The bare iron was dull gray except where the bird-headed hammers had struck silver. Here and there were flecks of white, holidays, and in many places the dents lost all the light.

I used my jacknife, placing the blade lengthwise and still closed, in under the lid. Working around to the opposite side broke the suction, and the strong smell of red lead filled the air. I took the dripping screwdriver Flap had already used and began stirring.

"Tomato soup," said Flap.

"Don't play with it all afternoon, boys."

"Everywhere I look today, it's tomato soup."

I dipped my brush home.

"Keep her thin, boys. Brush her out."

It was a good change to be brushing instead of chipping. I felt that my arm wouldn't have ached so much if only I had been brushing all morning. Brushing was a soft, voluptuous act, and the results—a smooth red world over the gray pockmarks—an added delight. It must have been all of twenty minutes before my hand began to feel its veins and a full half hour before the paint was oozing between my fingers, glueing my webs. It was an hour before it dripped from my cuff, another half hour before I longed for the austere ring of the morning's hammer.

"Who's leavin all these runs?" Okrastone was no longer working his own section, which was back by the shelter.

"Not me," said Flap. His section was by the window, which looked in on the washing machine. "I've been very careful about that. My Dad always taught me how to paint back on the old homestead."

"What's the matter with you, Bo? Your Pa you said was a boat man."

"*Put a lot on the brush,*" I said, "*then pull it all out.*"

"Then how come all these runs back here?"

"They must have done that when I turned my back."

"You got to brush them out."

"It's too late now," said Flap, cheerfully picking at one. "Look at that: set-right-up."

"On a day like this, son, stuff drys real fast." He put his hand on my shoulder.

"It is a pretty day," I said.

"It's been a pretty day *all* the day," said Okrastone and he looked away from the wall, away from the runs and out over the harbor toward the shore. There was a sand spit back there just under the Maritime Exchange Tower, and it had moved fifty yards in the three days of the storm. The aids to navigation people'd already sent a message that they were sending a boat with a big red pane of glass to expand the red sector up in our lantern. "Yes, sir," continued Okrastone, "I figure we can get another coat on her before the sun goes damp on her."

"I thought we were going to wash it down between coats with detergent," I said.

"Ya," said Flap, and as he looked up he shook a cramp out of his painting hand, flaunted it. "What was all that about anyway, Boats?"

"Oil," said Okrastone. "All that oil in the air." He rubbed his hand across the sky. "Well, it's a little early yet. We still got a northeast wind from the open water, but that's why we got to get her all done up before the wind hauls south over the land and that fish factory."

"I still don't see how it gets out here," said Flap. "I mean we still got the sea."

"Boys," said Okrastone, "you got to learn—the sea can't do everything for you."

When they were done at the far end of the patch, the beginning was, as Okrastone had predicted, already dry, and he ran his hand over it and gave it a soft pat. "If we hurry, boys," he said. "Before the oily air slurps up onto it."

"Why?" I said and looked toward shore. "You think it's going to haul around today?"

"The second coat's going to go on like water," he said, and began.

It did go on easier, but it wasn't as dramatic as the first, being a study in monochromatics, and sometimes even Okrastone had to cock his head to catch the light right which separated the older, dried work from the new. When we'd finished, my hand was stuck to the brush and my sneakers laced with soup. Since I was the messiest, I got the job of cleaning the brushes.

I took them down on the stage because that was where the thinner was and I simply walked over there, not even thinking of it as *out* there, just as if the stage were as sound as it had been last summer. In fact no deedle-doodle did begin, and I never even realized it should have until my hands were rolling free from the red lead and the brushes were all soused, wrung, and bashed free from the afternoon.

It was late by now, but still not raw. Okrastone was up on the balcony sweeping paint chips, an act which he admitted we should have completed before painting as the red lead had dripped onto the chips and in some cases gone through onto the deck, et cetera. Flap was in the galley getting his specialty ready. I put the paint and hammers and brushes and thinner away, hasped the box and walked up. The low sun warmed the planks of our wrecked boat so that it seemed not so much an ominous reminder of the futility of our escape as a trophy of the maritime life fit for a restauranteur's décor.

Okrastone had swept up all the chips into a big pile and was arranging them in the shape of a woman. She was about four feet tall, but as yet had no head. Her neck stretched toward the tower, her legs, very plump and footless, were slightly spread toward the southwest.

The climb back up from the landing stage had made me even warmer, and I wiped my brow. Okrastone heaped up her bosoms, pouring the white chips as delicately as if they were sand in an hourglass. The breasts swelled. The problem was to keep them even. On his knees, he'd reach over and give a pat here, a pour there. In his beard, which was noticeable since in the excitement he had not that day shaved, were fine white flakes the same as made up her body. Around his eyes sparkled even finer chips, and his cap was soaked with sweat against which the chips shone. Flap came out, wiping his hands on a dish towel.

"Make her breasts bigger," he said.

"Cot-damn, boy, you want them glands ab-normal?" He obliged, however, pouring with both fists. "There's more to a woman than just ab-normal milkers, right, Bo?"

I agreed.

"Aw, you family men don't know everything," said Flap.

"You got supper going, boy?" said Okrastone.

"I still say she looks flat-chested."

"You ain't got no imagination," said Okrastone. He leaned back on his ankles. "Still, there *is* something missing."

He swung around on his knees and fumbled in the stray chips.

From the southwest, Cape Henlopen, a cat's paw came, darkening the water, running the harbor's nap the wrong way.

"Wind's coming up," I said. "I knew this weather was too good to be true."

"It's already cold around to the northeast," said Flap.

"That's why I had you boys work this side of the tower. We got the sun and the lee."

"Not any more," I said. "Look at the wind come."

"Well, that's south, isn't it?" said Flap. "That wind's coming from the south."

"That's south all right," said Okrastone. "That's bringing the land, and it's going to bring the oil."

"It's going to bring the warm, too," said Flap. "It's going to bring the springtime."

It was about halfway out, a big carpet unrolling.

"Well, I still say she's flat-chested," said Flap.

"You just watch this." Okrastone had found two chips the size of strawberries and dipping them in a spatter he made them that color, too, and placed them, one to each breast.

"Nipples," said Flap.

"Nipples," said Okrastone. "Now she's complete."

"She hasn't any head," I said.

"For that matter, she hasn't any feet," said Flap.

"Now she's complete," said Okrastone and he got up. Dusted his hands.

Flap hung his head so he could see her right side up.

"She's a chunk of meat," I said.

"Look at this, boys," said Okrastone. He wiped his hand upon the sky and this time the balls of his fingers were rolling. "Oil all right," he said.

"But it's so warm," said Flap. "It's warmer than all day."

"Wash her all down tomorrow," said Okrastone.

"A real hunk of meat," I said.

"What's all this meat?" said Okrastone and he huffed up. "She's the belle of the bay." He was still watching the carpet of wind, too, and it had reached the base of the tower and stretched back all the way to the shore, to the spit that had moved out, they said, fifty yards the night of the storm, to the Maritime Tower among the dunes and the Coast Artillery towers, the fish factory, and the lifeboat station, to all that land of canals and alleys, to the trees that would soon be having leaves, red buds, and magnolias, all dancing. When the breeze hit it was warmer than Flap had said, warmer than he'd ever hoped a southern spring might be, and it traveled up our sleeves and bell bottoms, up the woman's legs and riffled her, our lady, swirled into her, catching her, and she rose, no longer meat, but a great fan of confetti, red and white chips fluttering into butterflies, a whole field of them rising, dancing, floating off around the balcony, sifting through the guard rails, over the top one, spilling down wind on the oily, warm, sou-wester, first of the year, into the sunlight, into the water which was all velvet now, all covered from cape to cape so that our lady was at last in all the warm sea.

FINAL DISPOSITION

Aboard the fishing boat hot blankets and the usual restoratives were in readiness.
Within an hour Willis was able to speak. "Thought I was a goner that time," he said
weakly. The keeper looked at him sternly. "The sperrits don't lie," he muttered and
went on deck.

—John J. Floherty, *Sentries of the Sea*

The Harbor of Refuge Light is now automatic.

The storm that began on March sixth was later declared by the *National
Geographic* to be "the Atlantic seaboard's worst winter storm in maybe half a
century." Unheralded, a freak, it lasted four days, caused over half a billion
dollars in damage, and killed forty people. North-Atlantic storms usually
travel north-eastward, but this one, made up of two relatively weak storms,
stalled and turned back on the land over a thousand mile fetch of open sea.

It was never named.